Cases on Global E-Learning Practices:
Successes and Pitfalls

Ramesh C. Sharma
Indira Gandhi National Open University, New Delhi, India

Sanjaya Mishra
Indira Gandhi National Open University, New Delhi, India

INFOSCI Information Science Publishing
Hershey • London • Melbourne • Singapore

Acquisition Editor: Kristin Klinger
Senior Managing Editor: Jennifer Neidig
Managing Editor: Sara Reed
Assistant Managing Editor: Sharon Berger
Development Editor: Kristin Roth
Copy Editor: Kim Barger
Typesetter: Jennifer Neidig
Cover Design: Lisa Tosheff
Printed at: Integrated Book Technology

Published in the United States of America by
Information Science Publishing (an imprint of Idea Group Inc.)
701 E. Chocolate Avenue
Hershey PA 17033
Tel: 717-533-8845
Fax: 717-533-8661
E-mail: cust@idea-group.com
Web site: http://www.idea-group.com

and in the United Kingdom by
Information Science Publishing (an imprint of Idea Group Inc.)
3 Henrietta Street
Covent Garden
London WC2E 8LU
Tel: 44 20 7240 0856
Fax: 44 20 7379 3313
Web site: http://www.eurospan.co.uk

Library of Congress Cataloging-in-Publication Data

Cases on global e-learning practices : successes and pitfalls / Ramesh C. Sharma and Sanjaya Mishra, editors.

p. cm.

Includes bibliographical references and index.

Summary: "This book has been developed to look into the global practices of e-learning, getting to know what have been the success stories or otherwise as experienced by the implementers. The unique feature of this book is providing a judicious mix of practical experiences and research based information in the form of case studies"--Provided by publisher.

ISBN 1-59904-340-8 (hardcover) -- ISBN 1-59904-341-6 (softcover) -- ISBN 1-59904-342-4 (ebook)

1. Computer-assisted instruction--Case studies. 2. Internet in education--Case studies. 3. Distance education--Case studies. I. Sharma, Ramesh C., 1962- II. Mishra, Sanjaya.

LB1028.5.C375 2007

371.3'58--dc22

2006027719

British Cataloguing in Publication Data
A Cataloguing in Publication record for this book is available from the British Library.

Cases on Global E-Learning Practices: Successes and Pitfalls

Table of Contents

Preface

Introduction

Today, e-learning is used in more countries and educational institutions than ever before. Most of the time, the leadership and enthusiasm of a single individual or a group of people have paved the way to use e-learning for delivery of education and training. And of course, everyone in their own enthusiasm, after having jumped into the bandwagon, tries to tread their own path without giving consideration to what paths others have followed, and how others have succeeded or failed. As such, every e-learning venture faces the challenge of sustainability, and the danger of being closed. Today, we have a huge amount of information and literature on the theory and practice of e-learning that can help organizations in all sectors take appropriate decisions on how to implement e-learning in their organizations.

Objectives

The objective of this book is to provide learning opportunities through a set of case studies on implementation of e-learning in different context. It is intended to serve as a guide to all those involved in the design, development, and implementation of e-learning. Literature on e-learning and research literature on e-learning is found in abundance through a simple search on the net. However, this book has been planned with a different concept and in a different manner to give practitioners an insight into the world of e-learning in a case study format. Thus, the book presents a judicious mix of practical experience and research-based information.

Case Study

Case studies are effective instructional tools. These are useful sources of authentic learning that help to analyze situations and enable understanding of issues in context to apply the new learning in other similar situations/contexts. Thus, case studies present realistic situations with a balance of theory and practice. In our case, writing a case study is to faithfully record and reflect on what, when, why, and how an organization has planned, designed, and implemented e-learning. As the book has been conceptualized with the objective of having an understanding into what e-learning practices have been followed by different institutions or organizations, what problems they encountered, or what were the success stories, we have followed a case study framework. To keep the structure of the cases uniform, a framework was designed and provided to all the contributors (see Appendix) so that they may provide their experiences in such manner so that a proper paradigm can be charted out on the basis of their success stories or pitfalls. These case studies will not only serve as a source of stimulation but also bring forward some challenges, which the institutions or organizations have faced. Such challenges and problem areas were tackled keeping in view different pedagogical issues and in response to the learners' requirements. In spite of the guidelines, some of the contributors have followed different presentation styles, and we have accepted these in order to give scope to different ways of presenting the cases. As far as possible, the original style has been retained with required editing. The common thread in these cases is the conscious "reflective thinking" on the part of the authors so far as the e-learning is concerned in their own institution. This is in line of the Schon's "reflection on practice," where the practitioner is asked to think about what they do, how they do, and why they do. The combined learning in this volume is enormous, as we have analyzed in the last section of this book. Individual cases are vivid presentations of the experiential learning of individuals and groups, and are reflective of how others can learn from those experiences.

Overview of the Book

The case studies in the book are organized in three sections: (1) Cases on completely online learning systems; (2) Cases on blended online learning systems; and (3) Cases on resource based online learning systems. In the introduction chapter, we present an overview of the e-learning concept, theory, and practices. It emphasizes how e-learning is perceived and used around the world. As a growing field of knowledge, the term "e-learning" itself has been interchangeably used with Web-based learning, online learning, Internet-based learning, virtual education, and so on. Whatever may be the term used, it is important to note that it is a system based on technology that provides opportunity for both synchronous and asynchronous interaction between the learners and the teachers. Thus, it has a new paradigm of teaching and learning—beyond—the print-based distance education (asynchronous) and tele-learning model of distance education (synchronous). It has the best of both and, therefore, it is a "new generation of distance education" (Mishra, 2001, p. 2). In order to use e-learning effectively, it is essential that a systematic approach is adhered to, and the online courses are planned, designed, and implemented according to sound pedagogical principles.

Cases on Completely Online Learning Systems

In Section I, there are 10 cases that discuss the use of online/Web-based/learning management systems (either off-the-shelf product or self-designed systems). Within the Web-based environment, these cases share their experiences and highlight what they did, how they did, and why they did the way they did. Most of these share some practice of program evaluation, and user feedback and critical reflection as lessons learnt. In Chapter I, Alina M. Zapalska and Dallas Brozik argue that the use of WebCT strongly contributes to the effectiveness of distance learning by improving the quality of students' learning in the areas of critical thinking, problem solving, decision making, attention to detail, written communications, and organizational and analytical skills. Ilias Maglogiannis and Kostas Karpouzis in Chapter II present a case study of e-learning implementation in a military training course, and highlight the benefits accrued because of the use of both synchronous and asynchronous technologies. The third case study is by Gunnar Martin, August-Wilhelm Scheer, Oliver Bohl, and Udo Winand from Germany, and showcases a full-fledged online masters program on information systems initially developed in a collaboration model by four universities. While the online programs are useful to the learners, it is also important to enhance the capacity of the tutors by providing appropriate training on needed competencies. In the next case, a team of researchers from New Mexico State University presents their model of teacher preparation to teach online through an online program of staff development. The next case presents another model of collaborative online program development by two universities, one in the U.S. and the other in Africa. In this case, Hilary Wilder shows us the issues related to academic program planning and administrative issues in developing programs for learners with low-tech access. In Chapter VI, Shobhita Jain presents her experience of developing and running India's first social science online program at the Indira Gandhi National Open University. She shares with us how continuous feedback from the learners was useful in improving the functionality of the system developed by the University. This case also presents to us the idea of alternative ways of assessment in online world by using the peer assessment in discussion forum. In order to promote reflective practice, this case also demonstrates the use of online diary (a primitive form of blogging). And when it comes to assessment, it is also a good idea to keep record of the work by the learners online in the form of portfolios. In the next chapter, Madhumita Bhattacharya presents a description and analysis of salient issues related to the development of an integrated e-portfolio application implemented at Massey University to help students track and accumulate evidence of skills developed over their period of study using the online distance education course in the background. Continuing the issue of online professional development, Donna Russell in Chapter VIII presents the experience of an activity-theory-based online learning program (eMINTIS) using a network space technology. This experiential learning model provides us an opportunity to see online learning as a vehicle of change and quality improvements. John Beaumont-Kerridge in the next case in Chapter IX showcases the experience of the use of Internet phone technology for synchronous group based e-learning and reports the experience of both students and tutors, who find the technology as a useful medium to increase communication and provide remedial learning. In the last case of this section, Lucio Teles and Nancy Johnston present the online program on co-operative education. Participants in the pilot project found the online version to be a valuable tool to support co-op students in learning and developing employability skills, including problem defining and solving, planning and goal setting, improved interpersonal communication skills and self-assessment, and peer feedback skills.

Cases on Blended Online Learning Systems

Section II has eight case studies where e-learning has been used in a blended learning scenario as a matter of design and delivery. The cases in this section cover subject areas as diverse as sports management to criminology. In Chapter XI, Alistair Inglis, Matthew Nicholson, and Clare Hanlon describe a case study based program on learning sports management. This case is unique in the sense that it uses the case study approach used in this book as the learning design to deliver the whole program, where learners study materials supplied in CD-ROM, and then interact online and also face-to-face to learn the subject matter content. In the next case, Raffaella Sette presents the complexities of developing a blended course on criminology at the University of Bologna. In Chapter XIII, Jarkko Suhonen and Erkki Sutinen from Finland present the digital learning environment to teach computer science and support the face-to-face teaching. Elspeth McKay in Chapter XIV presents a case study of school level application of online learning in Fiji. It discusses the institutional and national context of the e-learning program offered by a school in Fiji that is accredited by the International Baccalaureate Organization. A zoom-lens approach is taken by the year-5 classroom teacher to encourage her students' experiential learning. She points out that alternative instructional strategies are required when the Internet becomes unstable. Using the chemical engineering subject background, Katia Tannous in Chapter XV exhibits the experience of applying project-based learning methods through online learning, while in Chapter XVI, Mary Griffiths and Michael Griffiths describe how they developed intercultural, pastoral pedagogies suited to contrasting "internationalized" cohorts, despite trends in new "market-driven" universities. They used Michel Foucault's framework of "pastoral" power, as modeled by Ian Hunter in studies of the milieu of the face-to-face English classroom. They emphasize that the development of valuable intercultural skills in the student depends in part on the composition of the "internationalized" student groups themselves, and on their and their teacher's awareness of the formative nature of the software being used. Chapter XVII by K. C. Chu presents the use of scenario-based learning strategy in designing e-learning for vocational education. This online environment provides chances to all students to virtually immerse in a scenario to enhance their learning and knowledge. In Chapter XVIII, Yan Hanbing and Zhu Zhiting from China present their e-workshop model of teacher training to solve problems of time, quality materials, work relationships, and mentoring. They also use e-portfolios, synchronous chat, and community bulletin boards to develop teacher competencies.

Cases on Resource-Based Online Learning Systems

In Section III, there are five cases analyzing how online resources can be organized, designed, and delivered to optimize learning. Mitchell Weisburgh in Chapter XIX presents a systematic approach to development of an online resource center on pain medicine using the power of a multimedia-based online learning system. This case is a lesson for how to critically look into the issues of scripting, content development, and technology choice. In Chapter XX, Colette Wanless-Sobel analyzes online community problem solving using the power of the Web, particularly through blogging. Colette recognizes that success of the online learning resource is largely due to the intrinsic motivation and cognitive engagement afforded through civic engagement, allowing learners to pursue personally relevant knowledge in familiar milieus. Technology plays a role in increasing intellectual self-esteem and digital literacy by allowing students the opportunity to become bloggers and Web publishers. Patrick J. Fahy and Patrick Cummins in Chapter XXI present a case on an employment readiness online system titled "ESPORT" in Canada. The system assists users with choosing an occupation, assesses their enabling skills in respect to the chosen occupation, identifies and (optionally) remedies skills gaps, and documents in a resume their abilities for prospective employers. They have also developed an e-portfolio as a part of the learning package to record the learning development of individuals. In Chapter XXII, Byung Ro Lim presents the e-learning systems of educational broadcasting system in Korea to prepare students for the Korean College entrance test. The system uses the power of the Web, and delivers video on demand services through satellite-based Internet services through cable TV and direct satellite receivers. In the last case of this book, a team of scholars from the Simon Fraser University presents their e-learning ecosystem model for e-learning based on analyses of their experiences in various cases. Taking cue from biology, where ecosystems are characterized by the interactions and the flow of matter and energy among biotic and abiotic elements, they say that e-learning can also be treated as an ecosystem characterized by the interactions and the flow of information across activities related to learning. They see clearly two sub-systems: instructor and learner in the process, and emphasize the role of faculty development in the e-learning eco-system.

Conclusion

E-learning has gained popularity in all kinds of educational settings (with rich and low access to technology). What is more prominent that the Internet and PC penetration, which is essential to a large extent for e-learning, is increasing all over. E-learning can be treated as those learning activities where computers, networks, and multimedia technologies play pivotal roles. Use of ICT (information and communication technologies) is crucial here to support, deliver, and/or facilitate learning opportunities. Most of the universities across the globe have found this mode of offering instruction quite beneficial and have adopted e-learning either as a single mode or as a complementary mode for delivery of educational services.

In this volume, practitioners of e-learning have brought out different dimensions of adopting e-learning strategies in diverse settings. They have shared their success and failure stories and what solutions they adopted for their problems or challenges faced. We understand that such success or failure factors or solutions may not be applicable to all situations as each e-learning project is unique in itself, because of the target group, social context, and environment of the institution, resources available, and so forth. But certainly these cases do provide learning opportunities for students of educational technology/e-learning, planners, and policy-makers as well to take note of others' experiences critically and design their own e-learning systems. We do not intend to compare one case with the other, to indicate which one is superior or what is not good. It is for the readers to see what they can use and what they would like to avoid. Our intention is to help the readers gain an insight into what makes an effective practice and solution, and thus in the last section we synthesize some of the lessons learned and best practices.

We hope that this volume would provide relevant insights into the practices and approaches of planning and management of e-learning all over the world with cases from Australia, Brazil, Canada, China, Finland, Germany, Greece, Hong Kong, India, Italy, Korea, New Zealand, the U.S., and the UK. We are sure the rich experiences of the contributors of this volume would be beneficial to various stakeholders of e-learning to understand, examine, determine, and select solutions to what, how, why, when, and where e-learning can be best deployed.

Reference

Mishra, S. (2001). *Designing online learning*. Knowledge Series. Vancouver: The Commonwealth of Learning. Retrieved March 24, 2006, from http://www.col.org/Knowledge/pdf/KS_online.pdf

Acknowledgments

We have been closely observing various developments and changes in this field of e-learning for quite sometime now. Many institutions and organizations across the globe are engaged in developing e-learning technologies. Educational institutions are either using packages and technologies developed by commercial houses or developing their own technologies in-house. Continued interactions with friends and colleagues involved in designing, developing, and training for e-learning provided us necessary input to translate those experiences to this present volume as a compendium of case studies on successes or pitfalls of e-learning practices.

This has been a most rewarding experience for us, as we express our heartfelt thanks and gratitude to all our contributing authors for their excellent contributions and insights. During the long course of development of this book, some of the contributors due to their other engagements could not submit their work on time. We thank them also for their association, encouragement, and support provided for this work.

Any work of this magnitude and quantum certainly needs high quality standards, which were obtained through a double-blind peer-review process of the submissions. The authors of the chapters included in the book were kind and supportive enough to review and provide suggestions, constructive comments on the chapters for maintaining high quality submissions. In addition to our authors, we have our most sincere thanks to Dr. Kinshuk, Massey University, New Zealand; Professor Paul Kawachi, Kurume Shin-Ai Women's College, Japan; Dr. Lynn Hunt, Massey University, New Zealand; Dr. Michael Sankey, University of Southern Queensland, Australia; Dr. Geraldine Torrisi-Steele, Griffith University, Australia; and Mr. Karthik, Bangalore, India. Their critical and constructive comments on the chapters are deeply appreciated and acknowledged.

This is our second edited book with Idea Group Inc. We would like to place on record our special thanks and appreciation to the publishing team at Idea Group Inc. We are deeply grateful to Dr. Mehdi Khosrow-Pour, DBA; Ms. Kristin Roth, Development Editor; and Mr.

Andrew Bundy, Assistant Marketing Manager. We found them ready to help at all times. Their quick support and attendance to our queries enabled us to keep the book development schedule on right track. Ms. Kristin Roth deserves a special thank you note for the continuous interactions through e-mails as a result of which the project was managed in time. Dr. Ramesh Sharma would like to express his gratitude to the Idea Group Inc. and his co-editor, Dr. Sanjaya Mishra, for the support received during his illness, at the crucial finalization stage of the book. Dr Sharma further thanks his wife, Madhu Sharma, and kids, Aakanksha and Apoorv, for being there and giving the best kind of support.

We also thank our employer, the Indira Gandhi National Open University, and its staff members for providing us support and encouragement to bring out this quality work. We also wish to thank our respective family members and friends who have been fully supportive, without which this work would not have been brought to fruition. Especially Dr. Mishra would like to say thank you to his wife, Dr. Sweta Panigrahi, for all the support and understanding she has shown, without which the task would have been quite difficult.

It is also worthwhile to mention here that all the software and trademarks mentioned in the book chapters or referenced therein are the property and trademarks of their respective owners.

Last but not least, we once again express our sincere thanks to our contributing authors for sharing their experiences in an excellent manner. They have been very accommodating, in spite of their preoccupations and engagements, and obliged us by submitting chapters well within the schedule.

Ramesh C. Sharma

Sanjaya Mishra

Introduction

Global E-Learning Practices: An Introduction

Ramesh C. Sharma, Indira Gandhi National Open University, New Delhi, India

Sanjaya Mishra, Indira Gandhi National Open University, New Delhi, India

Introduction

No other educational technology has ever captured the imagination and interests of so many educators around the world simultaneously than Internet and the World Wide Web (Owston, 1997). The interest in the educational use of the Internet and its World Wide Web (WWW) has been so that today the e-learning industry is the fastest-growing sub-sector of a $2.3 trillion global education market, and the market for online higher education is estimated to exceed $69 billion by 2015 (Hazel Associates, 2005). The increased demand for and just in time need for higher education and training coupled with a shift from the labor intensive workforce to a more globalized knowledge intensive workforce has resulted in the rapid growth and expansion of e-learning. The demand to go online has become so significant that universities developed generic learning management systems. Most of these initially looked like a system to manage the existing classroom model of teaching and learning. The teaching community, largely for its simplicity and user-friendliness, accepted these systems quickly. However, soon they realized that what are delivered as e-learning courses are nothing more than lectures notes and PowerPoint files uploaded to the net. Weigel (2000, p. 12) says these courses are "little more than an exercise of posting on the Internet an enhanced syllabus that includes lecture content, reading assignments and practice tests, along with using discussion groups and e-mails to respond to students' questions," with very little thought on the pedagogical models relevant to the new medium. Carr-Chellman and Duchastel (2000) also expressed similar concern for the Web courses:

It is also evident that many online courses lack basic design consideration and that the Web is simply being used as a medium for delivery of instructions created within another framework. Such transposition from one medium to another may have some value in reaching certain outreach goals, but it also runs serious risks of diluting the original instruction and possibly rendering it ineffective. (p.229)

Although we can find universities that were established to exclusively offer online courses and are still running successfully (e.g., University of Phoenix Online), there are some instances of online universities and courses having started and closed down. A major setback, and often cited by the skeptics of e-learning, is the shutting down of the United Kingdom eUniversity (UkeU) in 2004 for want of sufficient students after considerable resource spending. Besides student recruitment, other problems faced by UkeU were the wrong timing of the opening of the university (just after the dot com bubble burst in 2000), platform development, and impatience to see results immediately (Garrett, 2004). A huge amount of literature is now available before us to study, review, and learn from the mistakes and best practices. A close look into the e-learning use in the educational institutions reveals three typical manners (Bates, 2001; Berge, Collins, & Dougherty, 2000; Laurillard, 2002; Mason, 1998; Mayes, 2000; Mitra, 1999):

1. As integrated in the classroom teaching that works as a supplement to the face-to-face teaching;
2. As a "mixed mode" approach to complement face-to-face teaching, normally called "blended e-learning"; and
3. As an independent mode for teaching and learning as a replacement for face-to-face teaching.

These different ways of using the Web are an expression of new models of learning and teaching, indicating the emergence of a paradigm shift from teacher- to student-centered learning, transmission of old knowledge to the construction of new knowledge, behavioristic to humanistic, inauthentic and context free to authentic and context specific tasks. But such a paradigm shift calls for a new assortment of skills, knowledge, talents, and competencies (Ryan & Woodward, 1998; Salmon, 2000). Berge (2001) and Willis (1992) discuss such skills needed for online learning, requiring new communication patterns and refined time management skills. In addition, they point out the necessity of proper orientation for students to be able to adjust to the new online environment in order to facilitate their success. The global practice of e-learning and innovations by practitioners present a wide spectrum of thinking and use, as we can see in this volume. But, before that, let us deal with the interchangeable use of a variety of terminologies in the field of e-learning.

E-Learning Defined

The field of e-learning is inundated with a number of terms used either interchangeably or with little difference as defined by the contributors. Nick Rushby, editor of *British Journal of Educational Technology* says, "E-learning by any one name would smell as sweet—or at least smell no different" (Rushby, 2001, p. 509); though everyone is speaking about it, there is no common terminology or agreement in the definition. Rushby goes on to relate the situation with that of the semantic debate on computer and its application to learning in the 1970s, and the buzz of phases around this: Computer {aided/assisted/based/managed/enabled} {instruction/learning/education/training}, without much difference (Rushby, 2001). We see a similar situation in the field of e-learning today and thus list a set of definitions and terms to make the point obvious to all:

Web-Based Instruction

Khan (1997, p. 6) described Web-based instruction as a "hypermedia based instructional program, which utilizes the attributes and resources of the World Wide Web to create a meaningful learning environment where learning is fostered and supported."

Virtual Learning

"The educational process of learning over the Internet without having face-to-face contact is known as virtual learning" (French, Hale, Johnson, & Farr, 1999, p. 2). However, for some virtual learning may also include tele-learning.

Online Learning

It is synonymous to Web-based learning where learning is fostered via the WWW only, in an intranet or Internet. It has been recognized as the new generation in the evolutionary growth of open, flexible, and distance learning (Mishra, 2001).

E-Learning

"E-learning can be defined as the use of digital technologies and media to deliver, support and enhance teaching, learning, assessment and evaluation" (Armitage & O'Leary, 2003, p. 4).

"E-learning refers to the systematic use of networked information and communication technology in teaching and learning" (Naidu, 2003, p. 5).

The American Society for Training and Development (ASTD) defines e-learning as teaching and learning "delivered, enabled or mediated by electronic technology for the explicit purpose of learning" (Rossen & Hartley, 2001, p. 2). They include online learning, Web-based learning, and computer-based learning within e-learning.

Figure 1. What is e-learning?

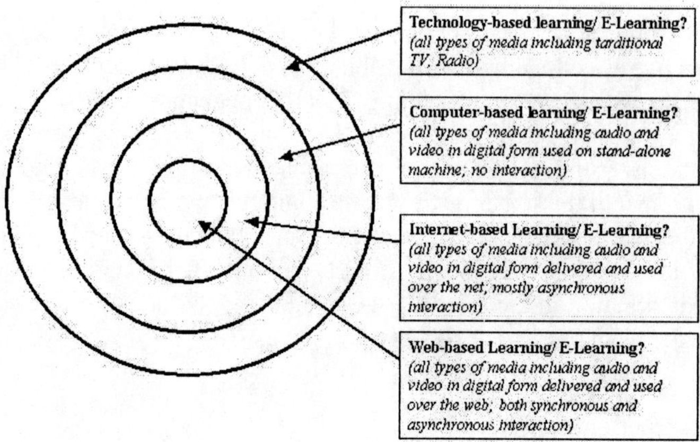

In the Corporate E-Learning report, e-learning has been defined as "a wide set of applications and processes including computer-based learning, Web-based learning, virtual classroom, and digital collaboration" (WR Hambrecht & Co., 2000, p. 8). Here e-learning has been equated with "technology-based training."

Thus, we can see a wide variation in the usage of the terms, with little difference in semantics. E-learning has gained popularity as a term also because of the notion of e-business, and the hype surrounding the word "e." Having looked at the usage of these terms, we map them in Figure 1 for better understanding and meaning making by the readers. While readers are free to use their own description and definition of the terms, we believe that e-learning is teaching and learning in a networked environment with or without blending of face-to-face contact and other digital media.

Benefits of E-Learning

E-learning has become popular amongst educationists because of the inherent strengths and advantages it provides to the instructional process. Some of these are:

- Access to educational resources from outside the institution on a global and instant basis;
- Quick and easy way to create, update, and revise course materials through low-cost off-the-shelf software;
- Increased and flexible interaction with students through e-mail and discussion forums;
- Location and time independent delivery of course materials such as course notes, diagrams, reading list, and so forth;

- Ability to combine text, graphics, and a limited amount of multimedia, enabling instructional designers to prepare quality learning materials;
- Ability to allow real-time access to subject matter experts with minimal loss of their productivity;
- Interactive and dynamic learning experience through online assessment tools, simulations, and animated learning objects;
- Platform independent delivery, accessible through any computer with a simple browser interface;
- Increased learner control through hypertext based presentation of information;
- Opportunities for international, cross-cultural, and collaborative learning; and
- Ability to serve a large number of students at a potentially reduced cost (Bates, 2001; Goldberg, Salari, & Swoboda, 1996; McCormack & Jones, 1998; Piskurich, 2006; Rossen & Hartley, 2001; Starr, 1997; Weller, 2000).

Design and Development of E-Learning Systems

A good understanding of Internet pedagogy, students' needs, and technologies are quite essential for the designing and developing of e-learning (Garrison, 2004; Mayes & Frietas, 2004). Collis and Moonen (2001) suggested institution, implementation, pedagogy, and technology as the chief components. Stick and Ivankova (2005) and Lieblein (2001) identified the factors that have been important to the online programs including the issue of on-campus visits by online students, the importance of conveying a sense of class, school, and university, approaches to pedagogy, synchronous versus asynchronous methods, administrative and technical support, and faculty issues.

HEFCE (2004) identified six key dimensions of effective e-learning design: connectivity (global access to information); interactivity (spontaneous assessment); motivation (enhanced learning); flexibility (anytime/any place learning); collaboration (through online discussion tools); and extended opportunities (reinforced learning). On the basis of these key dimensions, JISC set guidelines for effective e-learning design, viz. to develop learner's skills and knowledge; engage learners in the learning process; development of independent learning skills and to motivate learners.

Levy (2003) suggested following six factors to consider when planning online distance learning programs in higher education: (1) vision and plans, (2) curriculum, (3) staff training and support, (4) student services, (5) student training and support, and (6) copyright and intellectual property.

Some other aspects of designing and administration for online education have also been highlighted such as the importance of faculty support (Moskal & Dziuban, 2001; Truman, 2004); the selection of technology for its online programs (Dringus & Scigliano, 2000; Gibson & Herrera, 1999); and the importance of collaboration among different components of the system (Robinson, 2001; UT TeleCampus Overview 2004, 2004).

Mishra (2001) suggested the following key components to be kept in consideration while designing for online education:

1. Needs analysis (to look into the demand for online courses, whether they shall be cost-effective, what is the best option available, transfer of course credits, certification from an accreditation body);
2. Learner profile (understanding who the potential learner is, what technological skills he or she has, access to what hardware or software, access to Internet bandwidth, availability of educational loans, access to learning resource center, and so forth);
3. Organizational profile (if the organization has adequate infrastructure and expertise in terms of qualified faculty, what measure are taken for faculty compensation, availability of training facilities, and so forth);
4. Blueprint (it should contain detailed information on needs of the target learner group and how to apply learning theories [behaviorism, cognitivism, constructivism] to the online teaching; decision on media-mix; interactions; assessment and evaluation of learner performance in online settings; self-motivation of learners; orientation of learners and suitable decisions on developmental strategies like adoption of learner tools [course tools, collaboration tools, support tools]; developer tools [administrator tools, designer tools]; and learning management tools);
5. Institutional preparation (this pertains to installation and testing of hardware and software, staff training for system handling);
6. Learning materials development (to check for consistency particularly in multi-user environments, checking existing material's suitability);
7. Evaluation (this involves field trial of the learning materials and usability testing of the Web site. This would help examining on how effective the learning was as compared with face-to-face or other distance delivery methods. What were the cost-effectiveness issues? Adaptability of learners to the learning environment, issues of accreditation of online learning, and improvement in evaluation practices);
8. Promotion (course promotion through off-line and online modes to its intended learners); and
9. Maintenance and updating (continuous updating and maintenance of the system, regular feedback, constant monitoring, and so forth).

Pedagogy of E-Learning

As we know, pedagogy is the science and art of teaching and learning in general. And, every new technology brings in its own set of rules that needs to be followed and adapted to use that technology in a better way for teaching and learning. The Internet and the WWW can be effectively utilized in education, if we understand their unique features. Wiley and Schooler (2001) identify the following characteristics of the Web:

- Physicality of the media (no more paper-based);
- Social interactions (lack of physical co-presence both increases and limits interaction);
- Conversational pragmatics (being online, time independent, and flexible, increases participation and dialogue);

- Diversity of resources (available on the net);
- Lack of permanence (of the materials);
- Questionable authenticity (of materials);
- Multimodality (of learning resources; available in different forms: text, graphics, audio, video, animation);
- Hypermedia-based (not linear); and
- Customization and personalization (possibilities).

All these features bring in issues of designing appropriate pedagogical designs, and available literature suggests a variety of use of the Web for teaching and learning within the three major schools of thoughts (behaviorism, cognitive psychology, and constructivism). However, constructivism has been identified as the most suitable for online learning (Hung, 2001; Hung & Nichani, 2001; Oliver, 1999). An important issue while designing instructions has been of constructivism in terms of cognition. Basiel & Hatzipanagos (n.d., p. 1) suggested "Web-constructivism as a new e-learning paradigm, by taking knowledge acquisition as a process instead of as a product. Main emphasis in this paradigm is on problem solving approach as in real world context, where the tutor acts as a facilitator and the learner actively experiences the learning." Mishra (2002) suggested an eclectic approach in instructional design for Web-based learning based on his design experience in a social science online program (refer to Chapter VI). The design framework is depicted in Figure 2.

Based on the literature of e-learning and our own experience, we would like to present here another pedagogical framework of e-learning: experience-reflect-interact-construct (ERIC). We believe the pedagogy of e-learning should take into account the flexible delivery option

Figure 2. Design framework for online learning environment (Source: © Mishra, 2002)

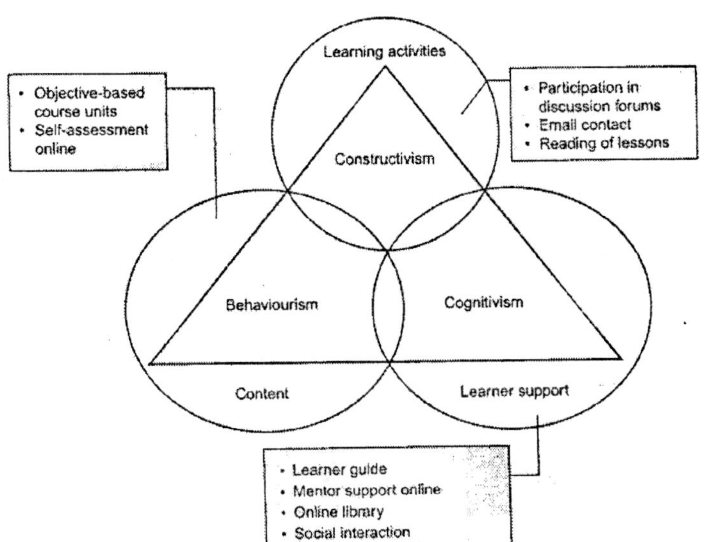

and provide learning experience to be accessed by the learner anywhere, anytime. This will include reading of materials on the Web, listening to audio, watching video, and experiencing animations and simulations. This will be followed by learner reflection activity that should be designed *a priori*. Having performed the reflective activities, the learners should now be given opportunity to interact both in synchronous and asynchronous mode. The last phase is to facilitate construction of knowledge by the learners though group work, projects, presentations, and other creative activities.

There are many other pedagogical designs applied in e-learning environments: "learning by doing" (Schank, 1997), "problem-based learning" (Barrows, 1994), "case-based learning" (Chen, Rong-An, & Harris, 2006; Lynn, 1996), "learning by designing" (Naidu, Anderson, & Riddle, 2000), and "role-play-based learning" (Ip & Linser, 1999).

Global Practices

During the initial wave of e-learning, the e-learning solution providers highlighted it as cost effective, advanced, and as an alternate to the traditional training. Thus, institutions and organizations were quick enough to embrace this new technology by making it a part of their staff training and learning strategy. From small universities to large multinational companies, everyone is trying to reach global audiences through Internet and multimedia applications by migrating from traditional classroom instruction or training to remote delivery models. E-learning practices have carved a niche for themselves in areas like health, education, military, entertainment, management, and scientific disciplines.

Some of the learning initiatives have been documented through the publications of the Commonwealth of Learning (COL) and the International Institute for Educational Planning (IIEP). There are major initiatives like the African Virtual University (AVU), Universiti Tun Abdul Razak (UNITAR), Malaysia, Athabasca University, Canada, Universitat Oberta de Catalunya, Spain, University of Southern Queensland, Australia, NetVarsity, India, and elsewhere (D'Antoni, 2003; Farrell, 1999, 2001). The Hewlett Foundation recently provided a grant to support the Teacher Education in Sub-Saharan Africa (TESSA) initiative, for an "open content" resource bank of educational materials to train teachers in basic curriculum areas including literacy, numeracy, science, and life and health skills. TESSA is a consortium of African and international organizations, led by the African Virtual University (Nairobi) and the Open University (UK). We present many other initiatives as case studies in this volume as exemplar of innovative practices in a structured format to help us draw our own conclusions.

References

Armitage, S., & O'Leary, R. (2003). *A guide for learning technologists (LSTN E-Learning Series No. 4)*. York: LTSN.

Barrows, H. S. (1994). *Problem-based learning applied to medical education.* School of Medicine. Springfield: Southern Illinois University.

Basiel, A., & Hatzipanagos, S. (n.d.). *Online pedagogy for Web-based videoconferencing: Guidelines of good use.* Retrieved August 29, 2006, from http://www.elearning.mdx.ac.uk/research/Skip_StylianosV4a.doc

Bates, T. (2001). *National strategies for e-learning in post-secondary education and training.* Paris: UNESCO, IIEP.

Berg, Z., Collins, M., & Dougherty, K. (2000). Design guidelines for Web-based courses. In B. Abby (Ed.), *Instructional and cognitive impacts of Web-based education* (pp. 32-40). Hershey, PA: Idea Group Publishing.

Berge, Z. (Ed.). (2001). *Sustaining distance training.* San Francisco: Jossey-Bass.

Carr-Chellman, A., & Duchastel, P. (2000). The ideal online course. *British Journal of Educational Technology, 31*(3), 229-241.

Chen, C. C., Rong-An, S., & Harris, A. (2006). The efficacy of case method teaching in an online asynchronous learning environment. *International Journal of Distance Education Technologies, 4*(2), 72-86.

Collis, B., & Moonen, J. (2001). *Flexible learning in a digital world: Experiences and expectations.* London: Kogan Page.

D'Antoni, S. (Ed.). (2003). *The Virtual University.* Paris: UNESCO, IIEP. Retrieved May 19, 2004, from http://www.unesco.org/iiep/virtualuniversity/

Dringus, L. P., & Scigliano, J. A. (2000). From early to current developments in online learning at Nova Southeastern University: Reflections on historical milestones. *Internet and Higher Education, 3*(1-2), 23-40.

Farrell, G. (1999). *The development of virtual education: A global perspective.* Vancouver: The Commonwealth of Learning.

Farrell, G. (2001). *The changing faces of virtual education.* Vancouver: The Commonwealth of Learning. Retrieved from http://www.col.org/virtualed/index2.htm

French, D., Hale, C., Johnson, C., & Farr, G. (Eds). (1999). *Internet-based learning: An introduction and framework for higher education and business.* London: Kogan Page.

Garrett, R. (2004). The real story behind the failure of UK eUniversity. *Educ. Quart., 27*(4), 4-6.

Garrison, D. (2004). *E-learning in the 21st century.* London: RoutledgeFalmer.

Gibson, J. W., & Herrera, J. M. (1999). How to go from classroom based to online delivery in eighteen months or less: A case study in online program development. *T.H.E. Journal Online, 6,* 57-60.

Goldberg, M. W., Salari, S., & Swoboda, P. (1996). World Wide Web Course tool: An environment for building WWW-based courses. *Computer Network and ISDN System,* 28. Retrieved May 17, 1999, from http://www.webct.com/papers/p29/

Hazel Associates. (2005). *Global e-learning opportunity for U.S. higher education.* Retrieved March 24, 2006, from http://www.hezel.com/globalreport/

HEFCE (2004). *Effective practice with e-learning.* Bristol: Higher Education Funding Council for England. Retrieved March 24, 2006, from http://www.jisc.ac.uk/uploaded_documents/jisc%20effective%20practice3.pdf

Hung, D. (2001). Design principles for Web-based learning: Implications for Vygotskian thought. *Educational Technology, 41*(3), 33-41.

Hung, D., & Nichani, M. (2001). Constructivism and e-learning: Balancing between the individual and social levels of cognition. *Educational Technology, 41*(2), 40-44.

Ip, A., & Linser, R. (1999). *Web-based simulation generator: Empowering teaching and learning media in political science.* Retrieved http://www.roleplaysim.org/papers/rpsg.htm

Khan, B. H. (1997). Web-based instruction: What is it and why is it? In B. H. Khan (Ed.), *Web-based instruction* (pp. 5-18). Englewood Cliff, NJ: Educational Technology.

Laurillard, D. (2002). *Rethinking university teaching: A conversational framework for the effective use of learning technologies*. London: Routledge.

Levy, S. (2003). Six factors to consider when planning online distance learning programs in higher education. *Online Journal of Distance Learning Administration*, *6*(1). Retrieved February 15, 2006, http://www.westga.edu/~distance/ojdla/spring61/levy61.htm

Lieblein, E. (2001). Critical factors for successful delivery of online programs. *The Internet and Higher Education, 3*(3), 161-174.

Lynn, L. E. (1996). *What is the case method? A guide and casebook.* Japan: The Foundation for Advanced Studies on International Development.

Mason, R. (1998). Models of online courses. *ALN Magazine, 2*(2). Retrieved March 24, 2006, from http://www.aln.org/publications/magazine/v2n2/mason.asp

Mayes, T., & de Frietas, S. (2004). *Review of e-learning theories, frameworks and models.* JISC E-Learning Models Desk Study. Retrieved March 24, 2006, http://www.jisc.ac.uk/uploaded_documents/Stage%202%20Learning%20Models%20(Version%201).pdf

Mayes, T. (2000). *Pedagogy, lifelong learning and ICT.* Retrieved March 24, 2006, from http://www.ipm.ucl.ac.be/ChaireIBM/Mayes.pdf

McCormack, C., & Jones, D. (1998). *Building a Web-based education system*. New York: Wiley Computer Publishing.

Mishra, S. (2001). *Designing online learning*, COL knowledge series. Vancouver: Commonwealth of Learning. Retrieved 2004 http://www.col.org/Knowledge/ks_online.pdf

Mishra, S. (2002). A design framework for online learning environments. *British Journal of Educational Technology, 33*(4), 493-496.

Mitra, S. (1999). Virtual institutions in the Indian subcontinent. In G. Farrell (Ed.), *The development of virtual education: A global perspective* (pp. 125-134). Vancouver: The Commonwealth of Learning.

Moskal, P. D., & Dziuban, C. D. (2001). Present and future directions for assessing cybereducation: The changing research paradigm. In L. R. Vandervert, L. V. Shavinina, & R. A. Cornell (Eds.), *Cybereducation: The future of long-distance learning* (pp. 157-183). Larchmont, NY: M.A. Liebert.

Naidu, S. (2003). *E-learning: A guidebook of principles, procedures and practices*. New Delhi: CEMCA.

Naidu, S., Anderson, J., & Riddle, M. (2000). The virtual print exhibition: A case of learning by designing. In R. Sims, O'Reilly, & S. Sawkins (Eds.), *Learning to choose: Choosing to learn (short papers and works in progress)* (pp. 109-114). Lismore, NSW: Southern Cross University Press.

Oliver, R. (1999). Exploring strategies for online teaching and learning. *Distance Education, 20*(2), 240-254.

Owston, R. D. (1997). The World Wide Web: A technology to enhance teaching and learning? *Educational Researcher, 26*(2), 27-33.

Piskurich, G. M. (2006). E-learning: Fast, cheap, and good. *Performance Improve., 45*(1), 18-24.

Robinson, R. L. (2001). Assuring quality in collaborative distance education programs: The experience of the University of Texas System TeleCampus. *Higher Education in Europe, 26*(4), 567-575.

Rossen, E., & Hartley, D. (2001). Basics of e-learning. *Info-Line, 109.*

Rushby, N. (2001). Editorial. *British Journal of Educational Technology, 32*(5), 509-511.

Ryan, M., & Woodward, L. (1998, June 20-25). Impact of computer mediated communication (CMC) on distance tutoring. In T. Ottman & I. Tomek (Eds.), *Proceedings of ED-MEDIA/ED-TELECOM '98 World Conference on Educational Telecommunications* (pp. 1203-1207). Freiburg, Germany: AACE.

Salmon, G. (2000). *E-moderating: The key to teaching and learning online.* Kogan Page: London.

Schank, R. (1997). *Virtual learning: A revolutionary approach to building a highly skilled workforce.* New York: McGraw-Hill.

Starr, R. M. (1997). Delivery instruction on the World Wide Web: Overview and basic design principles. *Educational Technology, 37*(3), 7-15.

Stick, S. L., & Ivankova, N. V. (2005). A decade of innovation and success in virtual learning: A World-Wide asynchronous graduate program in Educational Leadership and Higher Education. *Online Journal of Distance Learning Administration, 7*(4). Retrieved December 23, 2005, from http://www.westga.edu/~distance/ojdla/winter74/stick74.htm

Truman, B. E. (2004). UCF's exemplary faculty support: An institutionalized ecosystem. *Journal of Asynchronous Learning Network, 8*(3). Retrieved February 15, 2006, from http://www.sloan-c.org/publications/jaln/v8n3/v8n3_truman.asp

UT TeleCampus Overview 2004. (2004). Retrieved February 22, 2006, from http://www.telecampus.utsystem.edu/

Weigel, V. (2000). E-learning and the trade off between richness and the reach in higher education. *Change, 33*(5), 10-15.

Weller, M. J. (2000). Creating a large-scale, third generation distance education course. *Open Learning, 15*(3), 243-251.

Wiley, J., & Schooler, J. W. (2001). The mental Web: Pedagogical and cognitive implications of the net. In C. R. Wolfe (Ed.), *Learning and teaching on the World Wide Web* (pp. 243-257). San Diago: Academic Press.

Willis, B. (1992). *Strategies for teaching at a distance.* (ERIC Document Reproduction Service No. ED351008)

WR Hambrecht & Co. (2000). *Corporate e-learning: Exploring a new frontier.* Retrieved March 19, 2001, from http://www.wrhambrecht.com/research/coverage/elearning/ir/ir-explore.html

Section I

Cases on Completely Online Learning Systems

Chapter I

Online Learning with the Use of WebCT Vista

Alina M. Zapalska, U.S. Coast Guard Academy, USA

Dallas Brozik, Marshall University, Huntington, USA

Abstract

The primary goal of this chapter is to offer reflections on various aspects of the use of WebCT Vista in online business education at Marshall University, Huntington, West Virginia, U.S. The chapter argues that with the proper systems in place, including adequate technology and support and the cooperation of educational administrators, WebCT Vista can augment current educational systems in remarkable ways. The chapter also argues that the use of WebCT strongly contributes to the effectiveness of distance learning by improving the quality of students' learning in the areas of critical thinking, problem solving, decision making, attention to detail, written communications, and organizational and analytical skills. The assessment tool presented in this chapter was used to obtain students' feedback concerning their learning outcomes with and without the use of WebCT Vista. In general, most students positively evaluated the effect of WebCT Vista on their learning within areas such as critical thinking, problem solving, decision making ability, oral communication, written communication, knowledge of information, and the ability to organize and analyze. As the results of this analysis indicate, almost all students benefited from using WebCT.

Introduction

Today, many college students can complete their education without setting foot onto the college campus (Hutchins, 2001; Lynch, 2002). Online education has become an effective and efficient pedagogical tool that can be integrated successfully into college curricula as the standard method of distance learning (Lane, 2001; Lu & Chun-Sheng, 2003). Courses offered through the Internet using Blackboard, WebCT, and WebCT Vista allow students more flexibility to learn at their own pace as their schedules permit, reduce or eliminate travel time, and provide additional opportunities for reviewing course materials while being distant from in-class lectures (Kendall, 2001).

WebCT or WebCT Vista (the most recently updated version of WebCT) open educational access to nontraditional and geographically distributed students and can improve the overall educational process by reducing time, labor, and costs (Lichtenberg, 2001). Numerous studies have been conducted and show that the rich environments of Blackboard, WebCT, or WebCT Vista:

1. Promote study and investigation within authentic, realistic, meaningful, relevant, complex, and information-rich contexts (Hutchins, 2001; Wentzell, 2002);
2. Encourage the growth of student responsibility, self-motivation, initiative, decision making, and intentional learning (Smith, Ferguson, & Caris, 2001);
3. Cultivate an atmosphere of cooperative learning among students and teachers (Meyer, 2003);
4. Generate learning activities that promote written communication (Lynch, 2002);
5. Develop level thinking process (i.e., analysis, synthesis, critical thinking, decision making abilities, problem solving, experimentation, and creativity among many others) (McEwan, 2001; Scott, 2003); and
6. Enhance the quality of learning by enabling students to take new and more active roles in their learning process. (Smith & Rose, 2003; Smith et al., 2001)

It is clear that these tools provide real educational benefits and can be a valuable addition to any portfolio of teaching techniques.

Marshall University is a state-supported university providing undergraduate and graduate programs at several locations throughout West Virginia. The enrollment at Marshall is approximately 16,000 students, including 4,000 graduate and medical students. A major goal of Marshall University is to create teaching excellence by enriching student skills in communication, critical thinking, and problem solving to ensure that all students receive the best possible instruction. The Lewis College of Business offers business and economics courses through traditional classroom delivery and distance education to students in rural communities in West Virginia. The distance education program is comprehensive in that it enables students to obtain undergraduate business degrees without coming to campus. The primary mode of course delivery, before introduction of WebCT Vista, was a satellite course or instruction based on an e-mail system. While these techniques allowed the delivery of courses to remote areas, each lacked certain features necessary for a comprehensive program.

Marshall University introduced WebCT in beta format in the fall of 1996 as a test project. In the fall of 1997, the university officially adopted WebCT as its Web-based course delivery tool. Marshall University's electronic course policy states that all e-course materials are to be housed and used on Marshall University's WebCT server, so that the university can provide common support for course developers, instructors, and students taking courses from Marshall University. This university-wide standardization has facilitated a more efficient and cost-effective use of computers and distance-learning software.

Marshall currently has more than 1,000 courses that use or have used WebCT Vista for curriculum delivery. Twenty-seven of these were fully online courses for the fall 2000 semester. Over 12,000 students used WebCT for the delivery of instructional material since 2000. Of this number, more than 3,000 were enrolled in WebCT courses for the fall 2001 semester. All online distance education courses are offered via WebCT Vista, and about 20% of WebCT Vista supported courses are delivered online.

The primary goal of this chapter is to offer reflections on various aspects of the use of WebCT Vista in online business education at Marshall University. The chapter argues that with the proper systems in place, including adequate technology and support and the cooperation of educational administrators, WebCT Vista can augment current educational systems in remarkable ways. This chapter also argues that the use of WebCT strongly contributes to the effectiveness of distance learning by improving the quality of students' learning in the areas of critical thinking, problem solving, decision making, attention to detail, written communications, and organizational and analytical skills.

Online Learning Program

All WebCT Vista users, both instructors and students, access WebCT Vista using a Web browser. Other than the browser, there is no special software needed to access a WebCT-based course. All that is required is that the user can access a computer that has a modem or is connected to a network. The instructor creates and edits the course and marks students' work using WebCT tools. Students read notes, take quizzes, perform exercises, and communicate with the instructor or other students using a chat room. The program does require a general familiarity with the World Wide Web, but this is a skill that most students already have. Since specialized software or knowledge is not necessary, WebCT Vista provides a transparent and painless way to access educational resources.

WebCT Vista provides structure, interactivity, and course tools. The instructor provides course content. Course tools are accessed through an icon from the course Web page. Examples of tools include a conferencing system, timed quizzes, grade storage and distribution, e-mail between course participants, student self-evaluation, student presentation areas, a student annotation facility, student progress tracking, a course glossary, and an index. Progress tracking, student management, and access control tools are also available. WebCT Vista provides a robust, Web-based platform for discussions and document sharing and allows the students to work together via the WebCT Vista in groups. Students use the Web-based tools to discuss course concepts, to share work experiences, and to offer one another suggestions for carrying out assignments and improving learning. It is important to guide students as to what resources are available, pertinent, and accurate.

WebCT Vista allows students to share ideas and exchange information and knowledge with each other while working collaboratively. Students can review their lessons and do exercises at their convenience. They must receive feedback from the exercises quickly so that they know where they need to focus, thereby saving traditional classroom time that otherwise would have been used to correct and review homework assignments. Students are encouraged to use the discussion area, and postings can be counted toward the student's class participation grade. This helps assure that all students take part in this virtual classroom.

Students also use the WebCT Vista quiz program to assess their knowledge of the topic before the actual exam. Ten questions are randomly selected from a database of approximately 100 questions per topic. Along with the grade for the quiz, each student receives corrected answers to all questions and is provided with specific advice concerning mastery of the subject matter. Due to the random selection of questions students can take the quiz a number of times before all questions are viewed, and students are encouraged to retake the quizzes until they master the subject material.

Effective WebCT Vista-based education requires the same, if not more, faculty involvement as in face-to-face courses. In order to stimulate critical thinking, activities must be provided throughout the course that included discussions, individualized attention to students who need more help, timely and thorough feedback of assignments, and ad-hoc problem solving. Web-based education must not be thought of as a machine assisted replacement for traditional teaching. It must be considered as a technology-augmented method of educational content that requires a dedicated effort on the part of the instructor to be successful.

Program Evaluation

The curriculum structure in the College of Business at Marshall University presented a unique opportunity to evaluate the effectiveness of WebCT-based instruction. All business students are required to take a two-term sequence in economics. The students involved in this study had all taken their first economics course in the traditional classroom and took their second economics course using WebCT. These students were thus able to draw on their personal experiences to compare the two methods of delivery.

A questionnaire was used to collect feedback from students to help the instructor gain an in-depth perspective of the range of attained learning, as well as student competence. This type of assessment was beneficial because it allowed the evaluation of WebCT Vista and its effect on improving the quality of students' learning in areas of critical thinking, problem solving, decision making, communications, and subject knowledge. Forms were designed so that students were not required to identify themselves while answering the questions. Anonymous feedback offered the students the opportunity to make comments they might not ordinarily have made during face-to-face or group meetings.

The data were collected at the course's beginning and conclusion. The questionnaire at the beginning of the course focused on the previous classroom course, and the questionnaire at the end of the course focused on the WebCT delivery method. Students were given the same questionnaire that evaluated how strongly, if at all, the method of instruction influenced each area of the students' learning outcomes. Students had to rate the influence on a scale

Table 1. Course delivery assessment

Area	Positive Influence ←----		No Influence ----	Negative Influence ----→	
Critical thinking	5	4	3	2	1
Problem solving	5	4	3	2	1
Decision making ability	5	4	3	2	1
Oral communication	5	4	3	2	1
Written communication	5	4	3	2	1
Knowledge of information	5	4	3	2	1
Ability to organize and analyze	5	4	3	2	1

of one to five, with the most positive influence rated a "5," no influence rated a "3," and a completely negative influence ranked as a "1" (Table 1).

The survey was conducted in the Principles of Macroeconomics course in the spring 2004 semester. Because all 55 students who were enrolled in the course participated in the survey, the survey data is not represented by a simple random sample. However, because all of the students who participated in our course were typical business students, there is no source of potential bias in a student sample, and this group of participants has been treated as a fair representation of students who take Principles of Macroeconomics courses.

Since the same seven questions were asked each time, the matched pairs data allowed the use of each participant's differences to evaluate the impact of WebCT on the pedagogical performance. After converting the data into the "differences" representing the positive distance between categories selected on both occasions, the values ranged from –1 to 4. This implies that in most cases there was either a positive shift in categories selection (1 to 4) or no change noticed (0).

Statistical analysis was performed with two goals in mind. First, by analyzing positive differences in student responses and looking for evidence of improvement, it could be determined how students benefited from the use of WebCT-based instruction. The distributions were then examined across the student group to see if most of the students benefited in a similar way or if there were groups of students who benefited strongly from WebCT-based instruction while others did not benefit as much.

Second, all seven areas were examined to determine if the changes were similar, or if there were some areas where the improvement is more obvious than in the others. For each participant who reported an improvement in at least one of the seven areas, a number that represented the magnitude and the direction of the opinion shift was obtained, and based on these values the number of areas in which there was a positive shift for each participant was determined. The frequencies of positive shifts are presented in Table 2. Only 2 of the 55 students indicated no benefit in any area, while more than half of the students (42) benefited in majority (at least 4) of the seven areas (76.4% +/– 11.2%).

The next step in the analysis was to identify the number of students who reported an improvement in each of the seven areas. Initially, the magnitude of the improvement was

Table 2. Frequencies of students who reported positive changes

Number of areas in which student benefited	0	1	2	3	4	5	6	7
Number of students	2	4	3	4	5	11	9	17

Table 3. Numbers and percentages of students reporting positive change for each area (A1-A7)

Areas	Number of Students	Percentages
A1: Critical thinking	36	64.6% +/– 13.2%
A2: Problem solving	48	85.1% +/– 9.6%
A3: Decision making ability	37	66.3% +/– 13.0%
A4: Oral communication	37	66.3% +/– 13.0%
A5: Written communication	41	73.2% +/– 12.2%
A6: Knowledge of information	40	71.5% +/– 12.5%
A7: Ability to organize and analyze	31	56.0% + /– 13.7%

ignored and only the positive shift during the time period of the WebCT-based instruction was considered. The number of students reporting positive changes is reported in Table 3, with the 95% confidence intervals for the percentages provided in column 3. Since the confidence intervals overlap, there is no evidence that the true percentages of students who benefited from the WebCT Vista instruction vary across all seven areas. The observed differences could be random.

To gain further insight, a comparison of the changes within all seven areas for all students was made. The change frequencies are reported in the contingency Table 4. As mentioned earlier, each change was recorded within the range of –1 to 4. However, because of many small counts in two outside columns, the two first and the last two columns were collapsed for chi-squared analysis to be valid.

The chi-square analysis of homogeneity in distributions across all areas for the data in Table 4 yielded a p-value of 0.082 (chi-square = 26.831, 18 df) providing some, although not very strong, evidence of heterogeneity of the distribution of the magnitude of change across the seven areas. Frequency counts marked with stars indicate cells with standardized residuals –2.33 (count 7) and -2.08 (count 5). They indicate that the lack of homogeneity is mostly due to both counts being significantly less than expected for this contingency table. In area 2, there were fewer students than expected who did not benefit from the WebCT-based instruction. In area 4, the number of students who strongly benefited from the WebCT instruction is significantly lower than expected. Except for these two cases, the improvement is similar for all seven areas.

Both the frequency counts and the statistical analysis imply that content delivery by WebCT resulted in better learning outcomes than traditional classroom delivery. Students were posi-

Table 4. Classification of students according to their magnitude of the positive change

Areas	−1 or 0	1	2	3 or 4
A1: Critical thinking	19	14	13	9
A2: Problem solving	7*	16	17	15
A3: Decision making ability	18	10	12	15
A4: Oral communication	18	16	16	5*
A5: Written communication	14	17	10	14
A6: Knowledge of information	15	14	12	14
A7: Ability to organize and analyze	24	11	6	14

tively influenced by the use of WebCT in the majority of the areas examined. This indicates that a well-designed WebCT course is not merely a technological feat but that it also results in improved student learning.

Policy Implications

The success of the use of WebCT Vista suggests that this method of teaching must be considered alongside traditional classroom techniques as a valid pedagogical style. It will be necessary for institutions to identify their overall attitude to this type of teaching, and if it is favorable assure that the necessary resources are made available. Institutions will also have to develop systems to evaluate both instructors and courses for their effectiveness using this teaching method. It will also be necessary for faculty members to develop the skills necessary to deliver courses using Web-based protocols. Individual instructors will need to devote the time and effort to master the courseware and develop appropriate course materials. It may be that those programs that prepare individuals for college teaching develop and require courses that teach the use of this type of technology.

Lessons Learned

In traditional as well as online technology-based courses, there is a gap between what is taught and what is learned. Methods of assessing the teaching and learning experience that are generally used in college education are not sufficient to evaluate how well a faculty member performs in a virtual classroom. The assessment tool presented in this paper was used to obtain students' feedback concerning their learning outcomes with and without the use of WebCT Vista. In general, most students positively evaluated the effect of WebCT Vista on their learning within areas such as critical thinking, problem solving, decision-making ability, oral communication, written communication, knowledge of information, and the ability to organize and analyze. As the results of this analysis indicate, almost all students benefited from using WebCT.

The percentages of students who benefited in a particular area are not significantly different across all seven areas. The extent of the improvement made in each area is fairly consistent with two exceptions: fewer students than expected did not benefit from the WebCT Vista technology in the area of problem solving, and fewer than expected students benefited strongly in the area of oral communication. It is also noted that by including content delivery assessment as part of the course evaluation student motivation has increased. This is possibly because the students realized that faculty were interested in their success as learners.

The success of distance education requires encouraging learners to take an active role in the educational process. Students need to learn to rely on themselves to access and master the use of the technology. The careful, gradual introduction of Web-based technologies can guide and enhance learners' transition from a traditional model of pedagogy to a model in which they take a full, active role in directing and achieving their own learning. New tools like WebCT Vista allow instructors to add a level of interactivity that makes students monitor their own progress in the class and concentrate on these areas that require improvement. This type of progress checking can lead to more specific and in-depth questions and more meaningful discussion during the lecture.

Chat facilities have been implemented to promote communication similar to that found in traditional lecture classes. The use of WebCT Vista enhances students' collaboration and cooperation. Students are able to work with one another more often because of enhanced communication. Barriers of time, place, and distance between and among students are more easily overcome or eliminated. WebCT Vista also allows students to work together with simulations and "real life" projects. Learning activities can become increasingly real. Not only can instructors notify students of their homework or exam marks outside of class time, but instructional time is also saved because it need not be used to collect and redistribute assignments. Web pages within the WebCT Vista course deliver course content and give students feedback. WebCT Vista instructional technology can improve student learning by helping students use their time more efficiently. Students can learn at their own pace at different times of day.

This analysis of teaching with the WebCT Vista courseware has identified several specific factors that should be considered.

1. Proper use of Web-based teaching can enhance the student's ability to learn.
2. Improvement in educational outcomes can be seen in all areas of instruction.
3. Students must receive ongoing training related to courseware and other support functions so that they can efficiently utilize the materials provided via WebCT Vista courseware.
4. Effective use of WebCT Vista-based courses requires significant time and commitment to instructor training.
5. Preparation and implementation of a WebCT Vista course requires the instructor's commitment to continued training in instructional strategies for Web-enhanced courses.
6. The technical training is critical to the implementation of Web-enhanced courses.
7. University-based support for faculty, staff, and students is essential for successful distance and distributed learning.

8. Technical support is necessary and must be integrated with changes in instructional methods and course design.

These factors indicate that Web-based instruction is not merely an extension of the traditional classroom. It requires a different approach to the educational process and can deliver a different level of educational results.

The use of Web-based teaching technology, such as that offered by WebCT Vista, is not merely a technological extension of using computers in the classroom. It is an entirely new type of pedagogy that has demonstrated positive benefits for those involved in the class. As future developments continue to refine the methodology of Web-based instruction, it should become more widely accepted by both instructors and students. The power of the process cannot be denied, and the entire structure of higher education will need to adapt to accept this new way of delivering educational content.

References

Hutchins, H. (2001). Enhancing the business communication course through WebCT. *Business Communication Quarterly, 64*(3), 87-95.

Kendall, M. (2001). Teaching online to campus-based students: The experience of using WebCT for the community information module at Manchester Metropolitan University. *Education for Information, 19*, 325-346.

Lane, K. (2001). Report examines shortfalls of distance learning. *Distance Education, 14*(3), 14-19.

Lichtenberg, J. (2001). Going the distance. With the help of technology, correspondence courses evolve into electronic learning. *Publishers Weekly, 25*(4), 37-40.

Lu, J., & Chun-Sheng, C. (2003). Learning styles, learning patterns, and learning performance in a WebCT-based MIS course. *Information and Management, 40*(6), 497-508.

Lynch, D. (2002). Professors should embrace technology in courses. *The Chronicle of Higher Education*, January 18.

McEwan, B. (2001). Web-assisted and online learning. *Business Communication Quarterly, 64*(2), 98-103.

Meyer, K. (2003). The Web's impact on student learning. *THE Journal*, May 20(10), 14-19

Scott, K. (2003). Online education expands and evolves. *EEE Spectrum*, May 40(5), 49-52.

Smith, A., & Rose, R. (2003). Build and teach a successful online course. *Technology and Learning,* April 23, 16-19.

Smith, G., Ferguson, D., & Caris, M. (2001). Teaching college courses online vs. face-to-face. *T.H.E. Journal*, April.

Wentzell, C. (2002). Reaping the benefits of online learning. *Benefits Canada, 26,* 9-12.

Chapter II

Combining Synchronous and Asynchronous Distance Learning for Adult Training in Military Environments

Ilias Maglogiannis, University of the Aegean, Greece

Kostas Karpouzis, National Technical University of Athens, Greece

Abstract

A major issue problem in military training is the territorial dispersion of military personnel in a wide geographical area. Typically in every military training course, officers are gathered in training camps and attend the lessons. The specific model obliges officers to leave their position, their units to lose their services, and is extremely costly, as the learners have to move and reside near the training camp during their training. The application of distance learning techniques seems in a position to solve such problems. The School of Research and Informatics for Officers of the Greek Army in cooperation with the academic community in Greece studied the possibility of training military personnel via a computer assisted distance-learning system and then implemented a pilot program in operational business management. This chapter describes the results of this study, the experience acquired during the implementation, and an overall assessment of the pilot program.

Introduction

The increasing degree of technology shift and the growth of available information for consumption transform education into an incessant process. Furthermore, managerial needs impose the continuous strengthening of the capacities of human resources, since the human capital provides the impetus of any organization. As a result, the utmost priority of any modern army is the constant training and education of the military personnel in a wide gamut of issues.

Current telecommunications and information technologies provide the indispensable capabilities for lifelong education without the need for presence at a physical classroom; this is defined as "distance learning" (Moore & Kearsley, 1996). In essence, this is a form of open education, in which the teacher and the learner need not be in the same space, since they are in touch by means of synchronous or asynchronous communication. In general, distance learning comes in many forms: some try to simulate the classroom paradigm's two-way, synchronous communication in real time, while others support independent study controlled by the learner. The latter scheme is supported by most current distance learning environments (Broady, 1996).

One of the goals of open distance learning is to provide access to all levels of education to individuals that distance or personal circumstances make it very difficult for them to attend conventional classes. Another goal is to teach courses to remote locations or military camps that are difficult for teachers to access. Consequently, the military environment is one of the best suited for distance learning, since learners are geographically dispersed and absence from their positions usually causes additional problems in the operation of their units (Maglogiannis, Mpourletides, & Karpouzis, 2003). Several studies have proven the efficiency of distance learning in vocational training of the personnel in big public organizations (Folkman, 2002; Gemeinhardt, 2002; Sampson, Karagiannidis, Schenone, & Cardinali, 2002). This chapter sums up the results of a pilot distance learning course, taught to military personnel.

Fundamentally, distance learning is education delivered over a distance to one or more individuals located in one or more venues. Distance learning includes two modes of operation: "synchronous distance learning," which occurs when teacher and student are present at the same time during the instruction, even if they are in two different places, and "asynchronous communication," which occurs when students and teachers do not have person-to-person simultaneous interaction during teaching. Asynchronous distance learning is delivered through open networks such as the World Wide Web, private intranets, or home computer-based study applications, while student faculty communication occurs via e-mail, including comments on homework assignments.

Academic Issues

Models of Learning Environments

A distance learning training program may be directed to learners of different degrees of educational level, minors or adults. In the case of learners in military service, the special circumstances of their profession impose special requirements, as well as special demands, on a distance learning environment. As a result, it is extremely necessary to pinpoint their individual needs, so as to prepare measures for satisfying them to the greatest extent. According to Knowles (1990), some of the most important "counter-measures" are:

- Introduction of cooperative learning climate
- Establishment of mechanisms for teachers' and learners' mutual planning
- Identification of learner needs and interests
- Identification of learning objectives based on the diagnosed needs and interests
- Preparation of sequential activities for achieving the objectives
- Execution of planning via careful choice of methods, educational material, and required resources
- Evaluation of the quality of the learning experience while rediagnosing needs for further learning (Flottemesch, 2000)

For distance learning application to succeed in meeting the demands of all kinds of learners and be successful as a new educational paradigm that supports synergistic learning and active participation of learners, there have to exist a number of key elements and principles to be followed. These principles can be classified in five axes (Broady, 1996):

1. Learning goals and content presentation
2. Interactions
3. Assessment and measurement
4. Instructional media and tools
5. Learner support and services

As far as realization of a distance learning environment is concerned, one can assume three fundamental models. The distinctive characteristic of these models is the means of control with respect to the actual teaching space and the pace of training (Blythe, 2001; Cronjé, 2001; Dzakiria, 2004; Schellens & Valcke, 2005).

For example, in some models learners possess complete control and responsibility over their progress, while other models are based on stricter control enforced by the teacher or another central party (Bourdeau & Bates, 1996; Massicotte, 1997).

The "Distributed Classroom" Model

This model essentially extends the educational curriculum offered in a traditional classroom to a group of learners in one or more distant locations, using advanced interactive means of communication. This form of teaching imitates that of the conventional classroom as far as both the teacher and the learner are concerned. As one may deduce, control over the learning process is centralized in this model, thus the control rests with the teacher.

The "Independent Learning" Model

This model alleviates the burden of the learners' presence in a particular location for a long time. Learners are provided with a wide variety of learning material, including a study guide and access to members of the teaching staff. This member acts as a tutor, offering guidance, solving problems, and evaluating the learner's performance. Communication between the learner and tutor may include both conventional means (telephone, postal mail, etc.), as well as electronic (e-mail, teleconferencing, online forums, etc.).

The "Open Learning and Classroom" Model

Utilization of this model combines the usage of a print study guide with additional educational material in electronic form, enabling individual learners to complete studying in their own pace. This model is integrated with modern communications technology so as to facilitate virtual class meetings between the learners.

Table 1. Models of learning environments and their characteristics

The "distributed classroom" model	The "independent learning" model	The "open learning and classroom" model
• Class sessions involve synchronous communication; students and faculty are required to be in a particular place at a particular time (once a week at a minimum) • Number of sites varies from two (point-to-point) to five or more (point-to-multipoint); the greater the number of sites, the greater the complexity—technically, logistically, and perceptually • Students may enroll at sites more convenient to their homes or work locations than the campus • Institutions are able to serve small numbers of students in each location • The nature of the experience mimics that of the classroom for both the instructor and the student	• There are no class sessions; students study independently, following the detailed guidelines in the syllabus • Students may interact with the instructor and, in some cases, with other students • Presentation of course content is through print, computer disk, or videotape, all of which students can review at a place and time of their own choosing • Course materials are used over a period of several years, and generally are the result of a structured development process that involves instructional designers, content experts, and media specialists; not specific to a particular instructor	• Presentation of course content is through print, computer disk, or videotape, all of which students can review at a place and time of their own choosing, either individually or in groups • Course materials (for content presentation) are used for more than one semester; often specific to the particular instructor (e.g., a videotape of the instructor's lectures) • Students come together periodically in groups in specified locations for instructor-led class sessions through interactive technologies (following the distributed classroom model) • Class sessions are for students to discuss and clarify concepts and engage in problem-solving activities, group work, laboratory experiences, simulations, and other applied learning exercises

In this model, the teaching material is available in different forms and can be studied in a place and time that learners themselves choose. Usually, the same material is employed in more than one educational term and may be directly associated to a specific teacher. In some occasions, learners are gathered in pre-defined locations to attend lectures via interactive teleconferencing environments. Aim of these meetings is to discuss concepts and principles, inspire activity to solve specific issues, engage in laboratory work, and carry out educational exercises (Koumpouros, Maglogiannis, & Koutsouris, 2000).

The characteristics of each model are presented in Table 1.

E-Learning Program

The distance learning program described in this chapter was in the field of operational business management for the Greek Army personnel. The specific program was realized using an adaptation of the open learning and classroom model, with strictest rules for the learners, aiming to the provision of better guidance and control. This concept is congruent with the basic principle of discipline, which dominates the military environment. More specifically, the educational model is summarized in the following points:

- An adapted curriculum was formed using a combination of synchronous and asynchronous distance learning. The asynchronous part comprised of six courses, and each one of them was divided in several teaching units. The synchronous part included 15 lectures and presentations; some of them were reviews of the course material, thus these lectures were closely linked with the asynchronous course, while others dealt with subjects in the scientific area of the operational business management curriculum.
- The teaching material that supported the program was produced with the basic principles of open distance learning for adults in mind. This material was user friendly, included a multitude of self-evaluation exercises, as well as a study guide for each teaching unit, besides six printed books that were shipped to the learners. These books matched the six courses of the program, providing learners with the conventional print material, which they are usually more comfortable with, besides the online pages.
- Specific educational objectives were identified so as to promote the cooperative learning climate. A fundamental objective was to familiarize the Greek Army staff with the exploitation of a computer and the Internet as an educational medium. Thus, the staff was not merely trained in operational business management issues, but also in self-training and evaluation using computers.
- For every asynchronous teaching session, an academic and an Army staff representative were appointed to overlook the procedure. Every learner had mail and phone access to them so as to make specific questions, requests, or suggestions either on the process or on the actual content of the course.

Figure 1. Distance learning integrated architecture

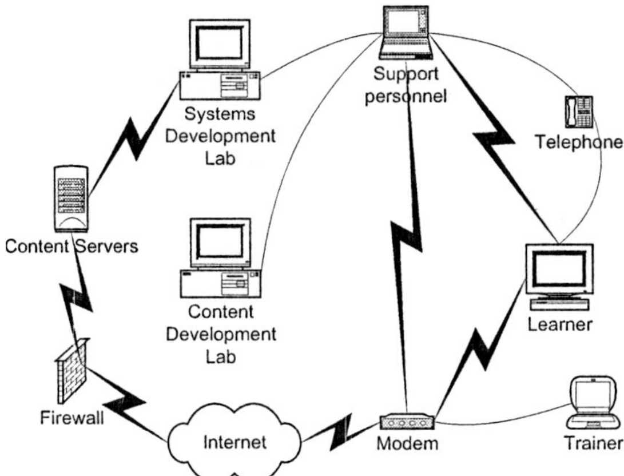

Networking and Collaboration

The network architecture of the distance learning environment is described in Figure 1.

All learners had personal Internet accounts in independent ISPs. This scheme provides a number of advantages:

- Low deployment cost
- Deployment was based on existing ISP infrastructure
- Inexpensive access to the material for the learners, at a place and time of their choice, without the need for extra hardware besides a PC and Internet access

However, this open architecture imposes a number of security measures during data transfer.

In a nutshell, the network architecture consists of the distance learning software and systems development laboratory, the content development laboratory, and the teaching support group. The latter includes personnel supporting the educational material, as well as technical support staff that help on matters related to the utilization of PCs and the distance learning environment. The distance learning environment that was employed for the operational business management course was Topclass from WBT (www.wbtsystems.com). Advantages of this system include:

- AICC (Aviation Industry Computer-Based Training Committee) certification
- Secure user management, organization in different classes, preparation of progress reports and tests
- Facility to use multimedia applications as educational material

Figure 2. The asynchronous distance learning platform

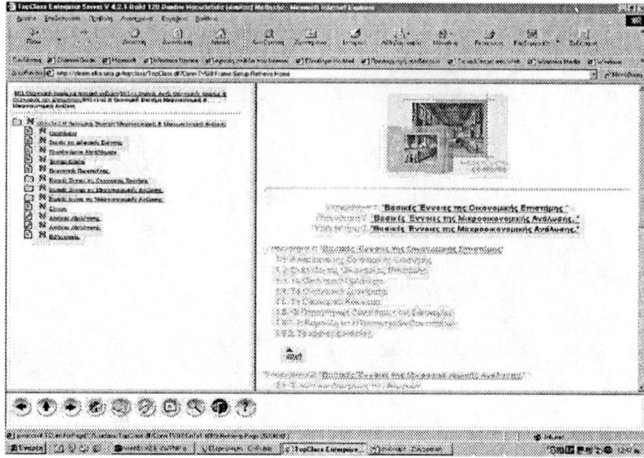

- E-mail-based communication between learners and teachers
- CSCW-oriented tools, such as bulletin boards, attachments, forums, and so forth
- Straightforward test compilation and paper assignment based on actual progress of the learners
- Reporting that includes progress of the learners, total study time and coverage of material, and so forth

The educational material that learners had access to was partitioned to distinct teaching units, each covering about 15 pages of a standard textbook. Each teaching unit included expected results and key concepts, as well as solved exercises, self-evaluation exercises, and case studies (see Figure 2).

In order to extend asynchronous teaching with constructive activities, synchronous teaching was implemented in the form of online presentations. Learners were able to attend high-level lectures by members of the academia or established business people, ask questions on scientific or applied matters, and, in general, comprehend the teaching material by participating in a distance education virtual classroom. This part of the curriculum consisted of 15 lectures, delivered by the Centra symposium application, part of the e-class services of Otenet, a major Greek ISP. The lectures were of perorational nature, but also gave the presenters the opportunity to elaborate on current socio-economical issues or answer learners' questions on the curriculum (see Figure 3).

This service provided users with:

- Integrated audiovisual teleconferencing
- Use of Windows applications in a multi-user environment

Figure 3. Screenshot from the online virtual classroom

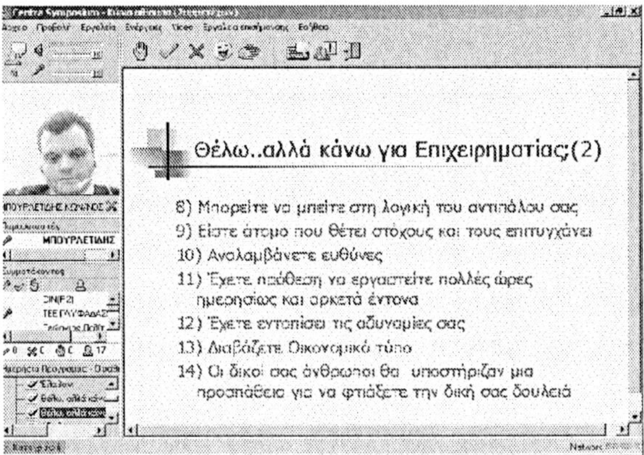

- Interactive chatting
- Provision of co-instructors (the main instructor was able to pass this role to any of the participants)
- Division of the e-class to breakout groups
- Lecture recording and playback on demand
- Recording of learners' responses for further evaluation
- Tracking and recording of participation

Besides these, the learners were provided with a business plan preparation application and given access to a related digital library, with plenty of material for further study.

Administrative Issues

Evaluation of acquired knowledge was performed both in-course and afterward. More specifically, following each of the six courses of asynchronous learning, learners took a two-hour online test and submitted a written paper, based on the curriculum of the course. After the completion of the six courses, learners took a written test in the UoA premises and submitted a final thesis, the subject of which was chosen amongst six possible subjects.

Control of the learning process was centralized. Every two weeks, members of the teaching staff of UoA met with personnel of the School of Research and Informatics Officers of the Hellenic Army to address issues raised from the process or from the learners. Participants of the pilot program included 60 professionals of the Greek Army, widely dispersed with respect to their rank and academic background, as well as the particular object of their everyday occupation. All successful participants were presented with a relevant training certificate.

Program Evaluation

Evaluation Criteria

The pilot distance learning course was successfully completed by 48 participants, while 12 failed to pass the final examinations. The assessment process was twofold:

a. Technological evaluation of the system, with respect to the functionality and the reliability of the platform (software problems, stability, response speed, etc.)

b. Academic assessment of the system, with respect to its effectiveness from an educational point of view (material comprehension level, acceptance from learners, teaching staff, etc.) and was completed via:
   - questionnaires filled in by the learners
   - statistical data amassed by the e-learning platforms, regarding the stability and utilization of the system
   - taking into account test results and other means of learner evaluation

Technological evaluation of the system was based on system reports and notes by the system administrators. The 60 participants did not encounter any particular problems regarding their access to the distance learning platforms. The reports showed that e-class participation was about 75% average, essentially indicating that each learner dedicated about four hours of study daily. It has to be noted that since learners were provided with printed material, they were able to put in additional study hours without utilizing the asynchronous e-learning platform, which was particularly overloaded during weekends and public holidays. Usage statistics of the synchronous learning platform display quite interesting results; therefore, they are discussed separately in the following subsection.

Statistics from the Synchronous Learning Platform

The participation figures during the synchronous virtual meetings fluctuated from 68% to 100%. The highest percentages refer to the beginning of the course, while the lowest occurred after three months. The figures increased again as the courses were close to the end but did not reach 100%.

The most popular application was the *"playback on request"* utility. According to the reports 39 out of 60 participants used this service a few hours or a few days later to recite the session. Other popular utilities that were used thoroughly are the *"chat service," "evaluation tests,"* and *"application sharing."*

A significant conclusion extracted from the technical reports is that although 35 learners used the chat service to set a question for the instructor or other participants during the online lectures, only 20 of them asked to take the floor in order to speak online. This figure, along with the 21 learners that did not communicate at all in the virtual classroom (they only indicated their presence by answering yes or no to typical questions), shows a relative reluctance in using the new interactive communication tools for speaking with the instructor. Therefore the corresponding speaker should always encourage the learners to participate, so as he was in an actual classroom with physical presence.

A more complete figure of how the participants used the synchronous platform is displayed in Table 2.

Questionnaire Supported Overall Assessment of the Project

Evaluation of the questionnaires filled in by the learners was extremely useful in recognizing potential malfunctions in the distance learning process. The input consisted of questions concentrating on general issues on the program methodology, the quality of the material, and the availability of the instructors, interactive questions, and questions regarding the teaching material itself. Results from gathering and processing the learners' responses indicated that:

- Ninety-eight percent of the participants experienced distance learning for the first time.
- Sixty-one percent were particularly satisfied with the course, 30% mildly satisfied, and only 9% were not satisfied at all.
- Forty-three percent of the participating military personnel declared that delivery via distance learning platforms is appropriate, because job obligations do not leave much time for continuing education. A major part of the participants also stated that one of

Table 2. How the participants used the synchronous platform

E-Class Services	Number of Participants Used the Service	Expression as Part of Total
Playback on Request	39 participants	65%
Chat Service	35 participants	59%
Evaluation Tests	32 participants	54%
Ask to participate	20 participants	34%
Other Tools	9 participants	15%
Web Safari	8 participants	12%
Application Sharing	41 times	2.7 PER SESSION
PowerPoint presentation	12 presentations	0.8 PER SESSION

the main reasons for enrolling in the program was that it was offered by an established, non-military academic institution and not by an internal military office.

- For most participants, distance learning and especially synchronous sessions were quite entertaining and original, since they offered a means of communication and interaction with colleagues. When this process was supplemented with academic activities (papers, test, etc.) the learners realized that synchronous teaching was not merely a communication tool, but part of the greater image.
- Eighty percent of the participants stated that quality of the material was exceptional, but requested more in-depth analysis on concepts that the authors regarded as self-evident, as well as wider access to specialized digital libraries. Sixty-five percent mentioned that self-evaluation exercises should indicate correct answers, while 30% thought that the duration of the program was less than necessary.
- In the question "how many hours did you spend on the program on a weekly basis," 45% answered 15-20 hours, 38% 10-15 hours, 10% over 20 hours, and only 7% dedicated less than five hours per week. These responses prove the interest displayed from the part of the learners.
- An important part of the questionnaire concerned the direct communication between learners and instructors. Fifty-three percent of the participants mentioned that they used this feature extensively, while 47% hardly resorted to e-mails for questions and other problems. Indeed, the platform statistics show that 123 e-mail messages were answered monthly, which account for 2.5 messages per active participant. This essentially means that almost half of the participants did not need any additional help with the course or the platforms, at least besides any assistance provided during the synchronous sessions.

As a general rule, questionnaire evaluation showed that 90% of the participants were satisfied from the online sessions and requested additional online meetings with instructors. This form of distance learning is closely related to conventional classroom teaching. Combination of synchronous and asynchronous teaching seems to be indispensable to eliminate the feeling of isolation, which is common in distance learning learners. Besides this, synchronous teaching served instructors' needs as well, since it provided the opportunity to contact the learners every two weeks, solve any group questions, and track their progress.

Best Practices

Successful practices of the pilot program include the combination of synchronous and asynchronous distance learning and the limited number of participants, which facilitated performance tracking and evaluation. More specifically, the platform combination seems to be the optimal teaching scheme, since it combines advantages from both distributed and open learning classroom models. The requirement of the learners for more online lectures indicates the significance of the synchronous part in a distance learning environment.

Moreover, regarding the synchronous part, the questionnaires showed that the opinion of the learners for their instructors was reflected on their participation and their interaction in the virtual class. The instructors that had better performance according to the answers had also bigger participation in their synchronous classrooms according to the extracted reports. This fact shows the criticality of the instructor's competence for the success of the synchronous learning.

The weak point of the program was the procedure followed for the selection of the trainees and the absence of a preparatory phase. Interrelating the trainee's background with their performance, it became evident that the students with the lower participation and performance were those that exhibited low motivation when they applied for the course or were not familiar with the new technology. Therefore, before the start of a course, the learners must be selected and informed carefully, checked for their motivation, test the necessary infrastructure, and become familiar with the tools to be used within the course, as it is very easy for them to feel disappointed and abandon the education procedure.

Sustainability and Conclusion

Problem and solution tracking can assure the viability of any educational system. The correct evaluation of the integration of material, platforms, and architecture will guarantee identification of correct practices, room for possible improvement or expansions, and conclusions for similar future programs.

During the specific pilot course it was proved that distance learning can be successfully applied for military training. The trainees liked very much the facts that an academic institution organized the course, they could attend the lessons without leaving their positions, and they could communicate with their colleagues located in distant units. The overall percentage of learners that successfully completed the distance learning course was approximately 85%.

Future expansion of the project should include the enhancement of asynchronous teaching material with adaptive multimedia information, which is essential with respect to keeping learners focused and stimulating their interest. With respect to the course content itself, possible ideas for enrichment include concepts deemed fundamental for any military organization, for example, document management, human resource management, foreign languages, and ICT basic skills.

References

Blythe, S. (2001). Designing online courses: User-centered practices. *Computers and Composition, 18*(4), 329-346.

Bourdeau, J., & Bates, A. (1996). Instructional design for distance learning. *Journal of Science, Education and Technology, 5*(4), 267-283.

Broady, E. (1996). You are your own best resource: Promoting confidence and autonomous learning in teacher education at a distance—a case study. In E. Broady & M. M. Kenning (Eds.), *Promoting learner autonomy in university language teaching* (pp. 49-65). London: CILT.

Cowan, J. (1995). The advantages and disadvantages of distance education. In R. Howard & I. McGrath (Eds.), *Distance education for language teachers* (pp. 14-20). Clevedon: Multilingual Matters Ltd.

Cronjé, J. (2001). Metaphors and models in Internet-based learning. *Computers & Education, 37*(3-4), 241-256.

Dzakiria, H. (2004). Models for open and distance learning. *International Journal of Educational Development, 24*(5), 575-576.

Flottemesch, K. (2000). Building effective interaction in distance education: A review of the literature. *Educational Technology, 40*(3), 46-512.

Folkman, K. (2002). Integrating distributed learning in work situations: A case study. *Educational Technology & Society, 5*(2), 75-80.

Gemeinhardt, G. (2002). Best practices in technology-mediated learning in American business education. *Educational Technology & Society, 5*(2), 39-46.

Knowles, M. (1990). *The adult learner: A neglected species*. Houston: Gulf Publishing.

Koumpouros, Y., Maglogiannis, I., & Koutsouris, D. (2000). A new tool for distance education. In E. Wagner & A. Szucs (Eds.), *Research and innovation in open and distance learning* (pp. 91-93). Budapest: European Distance Education Network.

Maglogiannis, I., Mpourletides, C., & Karpouzis, K. (2003). Combining synchronous and asynchronous distance learning for adult education: The Greek Army case. In V. Devedzic, J. Spector, D. Sampson, & Kinshuk (Eds.), *Proceedings of the 3rd IEEE International Conference on Advanced Learning Technologies (ICALT-2003)* (pp. 358 -359). Athens, Greece: IEEE Computer Society Press.

Massicotte, G. (1997). Groupware as a way of integration of classical and distance learning models in higher education. *European Journal of Engineering Education, 22*(1), 3-9.

Moore, M., & Kearsley, G. (1996). *Distance education: A systems view*. Belmont, CA: Wadsworth Publishing Company.

Sampson, D., Karagiannidis, C., Schenone, A., & Cardinali, F. (2002). Knowledge-on-demand in e-learning and e-working settings. *Educational Technology & Society, 5*(2), 107-112.

Schellens, T., & Valcke, M. (2005). Collaborative learning in asynchronous discussion groups: What about the impact on cognitive processing? *Computers in Human Behavior, 21*(6), 957-975.

WBT Systems. (n.d.). Retrieved May 1, 2006, from http://www.wbtsystems.com/

Chapter III

A Case Study on Education Networks and Brokerage

Gunnar Martin, German Research Center for Artificial Intelligence, Germany

Oliver Bohl, University of Kassel, Germany

August-Wilhelm Scheer,
German Research Center for Artificial Intelligence, Germany

Udo Winand, University of Kassel, Germany

Abstract

In the context of the development on the educational market—which is especially influenced by an increasing importance of knowledge in society—universities and professors stand the chance to serve existing customer segments better and to develop new business segments. Experiences made in traditional teaching as well as in the field of e-learning and e-teaching facilitate a target group-specific configuration of educational services and offers with academic contents according to the principle of "assembling on demand." Educational contents and services can be distributed beyond the physical barriers of the university to globally acting target groups and customer segments. Acquired core competencies and approved marketable educational services can be transformed into profits and economic success. Despite these promising market conditions, the active participation of universities on the global education market is insufficient. This chapter describes in terms of a case study different action alternatives, especially but not exclusively, for the German-speaking area, which can put public universities in the position to be able to transfer their competencies to the further education market, which is globalizing and increasing in competition, and thus market their competencies. Starting points for a new positioning and the development of a profile in the educational sector are shown by the example of an e-learning network and brokerage model among universities.

Introduction

Structure of the Education Network WINFOLine

The development of the market for educational trainings, which is especially influenced by an increasing importance of knowledge in society, forces universities to serve existing customer segments better and to develop new business segments. Existing experiences made in traditional teaching as well as in *technology-enhanced learning* (TEL; e-learning) and teaching facilitate a target group-specific configuration of academic contents according to the principle of "assembling on demand."

The *education network WINFOLine* (http://www.winfoline.de) serves as an example for the design, marketing, and distribution of academic, e-learning-based educational offers in the field of information systems, which will be presented in this chapter. The co-operation contributes to the reformation of university structures and was funded in 1997 by four professors of information systems in University of Leipzig, University of the Saarland, University of Goettingen, and University of Kassel. These partners constitute the WINFOLine core consortium. Initially, from 1997-2001, the project was funded by the German Bertelsmann foundation and the Heinz-Nixdorf foundation. In the beginning, WINFOLine started with designing and building e-learning-enhanced academic courses in terms of Web-based trainings, which were integrated in the curricula of all the participating universities. Thus, an inter-universities network for the consensual exchange of educational contents and services was created in partnership (Bohl, Grohmann, & Martin, 2002).

From 2001-2003, WINFOLine was funded by the German Ministry of Education and Research and was focusing on the aspects of broadening the network (more than 20 new partners from academia and industry were integrated), of broadening the spectrum of marketable educational contents and services, therefore a master degree and other more granular offers were created, and last but not least of achieving a sustainable maintenance of the project. Since 2004, WINFOLine is financed by revenue streams created from different sources: the non-monetary engagement of the participating partners is still important; most of them are still remunerated only on a basic level, that is, not in line with the market. Furthermore, the offered educational services and contents help to finance an employee who is responsible for the administration of the "Executive Master Degree Program."

To ensure the sustainability of WINFOLine, a content and educational product pool forms the center of the education network (see Figure 1).

Figure 1. Structure of the education network WINFOLine

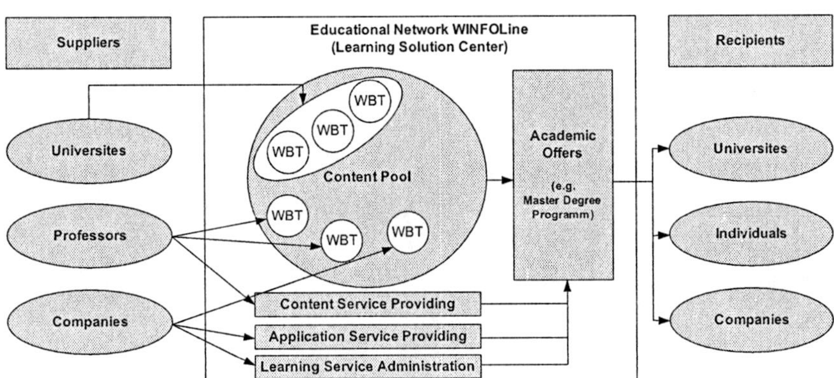

This pool contains Web-compatible educational offers of different providers. Their modular structure in combination with consumer-specific determined support services facilitates the configuration of various educational offers, for example, the distributed organized *Executive Master Degree Program* "WINFOLine Master of Science in Information Systems" (for details see Table 1). On the suppliers' side companies act beside universities and professors and, for example, bring in case studies or seminars for students studying at the partner universities or in the master program. On the recipients' side the consumers can have an individual educational offer configured for them from the services offered to integrate it into their existing educational organization and educational activities or, as a retailer, to transfer it on to further target groups (employees, students).

Thus, the *education network* acts as a broker in the sense of an inter- or cybermediary and coordinates the levels of providers and consumers. The role of *cybermediaries* "... has been to select among various choices in the world. They act as gatekeepers, filtering and analyzing choices in order to help users reach a specific outcome" (Bollier, 1996, p. 16). Models for

Figure 2. Transaction model of the education network WINFOLine

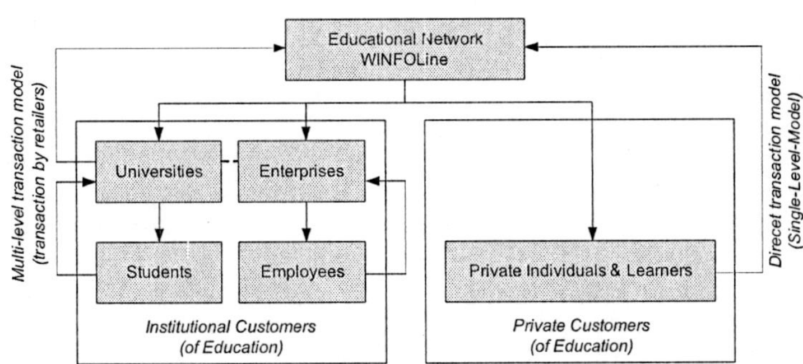

the settling of accounts, financing, exchange, and organization flank the service spectrum. These services contribute to the creation of transaction-oriented general frame (Figure 2) the exchange of educational services among the partners.

An important profit potential is the increase in the number of possibilities to choose partners who obtain services. The following are counted among the defined consumer groups:

- *Universities* that do not offer a course of studies in information systems but build it with the help of WINFOLine services and thus want to broaden their course portfolio horizontally.
- *Universities* that already offer courses of studies in the field of information systems and want to extend their offer with the help of WINFOLine practice vertical extension.
- *Private individuals* who want to continue their academic education in the field of information systems and who get the certified educational contents from the education network WINFOLine.
- *Enterprises* that employ the contents of information systems in training and further education and procure these educational services externally due to economic externalization and outsourcing decisions.
- *Enterprises* that market the contents of information systems in extended scenarios to end customers and procure parts of their services externally.

As can be seen, the services of WINFOLine are directed at a multitude of consumers to satisfy their specific needs for education. Corresponding to the structure of a network, the providers of services are recruited from different fields (Bohl, Winand, Grohmann, & Scheer, 2002). The virtuality of the WINFOLine educational offers serves as a unique selling proposition compared to other approaches in academic education. The decentralized sources of supply for the educational offers are a result of the virtualization and cause an increase in efficiency of the whole educational process. Also, discontinuously starting qualification measures can be carried out and insufficient qualification offers can be adjusted (Kortzfleisch, 1998). This means that the resource problem of the traditional academic education system can be counteracted and, due to their modularity, the offers can be marketed further. One prominent offer of WINFOLine will be described within the following section.

E-Learning Program: Master of Science in Information Systems

The "WINFOLine – Master of Science in Information Systems" is a job-related course of further education studies, which takes 15 months in full-time and addresses interested persons of all subject areas, who already hold a diploma, bachelor's, or master's degree and aim for further qualification in the field of information systems.

The *goal* of the WINFOLine Master is the mediation of knowledge, abilities, and skills for the development of solutions of economic tasks on the basis of modern information and

Figure 3. (Competency-oriented) curriculum of the WINFOLine MScIS

Semester	Master-Curriculum (WINFOLine Master of Science in Information Systems)			Workload (Credits)
	Master-Thesis			15 CP
2	Infomation Systems - Major -	Business Administration - Major -	Computer Science - Major -	42 CP
1	Infomation Systems - Basics -	Business Administration - Basics -	Computer Science - Basics -	18 CP

Semester	Master-Curriculum (WINFOLine Master of Science in Information Systems)			Workload (Credits)
	Master-Thesis			15 CP
2	Infomation Systems - Major -	Business Administration - Major -	Computer Science - Major -	48 CP
1	Infomation Systems - Basics -	Business Administration - Basics -		12 CP

Semester	Master-Curriculum (WINFOLine Master of Science in Infomation Systems)			Workload (Credits)
	Master-Thesis			15 CP
2	Infomation Systems - Major -	Business Administration - Major -	Computer Science - Major -	48 CP
1	Infomation Systems - Basics -	Computer Science - Basics -		12 CP

communication technologies. In 2005 about 80 students have been studying in this program; 18 of them are women.

The course of studies is subdivided into the basic course of studies and the main course of studies and the master's thesis (see Figure 3). Within the scope of the course of basic studies, the students are taught basic knowledge of information systems, business administration, as well as computer science. In the consolidating part, several modularly built major fields of study can be chosen according to previous personal knowledge and individual areas of interest. Course contents of the basic course of studies are as follows:

1. In the first stage of studies (*basic course of studies*) basic knowledge is conveyed to the students via the courses titled Introduction to Information Systems, Introduction to Business Administration and Management, Introduction to Computer Science. The contents serve to compensate for heterogeneous knowledge levels respectively the refreshment of already available previous knowledge.
2. In the second stage of studies (*main course of studies*) the students can choose several focal modules, which consist of individual, thematically grouped "courses," alongside the mandatory course Project Seminar: Science in Information Systems. Hereof several modules of the individual specialist courses in the fields of Information Systems, Computer Science, and Business Administration have to be taken. The sum of the modules to be taken depends on the target-specific course of studies.
3. In order to receive the master's degree, a *master's thesis* has to be written successfully within a period of three months in general.

Studying takes place online by means of practice-oriented and problem-oriented Web-based trainings (WBT). The online lectures, which have been approved and developed further for

Table 1. WINFOLine MScIS profile

Domain	**Information Systems**
Designation	Executive/post-graduate Master of Science Program
Certification	University degree "Master of Science in Information Systems" (MScIS)
Duration of Instruction Period	15 months. Standard period of study (full time) including the master's thesis
Application Deadline	Two application periods per year. Compulsory deadlines are: • Summer term: February 1st • Winter term: August 1st Capacity is limited to 30 students per period.
Tuition Fee	12,500 euro
Language Requirements	Proof of sufficient knowledge of the German language.
Academic/Other Requirements	Following enclosures have to be provided with the application form: • Bachelor's, master's, or an—for Germany—equivalent (university) diploma certificate • proof of work experience (minimum 12 month) • proof of sufficient knowledge of the German language, if this has not already been adduced with the presentation of the pre-mentioned proofs • a short resume with a depiction of the course of education and an occupational history If the leaving certificate is not available: • the high school graduation certificate or an equivalent certificate acknowledged by legal provision or by the responsible government facilities • an informal consent to the payment obligation, which resolves of the fee scale for this course of studies • documents that are certificates or official documents have to be presented as certified copies • applicants whose application for admission is not present, belated, incomplete, or bad in form, are excluded from the admission procedure
Forms of Assessment	All exams (tests, case studies, group work) are to be passed parallel to the studies. The working period for the master's thesis is three months as a general rule.

years, are completed by regular project seminars and lectures at the educational institutes. After the completion of the basic course of studies the participants can organize their main course of studies and their elective subjects to the greatest possible extent themselves, through an individual combination of multi-faceted online courses. They are supported by experienced (tele-)tutors from the WINFOLine network or its involved partner universities at any time.

All exams (tests, case studies, group work) are to be passed parallel to the studies. The working period for the master's thesis is three months as a general rule. After passing the exams, the university degree of Master of Science in Information Systems (MScIS) is awarded to the students. Until 2005, 12 students had finished their studies with an average grade of 1.77 (very good - good) with an average length of study of 27 months. Table 1 provides a brief overview of the master's profile.

Academic and Administrative Issues

Academic contents and educational services can be distributed beyond the physical barriers of the university to globally acting target groups and customer segments. Acquired core competencies and approved marketable educational services can be transformed into profits and economic success. Despite these promising market conditions, the active participation of universities on the global education market so far is insufficient.

In the context of the formation of the knowledge society, the knowledge acquired in phases of further education is subject to increasingly massive and fast moving processes of change (Kraemer, Sprenger, & Wachter, 2001). The creation of awareness concerning the importance of knowledge leads to lifelong learning approaches, which soften the boundaries between tertiary education and the following further education. Knowledge acquired according to the principle of building knowledge reserves, which does not lose in importance over the whole period of a working life, are a thing of the past (Scheer, 2000). The integration of different ways for imparting knowledge into the individual learning process proceeds from schooling to advanced vocational training, from traditional seminars via tele-teaching to Web-based courses and learning management systems.

Following these assumptions, knowledge is to be denominated as an economic good and the performance of knowledge building learning processes as a product, respectively a service, of specialized education providers. Education, and especially further education, is developing into a classic market where supply and demand meet and prices function as a market mechanism (Macharzina, 1999). For universities, this means "that a student is not only a potential customer for the university for a period of five to six years but is interesting as a consumer of educational or further educational services practically life-long, for a period of 30 to 35 years" (Scheer, 2000, p. 182). A global, market-oriented view of the customer segments of private demand (*education-to-customer*) and institutional demand (*education-to-business*) for education and further education seems advisable, if the universities do not want to cede segments of the changing education market, which correspond to their core competencies, to an increasing number of university-related or other commercial providers. German universities, especially compared to, for example, American universities, behave with restraint toward private as well as institutional demand on the growth market of further education (Hutzschenreuter & Enders, 2002).

The reasons for this, among other things, lie in an only marginally defined market economic orientation of German universities and the lack of equivalent incentive systems and marketing opportunities. Knowledge about potential customer segments and their specific educational needs is scarcely existent and neither are there central contact points in the sense of a university-wide marketing organization (Scheer, 2000). Instead, bilateral negotiations between private as well as corporate customers of education and professorial providers of education shape the phase of designing offers.

In addition to the creation of legally certain and acceptable incentive systems, German universities need to strategically reorient themselves toward taking the chances on the market. This means that educational offers orientate primarily toward expectations, needs, wants, and quality concepts of the customer (Kotler & Bliemel, 1995). Universities must learn to identify their customers, to build knowledge about them, and provide them with customer-oriented, individualized educational offers (Scheer, 2000). This applies in equal measure to the process of education and to the following phases of in-firm further education. For this purpose, and with the help of flexible organization structures, including the professorial level, as well as innovative technologies, strategies must be developed that implement intelligent solutions, which are suitable for everyday use. The core competencies of the providers at university must be analyzed and used efficiently by co-operations within the university, between universities respective between universities and enterprises (O'Hara-Devereaux & Johansen, 1994). A concentration on core competencies generally implies an increasing number of co-operations between providers to be able to produce services adequately and in line with the market (Hamel & Prahalad, 1995). Support for the formulation of the technology needed can be deduced from the following.

Technology Aspects

WINFOLine uses standard and state of the art *Web-based trainings* and personal devices with multimedia capabilities and plug-ins (Grohmann, Hofer, & Martin, 2005). For the creation of new e-learning offers following the "assembling on demand" paradigm XML-structures and metadata are needed. To ensure the content representation on any device and provide a multi-channel access, the content should comply with semantic Web standards, like RDF, SOAP, or WSDL. Distributed learning management systems (LMS) with single sign-on connections and (peer-to-peer) content server infrastructure are useful but not mandatory for the education network's activities.

The systems solution based on Perl, PHP, and mySQL integrated all network-wide distributed WBTs in one single platform and made comfortable dealing with the user administration, students and course administration as well as the use of additional, database-supported services possible, like the modularization of studying contents, offering studying accounts and performance reviews, testing, and so forth. An integrated entity relationship data model (ERM) on the requirements definition level was the basis for the development of the central platform with which decentralized contents could be accessed.

This was based on a typical matriculation and administration process and, in addition, included user, content, learning progress, and exam administration as core elements of the data model.

Nevertheless, it had to be realized early on that the regular maintenance, extension, and further development of the self-made platform solution was resource-intensive and detrimental for the attainment of project goals, which were the development of online education offers and inter-university organizational structures. Furthermore, the prototype was not multi-client capable. The claim for a location-specific, respectively personalized, view on the course spectrum of WINFOLine in accordance with the respective specifications of the home universities could not be accommodated. It has to be highlighted positively, though, that the problems in dealing with the platform prototype defined independent research and development questions and brought with them findings that contain perspectives for the development of a marketable product.

To meet the requirements, the learning management system CLIX Campus® of the IMC AG, together with an Oracle user database, was first implemented and hosted on a central platform server in Leipzig, later in Goettingen. Through the open structure of the network it is incumbent on each of the partner universities to configure the hardware and software via FTP and SSL connections and guarantee operation themselves. In former years standard solutions based on the operating systems Windows NT, UNIX, and Linux (derivates) were resorted to. The usually locally stored WBTs, which are used for the WINFOLine education offers, are directly linked to. The WINFOLine Web site is hosted on an additional Web server in Saarbruecken. Like it is the case with the WINFOLine core team the WBTs of the partners of the extended education network are on servers of the respective universities and (research) institutes that offer them, that is, several elements of the WINFOLine "Master of Science in Information Systems" course of studies physically exist on CLIX Campus® platforms of other universities like, for example, Freiburg and Cologne. The access to, respectively the aggregation of heterogeneous content into, an offer is also done by linking from the central WINFOLine homepage. More than 15,000 students were registered in the operating learning management system of the WINFOLine core network in 2005.

To guarantee multi-user operation with acceptable data rates, some partner universities facilitate parallel access and use streaming technology to make data-intensive elements available to students. It is the purpose of this technical design to burden the user with only a minimum of configuration efforts.

Therefore, it is stated in WINFOLine guidelines for the development of WBTs that all education offers must run on HTML including JavaScript and must be compatible with the important browsers of this and the last two generations. Compatibility is guaranteed for Netscape browsers from version 4.03, Microsoft's Internet Explorer from version 4.01, and Netscape/Mozilla from version 6.0 on. In addition, it was specified that only a minimum of plug-ins is to be installed, that is, at maximum the RealPlayer, Flash player, and Shockwave player are used. The production of learning contents is also subject to the didactic discretion and the technological possibilities of the network partners. The WINFOLine guidelines only define the framework layout and the functionalities of the WBT. The partners in the project can shape the production process freely or resort to already established and documented procedures. The open network (Figure 4) is also characterized by a great variety of choice concerning the production tools. According to the preference structure of a partner, standard authoring tools, individually developed tools, or hand-made solutions can be used. To guarantee a high quality of education offers a quality assurance concept has been developed in the frame of which potential partners have to meet formal as well as qualitative minimum requirements.

The education network is here geared to the guidelines of international standardization efforts, for example, the approaches of the Institute of Electrical and Electronics Engineers (IEEE) and the Aviation Industry Computer Based Training Committee (AICC). Special emphasis must be placed on the comprehensive shareable content object reference model

Figure 4. Basic platform architecture of WINFOLine

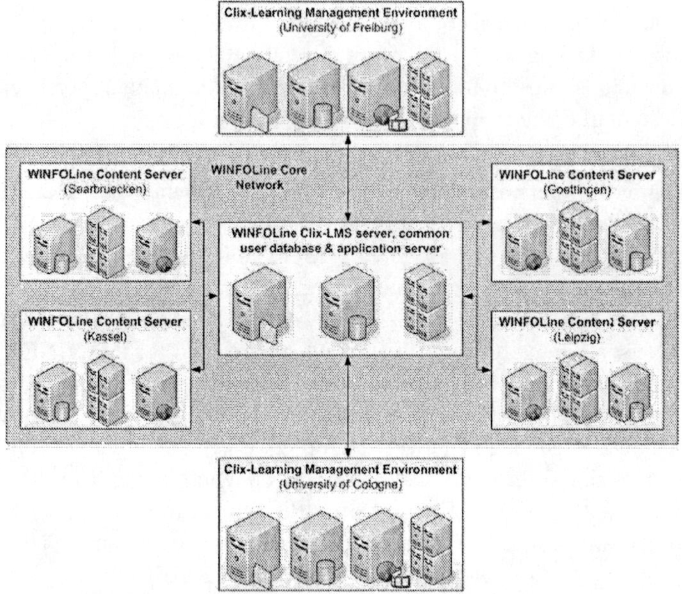

(SCORM) of the advanced distributed learning (ADL) organization and the learning object metadata (LOM) approach. The WINFOLine guidelines' rule set was extended by media pedagogical and didactical elements.

Program Evaluation

Since 1997, *WINFOLine* has been operating in the field of higher education. The focus is on Internet-based training in the field of information systems through a range of high-quality educational products. A pool of Web-based trainings was created for an open network (see Figure 1). For the extension of the pool new educational products are being created in co-operation with academic partners. Furthermore, existing WBTs and contents are being acquired. These WBTs can be combined with several support services, in order to create customised Web-based trainings.

Suppliers of content can choose from the pool and create individual trainings, in order to integrate these contents into their virtual lectures or to create completely new Web-based trainings. The Education network WINFOLine increases the choice for other suppliers of Web-based trainings. The wider range of content, even of previously inaccessible content, can also create immediate benefit for the students, university graduates, or employees. In 2000, WINFOLine was evaluated by an external auditor of the University of Giessen, Germany. In 2002, the ongoing external evaluation process was finalized. In 2005, there are more than 5,000 alumni, more than 800 new students per semester at the universities, and about 80 students are contemporary studying in the offered master's program. Figure 5 shows the history of WINFOLine.

Figure 5. WINFOLine's history

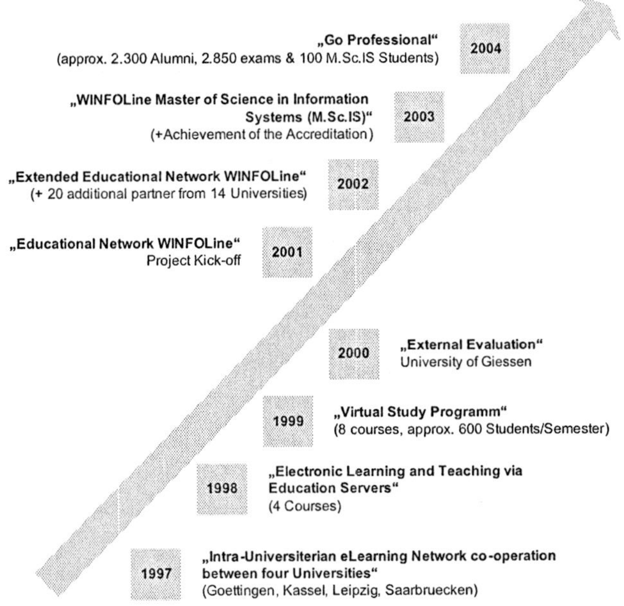

Sustainability and Conclusion

Policy Implications

For universities, research projects in the field of Web-based education are a starting point to gain experience with the planning and realization of corresponding educational offers. Here, the identification of potential customers, the satisfaction of their needs with the help of diversified educational products, as well as intelligent organizational structures can be tested without being under the pressure of acquiring customers or developing suitable products to meet the demand. The danger of the so-called "short time horizon," the misestimation in dealing with problems that are rather being solved according to a short-term effectiveness instead of an analysis of future conditions can be counteracted (Porter, 1997).

The classification of intelligently structured teaching organizations is illustrated by means of the displayed adaptation of the knowledge intensity portfolio according to Porter and Millar (1985). Analogous to the original procedure, the virtualization of the academic way of imparting knowledge has the intention of contributing to a market-oriented design of educational offers and of creating new business segments and profits. The classification is done by estimating the intelligence in the chosen distribution channel as well as the intelligence of the educational service. In this context, innovative systems and educational products are considered to be intelligent.

Figure 6. Intelligence in the distribution process and the (educational) services

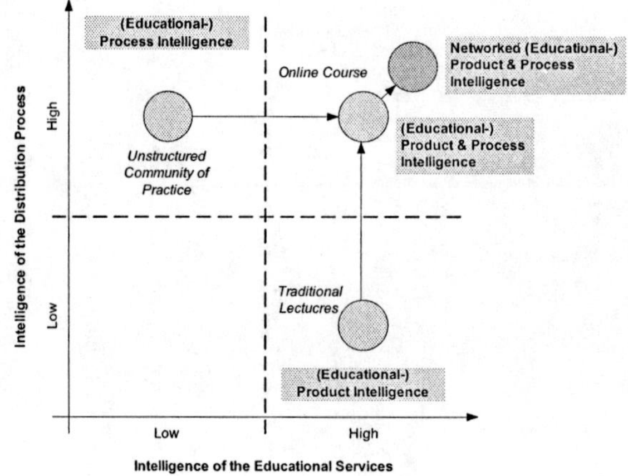

As Figure 6 shows, intelligence regarding the distribution process is low in the original academic process of imparting knowledge, although the services, and thus the intelligence in the educational service in general, have to be rated high. The reason for this is that the process of imparting high-quality academic contents through classic seminars or lectures is relatively inflexible because of fixed times and places. Out of the passivity of the service recipients, which is characteristic for lectures, the design of contents presents itself as a transference of the teacher's perspective to the learners (in/out view) (Winand, Kortzfleisch, & Heller, 1998). The interest cluster respectively the freedom of choice only take place in a corridor that is limited by the available course offers in the course of studies of the home university as well as by the available resources (e.g., lecture halls). Restrictions on capacities and supply are counterproductive to the flexibility favored on part of the learners. Interaction points for a coordination of the learners' and teachers' demands are used only sporadically. The low intelligence in the performance of the "unstructured communities of practice" in the sense of a Web-community is determined by the unstructured presentation of content and the lack of editorial intervention to avoid information redundancies and remove out-dated information. This can result in frustration, high costs for searching, and in an information overload.

A Web-based medium for the distribution of information, however, facilitates an on-demand access independent of place and time to solve problems at the time they appear (O'Hara-Devereaux & Johansen, 1994). Compared with classic lectures, the use of electronic media holds the perspective of a stronger overlapping of phases of working and learning, which is in line with the market (Euler, 1992). Web-based studies integrate the complementary strong points of both systems into an all-embracing offer while largely avoiding specific weaknesses. The high-quality contents are delivered to the customer on demand via innovative infrastructures.

The value added for the consumer lies in the up-to-dateness and richness of the contents, and the freedom to choose from a wide variety of courses and accompanying services. This flexibility reaches from the mass customization of educational offers, for example, in the context of master's studies, to the configuration of educational offers for in-firm further education centered on needs. When viewed as a whole, the virtualization of academic education processes presents itself as business process (re-)engineering for universities (Hammer & Champy, 1993). The reorientation and repositioning through elements of e-learning can be denoted as *learning process (re-)engineering*.

Because of the connection of the academic background of universities and the existing possibility of certification, universities have the opportunity to position themselves on the e-learning education market as *learning service providers* (LSP). What LSPs offer covers several areas, which can be provided individually or as a package, depending on the target consumer segments (private or institutional customers).

- **Application service providing:** The provision of professional learning management systems and undertaking the technical operation. At this point, partnerships with commercial providers seem advisable.
- **Content providing:** The provision of (academic) learning contents. In most cases employees of the university, for example, professors, will have to take over the providing of content because they are the ones who have to work out the content first.
- **Content service providing:** The provision of services for the organizational and editorial handling of learning processes, their handling as regards content as well as their certification.
- **Learning service administration:** The provision of administrative services for the operation of the learning management system. These are not prime tasks of traditional universities.

In the case of a complete delivery of all services we must speak of full learning service provision. Co-operations with partners from the academic as well as the business sphere are thinkable for all areas and to be aspired. At this point, concentration on the core competence of each supplier of services seems indispensable.

Lessons Learned

The main focus of the relationship marketing lies in the creation and implementation of customer relations, which are difficult to imitate. In the case of a change of the provider or partner, high costs result from the respective change barriers.

Consequently, a success factor of academic education products is the integration of the customer into the whole value-added process. Knowledge of customer target groups as well as the interaction between market actors and the integration of customers are to the fore. The knowledge to be gained from this puts education providers in the position to realize customer needs and structures of needs and to supply services for their precise satisfaction (Drucker, 1995). This approach can be understood as "customizing the relationship," which is characterized by the existence of the following principles (Hildebrand, 1998):

- The *interaction* between provider and consumer of education presupposes mutual communication. Explicit mentioning of specific needs, suggestions, and desires as well as the "active listening" of the provider, which becomes apparent in the openness in the information behavior toward the customer and encourages confidence, can be identified as critical for success. Directness and intensity of the interaction are of particular significance. As a special characteristic of institutional (education-to-business) relations the spectrum of the achievement of objectives of joint activities is relevant for decisions.
- The *integration* of the customer means his or her inclusion in the whole development process of services on the basis of the described interaction between the partners. This process comprehends the interaction along the value-added process from product planning, product development, and production to the technological linking of the value-adding processes of the participants. This behavior broadens the value-added chain beyond the bounds of the providers. Thus we must speak of a value-added network. The knowledge gain from the mutual information exchange puts providers of education in the position to realize customer needs and structures of needs and to supply services for their precise satisfaction (Grohmann & Martin, 2002). If this approach is transferred to the design of academic education measures, consumers of education become long-term co-operation partners of the universities regarding design, development, testing, and promotion of the quality of education products.
- The *individualization* of the services constitutes the core of relationship marketing. In the context of the design of the education offers considered, this approach results in the design of target group-oriented individual education offers. In the long run this results in a change of the quality of the education offers from a turning away from the mass product education via mass customization to a complete tailoring of education offers according to the desires of potential target groups.
- In the context of this chapter, *selection* means that a complete individualization of the design of education offers cannot be justified from efficiency viewpoints. Moreover, not all customer segments do have the same profitability. Rather, it is decisive to identify target customer segments promising in the long run and to provide them with integrated education offers. Additionally, gained criteria for efficiency must flow into the individualization of the design of the services.

To be able to accommodate the claims of different target group segments more precisely an economically sustainable middle course between a mass and an individual appeal must be found. Starting points are the identification of segment comprehensive demands on the supply of education and further education services. According to Bentlage and Hummel (2001) on the part of the education consumers, demands on the taking of the "*high quality education*" into consideration mainly consist in the securing of:

- up-to-dateness of contents,
- individuality of learning relations,
- just-in-time provision of learning contents,

- richness of method knowledge, and
- the provision of integrated educational offers and programs.

A differentiated view regarding the different potentials of the respective target segments could lead to more differentiated offers in these fields. It seems advisable to view the learning process from schooling via university education to in-firm further education as a whole.

Best Practices

The network has a leading role among universities in the research concerning e-learning. Constructed as an open network, it realizes an organizational structure that guarantees the highest possible flexibility for all participants. New partners can be affiliated at any time as well as leaving the network is possible for present partners. Therefore, the range of Web-based trainings is flexible and various. New topic areas can be covered at any time by affiliating new partners. To ensure a high quality of the offered trainings at any time, a concept for quality assurance is required to guarantee a minimum standard with regard to formal and qualitative aspects. The network follows international standardization efforts in e-learning. Partners have direct access to an extensive know-how network to support their efforts. This know-how network is supposed to encourage the knowledge exchange within the whole community.

Corresponding to the structure of a network, the providers of services are recruited from different fields. The virtuality of the educational offers serves as a unique selling proposition compared to other approaches in academic education. The decentralized sources of supply for the educational offers are a result of the virtualization and cause an increase in efficiency of the whole educational process. Also, discontinuously starting qualification measures can be carried out and insufficient qualification offers can be adjusted. This means that the resource problem of the traditional academic education system can be counteracted and, due to their modularity, the offers can be marketed further.

Further profit results from a consolidation of chair-specific competencies due to the underlying idea of a network. The consumers of educational offers benefit from the various competencies of renowned professors who are affiliated with the education network (best-of-peer). This contributes positively to the educational services' profiles and is a distinguishing feature in the market. Furthermore, the education network realizes a dynamic offer of courses of studies, which, on the one hand, contributes to up-to-dateness and quality assurance of teaching, and, on the other hand, offers consumers a broad spectrum of fundamental as well as more sophisticated courses.

Due to important experiences during the implementation of the open network, the technical, pedagogical, and didactical creation of Web-based trainings, the support service, organization, and administration of learning processes, the education network WINFOLine can be considered as a reference model for virtual studies.

References

Bentlage, U., & Hummel, J. (2001). Maerkte in den USA und in Deutschland im Vergleich. In U. Bentlage, P. Glotz, I. Hamm, & J. Hummel (Eds.), *E-Learning—Maerkte, Geschaeftsmodelle, Perspektiven* (pp. 121-153).

Bohl, O., Grohmann, G., & Martin, G. (2002). Case study: Education network WINFOLine. In E. Wagner & A. Szucs (Eds.), *Open and distance learning in Europe and beyond: Rethinking international co-operation. Proceedings of the 2002 EDEN Annual Conference*, Granada (pp. 511-513.). Granada: EDEN

Bohl, O., & Winand, U. (2005). Requirements for operating models of virtual educational networks. In M. Khosrow-Pour (Ed.), *Managing modern organizations with information technology* (pp. 144-147). Information Resources Management Association International Conference, San Diego, CA. Hershey, PA: Idea Group Publishing.

Bohl, O., Winand, U., Grohmann, G., & Scheer, A.-W. (2002). Virtuelle Bildungsnetzwerke: Struktur- und Betreibermodelle am Beispiel WINFOLine. In M. Engelien & J. Homann (Eds.), *Virtuelle Organisation und Neue Medien 2002* (pp. 41-68). Lohmar, Koeln: Eul.

Bollier, D. (1996). *The future of electronic commerce.* Washington, DC: The Aspen Institute.

Drucker, P. (1995). Quoted in P. Kotler & F. Bliemel (1995). *Marketing-Management: Analyse, Planung, Umsetzung und Steuerung* (8th ed.). Stuttgart: Schaeffer-Poeschel.

Euler, D. (1992). *Didaktik des computerunterstützten Lernens. Praktische Gestaltung und theoretische Grundlagen.* Nuernberg: BW Bildung und Wissen.

Grohmann, G., & Martin, G. (2002). Ansatzpunkte zur Organisation virtueller Lernszenarien am Beispiel des Bildungsnetzwerkes WINFOLine. In S. Schubert, B. Reusch, & N. Jesse (Eds.), *Lecture Notes in Informatics (LNI). Proceedings: Informatik bewegt. Informatik 2002 – 32. Jahrestagung der Gesellschaft für Informatik e.V. (GI)* (pp. 319-324).

Grohmann, G., Hofer, A., & Martin, G. (2005). ARIS MOBILE: Helping to define the future of mobile learning. In IEEE (Ed.), *Proceedings of the 4th International Conference on Mobile Business (ICMB 2005)*, Sydney, Australia (pp. 213-219).

Hamel, G., & Prahalad, C. K. (1995). *Wettlauf um die Zukunft: Wie Sie mit bahnbrechenden Erfolgen die Kontrolle ueber ihre Branche gewinnen und die Maerkte von Morgen schaffen.* Wien: Ueberreuter.

Hammer, M., & Champy, J. (1993). *Business Reengineering—Die Radikalkur für das Unternehmen.* Muenchen: Campus.

Hildebrand, V. G. (1998). Kundenbindung mit Online Marketing. In J. Link (Ed.), *Wettbewerbsvorteile durch Online Marketing—Die strategischen Perspektiven elektronischer Maerkte* (pp. 53-75). Berlin: Springer.

Hutzschenreuter, T., & Enders, A. (2002, September). Gestaltung internetbasierter studienangebote im Markt für Managementbildung. In *ZFBF—Schmallenbachs Zeitschrift für Betriebswirtschaftliche Forschung, 54*, 543-561.

Kortzfleisch, H. F. O. (1998). Virtualisierung der betrieblichen Aus- und Weiterbildung, Arbeitsbericht Nr. 22, Universitaet-Gh-Kassel, Fachgebiet Wirtschaftsinformatik, Kassel.

Kotler, P., & Bliemel, F. (1995). *Marketing Management: Analyse, Planung, Umsetzung und Steuerung* (8th ed.). Stuttgart: Schaeffer-Poeschel.

Kraemer, W., Sprenger, P., & Wachter, C. (2001). Learning services als Bestandteil einer eHR-Strategie. In A.-W. Scheer (Ed.), *Die eTransformation beginnt! Lessons learned, Branchenperspektiven, Hybrid economy, M-Business* (pp. 191-228). Heidelberg: Physica.

Lynch, M. (2001) *The knowledge Web*. New York: Routledge.

Macharzina, K. (1999). *Unternehmensfuehrung: Das internationale Managementwissen: Konzepte—Methoden—Praxis.* Wiesbaden: Gabler.

Martin, G., & Grohmann, G. (2003). Geschaeftsmodell bildungsbrokerage: Perspektiven fuer hochschulen. In K. P. Jantke, W. S. Wuttig, & J. Herrmann (Eds.), *Von e-learning bis e-payment 2003—Das Internet als sicherer Marktplatz* (pp. 42-50). Tagungsband LIT'03. Berlin: Akademische Verlagsgesellschaft.

Martin, G., Grohmann, G., & Scheer, A.-W. (2005). WINFOLine—Ein Ansatz zur strukturellen Implementierung und nachhaltigen Gestaltung von eLearning-Szenarien an Hochschulen. In A.-W. Scheer (Ed.), *Veroeffentlichungen des Instituts für Wirtschaftsinformatik, Nr. 180*, Saarland University, Saarbruecken.

Martin, G., Bohl, O., Scheer, A.-W., & Winand, U. (2003). Ansätze zur marktorientierten gestaltung Web-basierter, akademischer bildungsprodukte. In W. Uhr, W. Esswein, & E. Schoop (Eds.), *Wirtschaftsinformatik 2003/Band II: Medien—Märkte—Mobilität. Heidelberg (Physika)* (pp. 699-714). Heidelberg: Physica.

Martin, G., Scheer, A.-W., Bohl, O., & Winand, U. (2003). Action alternatives and solutions for a market-oriented design of Web-based academic offers. In M. Khosrow-Pour (Ed.), *Information technology and organisations: Trends, issues, challenges and solutions, Proceedings of the 14th International Resources Management Association Conference 2003 (IRMA International),* Philadelphia (pp. 31-34). Hershey, PA: Idea Group Publishing.

O'Hara-Devereaux, M., & Johansen, R. (1994). *Global work. Bridging distance, culture and time.* San Francisco: Jossey-Bass.

Porter, M. E. (1997). *Wettbewerbsstrategie: Methoden zur Analyse von Branchen und Konkurrenten (Competitive Strategy).* New York; Frankfurt am Main: Campus.

Porter, M. E., & Millar, V. E. (1985). How information gives you competitive advantage. *Harvard Business Review, 63*(4), 149-160.

Scheer, A-W. (2000). *Unternehmen gründen ist nicht schwer...* . Berlin: Springer.

Winand, U., Kortzfleisch, H. F. O., & Heller, U. (1998). Electronic Learning Commerce, arbeitsbericht 21. Universitaet-Gh-Kassel, Fachgebiet Wirtschaftsinformatik, Kassel.

Chapter IV

Transitioning to E-Learning: Teaching the Teachers

Bethany Bovard, New Mexico State University, USA

Susan Bussmann, New Mexico State University, USA

Julia Parra, New Mexico State University, USA

Carmen Gonzales, New Mexico State University, USA

Abstract

This case study explores the ongoing development of an online instructor training program, initiated in spring 2002. Involvement of the learner-instructors (professional development instructors learning to teach online) in the design and development of this online instructor training program was key to its overall success. Significant outcomes of the program include a core group of experienced and highly dedicated online instructors, a new model for continuous professional development and support, and the formation of an active and dynamic learning community.

Introduction

RETA (Regional Educational Technology Assistance program) at New Mexico State University (NMSU) is a professional development program funded by agency partnerships, Technology Literacy Challenge funds, a Technology Innovation Challenge Grant through the U.S. Department of Education, other grants, and the New Mexico Legislature. Its primary mission is to expand the number of educators skilled in effective use of technology to support educational goals (Gonzales, 1998; Gonzales, Pickett, Hupert, & Martin, 2002). RETA has been very effective in reaching New Mexico educators. Between the 1998-1999 and 2001-2002 school years, RETA delivered over 1,400 workshops to almost 8,600 educators. In 2002, RETA extended face-to-face professional development workshops for K-12 teachers to include an online component. This change was motivated by the scope of work for RETA's Technology Innovation Challenge Grant (Gonzales, 1998) and was facilitated by institutional and national events.

Since 2001, NMSU has emphasized distance education as a way to better serve student needs. This focus began with the appointment of RETA's founder as NMSU's first vice provost for distance education. Since that time, NMSU rapidly expanded online course offerings and invested in distance education tools, including WebCT, a course management system, and Centra, an online classroom.

These events coincided with a national increase in Internet access. In 2001, 77% of instructional rooms in public schools had Internet access (National Center for Educational Statistics, 2001), and more than 50% of Americans were online with 2 million new users connecting every month (U.S. Department of Commerce, 2002). This growth in Internet access helped insure that our audience of K-12 educators could participate in online workshops.

RETA's expansion to online professional development also aligned with the 2001 Elementary and Secondary Education Act's (ESEA) *No Child Left Behind* (NCLB) and its emphasis on quality professional development and technology. The act emphasizes teacher professional development, requiring "ongoing professional development for teachers, principals, and administrators by providing constant access to training and updated research in teaching and learning through electronic means" (20 U.S. Code 6301, available at http://www.ed.gov/policy/elsec/leg/esea02/pg34.html). Because of this emphasis, we anticipated a need for online professional development.

E-Learning Program

The RETA online instructor training program is a blended program designed to transition RETA instructors from face-to-face to online teaching and learning. The primary goal of the program was to train the learner-instructors in technology skills, pedagogic challenges, and administrative issues related to online teaching and learning. Ideally, instructors in the program would have experience in online teaching and learning as well as strong written communication skills due to the primarily asynchronous nature of our program. This was unrealistic, and in the end instructors who made a commitment to the training had limited online teaching and learning experience. However, they did have strong written communication skills, and most importantly, attitudes conducive to risk-taking and self-advocacy related to individual and community needs.

The process we envisioned for training online instructors was designed to:

- Use the expertise of the learner-instructors in training to give us feedback on their training, and
- Enlist learner-instructor help as co-developers of the workshops they would lead.

We only met the first goal, however, because our expectations about involving the learner-instructors in online instructional design were unrealistic. Our final process focused on training the learner-instructor and evaluating the training program (Figure 1) as follows.

1. Train learner-instructors, via Centra, in online technologies, pedagogy, and workshop content.
2. Mentor and support learner-instructors as they teach online workshops.
3. Develop and revise RETA Online Certification Competencies (see Appendix A and B) based on feedback of the learner-instructors.
4. Provide additional face-to-face training based on the RETA Online Certification Competencies.
5. Repeat process as needed.

Figure 1. Our online training process

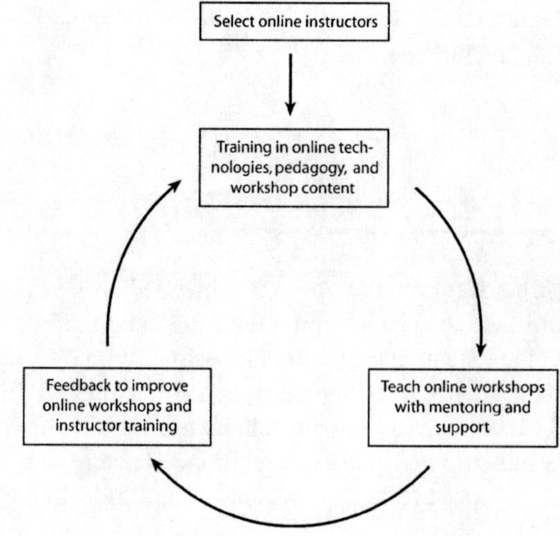

6. In training the learner-instructors, we went through this process twice and continue to use this process to introduce online workshops.

Academic Issues

Philosophical and Pedagogic Foundations

RETA professional development is learner-centered and based on constructivist learning theory as well as theories of brain-based learning, learning styles, multiple intelligences, and learning communities (Gonzales et al., 2002). The RETA professional development model is based on the teachers-teaching-teachers model and for instructors, a one-year apprenticeship. Most RETA instructors begin as participants, apply to become instructors through a competitive process, and apprentice with a team of two instructors before they form a team with another instructor. RETA online learner-instructors were recruited and trained from this pool of instructors to undergo further training and apprenticeship.

Collaboration and learning communities play a vital role in instructional improvement and empowerment of teachers as leaders and professionals (Dufour & Eaker, 1998; Riel & Fulton, 1998). RETA has used these techniques to develop an extended learning community with a supportive, familial atmosphere. The RETA extended learning community is supported by the RETA Web site (http://reta.nmsu.edu), two listservs, and two annual face-to-face events for professional development for instructors. During these events, the smaller group of RETA online learner-instructors attended regular sessions as well as workshops specifically developed for them to enhance skills in WebCT and online technology and teaching. Via Centra, they synchronously received training and communicated on topics, including summative assessment.

Since RETA's transition to online professional development is ongoing, RETA staff and instructors are encouraged to collaborate and improve their online teaching knowledge and skills by using the technology tools and learning communities available. Due to the challenges of online teaching and learning, RETA online learner-instructors formed a tight-knit learning community. Both personally and professionally, the larger and smaller RETA learning communities continue to serve as valuable resources for RETA members to take risks, to grow, to change, and to achieve.

Course and Program Development

Our goal in training instructors in online facilitation was to ensure they had the technology and facilitation skills to be effective online instructors. Because this skill set needed to meet their needs, we engaged learner-instructors as co-developers of their online training program. They provided continuous feedback to us (RETA office staff) via e-mail, surveys, and meetings (face-to-face and online). Although seemingly chaotic at times, the development of the online instructor training program was iterative, which helped stakeholders understand

Table 1. E-learning program overview

Online Instructor Training										
		Spring 02	**Summer 02**	**Fall 02**	**Spring 03**	**Fall 03**	**Spring 04**	**Fall 04**	**Spring 05**	**Summer 05**
Admin	Program policies		*e-mail:* program policy negotiations including instructor benefits and training requirements		*f2f:* program policy dissemination w/ e-mail follow up	*f2f:* revised program policy dissemination; e-mail follow up		*Centra:* instructor contract negotiations; e-mail follow up		
	Workshop management			*e-mail:* registration, security, record keeping	*f2f:* registration, security, record keeping; e-mail follow up	*f2f:* registration, security, record keeping; e-mail follow up	*e-mail:* registration, security, record keeping	*f2f:* RETA database	*Centra:* workshop specific	
Tech Tools	WebCT		*Centra:* orientation	*f2f:* interface and basics	*f2f:* discussion board, chat tool	*f2f:* new version	*f2f:* grade book			*f2f:* calendar & quiz tools
	Centra	*f2f:* orientation		*f2f:* interface and basics		*Centra:* troubleshooting markup tools				*f2f:* quick start tutorial handout
Pedagogy	Synchronous			Online Instructor Certification Competencies (Appendix A)	*Best Practices in Online Teaching Checklist (Appendix B)* *f2f:* moderating chats	*Centra:* interactivity, games, *WebCT & Centra:* competencies				*f2f:* mentoring
	Asynchronous			Online Instructor Certification Competencies (Appendix A)	*Best Practices in Online Teaching Checklist* *f2f:* facilitating & moderating	*f2f & WebCT:* facilitating & moderating	*f2f:* participation challenges			*f2f:* mentoring & testing

Training delivery method
e-mail: training and information delivered via e-mail
f2f: training and information delivered via face-to-face professional development workshops
Centra: training and information delivered via Centra, an online synchronous conferencing system
WebCT: training and information delivered via WebCT, an online course management system

goals (Schwen & Hara, 2004) (Table 1). In addition, involving online instructors in their training promoted ownership, allowed us to address individual and group concerns, and let learner-instructors control the learning pace (Elbaum, McIntyre, & Smith, 2002).

Our collaboration and community building was also essential to developing relevant content and quality interactive materials (Collison, Elbaum, Haavind, & Tinker, 2002). Early in the program, we oriented the learner-instructors to Web delivery tools and basic online pedagogy (Table 1). Then the learner-instructors apprenticed with us, teaching colleagues online the skills and information they had learned. For many of them, this was their first experience teaching online. These experiences gave us a common framework from which to collaborate further on the design. From there, training combined direct instruction (Table 1) and application of new skills as they continued teaching RETA Online workshops under our guidance.

Teaching and Learning Processes

We collaborated with online learner-instructors to create a community of learners. As per learner-instructor requests and with their guidance, a list of online instructor competencies (see Appendix A) was developed, in fall 2002, based on examples from organizations such as the International Board of Standards for Training, Performance and Instruction (http://www.ibstpi.org) and Western Governors University (http://www.wgu.edu). Learner-instructors used these competencies to assess and pursue their own learning paths (Brockett & Hiemstra, 1991). The competencies also provided us with direction in delivering continuous and relevant training. Directly engaging learner-instructors increased their self-awareness and their attainment of new skills (http://www.arl.org/training/ilcso/adultlearn.html). Once learner-instructors became familiar with the online instructor competencies, it became evident that further development of advanced online instructor skills was needed. Thus, in spring 2003, we incorporated RETA Best Practices in Online Teaching (see Appendix B) into training that delineated specific practices for the learner-instructors to advance skills in online instruction and further their growth as online educators.

Learner Support

The learner-instructors accessed RETA office staff members and resources via e-mail, postal mail, and phone. Instructor-only discussion boards were established in WebCT-based workshops for learner-instructors and office staff to communicate. Centra events were provided as needed.

Virtual Learning Environment

We were fortunate to have both WebCT and Centra as e-learning tools. WebCT (http://webct.com) is an online classroom environment with both classroom management (course administration, content management, and a grade book) and learning management features, including synchronous and asynchronous communication and collaboration tools. Centra (http://www.centra.com) is an online, synchronous conferencing system that allows students to communicate in real-time using voice and text chat. It also includes a whiteboard with real-time mark-up tools. Centra delivers virtual or "live" classroom presentations and other events through the Web. The powerful combination of these two tools in conjunction with face-to-face training provided rich opportunities for building the learning communities that were vital to this program.

Assessment and Evaluation

The primary assessment tool for this program was the online instructor competency checklist. It was developed by RETA staff to assess learning progress and feedback for program evaluation. After each training session, learner-instructors completed a section of the checklist to assess their progress in that area. They also used the checklist as a tool to reflect on their learning over time and assess their learning goals for the program. Finally, RETA staff also assessed the learner-instructors using the same tool to provide them with feedback.

Administrative Issues

Technical Infrastructure

Through NMSU, we have access to a well-developed technical infrastructure for distance learning. Additionally, because our organization is committed to technology integration, we have a strong technology infrastructure of our own that includes servers, computers, digital audio and video equipment, and Web development tools and software.

Our learner-instructors have access to most of the technical infrastructure that we do; however, stable Internet access is a challenge. Additionally, frustrating limitations in public school infrastructures prevented them from using some synchronous tools we provide such as Centra and WebCT chat.

Human Resources

RETA staff has extensive experience in distance education, online teaching, and learning. Additionally, several learner-instructors had limited online teaching and learning experience. Using a collaborative approach and the combined knowledge, skills, and experience of stakeholders (Figure 2) was imperative for successful program development. However, we had never managed such a program, and we developed these skills during the program. Skills and knowledge that we developed included project management, online instructional development, course development, quality control issues, WebCT and Centra technical skills, and online program development and delivery.

Figure 2. Organization chart

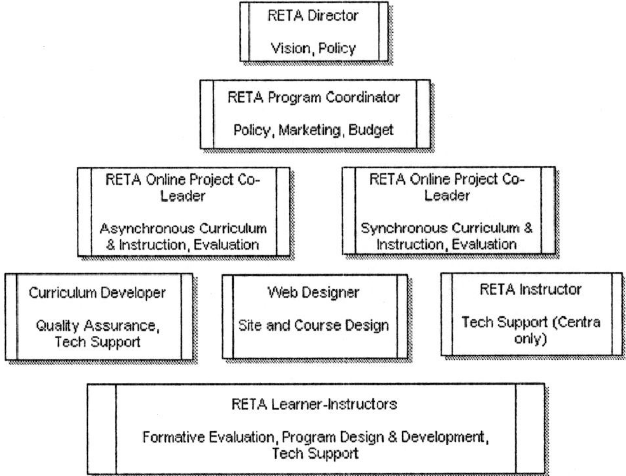

Budget

Costs for this program were covered under RETA's funding. Costs unique to this effort included learner-instructors stipends for training, assisting in the purchase of Centra for the university, and upgrading staff skills through conferences and workshops.

Intellectual Property and Copyright

This program had no intellectual property issues. RETA staff members and instructors routinely develop curriculum and workshop materials that are copyrighted by the Regents of New Mexico State University. Most are free and available at the RETA Web site (http://reta.nmsu.edu). These materials may not be used for monetary gain.

Quality Assurance and Standards

Quality assurance and standards for the RETA online instructor training program were based on RETA standards. Based on our needs and competency lists from other e-learning organizations, we developed the RETA Online Instructor Certification Competencies (see Appendix A) and the RETA Best Practices in Online Teaching (see Appendix B) to guide our teaching and learning efforts. Additionally, the online learner-instructors provided continual feedback as part of the process model to formatively assess, revise, and assure program quality.

Program Evaluation

Since we developed the program as we implemented it, we evaluated the program informally using online interviews and questionnaires. This ongoing process kept the program and us on track.

Our primary instrument for program goal evaluations was the online instructor competency checklist. The checklist was developed to provide us with learning and teaching paths for the program. As our group refined their knowledge, we used the checklist to help us stay on track with our training program: if a learner-instructor improved in the targeted area, we knew our training environment was sound. Finally, the instructor-learners also used the checklist to evaluate their progress as online instructors so they could set their learning goals. Additionally, the RETA Best Practices in Teaching Online was created and similarly applied for progress evaluation.

Networking and Collaboration

Most networking and collaboration for RETA's e-learning training program happened in-house among staff members. However, to run the technical part of the online program, we collaborated with Scholarly Technology, the NMSU unit that managed WebCT and NMSU's Centra Consortium to set up WebCT and Centra for online workshops and sessions. We also used the library and computer labs at Desert Ridge Middle School in Albuquerque for face-to-face training sessions.

Policy Implications

The RETA Online Instructor Training program used and incorporated RETA policies and procedures. The greatest effect of our RETA online training experience is that we now provide ongoing and continuous training and support as recommended by the National Staff Development Council (National Staff Development Council, n.d.). Previously, training and support was only provided at spring and fall instructor development sessions. Training and support is now ongoing, continuous, and provided online via Centra and WebCT instructor-only areas. All resources, rubrics, and materials are online. Our online training capabilities are now an integral part of our planning process when developing resources, training, and support. This blended approach to training, where we meet face to face and continue online, has strengthened the RETA online learner-instructors' learning community as well as the rest of RETA professional development.

Sustainability and Conclusion

Cost effectiveness and sustainability of RETA's online workshops are issues that we struggle to address, especially since we are operating with reduced funding. Financial constraints and

No Child Left Behind, which emphasizes test scores and proven, research-based programs, has created a dilemma for technology-oriented professional development programs, where there is little hard evidence that student technology use raises test scores. Although teachers are interested in online workshops for technology integration, the educational climate is not supportive. Other training opportunities take priority and consume the limited time teachers have for professional development.

New Mexico's inadequate technology infrastructure also challenges the sustainability of RETA Online. Even though the technology infrastructure of New Mexico's schools has benefited tremendously from E-rate funding, seamless, robust online access is still an issue for many schools. In October 2003, New Mexico ranked 47th in the nation in Internet use, with just over 50% of New Mexicans reporting Internet use from any location (U.S. Department of Commerce, 2004). The selection of New Mexico as an early beneficiary of funding from initiatives like Intel's *Teach to the Future* and the Gates Foundation underscores the high-need status of our state's education system.

Our online instructor training program requires online learners. These are not easily found in New Mexico: even free online workshops failed to generate sustainable enrollments. However, we are not giving up. Our survival strategies include targeting our limited resources to the development of highly marketable online workshops, cultivating partnerships, adding online components to our face-to-face workshops, and diversifying the format of our online workshops.

Lessons Learned

No matter how good the content, how well executed the plan, or how much expertise is available, significant challenges and discoveries exist in transitioning from face-to-face to online teaching and learning. These challenges present opportunities for learning the following lessons.

Lesson 1. Involve learners in course and program development

Program implementation would have been slower if we had not involved the learners. Their participation helped us create a customized program suited to our needs. More important, their involvement increased their buy-in and improved their overall comprehension of teaching and learning online:

The unknown is always scary ... Now, it would be really scary if RETA set off to conduct online sessions w/o instruction and practice! We will all get to the other shore together ... (Learner–instructor, RETA chat log, October 2002)

Lesson 2. The learning curve is steep

The learner-instructors in this program are among our most experienced RETA instructors. They have been teaching teachers how to integrate technology into curriculum for years and are technologically proficient in many areas. However, teaching online requires an entirely new set of skills; even with their background, many learner-instructors found the new teaching environment intimidating:

My initial response was pure fear. Fear that I might not figure out how to use [the technology] well, fear that I might be left behind, etc. (Instructor, RETA chat log, October 2002)

Gulp!!! I have not taken an online class previous to this one. As usual, the challenges RETA present to instructors takes us to territory I've not visited before. I find it exciting! I also get insecure that I don't quite know what I am doing (even right now are you receiving this?). But I do know that if I don't delve in I will become stagnant... (Learner-instructor, RETA chat log, October 2002)

Lesson 3. Plan for ongoing technical training and support

There is no point at which all learners are completely familiar with online technologies. They will learn key aspects of individual tools and spend time figuring out how to use them in pedagogically sound ways before adding to their technology repertoire. Then, just as they are becoming proficient, new versions of the technology will be launched requiring more learning. This never-ending process will have significant impacts on training and budget concerns.

Lesson 4. Capitalize on established models

Because we provided face-to-face professional development for many years, we had workable policies and procedures for communication, instructor training, and course development. Some policies were adequate for the new program, and others needed modification. Only a few policies were changed completely. We could not have implemented the RETA Online Instructor Training program as quickly as we did if we had needed a new organizational model.

Lesson 5. Be willing to change models when necessary

One reason for RETA's success is that we involve our instructors in design, development, and delivery of our professional development workshops. However, this model was not initially effective for RETA-Online. The online learner-instructors' lack of experience, ascertained after the program was already underway, frustrated our attempts at collaborative online course design and development. As a result, we had to employ a different model and wait until our learner-instructors had enough experience with online teaching and learning to once again attempt the previous ideal model.

Lesson 6. Teachers need time to adjust to their new roles in the online environment

Experienced classroom teachers often become frustrated when moving to an online environment. The roles they fulfill as an online teacher are, in many ways, very different from the roles they have in the classroom, and they are frequently uncertain how to react to their learners. Programs aimed at teaching teachers to teach online must recognize this frustration and allow learners to adjust to the new environment. When asked to provide advice to a hypothetical learner new to online teaching, the following RETA online instructor (with 2 years of experience) had this to say:

You will be asked to walk a fine line between sharing ... personal experience and expertise enough that you are human and accessible and not enough that it becomes about you and not your participants... You will play cheerleader, counselor, evaluator, advisor, devil's advocate, and slave driver, all in the course of a session—and all without ever seeing your students' faces... You will be in charge, from the back seat, without ever raising your voice. (Learner-instructor, Evaluation, Fall 2003)

Lesson 7. Allow new programs to influence other programs in organization

It can be easier to implement new ideas with new programs than it is to change existing models. Beginning a new program is the perfect opportunity to try new methods and models and then let those influence older programs. For example, the first time we implemented a blended training approach was for the RETA Online Instructor Training program. Initially, we used a blended approach out of necessity; however, the strengths of the model became evident through positive comments from our instructors. As we gained more experience with this method of training, we realized that other programs might benefit from the approach. Two years later, we implemented blended learning across our programs.

Lesson 8. Centralized program communications are more efficient

At the onset of the program, project leaders spent hours responding to e-mail regarding program policies, administration, training materials development, teaching and learning issues, and technical support. Often, we answered the same questions several times a day. We quickly realized that we needed more centralized communication. First, we established a listserv to discuss policy. Second, we set up a learning community in WebCT to discuss technical and pedagogic questions as well as to practice with the primary e-learning tool. Additionally, we created an area in the RETA Web site to post relevant program information. Finally, when program policies were fully established, we began to use formalized contracts rather than informal e-mail communications as our preferred method of communicating teaching and learning expectations.

Lesson 9. Be prepared with "Plan B"

Because our learner-instructors lived all over the state, we had many opportunities to learn about the technology infrastructure around New Mexico. Sometimes that infrastructure supported our learning plans; other times it thwarted them. At first, we were not prepared for this. We designed our program around WebCT and Centra, but many locations could not support Centra's technical requirements, resulting in canceled training. Later, we developed technology back-up plans. These were critical to our success because they allowed us to proceed with scheduled training even if we had technical problems.

Lesson 10. Learners support each other

We were all committed to the idea of designing this program with the participants, but it was initially difficult to change teacher-learner relationships from previous programs. Creating an area in WebCT for learners to support each other helped revise that relationship and put us on similar terms. The area provided learner-instructors with opportunities to act as online teachers early in the program and gave them space to try new things without asking for help. This was an essential component of our overall program goals.

Best Practices

Best Practice 1. Establishing a training program for online instructors should be a collaborative process between trainers and learners

Using both trainers and learner-instructors in a collaborative process ensures that (a) learning is appropriately scaffolded to meet learners' needs (Elbaum et al., 2002); (b) learners have buy-in and ownership over their learning activities and content (Senge, Roberts, Ross, Smith, Both, & Kleiner, 1999); and (c) we were more likely to include all necessary elements of the program.

Best Practice 2. The blended approach is essential

Using the blended approach for the RETA online instructor training program provided the venue for RETA to provide ongoing, continuous training and support with reduced costs and improved learning outcomes while supporting and sustaining learning communities and aiding in transforming RETA face-to-face instructors into RETA online instructors (Dziuban, Hartman, & Moskal, 2004).

Best Practice 3. Nurture a learning community

The learning community established by RETA trainers and learner-instructors provided a supportive environment for the development and social construction of new knowledge, understanding, and skills. Its development is appropriate according to the National Standards for Staff Development (National Staff Development Council, 2001) and is critical for the perpetuation of RETA's online ventures. Its value is recognized as RETA online instructors continue to take full advantage of the learning community fostered by the RETA Online Instructor Training program.

References

Brockett, R., & Hiemstra, R. (1991). *Self-direction in adult learning: Perspectives on theory, research, and practice.* New York: Routledge.

Collison, G., Elbaum, B., Haavind, S., & Tinker, R. (2000). *Facilitating online learning: Effective strategies for moderators.* Madison, WI: Atwood Publishing.

Dufour, R., & Eaker, R. (1998). *Professional learning communities at work.* Bloomington, IN: National Education Service.

Dziuban, C., Harman, J., & Moskal, P. (2004). Blended learning. EDUCAUSE Center for Applied Research. *Research Bulletin,* 7. Retrieved August 12, 2004, from http://www.educause.edu/LibraryDetailPage/666?ID=ERB0407

Elbaum, B., McIntyre, C., & Smith, A. (2002). *Essential questions: Prepare, design, and teach your online course.* Madison, WI: Atwood Publishing.

Gonzales, C. (1998). *RETA Technology innovation challenge grant: (RETA) Regional Educational Technology Assistance.* Las Cruces, NM: New Mexico State University.

Gonzales, C., Pickett. L., Hupert, N., & Martin, W. (2002). The Regional Educational Technology Assistance Program: Its effects on teaching practices. *Journal of Research on Technology in Education, 35*(1), 1-18.

National Center for Education Statistics. (2001). *Internet access in U.S. public schools and classrooms: 1994-2001.* Retrieved August 2, 2005, from http://nces.ed.gov/pubs2002/internet/ and http://nces.ed.gov/quicktables/Detail.asp?Key=535

National Staff Development Council. (2001). *NSDC standards for staff development.* Retrieved August 15, 2005, from http://www.nsdc.org/standards/index.cfm

National Staff Development Council. (n.d.). *NSDC resolutions.* Retrieved August 15, 2005, from http://www.nsdc.org/connect/about/resolutions.cfm

Riel, M., & Fulton, K. (1998). *Technology in the classroom: Tools for doing things differently or for doing different things.* Accessed August 15, 2005, from http://www.gse.uci.edu/vkiosk/faculty/riel/riel-fulton.html

Schwen, T., & Hara, N. (2004). Community of practice: A metaphor for online design? In S. Barab, R. Kling, & J. Gray (Eds.), *Designing for virtual communities in the service of learning* (pp. 154-180). Cambridge, UK: Cambridge University Press.

Senge, P., Roberts, C., Ross, R., Smith, B., Both, G., & Kleiner, A. (1999). *The dance of change: The challenges to sustaining momentum in learning organizations.* New York: Doubleday.

U.S. Department of Commerce. (2002, February). *A nation online: How Americans are expanding their use of the Internet.* Retrieved August 2, 2005, from http://www.ntia.doc.gov/ntiahome/dn/html/anationonline2.htm and http://www.esa.doc.gov/508/esa/nationonline.htm

U.S. Department of Commerce. (2004, September). *A nation online: Entering the broadband age.* Retrieved August 15, 2005, from http://www.ntia.doc.gov/reports/anol/NationOnlineBroadband04.htm#_Toc78020942

Appendix A

RETA-Online Instructor Certification Competencies

Why have instructor competencies for online learning instructors?

The instructor's role in the success of the course, the program, and student retention and achievement is clearly documented. In online learning, the instructor's role is even more critical because the instructor has to overcome potential barriers caused by technology, time, and place and help create an optimal environment for achieving educational goals. For the RETA program, the actions of a good online learning instructor fall into four areas: technical proficiency, course preparation, facilitation, and evaluation. Additionally, we will be asking for some anecdotal and reflective feedback.

Technical proficiency

General

- E-mail (sends & receives e-mail with and without attachments)
- Word (create, comment, save, save as)
- Internet browser (navigation, cache, bookmarks)

WebCT

- Discussions (manages topics, messages)
- Mail (send & receive)
- Content Module (add, edit, organize content)
- Chat (send & receive messages and URL, retrieve chat logs)
- Quiz (add, edit & delete questions or quizzes, force grade)

Centra

- Promoting co-presenters
- Presenting
- Recording presentation
- Publishing presentation
- Passing microphone
- Survey tool
- Text chat
- Breakout rooms
- White board

Course preparation

- Reviews course materials for accuracy, consistency, and viable resource links.
- Sends welcome e-mail to learners informing them how to access course, when to access course, and who to contact in case of technical or other issues.
- Prepares WebCT environment: adds students to course, sets up grade book, posts welcome info, and sets up discussion topics.
- Requests Centra session(s).
- Prepares Centra agenda for session(s).
- Posts Centra access information and link in WebCT Discussions.
- Establishes and guides participants in the use of synchronous (real-time) office hours.

Course facilitation

General

- Helps establish course rules and decision-making norms.
- Posts timely bulletins about changes and updates to course.
- During first week, assures that all learners are "on board" and responding (contacts privately by phone or e-mail if not).
- Returns learner calls/e-mails within 24 hours.
- Engages learners, fosters sharing of knowledge and experience.
- Contributes outside resources (online, print-based, others).
- Contributes advanced content knowledge and insights, weaves together discussion threads.
- Fosters learning and self-regulated learning.

WebCT

- Manages discussion and learner interactions and assists learners to do the same.
- Moderates discussion, models desired methods of communication.
- Minimum of 10% of discussion postings are from the instructor.
- Helps maintain an active learning community in WebCT (asynchronous and synchronous).

Centra

- Establishes event goals and objectives.
- Manages discussion and student interactions.
- Poses thoughtful questions related to the topic and appropriate to the desired cognitive outcomes (Bloom's Taxonomy).
- Fosters group learning in a synchronous environment.

Assessment and Evaluation

- Develops, utilizes, and revises an assessment plan.
- Provides students with clear grading criteria including examples as needed.
- Utilizes WebCT gradebook tool.
- Acknowledges receipt of assignments within 24 hours.
- Returns students assignments, with detailed notes and grade, within 96 hours.
- Encourages students to evaluate course content and instructor via anonymous feedback area, RETA course evaluation tool, and so forth.
- Uses assessment data to revise instruction and learning activities.

How will we ascertain that you are meeting these competencies?

- Instructor training
- Instructor evaluations
- Course evaluations
- Learner assessment data
- Communications with students

For Reflective/Metacognitive Consideration

- Consider your strengths and weaknesses and use that information to guide you in developing your own personal growth program. How can we help address your needs? What discussions, workshops, and so forth do we need to continue or add?

Appendix B

Providing Learner Support
Welcome e-mail with Workshop Materials Packet will be sent out by instructors.
Workshop Materials Packet will include PDF of Syllabus, Schedule, Resources, WebCT/Centra login instructions, Discussion & Participation rubric, and so forth.
Syllabus, Schedule, Resources will be available on RETA site.
Resources document will include specific instructions for downloading and installing any necessary software and plug-ins.
Backup methods of communication will be stated upfront by instructors.
Expectations of learner to learner, learner to instructor, learner to content communications (frequency, quality, etc.) will be provided.
A workshop orientation lesson covering help menus, attaching files, using WebCT discussions/e-mail, and so forth, communicating in discussions, and so forth will be in the first week of every workshop.
Syllabus will identify technical skills needed to successfully complete workshop (EX: "Participant must have access to and be able to use a scanner to complete this workshop").
Instructors will hold weekly office hours to address specific participant issues and to provide feedback.
Participants will have access to the student progress tool in WebCT in order to determine what they have completed/need to complete.
Self-quizzes at the end of every lesson of the workshop will be provided for the participant so that they can gage their understanding of the material.
A discussion area for participants to help each other with technical issues will be created.
A discussion area for participants to talk about non-course related topics will be created.
Discussion areas for participants to talk about specific themes related to the workshop topic will be created so that they might engage in dialogues of specific interest to them.
Workshop FAQs and Glossary will be available to participants.
Facilitating Learning Environment
Establish Communications
Obtain your participant list and participant contact info from RETA Web site.
Send welcoming e-mail: • welcome • introductions (yourself and the workshop) • expectations and requirements (type/amount of participation, etc.) • links to syllabus, schedule, and resources on RETA site • links and login instructions for WebCT/Centra • backup plan information (what to do if you can't login, etc.) • request response from participants so you can verify their e-mails, and so forth • attach workshop materials packet (.pdf of syllabus, schedule, resources, participation rubric, detailed login instructions for WebCT/Centra, etc.)

Appendix B (cont.)

Remember, your workshop communication plans need to compensate for the loss of face-to-face communications. It takes time, planning, and effort to communicate online, but it can be just as effective as face-to-face. • Most online communications are asynchronous. Expect it to take more time to plan events, distribute information, and hold discussions. • Plan ahead. Try to anticipate your participant's information and support needs. • Agree on a communication plan with your participants. • Maintain frequent, meaningful communication throughout workshop. If you do not have time to respond right away, let them know when you will get back to them.
Build Community
Remember: You are part of the community. In true constructivist fashion, you and the participants will be working together toward a deeper understanding of the learning topic. Allow learners to dominate the discussion. Remove yourself from the center of each communication, but do not withdraw from the conversation either. The workshops are not self-running. They require a "guide on the side" to keep things running smoothly and moving toward deeper understanding of the topic(s).
Agree upon deadlines, requirements, and expectations. Your participants need to understand both the big and small picture. Your participants need a clear picture of where they are going, what they need to do to get there, and when it needs to be finished. Without this information, participants may feel like they are lost and floundering.
Model high expectations and good practices. Your participants will follow.
Send deadline and meeting reminders.
Encourage participants to share. They should be sharing with each other and with you. Their insights and experience are meaningful and critical to the group learning experience. Remind them of that.
Provide and encourage timely, meaningful feedback. Participants need to be acknowledged for their efforts, and insightful comments will help participants to learn and improve. Participants also need to feel free to share their workshop comments, questions, and concerns.
Insist on a positive, respectful learning environment. Demeaning, threatening, coarse, vulgar language is not only disrespectful and damaging to learners; it is, in many instances, against NMSU digital communications policy. See http://ict.nmsu.edu/Guidelines/general.use.html for NMSU guidelines.
Hold office hours—WebCT chat is perfect for this. You can specify an hour each week in which you will be online to provide content assistance, clear up problems with assignments, and so forth. You could even build weekly chats into the course as an assignment.
Provide Basic Technical Support
Hold office hours—WebCT chat is perfect for this. You can specify an hour each week in which you will be online to provide technical assistance, clear up problems, and so forth.
Provide technical assistance—how to attach files in mail, how to navigate the course, and so forth.
Decide on a "backup plan" to deal with technical problems such as server down, and so forth.

Appendix B (cont.)

Moderating Discussions
Strive for three goals—community building, supporting a culture of respect, cultivating reasoned discourse of the topic.
Recognize three forms of dialogue—social, argumentative, pragmatic—so that you can plan interventions that will effectively promote active, collaborative, focused reflection. • Social dialogue—general, non-course related chitchat. Important for bonding and trust building, but have separate area set up for this. • Argumentative dialogue—strongly advocating a particular view, or distancing self from discourse ("This is too hard." "This is too new."). While people need to feel comfortable saying what/how they feel, the emphasis should be on critical thinking and opening up to new ideas and possibilities. • Pragmatic dialogue—process-oriented dialogue that serves ends beyond the dialogue itself. This type of dialogue engages, promotes enquiry, exposes assumptions, welcomes confirmation as well as challenges to data and interpretation of "facts."
Fulfill three roles—guide on the side, instructor, and group process facilitator. • Guide on the side—carefully crafts interventions in the dialogue, does not play a central role in dialogue, tries to move participants to a new conceptual level. • Instructor—sets course expectations, requirements, an so forth. • Group process facilitator—helps form and maintain group collaborative spirit through community building, nurturing, organizing posts, acknowledging diversity, and so forth.
Remember: Your job as guide on the side is to extend the thinking of your participants. To do this, you can use a variety of ***voices*** to help participants see their own thinking and facilitate their reflections of their own ideas with the purpose of moving the learning forward. Adopt various "voices" as you guide your group through the learning process by crafting those dialogue interventions mentioned previously: • Generative Guide—lay out spectrum of possible positions on a topic to indicate avenues of questioning that need to be explored. • Conceptual Facilitator—identify conceptual areas that need attention. • Reflective Guide—restate a message or series of messages for the purpose of highlighting fruitful lines of discourse or insights from participants that have extended key points in the discussion or to highlight tensions between competing thoughts. • Personal Muse—craft a post that shows your internal dialogue about central issues in order to hold your own opinions/beliefs up for questioning. • Mediator—maintain open spirit of dialogue. • Role Play—adopt a character to "voice" concerns, issues, and so forth, from a new/different perspective.
Remember: You are communicating in a primarily text-based medium. Messages can, and frequently are, misconstrued if you do not pay attention to the ***tone*** you use. Adopt various "tones" to support and encourage reflection and pragmatic dialogue. You might choose to be nurturing, curious, analytical, humorous, informal, and so forth, or a combination of them throughout your posts. Used in conjunction with the voices mentioned previously, your messages will serve to deepen critical thinking, understanding, and learning.
Remember: As guide on the side, your job is to deepen the understanding of a topic. Voices and tones are only two parts of a triad of advanced moderating skills you can use to do this. The third is critical thinking strategies. In combination with voice and tone, these strategies sharpen the focus of the dialogue and help participants dig deeper into the dialogue.

Appendix B (cont.)

Adopt various critical thinking strategies: • Identify direction of dialogue—help participants recognize goals and expectations of the current dialogue. • Sort ideas for relevance—help participants decide on the relative importance of active lines of thought based on stated goals of dialogue to be pursued. • Focus on key points—highlight essential concepts and connections made by the participants to date. • Full-spectrum questions—help participants examine their own hypotheses, thoughts, and beliefs, both as individuals and as a group. • Make connections—help participants explore inferences, tensions, and rationales in statements made to date in order to help them shift to deeper layers of meaning. • Honor multiple perspectives—help participants understand and appreciate varying points of view.
Promote Knowledge, Comprehension, Application, Analysis, Synthesis, and Evaluation in each of your participants (Bloom's Cognitive Domains).
Promote Receiving, Responding, Valuing, Organizing, and Internalizing in each of your participants (Bloom's Affective Domains).

Note: For a list of references used in creating this checklist e-mail the authors at reta@nmsu.edu.

Chapter V

Using E-Learning to Globalize a Teacher Education Program

Hilary Wilder, William Paterson University, USA

Abstract

This case study explores the use of online distance learning technology to bring an international component to a teacher education program. By converting a course in the program into a fully online offering, the author was able to include students from Namibian teacher education programs in the class along with her own students from New Jersey. The objective was to give all students a chance to interact with peers that they would not otherwise have the chance to meet, and to explore differences and commonalities in their respective education systems. This case study describes the pitfalls and successes in meeting that objective.

Introduction

Online distance learning technologies are being used in almost every field of study these days, providing students with flexibility, which is not possible in traditional face-to-face courses. In addition, these technologies can go beyond anytime, anywhere access to course material and discussions, and can be used to open the classroom up to global collaborations.

This is especially important in teacher education programs where students need to be capable of teaching in an increasingly diverse, multicultural classroom as well as being capable in preparing their own students for success in an increasingly interconnected, global community. As teacher educators strive to incorporate multiculturalism and international education into their programs, many have begun to explore the use of technology as a way of reaching this goal (Davis, 1999; Merryfield, 2000; Schoorman, 2002; Zong, 2002).

In this case study we will explore one such project in which an online teacher education course was offered to students in the United States and Namibia as the result of a collaboration between teacher educators at William Paterson University in New Jersey (WPUNJ), and the National Institute of Educational Development (NIED) and its partner Colleges of Education in Namibia. The College of Education at William Paterson University has been preparing teachers in New Jersey for 150 years, and over the past 10 years has provided faculty and students with a wide range of educational technologies, including the Blackboard online course management system. Many of the graduates go on to teach in disadvantaged urban school districts, which now have large numbers of non-native English speaking immigrants.

Since independence in 1990, the Colleges of Education in Namibia (located in Caprivi, Ongwediva, Rundu, and Windhoek) have been preparing teachers to provide basic education to a previously disenfranchised majority, which is still working to overcome the effects of decades of apartheid. In the past few years the colleges have been striving to bring educational technology into their classrooms and are particularly interested in using technology to quickly increase the number of qualified teachers there. Regardless of country, an expectation for teacher education programs is that their graduates are able to prepare primary and secondary school students for effective 21st century citizenship, which includes technological literacy as well as global understanding.

Rationale for Using Online Distance Learning

"Technology Across the Curriculum" is a required course in the undergraduate, primary-school teaching certification program offered to students at William Paterson. Although this is a course that covers the basics of how to teach with and teach about technology, in the past it had only been taught in a traditional, face-to-face mode. In the spring of 2004, it was decided that this course should be converted to be fully online and delivered via the university's Blackboard course management system, starting in the fall 2004 semester. This was done for a number of reasons, including the need to ensure that WPUNJ students had sufficient experience with online technologies and would be able to benefit from future oniine training as they continued their professional development after graduation, and also to ensure that they would be comfortable using similar technologies with their own students. Current state and national standards mandate that primary school students are able to use technology to find and process information, and to use technology to communicate their own ideas (International Society for Technology in Education [ISTE], 2000a; New Jersey Department of Education [NJDOE], 2004a; U.S. Department of Education [USDOE], 2005).

Similarly, in Namibia the Ministry of Basic Education, Sport, and Culture (MBESC) and the Ministry of Higher Education, Training, and Employment Creation (MHETEC) are in the process of developing technology literacy standards for students as a way of ensuring that they will be able to participate in the global marketplace and job force. As governmental and non-governmental organizations such as SchoolNet Namibia (http://www.schoolnet.na) equip primary and secondary schools there with networked computers, teachers will need to know how to support their students' use of this equipment. In addition, online technologies are seen as a way to provide badly needed teacher training at a time when the teaching population is being greatly reduced by the HIV/AIDS pandemic. Although the ministries do not currently have an online distance learning infrastructure in place, by having students from the Colleges of Education in Namibia enroll in the William Paterson course, they were able to trial something that could potentially meet both goals.

On the Namibia side, this project was coordinated by the National Institute of Educational Development (NIED), an arm of the MBESC that works with the Colleges of Education and develops curricula and resources for them, as well as educational standards. NIED contacted the colleges and asked that they identify one student who would like to participate in the program. They also asked the colleges to identify one faculty member who had participated in NIED's Initiative Namibian Educational Technology (iNET) project (Soule, 2005), which had introduced them to online distance learning technologies. These teacher educators would act as mentors to the students throughout the time the course was offered. It should be noted that within Namibia, three of the four Colleges of Education are located in remote rural areas in the country (in Rundu, Caprivi, and Ongwediva, with the fourth located in the capital city of Windhoek). For this reason alone, there was a great interest in exploring ways that an online technology could help "leapfrog" communication and collaboration between NIED and the colleges.

Furthermore, as previously mentioned, a major additional benefit of the technology was that it would allow teacher candidates at WPUNJ to collaborate and communicate with peers in Namibia and vice versa. For New Jersey students, there is a growing need for international education in the primary and secondary schools (NJDOE, 2004b). As Merryfield and others (Merryfield, Jarchow, & Pickert, 1997) point out, future teachers need to understand the diversity within their classrooms as well as the implications of global events on their classrooms. This is as important for teachers in developed nations such as the U.S. as it is for teachers in developing nations such as Namibia. In addition, by discussing educational issues with others, future teachers may be able to induce practices and trends that can be seen as commonalities across educational contexts and thus inform their own practices.

Academic Issues that Arose

Development of the online course syllabus and materials was done over the summer of 2004 and involved one professor of educational technology from WPUNJ and three instructional technologists from NIED. Since the professor from WPUNJ would be the primary instructor in this course and had already taught it in face-to-face mode before, she took the lead in developing the course material. The plan was that the NIED collaborators would then review all material as it was developed, with the goal of having a course that would meet the learning needs of both New Jersey and Namibian students. This process had mixed results, mostly due to the fact that communication between New Jersey and Namibia was limited to e-mail and online discussion boards. Without any synchronous, face-to-face meetings, it was difficult for the NIED collaborators to prioritize and find time to work on the course, and while these were predominantly administrative issues, they impacted on academic issues by limiting the amount of adjustments that ended up being made for Namibian students. For example, the term "unit plan," which was familiar to WPUNJ students ended up not being corrected in time and became a point of confusion for Namibian students.

In terms of course objectives, it was agreed early on these would be tied to the National Educational Technology Standards for Teachers (NETS-T) (ISTE, 2000b). Again, this favored the WPUNJ students, who had a much greater chance of being able to immediately apply these skills and concepts in their own classrooms than did the Namibian students. On the other hand, it could be argued that Namibian schools, when they were equipped with the technology, would have an even greater need for new teachers who could effectively use it since in Namibia, unlike in much of the U.S., technology support and resources are few and far between. So while the material for the WPUNJ students was more "just-in-time," the material for the Namibian students was more "just-in-case." Students were welcome to download and/or print out course material for future use.

In addition to course material, which consisted of weekly session, notes (designed as reusable learning objects in the form of pdf and html files), and links to other resources, there were also regularly posted asynchronous discussion forums in which students were required to participate. All of the course material was available from the first day of the course on and could be reviewed by the student at any time. Similarly, required assignment projects were also available from the first day on, and could be turned in at any time before the due dates at the end of the semester. Discussion forums, however, were tied to the syllabus schedule and were only available during the week that the related topics were covered. By having mandatory weekly discussions, the students were better able to stay on task and keep up with the class, and while participation in the forums was graded, the actual topic questions were open-ended without a real right or wrong answer. For example, in the third session, students were asked to read up on the technology literacy standards for primary school children and then comment on the digital divide and the importance (or unimportance) for students in developed and developing countries to be able meet these standards. Interestingly, even this type of interaction tended to favor WPUNJ students, because the Namibian students were not accustomed to just giving their own opinions, due to the fact that they had generally experienced a very rote form of learning under apartheid.

Discussion questions were designed to encourage the exploration of social, legal, and ethical issues that surround the use of technology in education. For example, students were asked to research copyright and fair use laws in the U.S. and Namibia and comment on how these laws would affect their teaching and affect what their students would need to know. It was hoped that these discussions would lead to a cross-cultural sharing of ideas and opinions and meet the global education objectives of the project. Assignments, on the other hand, were used to meet and assess the teacher technology (NETS-T) objectives of the course. In the past, when the course had been offered in face-to-face mode, the instructor was able to provide training and assessment in students' technology skills during hands-on computer lab periods. Since students would typically come with a wide range of technological abilities, many class periods would often become remediation sessions for students who did now know some of the standard office applications or computer basics.

By making the course fully online, the focus shifted from learning technology basics to ways of integrating technology into education and meeting technological literacy standards for primary and secondary grades. Assignments were carefully designed to have students use standard applications (which they were now on their own to pick up) for educational purposes. For example, in the past, a hands-on lab session might have been devoted to covering basic spreadsheet operations, but in the online course students were responsible for turning in a gradebook spreadsheet, which they created on their own, with the help of optional drop-in workshops, online tutorials, or office hours and telephone support from the instructor. The online nature of the course had the added side effect that students now had to assume more responsibility for their own learning. WPUNJ students were encouraged to use formal (e.g., the online tutorials) as well as informal (friends, books in the "Dummies" series, etc.) resources for additional support. For students in Namibia, where these informal resources are not typically available, the mentors at their respective colleges were expected to provide this support.

Administrative Issues that Arose

The collaboration between WPUNJ and NIED was the result of a rather informal social network (i.e., "a friend of a friend of a friend ..."), and while the administration in both institutions was aware of and approved of the project, there was no formal agreement or memorandum of understanding. On the positive side, this meant that something could be started quickly and flexibly. On the negative side, this meant that there were no formally assigned responsibilities or dedicated resources for the project. For example, as mentioned previously, NIED collaborators were expected to review the course material in addition to their regular job responsibilities, which often took them out of the office. The NIED collaborators as well as the teacher educator mentors from the Colleges of Education in Namibia were also expected to co-teach the course with the professor from WPUNJ, but again this was on top of their regular job responsibilities and so was given very low priority by them.

Furthermore, although WPUNJ students received credit for taking the course, there was no reciprocal arrangement with the Colleges of Education in Namibia. This meant that the students from there did not have to pay tuition, but it also meant that they had no leverage when the technology at their college was broken, or the mentors were not available. Often these students resorted to finding an Internet cafe and sending e-mail to the WPUNJ professor who would then send e-mails to NIED in the hopes of getting someone there who could help out.

For WPUNJ students, the technology was not an issue, as the university has a well-established network infrastructure, a robust Blackboard course management system, and a number of open computer labs for those who did not have computers at home. For students in Namibia, particularly those from the three rural colleges in Rundu, Ongwediva, and Caprivi, the technology was not quite there. There were significant delays in the MBESC's rollout of equipment to the colleges of education and getting IT support at the colleges, so NIED set up pre- and post-semester "computer camps," with the four students staying at NIED housing in Okahandja (in the middle of the country) and using the computers there to get started and finish up. The lack of reliable technology during the semester clearly had an impact on the online discussions, with Namibian students often posting their responses weeks after the WPUNJ students.

This aspect of the project was very frustrating for all, and especially frustrating for the Namibian students who were quite eager to participate, but had little clout when problems arose. On the other hand, the trial was useful in pointing out pitfalls and consequences for officials at the MBESC and MHETEC ministries as they move toward creating an online distance learning infrastructure of their own. In anticipation of this, all course material was developed as reusable learning objects and designated with a Creative Commons copyright license, with the hope that it would be used in future Namibian as well as WPUNJ courses.

Project Outcomes

All students, from both WPUNJ and Namibia successfully passed the course and were able to demonstrate achievement of the course objectives tied to the NETS-T standards, although Namibian students would not have been able to do this without the post-semester sessions at the NIED facility. Similarly, 22 out of 23 students rated themselves as having significantly higher scores on an end-of-semester NETS-T self assessment[1] (Johnson, 2002) as compared to one taken at the beginning of the semester. Student evaluations of the course revealed that students rated the course highly (mean = 5.2 on a scale of 1 to 6 [with 6 being "excellent" and 1 being "very bad"], n=20, std=1.4), although three students did comment that they would have preferred a face-to-face mode.

In terms of cross-cultural exchanges, preliminary evaluations of the online discussions reveal that WPUNJ students for the most part did not communicate with the Namibian students, although the Namibian students would reach out to them. This may have been due to the lag that sometimes occurred as Namibian students had technical difficulties—by the time they were able to post their responses, the WPUNJ students were already on another discussion topic. Similarly, an end-of-semester survey on awareness of Namibia and the Namibian educational system revealed that WPUNJ students did learn a little about Namibia (as compared to what they knew on a survey taken at the beginning of the semester) and generally saw that the expectations and needs in Namibian education were similar to those in New Jersey. Further investigation is underway to discover the impact that these exchanges had on the students' understanding of international education.

As mentioned previously, the networking and collaboration on this project happened in a very informal, *ad hoc* way and unfortunately, most communication between WPUNJ and Namibia was done via e-mail, which was easy to lose or misinterpret. This was further hampered by the time difference as well as cross-cultural differences that were difficult to understand given the sparse nature of the communication medium. At one point, when there was a particularly bad lag in e-mail responses, the professor from WPUNJ bought a telephone card in order to find out what was happening.

Implications for Internationalization Efforts

For WPUNJ, it is clear that the current technology infrastructure is capable of supporting international and cross-cultural collaborations that can benefit students. The use of technology to "globalize" the curriculum can be particularly helpful for a public university like WPUNJ that serves students who come from a lower economic background than students at private schools do, and who would not necessarily have the money to participate in a study abroad program. What is needed, however, is a commitment to building the relationships and formal agreements to support this, including the allocation of appropriate resources. Informal collaborations between faculty members can be the start of this, but administrative support, in terms of faculty release time or even money for international telephone calls, is needed to sustain it.

The following semester (spring 2005) the course was only offered to WPUNJ students. Two of the NIED collaborators were in the process of leaving NIED, and there were no available personnel there to continue it from that end. Again, since there had been no formal agreement or memorandum of understanding between NIED/Colleges of Education and WPUNJ, there was no commitment to continue the project. The administration of both institutions (NIED and WPUNJ) acknowledged that the project had potential and was beneficial to their respective students; however, neither were ready to commit resources or personnel to it. The hope is that if and when the administrations of both institutions are ready to formally pursue this that this project will be the basis for future collaborations.

Lessons Learned

1. An informal, *ad hoc* collaboration can be good in that a project can be put together quickly and flexibly. But ...
2. An informal, *ad hoc* collaboration can be bad in that there are no recognized deadlines, dedicated resources, or committed responsibilities. Furthermore, some stakeholders (students) may be left without any leverage at all unless this is explicitly contracted ahead of time.
3. It is easy to back-burner responsibilities in a virtual collaboration that relies solely on asynchronous communication (e-mail or discussion board). Instead try to also hold regularly scheduled synchronous meetings (teleconference or chat), which review project status and deadlines.
4. Teaching an online course is a lot of work, even if you have all the material prepared ahead of time. It is even more work if you have students in different time zones. You wake up in the morning and you are already behind the students who woke up seven hours before you.
5. Do not expect students to respond to each other's discussion board postings on their own. Student-to-student communication may need to be an explicit requirement if that is what you are hoping for.
6. Technology, personal, or other issues may cause a student to fall behind, and once this happens in a fully online course, it is hard for them to catch up to the rest of the class. Keep tabs on all students to make sure they are participating as expected. Recognize that some students do not have very good "self-regulated learning" skills and decide what you want to do about that.

7. Unique learner characteristics and/or students' technology limits may mean that material has to be presented in multiple formats. For example, pdf or Word documents may need to be converted into html.
8. If the course is fully online, try to get pictures of the students by the first or second session. This is especially helpful if students are from different cultures and prone to forming stereotypes of what each other looks like in the absence of real photos.
9. Expect lots of e-mails from students who are taking an online course for the first time and nervous about it. This includes an e-mail every time they post something to make sure that you see their posting. Be patient.
10. Getting "thank you" e-mails from students after the course ends feels great! It is easy to start to feel like you are not reaching them if you are not seeing them face-to-face, so the positive feedback goes a long way.

Best Practices

1. Open the course up to students from a developing nation—even though it was extremely frustrating at times, those in developed nations should be looking for ways to use technology to bridge the digital divide, not widen it.
2. Collaborate on development of course material—material should not be "U.S.-centric," and all parties should be producers as well as consumers.
3. Be flexible, especially if the technology infrastructure is unstable—be sympathetic when students have to access the course from an internet cafe (which can be noisy and expensive).

References

Davis, N. (1999). The globalisation of education through teacher education with new technologies: A view informed by research through teacher education with new technologies. *Educational Technology Review 1*(12), 8-12.

International Society for Technology in Education. (2000a). *NETS for students*. Eugene, OR: Author. Also available on the web at http://cnets.iste.org/students/

International Society for Technology in Education. (2000b). *NETS for teachers*. Eugene, OR: Author. Also available on the Web at http://cnets.iste.org/teachers/

Johnson, D. (2002). *CODE 77 rubrics, 2002 revision*. Retrieved August 1, 2005, from http://www.doug-johnson.com/dougwri/rubrics2002.html

Merryfield, M. (2000). Using electronic technologies to promote equity and cultural diversity in social studies and global education. *Theory and Research in Social Education, 28*(4), 502-526.

Merryfield, M., Jarchow, E., & Pickert, S. (Eds.). (1997). *Preparing teachers to teach global perspectives: A handbook for teacher educators*. Thousand Oaks, CA: Corwin Press.

Ministry of Basic Education, Sport and Culture & Ministry of Higher Education, Training and Employment Creation. (2004). *ICT policy for education: ICT integration for equity and excellence in education.* Unpublished policy paper.

New Jersey Department of Education. (2004a). *New Jersey core curriculum content standards for technological literacy*. Retrieved August 1, 2005, from http://www.nj.gov/njded/cccs/s8_tech.htm

New Jersey Department of Education. (2004b). *Why does international education matter in New Jersey's schools?* Retrieved August 1, 2005, from http://www.nj.gov/njded/international/

Schoorman, D. (2002). Increasing critical multicultural understanding via technology. *Journal of Teacher Education, 53*(4), 356-364.

Soule, H. (2005). *Online teacher professional development: Exploring lessons from Namibia and Uganda.* Unpublished report retrieved August 1, 2005, from http://www.dot-com-alliance.org/resourceptrdb/uploads/partnerfile/upload/293/Online_Teacher_Professional_Development_Uganda_Namibia.pdf

U.S. Department of Education. (2005). *National education technology plan*. Retrieved August 1, 2005, from http://www.nationaledtechplan.org/

Zong, G (2002). Can computer mediated communication help to prepare global teachers? An analysis of preservice social studies teachers' experience. *Theory and Research in Social Education, 30*(4), 589-616.

Endnote

1 Survey used with permission of the author.

Chapter VI

Delivery of a Social Science Online Program in India

Shobhita Jain, Indira Gandhi National Open University, New Delhi, India

Abstract

This narrative of an engagement with the open and distance learning system and its highpoint of launching an online learning package in 2001 reveals an attempt to integrate various components of the multimedia format of course development. The uneasy task of meeting the various needs of diverse learners became possible by using the information technology tools to communicate and interact more effectively. Well-structured architecture of the Web site of the program, including its peer-evaluated threaded discussion board has been well accepted by the learners. Rudimentary in its overall design, this first ever social science online program in India may be, it has generated in the institution a live interest in encouraging further attempts at launching online programs of study.

Introduction

In the globalized world of the 21st century, education has become a tool for growth of developing countries. In this sense, education is an economic necessity in a nation like India, where the numbers are large and resources available are fewer in relation to higher cost of education for all. Whether it is the ancient Gurukul system or the present-day classroom system, knowledge seekers have always gone to the place of learning for receiving education, but the classroom system is increasingly proving to be inadequate to meet the challenges of demands for universal education, continuing education, and equity in access to educational opportunities. With the entry of the open and distance learning (ODL) mode of education, instead of people going to the place of knowledge it has now become possible to take knowledge to people. The current educational scenario in India requires that ODL institutions strive to make full use of information technology to achieve higher productivity in a cost-effective manner. In this context this chapter narrates the story of the author's engagement with the open and distance learning system and its highpoint of launching of an online learning package in 2001.

Introduced at the Indira Gandhi National Open University (IGNOU) to the distance-learning mode of education in the late 1980s, the author became interested in the ODL's potential power for meeting the e-needs of India and educational needs of India, and after grasping, in the first five years of being at IGNOU, its unique features and their relevance to contribute substantially to the Indian educational system, an attempt was made to tap the potential of information technology tools to integrate within the ODL system. There were two challenges before us.

Encouraged by the results of dogged pursuit, in some other programs of study at IGNOU, of making course development a participatory exercise (Jain, 2001), the first challenge facing us was to create shared learning environments for making possible a sustained exploration by learners around critical issues in the subject of study. For this purpose we planned to appropriately integrate various components of the multimedia format of course development.

The second challenge was to meet IGNOU's objective of addressing the learning requirements of diverse target groups. The World Bank approached IGNOU to offer a learning package for resettlement and rehabilitation (R&R) managers working in the various development projects. The wide range of managers employed in government, private, and voluntary bodies to manage the R&R issues of displacement caused by development projects in India presented a wide range of potential takers of such a package. It was not easy to integrate the various needs of different groups of potential takers of this group in one learning package, and it seemed very useful to tap the information technology (IT) tools to communicate and interact more effectively with the learners employed in different institutions ranging from a non-governmental organization to the government of India both at central and state levels to financial institutions carrying out huge development projects of various kinds. The sociology and economics faculty of the School of Social Sciences at IGNOU accepted to develop the learning package, and the author of this chapter coordinated the project. In the light of these considerations, the goal of the collaborative learning processes focussing on the participation of learners became the underlying principle to conceptualize and develop the online learning package of a six-month post graduate certificate program of study in participatory management of displacement, resettlement and rehabilitation (PGCMRR, launched in July 2001).

The chapter has four parts: basic information about PGCMRR, academic and administrative issues, lessons learned and evaluation of the program, and concluding remarks that incorporate policy implications of promoting networking and collaboration in the world of knowledge.

E-Learning Program

As part of IGNOU's commitment to offer courses to diverse groups of learners, and the initiative from the faculty led to launching of an online post-graduate certificate in PGCMRR through a financial support of the World Bank. Its objectives, target groups, entry requirements, and other information are given next:

- **Objectives:** The main objective of the program is to provide participatory management skills to the personnel involved in R&R work. The word "participatory" is of critical importance because no R&R is feasible without participation of those displaced. The PGCMRR students learn in this program the skills involved in taking a participatory approach, and they are expected to apply the same in their project work of PGCMRR. This, in turn, will hopefully prepare them to carry forward the same in real life to their work in the field of R&R.
- **The target groups:** The program has been targeted to: (a) those engaged in resettlement and rehabilitation (or R&R) divisions of development projects of the government and private sectors as project officers, technical experts, field staff, and/or desk staff, and also (b) those working with the NGOs, industrial establishments, and other agencies involved in R&R plans of development projects.
- **Entry requirements:** The program is open to graduates with access to and basic competence in the use of computers and Internet. It is of six-month duration but can be completed in the span of two years. This flexibility refers only to the submission of the project work. Other course requirements have to be completed in the semester of enrollment. Those who cannot complete the online course requirements are by default the off-line learners of the program. To continue as an online learner, one has to pay a nominal fee to re-register. This option is available for four six-month cycles from the date of initial registration to the program.
- **Date of launch and mode of delivery:** The first batch of the program started in July 2001. All admissions in this batch were for online mode of delivery. From January 2002, admissions to the program were available in online as well as off-line mode.

Academic Issues

PGCMRR is the first social science online program offered by any Indian University. The online delivery of PGCMRR presumed that in the near future Web-based courses are going to be the most efficient and cost-effective mode of delivery in the ODL system. One is of course well aware of the prevailing infrastructure-related deficiencies in developing countries, and keeping them in mind one can argue for Web-based delivery mode to co-exist with other forms and hope for its increased use as and when better infrastructure takes roots. Having stated the bias in favor of using the Internet as a delivery mechanism, the chapter discusses the following academic issues pertaining to PGCMRR's online learning center.

- The underlying principles of the design of online learning environment
- Design constraints of the learning center
- The special features of the site

Underlying Principles of the Design of Online Learning Environment

Before designing the online learning center, the first task of the program coordinator was to identify some guiding principles, which were in line with the target audience and the nature of the subject. The online learning center of PGCMRR had the following underlying principles:

- Most learning tasks of the program need to be completed online requiring minimum face-to-face contact.
- Learners should be able to manage their own learning, share their experiences with other learners, and participate in discussions so that they are simultaneously both self-directed learners as well as participants in group learning process where they share with and care for fellow learners through online discussions.
- Not only do the learners need to manage their own learning, they also need the opportunity to construct their own knowledge, based on a variety of inputs. Sharing their insights and eliciting comments, the learners should submit their assignments after reconsidering their own views in the light of comments from the peer group.
- Teachers, or mentors as we refer to them in PGCMRR, should act as facilitators to ensure right educational advice at the right time in a right way. They need to give diagnostic as well as remedial help to the learners.
- Keeping in view the low bandwidth available to the learners, the learning center has to limit itself to minimum graphics and multimedia content to facilitate easy access.
- Going along with IGNOU's supplementary approach to audio/video components of its multimedia learning packages, the PGCMRR learning center would use CD-ROM to deliver audio/video inputs, with just brief annotations of them on the Web.

Design Constraints of the Learning Center

The Web-based technology has enabled us in designing the PGCMRR learning center to integrate two types of learning environments, namely, tele-learning-based, and Web-based, for both synchronous and asynchronous communication. In PGCMRR, the Web-based technology provides a learning process that is essentially hypermedia-based instructional system that uses the attributes and resources of the World Wide Web.

To develop this instructional system our second task was to build a framework or the theory guiding its structure. Mostly three schools of thought, behaviorism, cognitivism, and constructivism, have been widely used for this purpose. Of the three, constructivism has been most suitable for online learning environments. It demands continuous interaction among instructional designer, content expert, and technical support person. In PGCMRR our approach has been an eclectic blending of the three learning theories (Mishra, 2002).

Special Features of the Site

The program structure of PGCMRR comprises five courses with a total of 16 credits, and each credit is equivalent to 30 study hours for the learner. Of the five courses, four are theory courses and the last one is practical oriented project work. The project work is the application-oriented end of the four theory courses. The theory courses have a total of 48 lessons or units packed in 13 modules. All the five courses are available on the Web site. But in the light of low bandwidth and generally poor connection of the Internet in India, the media mix for PGCMRR has been so arranged that while course lessons are all available online, the audio and video components of the courses are on CD-ROM. As a result the audio/video section of the PGCMRR Web site has annotations only.

The learners use the online learning center for completion of their assignments-related work and for interaction with mentors and among themselves. Online help (a feature added later on), available for two hours daily from Monday to Friday, helps those learners who are relatively new to the use of the Internet, to easily negotiate the various sections of the Web site. Important topics of R & R have been discussed in a series of guest lectures, which have been recorded for telecast for the learners as well as general public.

The learning center for PGCMRR or the Web site http//www.rronline.ignou.ac.in (earlier domain http://www.rronline.org) has a simple but highly interactive design. Lest the learners get lost in the cyberspace, a constant panel on the left side helps them to navigate through the site. As we discovered that many learners had little skill of using the Internet for purposes other than e-mail, a help line button was added to facilitate them. Further, many learners miss the very first online activity of orientation program; another button of orientation program has been added to the menu. The design of the Web site in this sense is not a one-time activity. It is an ongoing process that incorporates new features as and when required for efficient running of the site and achieving the main objectives of PGCMRR in terms of participatory approach to R&R issues.

The learners mostly use the announcements section as a notice board. Learners have given their suggestions to modify its contents. Their participation has helped us to make it more learner-friendly. For example, they suggested that notices regarding too many deadlines confuse them. Deadlines should not be arriving too soon for too many activities.

The program guide section is used by learners to keep a check on their timetable and also to understand the IGNOU system of open and distance learning. Any visitor to the site can consult it. This section provides access to few sample courses for the visitors to have a feel of the program.

Only the registered learners of PGCMRR can access the section on courses. It has lessons in all the four courses and guidelines for project work. Design of each lesson promotes active learning as based on behavioristic approach each lesson has been divided into small chunks with self-assessment questions (SAQs) interspersed within it. As the learners work on SAQs and submit the answers, the system automatically provides immediate feedback about the correctness of the response. The learner can compare his or her answer with the one generated by the online system.

Synchronous communication takes place during e-counselling sessions, which are not compulsory to attend. Learners are however encouraged by their mentors to use the facility to clarify their doubts and share their views and experiences with the mentor and fellow learners. For purposes of completing assignments all learners of PGCMRR in a batch are divided into groups of 10 to 15. In the first cycle the same groups received e-counselling by separate mentors. In the second cycle, for counselling two to three groups were merged into one because the learner participation in each session was only 25% to 30%. Since most of PGCMRR learners are working in the field, they are not able to access the Internet for attending e-counselling sessions. They contact the mentors upon their return and through e-mail clarify all their doubts and discuss complex concepts and issues.

Completion of all assignments is a compulsory component of the program. All online learners complete them online only. The assignments are continuous in nature, and their main purpose is to test the learners' comprehension of the concepts and help them to go through the courses. More importantly, the Assignments button is so designed that the continuous process of assignments-related work establishes a community of learners who share their ideas and experiences among themselves, derive benefits from the points of view of fellow learners, and gain self confidence in articulating their own views in a congenial and friendly learning environment of one's own peer group. The three sets of assignments carry 50% weight in the total evaluation.

Of the three types of assignments in PGCMRR, namely participation in discussion forum (PDF), online computer marked assignments (OCMAs), and online diary (OD), the first one demands considerable participation by way of sharing of and commenting on each other's work. The learners have most enjoyed this part of their work and found it very useful. All learners, graduate and experienced in field, are able to learn better from peer interaction. The system works like this that each course has one discussion forum, and learners participate in it as a group of 10 to 15 in each group. Each learner is to provide an outline in the first instance to a PDF question and comments on the postings of the other members of the group and evaluate them. Then, in the light of comments received each learner submits the full answer to the question. The mentor evaluates this. The average of the marks given by the learners and the mentor makes the total marks in one PDF. There is only one PDF question for each course, and the learner reads all outlines submitted by group members as well as writes comments on them. All this adds up to quite a lot of work in a spirit of sharing and understanding each other's point of view. This is exactly what an R&R officer needs to do in relation to displaced persons, that is, share and understand their views on R&R. Overall the PDFs carry 20% weight in the evaluation of assignments. Each member of the group gets a different question to answer, and therefore participants in the discussion forum are able to cover the entire course by reading other members' answers.

OCMAs comprise an objective type multiple-choice test for all the four courses, with 25 questions for each course to be answered in 30 minutes. The tests are aimed and once completed cannot be modified. The questions appear one by one on the screen to be answered by the learner, and answers are evaluated by the system. No learner receives the same question. Overall the OCMAs carry 10% weight in the evaluation structure of assignments.

The online diary is a concept to facilitate reflective thinking and preparation for the project work. Making a daily diary entry online about their project-work related activities, the learners are able to document their field experiences, and often they critically respond to situations faced in the field. The learners have the option of typing their entries online or in a word processor and submit them at one go. This flexibility has been incorporated after many learners found it difficult to access the Internet every day. The mentors evaluate the diary entries, which receive 20% weight in the evaluation of assignments.

The program has no traditional three-hour paper test for term-end examination. The project work report is considered as final examination. It receives 50% weight in the overall evaluation. The project work report can be submitted any time after five months of the program cycle. Up to the period of two years from the date of registration, the learner has the flexibility of submitting the report in any one of the four semesters. This part of the program complements the online learning that takes place during completion of assignments. The learner has the option of submitting his or her report in different kinds of formats such as video film, audio, slides, pictorial depiction of an event, and so forth.

Other important features of the learning center are:

- The facility for online access to other related material on R & R searched, identified, and filtered by experts in the field.
- A private place for each learner with his or her complete details like name, address, enrolment number, log-in name, password, assignment grades, and so forth, with the facility of changing the password and address.
- A section on social chat among learners that emulates the cafeteria concept.
- The site has an in-built communication center for e-mail communication amongst the learners and mentors. This is the most used section of the site.

Administrative Issues

Content experts and the coordinator of PGCMRR prepared during a series of workshops the course outline, its scope, learning objectives, and content structure. In addition, they prepared the assessment items and discussion questions. Subsequently the program co-coordinator conceptualized and visualized the learning process in terms of experiential exercises.

Instructional designers played an important role by designing the front-end of the online course and identified course activities as per the need of the subject in collaboration with the program coordinator. Mishra (2002) designed a prototype of the Web site design, which was implemented for the delivery of the program. Digitalization of learning materials took place right from the beginning of the development process, and course writers prepared lessons and transmitted them electronically. The project coordination team completed the process of editing while a graphic artist prepared appropriate illustrations.

After the due process of inviting proposals from Web site developers, a committee of information technology specialists, set-up by IGNOU, selected one firm to carry out the task of Web site development for launching PGCMRR, the online six-month postgraduate certificate program of study. The Web site development firm in collaboration with the project co-coordinator executed the various tasks involved in technical production of the learning site as per the main structure of the prototype design. The faculty learned about the many challenges of online course development during its interaction with members of the Web site development firm.

Program Evaluation

We have access to the conclusions of the program evaluation, opinions of stakeholders, analysis of the use of virtual learning environment. After its two cycles, a team of an outside expert and an IGNOU faculty (who was not involved in planning, development, and delivery of PGCMRR) carried out the evaluation of PGCMRR (Swarnakar & Kumar, 2002). The evaluation experts used a variety of evaluation tools/methodologies including personal online interviews with both groups, namely the candidates that registered in the course and the course writer/editors, who prepared/edited the lessons (see Example 1).

The evaluation concluded that "PGCMRR course has fair level of sustainability as there remains demand for it by the candidates from government/private sectors/NGOs/donor agencies, and so forth. If the certificate course is upgraded to diploma level, the program will find more takers, thus it will sustain itself." (See Example 2.)

Later another IGNOU faculty undertook one more evaluation of PGCMRR's online delivery (Mishra, 2005). This study has the following to say:

This paper reports on the feedback study undertaken to learn from the experiences of the users of the online learning environment. All components of the program have been completed by 50% of the respondents, and from the rest, at least 50% were working on the project work. This is an indicator of the seriousness of the respondents and the usefulness of their views to the university. The majority of the respondents (87.5%) indicated that given an opportunity, they would like to join another online program, and 56.3% said their expectations of joining the program have been met. (p. 570)

The PDF section, which is a peer-evaluated threaded discussion (asynchronous) board, has been well accepted by the group. It is probably because of the nature of the target group of the program and the respondents, who are development workers, known for their ability to discuss issues emotionally and forcefully. At the same time, the synchronous sessions (e-counselling and social chat) did not receive much importance, as most of the development professionals are on tour in remote and difficult areas without access to computers and

Example 1.

An Excerpt from the Evaluation Report

All the online students were able to understand and appreciate the rationale behind the PDFs and online diary. One of them has stated, "The pattern of assignment is nicely structured and gives ample opportunity to improve by getting views from others also.

Use for social cause

One of the learners remarks, "PGCMRR course has really enlightened me about the knowledge of R & R, which is useful in the planning field. I can help my organization in resolving the displacement, R&R issues. Also, I can contribute by looking into the aspects where displacement could be avoided or minimized and mitigated. Guidelines enforce that R & R takes place in a proper way by involvement and participation of PAPs."

It gives an in-depth understanding of the development-induced displacement in the country, its vast impact on DPs and PAPs, and the interrelatedness of the issues. The concept of stakeholders, role of NGOs, and their importance are worth understanding. There is need to work for sustainable development to minimize the impacts of development induced displacement. The importance of participatory approach PRA exercise, RAP for better R&R program, and monitoring of R&R activities are imperatives.

Another learner says, "I am very glad that I have been given an opportunity to do something for displaced/project affected persons in the Jharia coal field."

Example 2.

An Excerpt from the Evaluation Report

Learning about project and people

Being my first time experience in the development field, I have begun to understand a lot from the discussion on the topic (as it happens in my office) and have begun to follow projects with R&R with keen interest. I have put to use this learning in my project work assignment. I intend to contribute actively in preparation/review of RAPs in a participatory manner. It needs considering and incorporating in views and comments of all stakeholders carefully. The course content gives the confidence and inculcates a desire to get associated with the working for affected people. The impacts of displacement are many and interrelated. So are the ways of rehabilitation and the need to minimize its impact in the national interest, says another candidate.

Internet. The respondents were satisfied with the role of the mentors in the e-counselling sessions, but they were not satisfied with the interaction amongst other learners. It shows that there was much room for improvement in the organization of the synchronous sessions. (p. 571)

Lessons Learned

The experience of running the program for the first two cycles provided us the following valuable lessons (Mishra & Jain, 2002):

- As most learners were new to the open and distance learning system, and many of them were also new to online learning, and they were also new to each other, the purpose of orienting them to the working of the Web site did not succeed. The learners used up the Internet time to get to know each other. As an alternative we have put all FAQs relating to the Web site, originally meant for the orientation program, in a separate button of the site menu. In addition, learners have now the facility of online help to facilitate the navigation through the site.
- Initially the learners were supposed to limit their answers to a PDF question to 8,000 characters. Almost all learners revolted to this limitation. Finding a solution to enable them to express themselves was our course of action. Both the faculty and students insisted that the Web site developer should provide the facility to prepare the answers in either text or word files and upload the same, with text and graphics and so forth on the site directly. This allows them to save their answers on their local machines. In addition, they can now download all answers of the group members to read and evaluate them off-line. This has reduced the Internet time spent by each learner.
- The mentors need to be proactive and provide continuous guidance to the learners. The tutors/mentors should provide them enough time to study and answer assignment questions.
- Students of PGCMRR have provided us useful feedback on learning materials and assessment questions. They have thus helped the faculty to remove errors in the course material. Students using unfair means to answer the questions revealed possible loop-holes in security systems. This led us to develop more secure systems to avoid unfair means.
- After holding a couple of such sessions we realized that mentors' training was not adequate and they required more specialized training to handle such sessions so that they can remind learners of the e-space and limited time of synchronous meeting.
- We also learned that online learners need continuous help; and for one to one problem solving a line of communication through e-mail is a very good mechanism available to us. This tool has, in fact, provided more contact between learners and mentors. Online learners are at times in contact with the mentors on a daily basis. In the process mentors have discovered that they have learned a great deal from their students.

Best/Worst Practices

The following are the three-actions/practices in order of priority in the program that should be taken note of by others:

- **Do not feel disheartened:** The program coordinator went through a fair amount of trials and tribulations during the planning and developing phases of the program. The final phase of its online delivery proved to be quite an ordeal in terms of kicks from both the learners and the university system. The latter has yet to come to terms with the requirements of online delivery of its programs. Yet, the students have again enrolled for the subsequent cycles, taking us to yet more learning from our experiment.

- **Face the reality of digital divide:** The program was also launched in off-line mode from January 2002. Comparing the outcomes of the two modes of delivery in terms of participation of learners in the interactive learning process one is able to appreciate the merits of online delivery that provides much more interaction among the learners and between the learners and their mentors. All off-line learners of PGCMRR are simply a part of IGNOU's faceless crowd of those enrolled in its various programs. We know for sure that counselling of off-line learners is a non-existent feature, and their learning is entirely based on their individual experience. It is completely devoid of group-based collaborative learning. The only sharing that occurs among off-line students is confined to copying out each other's assignments. Yet we have to make the online delivery to co-exist with off-line mode because the Internet facility is still the privilege of only a few in India.
- **Learn to continue to have faith in your vision despite criticisms of all kinds:** PGCMRR has a well-structured architecture of its Web site; it has a committed band of faculty members; each year some students enrol in it, yet PGCMRR has the reputation of a low-enrollment program. The institutional set-up does not feel interested in declaring results of those who have completed the courses in all respects. This discourages fresh enrollment in larger numbers. Though it is clear that upgrading the certificate into a diploma level program would attract more students, the usual delays of the institutional machinery have taken more than two years to take a firm decision on this matter. Yet the efforts are on to add some more inputs and offer the program as a post-graduate diploma.

Networking and Collaboration and Conclusion

Nature of Networking and Collaborative Arrangements to Run the Program

Initially a team comprising the IGNOU faculty, its computer division, and the Web site developer collaborated to run the program, and all its teething troubles were gradually sorted out to the satisfaction of its learners and other stakeholders. From 2003, the university decided to make only the computer division and the faculty responsible for running the program. This has resulted in slackening of efforts. As a result there is little or no availability of access to the Web site for e-counselling sessions. The faculty has implemented the idea of bringing even the off-line students to e-counselling. This has worked nicely at least for the Delhi-based students, but of late owing to the shifting of the campus from its earlier location to the new complex, the system has not been functioning efficiently and students have had to take recourse to the e-mail mechanism. Yet, the hope is that once all units of IGNOU have shifted to its new location, it will be possible to make use of the full capacity of the various features of PGCMRR's online delivery. Hopefully by that time the program will be offered as a diploma so that there will be more takers of the program. IGNOU has taken up the matter of training of its faculty in developing online programs. However rudimentary PGCMRR may appear in its design and delivery, it has the status of being a pioneer, and its spirit and dogged pursuit of objectives have brought the institution to offer further training to its faculty.

The Need for Professional Development

All of us in the R&R project team were highly committed to our work, but were not trained or qualified to do what we aimed to achieve. We learned our skills while we worked on this project and focused on developing effective collaborative mechanisms to facilitate collegiality among the learners, and we endeavoured to share information through the use of online networks. We had no access to professional development in the use of ICTs, but after launching PGCMRR our university did organize a series of workshops to train IGNOU faculty in application of ICT tools. In fact, the coordinator of R&R project was invited to share her experiences with the participants of these workshops. So PGCMRR acted as a harbinger to staff development. It made the need for such training visible and concrete. PGCMRR championed a new form of teaching, and IGNOU has now initiated steps to promote and nurture these forms of developing and delivering its new courses. Post PGCMRR period has witnessed changes in the sense that some of IGNOU faculty have learned to be "resource specialists" and "response specialists" and the effort is that learners are less teacher-dependent and they engage in self, peer and tutor guided, and resource-based learning. This has been the unintended consequence of developing PGCMRR that quite a few of IGNOU faculty have now adopted new technologies and technology-based work practices.

In terms of sustainability of PGCMRR, we need to pay heed to the considered opinions expressed in the program's evaluation report. However, we need not worry about its low-enrollment status. PGCMRR is not a commercial, job-market oriented learning package. It is a socially useful training program that will attract only a few. Yet it will serve its purpose of contributing to participatory development that makes all development projects more humane and equitable.

A pilot project of introducing an online program of study in social sciences has brought before us both our own naiveté about online learning processes and a variety of problems faced by the learners. It is only through the process that we are able to recognize the possible pitfalls and their remedies. The faculty and the students have been constantly revising their positions and views regarding the subject of study and also ways of studying it. Perhaps this is all that lifelong learning is about and during its course we can only learn more and not harm us in any way. With the hope of improving both contents of the course material and methods of learning them we intend to carry on our online learning system.

References

Jain, S. (2001). Participatory learning and discourse on local and global culture of the disadvantaged. *Indian Journal of Open Learning, 10*(2), 159-173.

Mishra, S., & Jain, S. (2002). *Designing an online learning environment for participatory management of displacement, resettlement and rehabilitation.* Paper presented at the 2nd Pan Commonwealth Conference on Open Learning held at Durban, South Africa from 28 July to 3 August 2002. Retrieved May 19, 2004, from http://www.col.org pcf2/papers/mishra.pdf

Mishra, S. (2002). A design framework for online learning environment. *British Journal of Educational Technology, 33*(4), 493-496.

Mishra, S. (2005). Learning from online learners. *British Journal of Educational Technology, 36*(3), 569-574.

Swarnakar, R. C., & Kumar, K. (2002). *Evaluation report of PGCMRR.* New Delhi: Internal Report, IGNOU.

Chapter VII

Introducing Integrated E-Portfolio across Courses in a Postgraduate Program in Distance and Online Education

Madhumita Bhattacharya, Massey University, New Zealand

Abstract

This chapter presents a description and analysis of salient issues related to the development of an integrated e-portfolio application implemented at Massey University to help students track and accumulate evidence of skills developed over their period of study, particularly associated with the three core papers in the program. The Web-based e-portfolio project was initiated to help students provide evidence required by employers and research supervisors in a progressive and reflective manner by identifying the links across different papers and demonstrating their own conceptual understanding. Administrative issues are discussed, as well as considerations for future developments based on the experiences of this study.

Introduction

This chapter reports on the conceptualization and implementation of the integrated e-portfolio project initiated at the College of Education, Massey University, New Zealand. The conceptual model of the integrated e-portfolio is based on the assessment related tasks and the graduate profile of students in the distance and online education postgraduate program in the College of Education at Massey University. The portfolio framework was designed to allow students to display a range of their work completed in three core papers/courses in the program. The e-portfolio became a means for students in the area of distance and online education to display key aspects of their expertise. The making of integrated portfolio supports a programmatic approach to assessment and knowledge development. Initially the digital portfolio platform of John Hopkins University has been used. It is a Web browser-based framework for e-portfolio for its use across different papers and subject areas. The framework for e-portfolio enables students to edit multimedia objects. The task of developing e-portfolio has been introduced initially for the three core papers only. The coordinators of the three core papers have designed the assignments, keeping objectives of the papers and graduate profile into consideration, interrelating and overlapping tasks so that students are able to visualize the links among different courses and understand the ways in which learning in one paper is complemented in another paper. The portfolio is a part of student's assessment. On completion of their study students will have a portfolio of assessed work that will provide a presentation of key knowledge and skills developed throughout the program of the postgraduate studies. The author envisages that the employers will be able to see students work in an electronic form that demonstrates their skills and knowledge. Through this process of learning students were led to reflect on their strengths and weaknesses in a manner that gave direction for future study. Creation and development of integrated e-portfolio also enabled students to learn and develop research skills useful for project/thesis work in the later part of their study.

E-Learning Program

E-learning is defined by the New Zealand Ministry of Education (2004, p. 3) as "learning that is enabled or supported by the use of digital tools and content. It typically involves some form of interactivity, which may include online interaction between the learner and their teacher or peers. E-learning opportunities are usually accessed via the Internet, though other technologies such as CD-ROM are also used in e-learning." It would be an extremely rare tertiary institution that does not have a learning management system (LMS) for online delivery, and a body of staff already using it in their courses (Nichols & Anderson, 2005).

At Massey University we have acquired WebCT as the LMS since 2002 for delivery of courses at a distance. At Massey University we also use CMC platforms such as Horizon Wimba and Macromedia Breeze for conducting real-time meeting sessions with the distance students. We have about 20,000 extramural (distance) students which is double the number of internal (on campus) students.

Figure 1. Massey University postgraduate qualification staircase

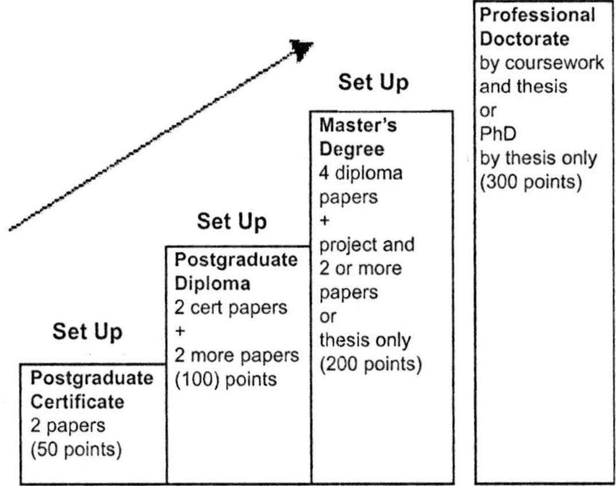

Massey University postgraduate qualifications staircase (Figure 1), in education, permits students to tailor courses and programs in ways that are suitable and which accommodate a wide range of circumstances and needs. On the staircase, the qualifications commence with two-paper postgraduate certificates (commonly for individuals just starting postgraduate study). Thereafter, the qualifications include general and endorsed 100-point postgraduate diplomas and a wide range of 200-point masterates, and they culminate with doctoral study, either the EdD or the PhD.

Since 2004 we have introduced a completely Web-based postgraduate program in distance and online education focusing on different aspects of e-learning. It is a new endorsement under the postgraduate qualifications in education offered by the College of Education. The program has three core papers ("Instructional Design and Learning Technologies in Distance and Online Education," "Teaching for E-learning," and "Policy, Practice and Trends in Distance and Online Education"). These papers are compulsory for students who wish to earn a postgraduate diploma or masterate in "distance and online education." The integrated e-portfolio project presented in this chapter has been implemented across the three core papers as mentioned previously. It is essential to discuss about electronic portfolios, its purpose, and its types before discussing about the concept of integrated e-portfolio.

What is an E-Portfolio?

The ever-advancing capabilities of computer technology and the increased need for portability of evidence related to qualifications, knowledge, and attributes mean that the "shoe-box" approach to storage is no longer adequate. An electronic version offers a different type of storage and a more flexible means of presentation—be it a PowerPoint, hyperlinked text, or an Acrobat PDF presentation. Also, as a career management tool to help write job applications, students can quickly and effectively store and access large amounts of information that are easy to update, reflect upon, and improve (Rogers & Williams, 1999).

Electronic portfolios focus on "growth and development over time, implemented through selection, reflection and inspection of skills, attributes and achievements, along with goal setting and self-evaluation" (Barrett, 2001, p. 2). Additionally the e-portfolios provide the capability of directly linking students' portfolio evidence to the standards for which they may need to demonstrate achievement. These standards include the recently introduced Massey University graduate attributes, employment or graduate studies selection criteria, or practicum and/or course assessment outcomes.

The electronic portfolio is a multimedia portfolio approach that allows the creator to present teaching, learning, and reflective artifacts in a variety of media formats (audio, video, and text). E-portfolios are sometimes referred to as e-folios, electronic portfolios, digital portfolios, or multimedia portfolios (Montgomery, 2004). Wheeler (2005) stated that e-portfolio is best defined by its purpose. Integrating many varied, published definitions, e-portfolio can be understood as a collection of purposefully organized artifacts that support backward and forward reflection to augment and assess growth over time. Artifacts could include any digital work, such as, a class-assigned report, transcript, diploma, video of a performance, audio of a speech, images of fieldwork, links to Web sites, and so forth. Early e-portfolio work has established key principles for e-portfolio practice:

- Individuals (students, faculty, etc.) rather than institutions have life-long ownership and control of their e-portfolio. Individuals retain the right and ability to grant limited access to portions of the e-portfolio and to move their portfolio among institutions.
- E-portfolios should ultimately support the reflective practices needed for life-long learning. This implies e-portfolio applicability and portability within K-12, to higher education, and on to career.
- E-portfolio users benefit from system- and faculty-based guidance in choosing learning artifacts and arranging them in views.
- Assessment against curricular rubrics is essential in establishing meaning for e-portfolio artifacts.
- Standards for portability of e-portfolios are essential for lifelong individual and institutional value.

Individual ownership of his or her life-long learning information is revolutionary. It shifts ownership of an educational record from passive management among many disparate organizational systems (e.g., K-12 schools, universities, professional career development in corporations, etc.) to active management by the individual. The individual assembles collections of artifacts from his or her e-portfolio into a view and grants access to that specific view to specific individuals/organizations for a period of time.

In the widely discussed quest for a society engaged in life-long learning, e-portfolios provide an essential tool to enable integration, meaning, and portability among the many educational experiences of an individual's life. At Massey University we are engaged in a number of e-portfolio projects. Based on our research findings we affirm that e-portfolio is one of the essential tools for transforming higher education.

Types of E-Portfolios

It can be helpful to think about e-portfolios in terms of when the work is organized relative to when the work is created. This results in three types of e-portfolios:

1. **The showcase e-portfolio:** Organization occurs after the work has been created.
2. **The structured e-portfolio:** A predefined organization exists for work that is yet to be created.
3. **The learning e-portfolio:** Organization of the work evolves as the work is created.

There are a variety of purposes for developing electronic portfolios: as an assessment tool, for marketing or employment, and to document the learning process and growth for learners of all ages, from pre-school through graduate school and into the professions. The purposes and goals for the portfolio determine the content.

- **Showcase e-portfolios:** With so much material in digital form, a common starting point for e-portfolio thinking is to organize and present work that has already been created. A showcase e-portfolio enables the author (student) to share specific examples of work and to control who can see these collections, most simply by setting and then distributing passwords for different audiences. Although a showcase e-portfolio may look like a personal Web page, it is much more than that. The e-portfolio author should be able to organize and manage documents stored on the Internet and to control access even without knowing how to use HTML or build Web pages. Ideally, showcase e-portfolios should go beyond simply sharing work that has been completed. They should provide a stimulating context for reflecting on a body of work in order to make new connections, personalize learning experiences, and gain insights that will influence future activities. Without supporting reflection, a showcase e-portfolio can be reduced to merely a collection of artifacts.
- **Structured e-portfolio:** Another approach is to use a structured e-portfolio to establish a predefined organization in anticipation of work that will be completed. In a structured e-portfolio, demonstrating accomplishments for certification or fulfillments of specific requirements is a common goal.

By clearly articulating requirements, a structured e-portfolio can effectively focus a student's time and attention. Furthermore, the predefined organization of a structured e-portfolio can make it easier for work to be systematically reviewed, evaluated, and compared. Because meeting a requirement or demonstrating a skill is not necessarily the same as taking a specific course, structured e-portfolios provide opportunities for developing new approaches to assessment.

Although some institutions are beginning to use a structured e-portfolio approach to assist with student advising and career planning, others are developing a "learning matrix" of formal learning objectives and student outcomes as a way to ensure that an institution's commitment to learning is being achieved by all students. Each objective has a descriptor of what the work should demonstrate, clarifying for the student what is expected and providing a common framework for advising on and assessing the competencies being demonstrated. Outside reviewers can play an important role in this approach by sampling student work to confirm that institutional goals are being achieved and by identifying curricular strengths and weaknesses.

Some professions like elementary and secondary teaching have formal standards and certification requirements that candidates must meet regardless of the institution they are attending. The Center for Technology in Education (CTE) at Johns Hopkins University has developed a standards-based e-portfolio for teacher education as a replacement for the paper portfolios used in the Master of Arts in Teaching program. In the CTE electronic portfolio (EP), prospective teachers demonstrate their evolving skills in the context of established standards, local or state certification requirements, or standards required for their field. Participants can share and discuss work with peers, request feedback from advisors, and use an online journal to reflect on their progress and growth as a teacher. At the end of a program, participants can submit their EPs for formal review and use them to showcase accomplishments for possible teaching positions.

Supported mentoring can significantly enhance structured e-portfolios. Guiding and encouraging students through a sequence of experiences will better enable them to develop the skills they need to demonstrate required competencies. Without supported mentoring, a structured e-portfolio can be reduced to a set of directions that students follow to meet seemingly arbitrary requirements.

- **Learning e-portfolios:** Whereas a showcase e-portfolio is used to organize and present accomplishments and a structured e-portfolio can ensure that specified work will be done, the organization of a learning -portfolio is dynamic.

The organization of work evolves over time as tasks are identified, worked on, and completed in response to the student's changing interests, requirements, and understanding. Students in the process of developing an e-portfolio can reach back in time across different activities to make new connections. This ongoing reorganization of work can be well thought out and clear, or it can be spontaneous and messy.

Barrett (2005) described that learning or process portfolios involve the focus on Plato's directive, "know thyself," which can lead to a lifetime of investigation. Self-knowledge becomes an outcome of learning. In a portfolio study conducted with adult learners who were developing portfolios to document prior learning, Brown (2002) found the following outcomes: increased students' understanding of what, why, and how they learned throughout their careers, and enhanced their communication and organization skills. The results of this study reinforce the importance of reflection in learning.

Primary motive of a learning portfolio: "to improve student learning by providing a structure for students to reflect systematically over time on the learning process and to develop the aptitudes, skills and habits that come from critical reflection" (Zubizaretta, 2004, p. 15). Zubizaretta borrows from Peter Seldin's work on teaching portfolios, and identifies three fundamental components of learning portfolios, as shown in the following diagram (Figure 2).

Figure 2. The learning portfolio (Zubizaretta, 2004, p. 20)

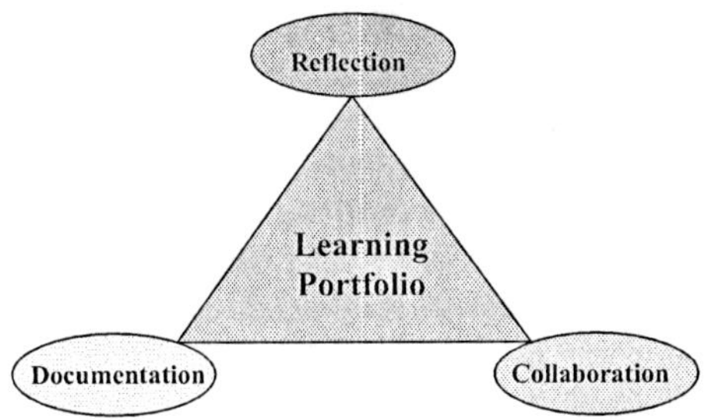

Integrated E-Portfolios: An Innovative Approach to E-Learning

Integrated e-portfolio can be described as a hybrid form of all the different types of portfolios described previously, having additional features that demonstrate learning in all the three domains of learning (cognitive, psychomotor, and affective) including interpersonal domain. Integrated e-portfolio special emphasis is on one's own integration and conceptualization of the process of learning through linking of learning in different papers to the graduate profile (Figure 3).

The basic concept of integrated e-portfolio is to allow students to understand the links between the different courses they study and its association with the concept of integrative learning. Integrative learning comes in many varieties: connecting skills and knowledge from multiple sources and experiences; applying theory to practice in various settings; utilizing diverse and even contradictory points of view; and, understanding issues and positions contextually. Significant knowledge within individual disciplines serves as the foundation,

Figure 3. Framework for integrated e-portfolio

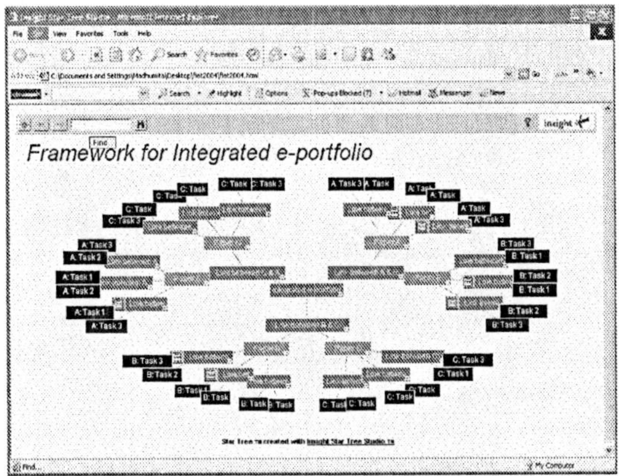

Figure 4. The rubric for identifying different phases of learning

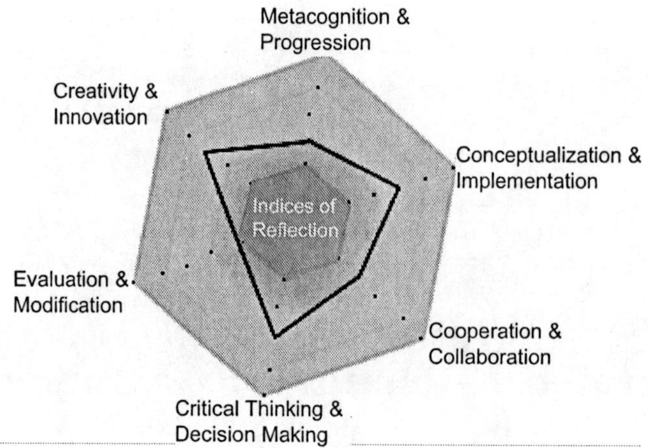

but integrative learning goes beyond academic boundaries. Indeed, integrative experiences often occur as learners address real-world problems, unscripted and sufficiently broad to require multiple areas of knowledge and multiple modes of inquiry, offering multiple solutions and benefiting from multiple perspectives.

The development of integrated e-portfolios allows students to self-evaluate their learning. This is a platform for "assessment for learning" as opposed to "assessment of learning." Students while creating their e-portfolios demonstrate their own understanding of the links between different assessment tasks of each paper and across the core papers. Through their thinking log and self-reflection students demonstrate the process of learning by providing evidences as per the rubric given in Figure 4 (Bhattacharya, 2001).

The present project has been initiated across three core papers in the new postgraduate program in distance and online education as mentioned. Assignment tasks for each of these papers were designed in such way that the students while working through these tasks would be able to visualize the connections between the learning in each of these papers. Students are required to provide evidence (artifacts) for linking them to the graduate profile of the program they are enrolled in. Students enrolled in one paper/course only may link the artifacts to the achievement objectives/learning outcomes of the individual paper/course.

Administrative Issues

Despite the many advantages of portfolios, there are also disadvantages, many related to their implementation: "Portfolios are messy to construct, cumbersome to store, difficult to score and vulnerable to misrepresentation" (Wolfe, 1999, p. 129), and there is always "the possibility of (portfolios) becoming a useless paper chase and a futile exercise" (Wheeler, 1996, p. 89).

Also, a lack of technical support and assistance (at both micro and macro levels) is seen as a major area of concern with Bloom and Bacon (1995, p. 2) "highlighting that especially new students may have difficulty with the lack of structure in the process."

In 2004 the integrated e-portfolio project received the grant under the Fund for Innovations and Excellence in Teaching from Massey University competitive internal research funds. In order to avoid some of the problems as mentioned previously, we decided to host the students' portfolio accounts through an external service provider. After some survey we decided to host students' portfolios at the John Hopkins University. In the future we intend to develop our own platform or create an open source platform for electronic portfolios.

The choice of a software tool can have profound effects on the nature of the interaction within a networked learning community. As theorists and researchers on situated learning have argued, cognition is a social activity that emerges out of a system comprising individuals, a context of intentions, and the tools available (Greeno, Collins, & Resnick, 1966). Tools shape and structure action (Wertsch, Del Rio, & Alvarez, 1995) by empowering or constraining particular activities of the individuals who use those devices—that is, tools have distinctive profiles of affordances and constraints (Gibson, 1979). We will need to conduct further research studies before deciding on a generic e-portfolio platform for the number of different ongoing projects.

In order to conduct any research where we need to quote students work on portfolios we will have to go through the process of securing ethics approval from the Massey University ethics committee. Copyright of the project remains with Massey University. Intellectual Property Rights remains with the authors of the products, for example, research publications, students' assignments, and so forth. Implementation of integrated e-portfolio across different disciplines and courses would definitely require organizing workshops, seminars, and demonstration of cases for faculty and administrative staff.

Evaluation of the Integrated E-Portfolio Project

The integrated e-portfolio project described in this chapter is a work in progress. We have conducted an evaluation study of a mini integrated e-portfolio project based on an intensive summer school program for postgraduate students at the University of Tartu in Estonia (Bhattacharya & Mimirinis, 2005). It was a real eye opener for us to see how different the individual perception of the same course is. Following are some of the conceptual maps developed by the participants of the summer school as part of their integrated e-portfolio (Figures 5 and 6).

This pilot study demonstrates the importance of individual's knowledge structure for making any decision or passing any judgments about individuals learning outcomes. We perceive and understand any new learning experience by relating and accommodating it with our previous knowledge structure, our motivation, and our interest. Therefore, each of us constructs individual meaning from the same course material or instruction.

Figure 5. Concept map 1

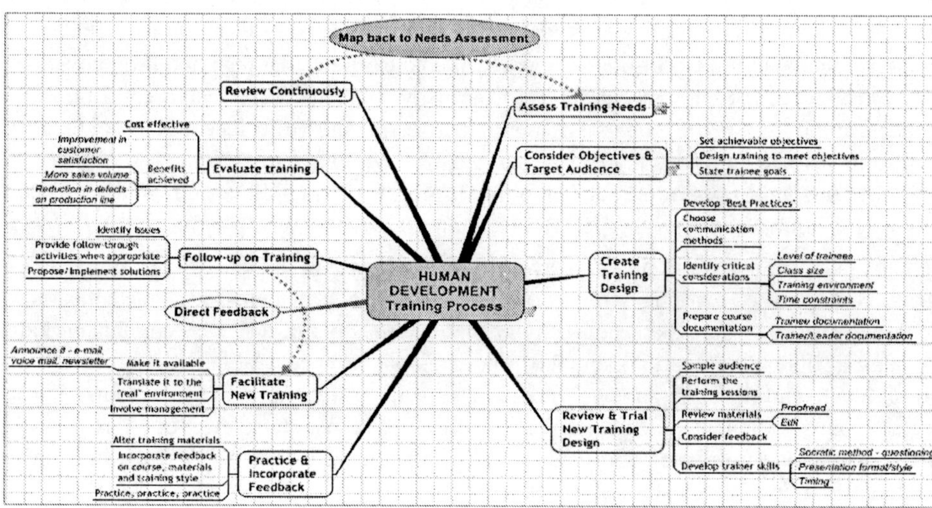

Figure 6. Concept map 2

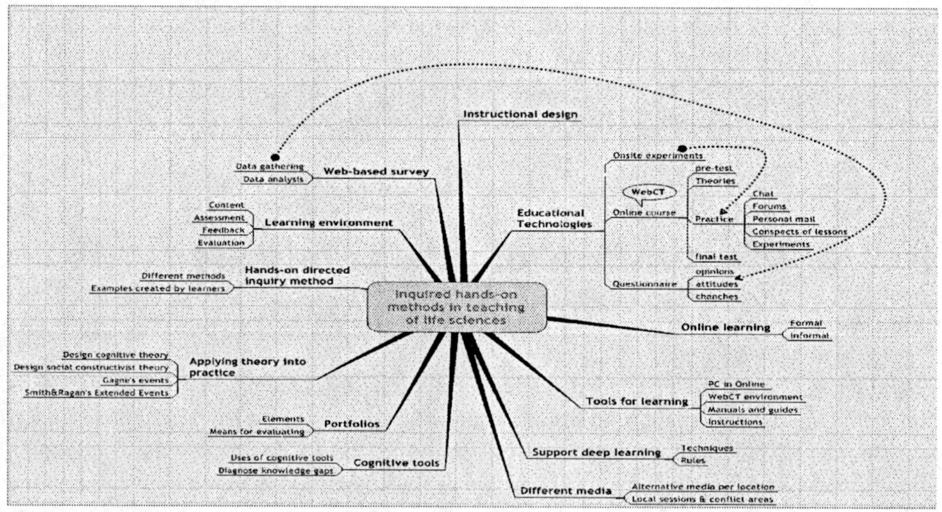

Students Reflection on the Process of Developing E-Portfolio

Following are excerpts from two students' responses to the usefulness of e-portfolio (posted online in a web-based course). Students have found developing e-portfolio and integrating the learning across different papers/courses in the degree program made it very useful for showcasing not only their work but also the progression in understanding and knowledge.

Student 1:

Until this paper—and in fact the arrival of our "digital portfolio guide" by The John Hopkins University—I had never heard of "e-portfolios" period. When I did, my mind immediately arrived at the "showcase" idea where I could use an e-portfolio to showcase myself as an individual from an array of dimensions far beyond the constrict of a traditional CV, including:

- *Personal philosophy of education*
- *Artifacts of actual work I have done*
- *Supporting reflective documents that describe the artifact mechanism*
- *Personal goals short term and long*

The biggest challenge for me was in actually sitting down—taking a look at myself and drawing up a personal philosophy in education—in writing, something I had never done before, something that felt personally "empowering" once completed.

The development of the e-portfolio thus far has given me a greater sense of direction in my research and work—and something to look back on, assess myself against, challenge myself against, and develop myself against. So now it seems so much more than just a "showcase" of my work.

Student 2:

Developing the e-portfolio provided an opportunity to reflect on studies to-date and the achievement of objectives at a paper and program level. Engagement with the task has highlighted and clarified the links between the core papers, motivated me to go beyond one assignment and develop my e-portfolio to include completed papers (PGDipEd), and provided a potential focus for future Masters studies.

Concluding Remarks and Future Plans

It will take at least another year to determine the usefulness of the integrated e-portfolios for students enrolled in the distance and online education core papers at Massey University. Expected outcomes of this project include that students will on completion of their study in the core papers of the MEd (DistOnEd) have a portfolio of assessed work that will provide a presentation of key knowledge and skills developed through their study. Employers will be able to see in an electronic form student work that demonstrates their skills and knowledge. Students will through this process be led to reflect on their strengths and weaknesses in a manner that gives direction for future study. Creation and development of integrated e-portfolio will enable students to learn and develop research skills useful for project/thesis work in the later part of their study.

Working through this project made it clear that it is important for the faculty to work as a team, to take initiative, and share each other findings in order to be successful in any innovative endeavor. Integrated e-portfolio development allowed both students and the faculty to visualize individual student's understanding of the different concepts and their links toward the formation of individual cognition. Finally the e-portfolios created through continuous activities and reflections demonstrated the process and the product of learning, which should be an integral part of any online course to minimize plagiarism.

At Massey University we are keen on introducing the e-portfolio as an integral part of all the undergraduate and postgraduate courses. The policy development toward this initiative is already underway. Some of the pedagogical, administrative, and technical issues remain to be addressed before we can introduce e-portfolios as a compulsory component across all the programs in the university. Evaluation studies showed positive remarks by the students about the portfolio approach in their learning. Interactions and collaborations during the process of learning provided opportunities to distance students to develop interpersonal skills and build communities of practice.

Acknowledgment

The design and development of integrated e-portfolio work has been undertaken with the grant recieved from the Fund for Innovations and Excellence in Teaching- 2004, Massey University, New Zealand.

References

Barrett, H. (2005). *Researching electronic portfolios and learner engagement* (White Paper). In The REFLECT Initiative: Researching Electronic portFolios: Learning, Engagement and Collaboration through Technology. Retrieved November 30, 2005, from http://www.taskstream.com/reflect/whitepaper.pdf

Barrett, H. C. (2001). *ICT support for electronic portfolios and alternative assessment: The state of the art.* Paper presented at the World Conference on Computers and Education (WCCE). Retrieved November 30, 2005, from http://transition.alaska.edu/www/portfolios/wccepaper.pdf

Bhattacharya, M. (2001). *Electronic portfolios, students reflective practices, and the evaluation of effective learning.* AARE2001, Fremantle, Australia. Retrieved November 30, 2005, from http://www.aare.edu.au/01pap/bha01333.htm

Bhattacharya, M., & Mimirinis, M. (2005). *Australian Association for Educational Research, SIG report* (p. 9). AARE News no. 52. Retrieved November 30, 2005, from http://www.aare.edu.au/news/newsplus/news52.pdf

Bloom, B., & Bacon, E. (1995). Using portfolios for individual learning and assessment. *Teacher Education and Special Education, 18*(1), 1-9.

Brown, J. O. (2002). Know thyself: The impact of portfolio development on adult learning. *Adult Education Quarterly, 52*(3), 228-245.

Gibson, J. J. (1979). *The ecological approach to visual perception.* Boston: Houghton.

Greeno, J. G., Collins, A. M., & Resnick, L. B. (1996). Cognition and learning. In D. Berliner & R. Calfee (Eds.), *Handbook of educational psychology* (pp. 15-46.) New York: Macmillan.

Horizon Wimba: http://www.horizonwimba.com/

John Hopkins University: http://cte.jhu.edu/epweb/

Macromedia Breeze: http://www.macromedia.com/software/breeze/

Massey University Elearning: http://elearning.massey.ac.nz/

Massey University GSE, CoE: http://education.massey.ac.nz/gse/study/postgraduate.htm

Ministry of Education (2004). *Interim tertiary e-learning framework.* Retrieved November 26, 2005, from http://www.minedu.govt.nz

Montgomery, K., & Wiley, D. (2004). *Creating e-portfolios using PowerPoint.* Thousand Oaks, CA: Sage Publications. ISBN 0-7619-2880-4.

Nichols, M., & Anderson, W. G. (2005). *Strategic e-learning implementation.* Distance Education Association of New Zealand (DEANZ) Electronic discussions. Retrieved November 30, 2005, from http://deanz-discuss.massey.ac.nz/july2005.html

Rogers, G., & Williams, J. (1999). Building a better portfolio. *ASEE Prism, 8*(5), 30-32.

Wertsch, J. V., Del Rio, A. & Alvarez, A. (Eds.). (1995). *Sociocultural studies of mind.* Cambridge: Cambridge University Press.

Wheeler, P. (1996). Using portfolios to assess teacher performance. In K. Burke (Ed.), *Professional portfolios: A collection of articles.* (pp. 74-94). Victoria: Hawker Brownlow Education.

Wolfe, E. W. (1999). How can administrators facilitate portfolio implementation. *High School Magazine, 6*(5), 29-33.

Zubizarreta, J. (2004). *The learning portfolio.* Bolton, MA: Anker Publishing.

Chapter VIII

The Mediated Action of Educational Reform: An Inquiry into Collaborative Online Professional Development

Donna L. Russell, University of Missouri - Kansas City, USA

Abstract

The purpose of this case study was to describe and evaluate how four teachers in four different cities in Missouri, U.S., collaborated online to implement an online constructivist-based learning environment that included an innovation cluster pairing and emerging online technology with a problem-based learning unit design framework. The design of this study originated from prior research on teacher reform efforts including the adoption of technology innovations in the classroom, new theories of constructivist-based learning and the principles of professional development for educators implementing reform. Using the methodology of cultural historical activity theory, the researchers collected and analyzed data to identify how effectively each of the teachers implemented the innovation cluster based on their goals for adopting the new innovations while participating in online collaborative professional development. As a result the researchers were able to evaluate the effectiveness of the online professional development model used to aid these innovative educators and develop concepts of best-practice professional development programs.

Introduction

The purpose of this study was to understand how teachers participate in online collaborative professional development in order to implement an innovation cluster of (1) an emerging online technology and (2) a framework for designing a constructivist-based learning environment (CBLE). This innovative pilot was developed as part of the Missouri Department of Elementary and Secondary Education's (DESE) online access system for K-12 districts titled the Missouri Research and Education Network (MOREnet). MOREnet sponsors a technology integration program called enhancing Missouri's Instructional Networked Teaching Strategies (eMINTS). eMINTS places a saturation level of technology in selected fourth grade classrooms in the state. The innovative program analyzed in this study was a one-year pilot called ePioneers. ePioneers was a new online program introduced in 2001-2002. This research studied four experienced eMINTS teachers who volunteered to collaboratively implement an online problem-based unit of study with four other teachers in classrooms across the state of Missouri. The units were collaboratively taught in an online Linux-based workspace called Shadow netWorkspace™ that was designed and hosted for the teachers by the University of Missouri's School of Information Science and Learning Technologies.

Theoretical Background

The theoretical grounding for this study is the socio-cultural theory of human interaction and development (Bruner, 1990; Vygotsky, 1978) with an emphasis on understanding the processes of mediated activity (Wertsch, 1998). This form of analysis identifies responses to complex social systems by making the interactions in the system explicit so practical and theoretical implications can be developed (Cole & Engeström, 1993). The researchers used activity theory (AT) in order to design a systems-based framework for understanding the interacting processes in context and over time (Engeström, Miettinen, & Punamaki, 1999; Il'enkov, 1977). Activity theory defines the elements of human interactions systemically and allowed the researchers to design analytical procedures that developed systemic and contextual relationships among the dataset (Barab, Hay, & Yamagata-Lynch, 2001; Schoenfeld, 1999). As a result of using AT as the framework for analysis, the researchers created *a priori* coding categories based on the AT model of work activity and the concept of mediational effects of new tools and integrated theoretical constructs from related fields (e.g., professional development, innovation, collaboration) into operationalized groupings of interactions in the local and collaborative work activity of the teachers (Engestrom, 1999).

This study looks at the implementation of two interrelated educational innovations as an innovation cluster that included an advanced online learning technology and an instructional design template used by the teachers to collaboratively implement an online constructivist-based learning environment. The researchers identified the AT work activity processes of the teachers as they designed and implemented the innovation cluster. The researchers focused on three progressive research issues that arose as issues of concern during their in vivo data structuring: (1) What factors in a teacher's school environments influenced the implementation of an innovation cluster? (2) How did a teacher's participation in collaborative professional development influence the implementation of an innovation cluster? (3) How does a teacher's belief about learning and technology influence the implementation of an innovation cluster?

E-Learning Program

The researchers studied four eMINTS teachers who work with students in fourth and fifth grades in four different cities throughout Missouri who were implementing a collaborative online problem-based unit during the final quarter of the 2001-2002 school year. The students represented inner city, small city, suburban, and rural students. An eMINTS classroom lab contains 12-14 IBM workstations and educational software. All of the eMINTS teachers in this study had three years of prior training in constructivist-based and inquiry-based learning from eMINTS. The goal of eMINTS is to transform how teachers teach and students learn with technology in order to illustrate the effective use of technology in classroom instruction and develop models of inquiry-based instruction (http://missouri.emints.org). These four eMINTS teachers were invited to participate in a pilot project called the ePioneers Program that involved learning a new online tool, Shadow netWorkspace™ (SNS), and implementing an online problem-based unit that incorporated constructivist-based learning methods and takes advantage of the many affordances of SNS. Table 1 identifies the characteristics of the classrooms for the four teachers.

Table 1. Classroom descriptions

<table>
<tr><th>Teacher</th><th>Grade</th><th>Community</th><th># Students</th><th>Technology Access</th></tr>
<tr><td>Teacher A</td><td>4th</td><td>suburban</td><td>22 students</td><td rowspan="4">As a part of their participation in the eMINTS program, each teacher has 12-14 Pentium3 LCD computers, a teacher workstation, laptop, a Smartboard and projector, a scanner, a color printer, and a digital camera. The eMINTS program also trained each teacher in technology usage and inquiry learning.</td></tr>
<tr><td>Teacher B</td><td>4th</td><td>rural</td><td>24 students</td></tr>
<tr><td>Teacher C</td><td>5th</td><td>urban</td><td>17 students</td></tr>
<tr><td>Teacher D</td><td>4th</td><td>mid-size city</td><td>19 students</td></tr>
</table>

Academic Issues

Researchers who both have a background and master's degrees in instructional design designed the authentic online problem-solving unit on "Improving Interstate-70." Interstate 70 runs across Missouri and is in need of repair and expansion. The instructional unit was developed as a problem-based unit design template, which was given to each teacher as part of their pre-unit interview. The researchers created the design template so that each teacher could develop their local resources as well as build on the online interactions among all four classrooms. The problem-based unit design template was created based on research in cognitive sciences (Russell, 2004). The I-70 unit was designed in three phases. In Phase 1 the students identified common elements to the authentic problem in their local classrooms. In Phase 2 the students worked in online groups to identify needed information and gather information to solve the problem. In online chat rooms the students studied and dialoged about this authentic engineering problem from their differing perspectives concerning their local use of the interstate. In Phase 3 the students work in their online workgroups to design a strategy to solve the problem. In this final phase each online group included students from each of the classrooms so each perspective is included in their final strategy for solution. The teachers identified their goal for participating in this pilot program as developing their students' ability to study a real-world problem from multiple perspectives. Online access through SNS was the necessary component of meeting this goal.

Administrative Issues

SNS allows the users to develop online workgroups where the users can log in and disseminate information and documents, edit the work of others, engage in discussion boards and chat rooms with others in their group, and contact experts online using a secure contact system. The administrators control all availability; in this case the teachers, so that the students can work collaboratively in a safe online environment. This middleware was developed at the University of Missouri at Columbia's School of Information Sciences and Learning Technology (SISTL). SNS is Linux-based, therefore free, and was served from SISTL (Laffey, Musser, & Espinosa, 2000). Each school had a local technology support person in their building to work with the eMINTS teachers. These local support personnel did not maintain SNS, but they were responsible for maintaining and supporting the building and district Internet connections.

Data Structuring and Analysis

The data collection process used interpretive research practices to capture the dynamics and complexity of learning processes at specific stages in their professional development: pre-unit, after Phase 1, after Phase 2, post-unit (Fraenkel & Wallen, 1996). The data collected from the teachers included initial and follow-up interviews, transcripts from a phone conference and seven chat room conferences, messages posted on discussion boards, reflective questionnaires related to their design of the unit and the principles of constructivist learning, an online journal, and documents the teachers produce related to the unit and technology.

The researchers designed interviews, online interactions, and videos of the work activity of the teachers in order to identify the components of the AT based work activity model for each teacher (Engestrom, 1999). Using AT to define the components, or nodes, of the work activity of the teachers, the researchers then used N*UDIST software to define the nodes of the AT model (e.g., subject, mediation, object, community, rules, division of labor, outcome) and integrated the theoretical constructs from several related fields (e.g., professional development, innovation, collaboration) into operational categories of interactions in and among the work activity of the teachers.

Each teacher's transformative processes were then analyzed through the hierarchical identification of contradictions in an AT model designed for each teacher. When external elements, such as new mediational tools, are inserted into a teacher's work activity system, internal contradictions, or tensions, result between two nodes of the activity system model these contradictions were identified within each individual teacher's activity setting using the AT model. Contradictions unresolved are shown as solid broken lines in each teacher's AT Model shown as Figures 1 to 4. Resolved contradictions are shown as dashed broken lines.

Program Evaluation

Teacher A: Each teacher had contradictions that constrained her efforts to implement the innovation cluster successfully based on her initial goals. Teacher A was able to overcome a departmentalization issue prior to the unit implementation (see Figure 1). She was able to negotiate with a collaborating teacher and keep her students in her classroom in order to implement the unit. However, she had two unresolved contradictions each related to her use and/or her perceptions concerning the use of the mediating tools (the unit design template and SNS). She removed her students from the Phase 2 scheduled SNS chats among all the classrooms because she found the online chat process "chaotic," a contradiction between a tool, SNS (coded as tool compatibility), and the object. She also did not complete the unit with the other teachers because she chose to complete into Phase 3 in her local classroom deciding that the unit design did not accomplish her goals, a contradiction between the tool, the unit design template (coded as tool applicability), and subject. She narrowed her object overall by not completing the unit in the online workspace.

Teacher B: Teacher B had two unresolved contradictions each between rules and division of labor and the object (see Figure 2). She was unable to develop her unit schedule with the other participating teachers (coded as community and object) in their online dialogs. As a result she delayed initiating her unit until the others were ready making it less likely that she could complete the unit. She teaches at a rural school district that starts before suburban or urban schools so her school year ended several weeks earlier than others. She also lost

Figure 1. Teacher A

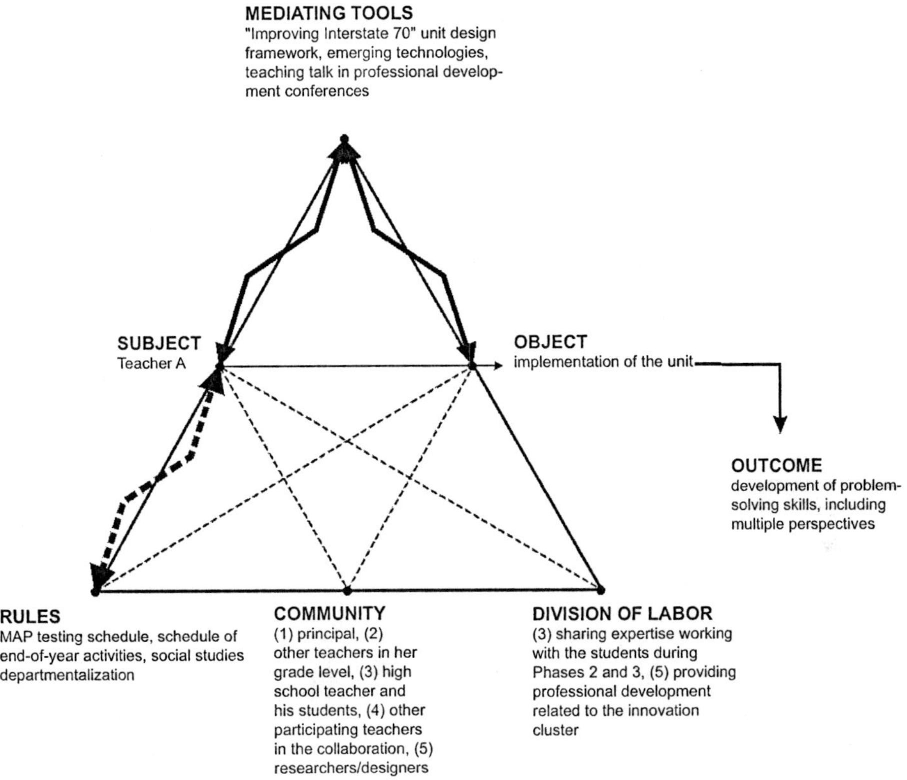

online access for over a week and did not discuss this with her building's technology support person (coded as a contradiction between division of labor and object). As a result, her students were off-line during the critical Phase 2 student chats. Ultimately she disintegrated her object overall when she was unable to complete the unit because of lack of time.

Teacher C: Teacher C encountered four contradictions but was able, as a result of her response to professional development processes, to resolve two contradictions coded as primary subject characteristics (see Figure 3). Prior to initiating the unit, she discussed a contradiction between the learning goals for implementing the innovation cluster (her outcome for her object was to develop higher-order problem-solving abilities in her students) and her belief that her urban students were unable to participate in an advanced problem-based unit coded as a contradiction between subject and tools. However, throughout the planning and implementation of the unit she used the professional development forums of the online community and her work with the researchers as a change agent and changed her beliefs about her students' ability in the problem-solving unit. She also resolved the

Figure 2. Teacher B

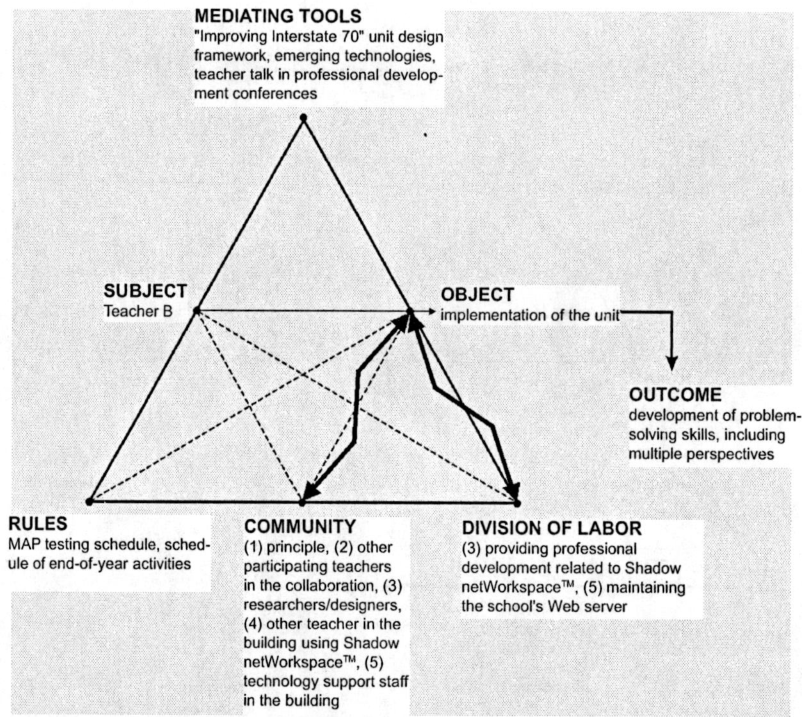

departmentalization issue before the unit began coded as a contradiction between rules and subject. However, during implementation two contradictions arose in her local context that she could not resolve. She was not able to get consistent access to SNS chat rooms in her building a contradiction between tool (accessibility) and object. During Phase 2 of the unit the science teacher in her building asked her to release her students for departmentalization and she agreed resulting in a contradiction between community and object. Overall she widened her object by completing the entire unit successfully with the result that her students participated in an advanced online problem-solving unit of study and developed advanced problem-solving abilities with multiple perspectives.

Teacher D: Teacher D also described reservations about the capabilities of her students in a pre-unit interview. Her students were a "class-within-a-class" structure, and she did not feel they would be successful with the complex interdisciplinary activities of the unit. This was identified as a contradiction between rules and subject (see Figure 4). This meant that her learning disabled and behavioral disabled students stayed in her class, and their teacher came into her classroom to work with them. She did not resolve this contradiction between subject and rules. She also did not like the structure of the unit and the types of activities

Figure 3. Teacher C

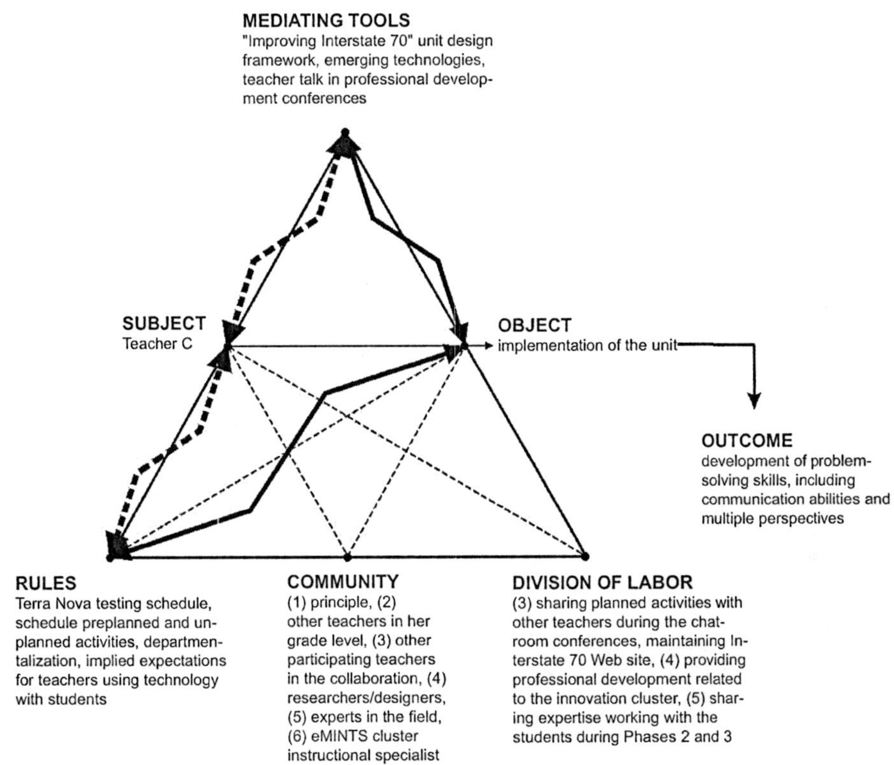

designed into the unit-a contradiction between tool (the unit design) and subject (coded as tool complexity). She stated in her pre-unit interview that she did not work collaboratively in her local setting and did not want to implement the unit as designed with the other teachers—a contradiction between community and subject. However she eventually developed all the unit activities as a result of working online with the other participating teachers. She stated post unit that she did not want to stop the online interactions because she did not want to "let the others down" by dropping out of the unit. She also worked with her local technology support to fix a server problem and gain better access to SNS resolving an issue between the tool, SNS, and the object (coded as tool accessibility). She overall widened her object by completing the entire unit despite her reservations about her students' capabilities but insisted in her post unit interview that this type of problem-based learning was "useless" to her students.

Collaboration Issues

The researchers developed evaluations of the effectiveness of the online professional development program based on the level of successful implementation of the online unit of

Figure 4. Teacher D

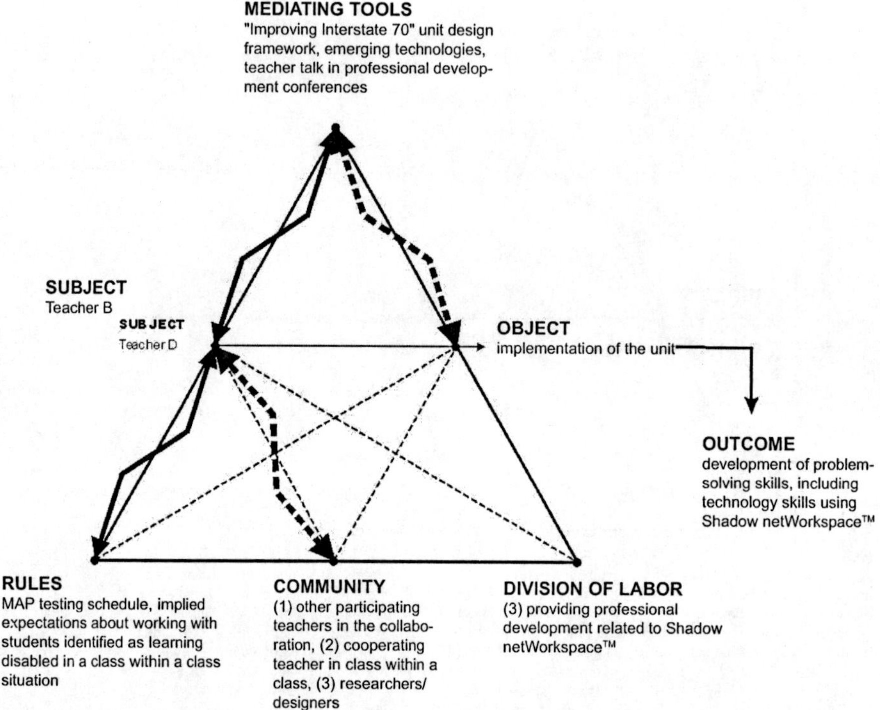

study. There were three issues that appeared in the online dialog of the teachers as they implemented the unit. The three questions were (1) What factors in a teacher's school environments influence the implementation of an innovation cluster? (2) How does a teacher's participation in collaborative professional development influence the implementation of an innovation cluster? (3) How does a teacher's belief about learning and technology influence the implementation of an innovation cluster? Each issue was expressed as a contradiction in the activity system, a form of tension between the interrelated elements of the system. There were three types of contradictions in the teachers' activity.

Secondary contradictions occur in the local context of the work activity setting and are depicted in the AT triangle made for each teacher. Three of the teachers in the study narrowed the object because of communication issues with people in their school environment who were important or necessary to successfully implementing the unit. Without a productive dialog about the teacher's goals for the innovation among her local division of labor and community members, none of the teachers were able to resolve contradictions in their local setting.

A tertiary contradiction occurs between interacting activity systems. This type of contradiction occurred when the teachers collaborated to define a common object in their online professional development processes, which included chat rooms, e-mail, and a discussion board. Three of the teachers reformulated their object, either widening or narrowing, because of these online collaborative processes. Teacher B shortened her schedule as a result of collaboration dialogs despite her own context-related concerns about the limits it placed on her schedule. She was not proactive in her work activity role online choosing to defer to the ideas of the other teachers. She stated in her post-interview that she had "...let her students down. They were ready for it (finishing the unit) but we ran out of time." Teacher C participated in the online collaboration as a receiver of information and added several new activities and evaluations to her unit as a result. Online Teacher D developed a strong social presence using the forum to develop productive social interactions despite her pre-unit statement that she did not like to collaborate. She completed all three phases of the unit in order to stay with the others. Teacher A made no changes in her unit as a result of her online dialogues and her social or work-related roles in the collaboration.

A primary contradiction is as negative tension between the concepts underlying the implementation of the object, the motive, and the ultimate result that the teacher hopes to achieve, the outcome. This type of contradiction defined the progressive issue, how do individual teachers' beliefs about learning and technology influence the implementation of an innovation cluster? Teacher A narrowed her object overall because she did not complete the unit on SNS with the other classrooms. Her ideas about how the learning activities the online problem-based unit would involve did not match up with the real-time activity of multiple chats going on simultaneously. She found the online chats among the students chaotic. Teacher C widened her object by adding new activities and completing the entire unit despite her initial premise that her urban students could not interact at this level. She resolved a contradiction between her beliefs about her urban students' abilities and their productive response to the online problem-based unit. Teacher D widened her object because she did complete the entire unit although she initially stated she did not want to continue past Phase 1 because the online problem solving was too complex for her students.

Policy Implications

In order to identify the overall functioning of the online professional development interactions the researchers looked at cross-case data to distinguish patterns of response among all four teachers. The researchers designed the transformation model (see Figure 5), which identified all transformation activities as they occurred among all four teachers over the course of the study. The model includes each teacher's individual AT Model in the center and a series of four AT models for each teacher that represent when the contradictions occurred in the five phases of collaborative professional development contact—pre-unit, Phase 1, Phase 2, Phase 3, and post-unit. Shown outside the circle is a widening or narrowing line connecting the four external AT models. This line represents the teacher's response to the contradiction, a widening represents a resolution of a contradiction, and a narrowing represents an unresolved contradiction. Turning point behaviors, actual classroom responses of the teachers to the contradictions such as adding new assessments in response to an online dialog, widening her object, or taking the students off the chats in response to online dialogs, narrowing

Figure 5. Transformational model

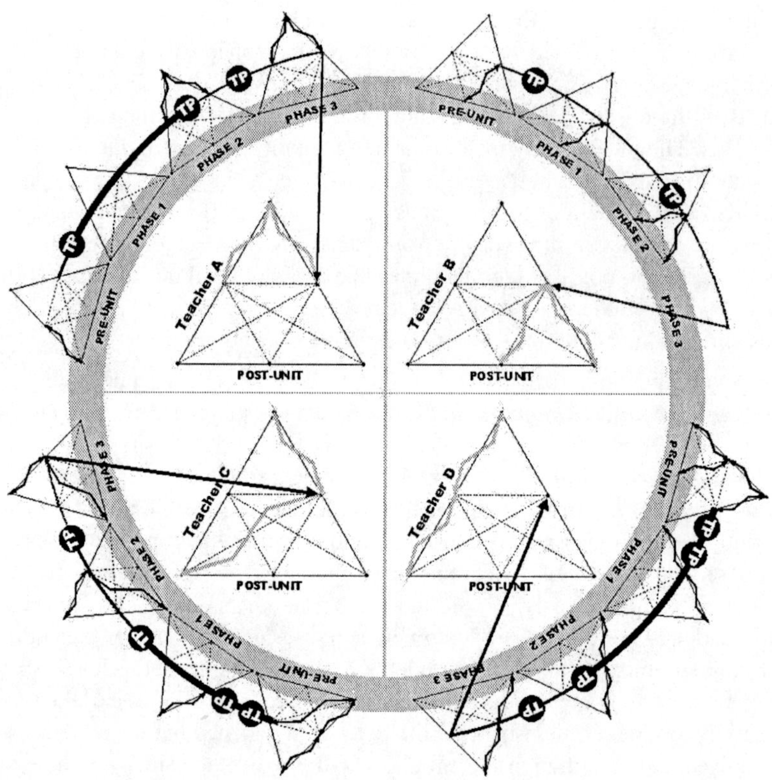

her object, are identified in the transformation model by a TP and placed on a line running through the outside AT models in reference to when the TP occurred in the classroom. The line narrows if the TP narrowed the object and widens if it widened the object.

Using the transformation model the researchers found that all the teachers narrowed their object during a difficult collaborative phase of the unit, Phase 2, when all their students were online in synchronous chat rooms. The online professional development forums available to the teachers, a weekly online chat, e-mail, and a discussion board, were insufficient to aid these teachers in resolving any contradictions that occurred during this phase. The model also identified that the two teachers who used the professional development processes most effectively to resolve contradictions, ultimately widening their objects overall, were the two teachers, C and D, who had identified a non-collaborative local work environment in their pre-unit interviews. Teacher A and Teacher B who stated in pre-unit interviews that they were currently working in collaborative local contexts that encouraged innovation did not benefit, resolve contradictions, from the online dialogs. Teachers A and B were online givers of information to the less collaborative and innovative teachers.

Sustainability and Conclusion

Lessons Learned

In response to the findings of this systemic analysis of the online professional development program, the researchers identified 10 lessons learned that impact the design of an online professional development model for innovative educators.

- Online professional development models for innovative educators should include problem-solving simulations to aid them in anticipating and identifying problems that may arise as they implement change. Problem solving is an important aspect of professional development for educators implementing new technologies.
- Teachers implementing new technologies should be able to reflect on and communicate their motives and questions regarding these new tools in their classrooms. These online dialogs can be private or with a trusted mentor but should ask the educator to address the questions of personal goals and motives for innovation. Understanding their motive, usually the development of an advanced learning process unavailable without the integration of technology, will help teachers understand their beliefs about the learning and technology.
- Online professional development interactions should be scheduled throughout the implementation of the innovation and based on the types of instructional activities occurring in the classroom.
- Prior to beginning the innovation, teachers' dialogs should focus on the overall learning processes involved in the innovation. These dialogs should focus the teacher on the cognitive processes that the new technologies can potentially affect.
- During the unit teachers need to address the logistics of the day-to-day operations of the classroom. Online interactions at this time should also include an immediacy that is essential as the instructional activities occur.
- After the unit, online dialogs should focus on reflection on what worked or did not work so curriculum redesign can occur. Reflection-in-action is a critical component of developing the potential for innovation.
- The online professional development model should include video of exemplar innovative classroom in order to help educators understand the practical aspects and myriad intended or unintended impacts of implementing advanced technologies. The use of online video vignettes of similar classrooms would help teachers understand how the innovation looks in real-time in the classroom and respond productively in the moment-by-moment decision-making process in the classroom.
- Innovative teachers need varied and ongoing access to change agents and other successful educational innovators including chat rooms, blogs, listservs, and e-mail in order to dialog about the potential of implementing innovation in educational setting.
- Online programs for innovative educators should include technology awareness and support including the identification of constraints and affordances embedded in new

technologies and the type and quality of technology support needed and available to them to realize their potential in their classrooms.

Best Practices

As a result of the systemic analysis of this online professional development program and the evaluation of the level of successful implementation of the online collaborative problem-solving unit, the researchers are able to identify three best practice processes that will improve the effectiveness of online professional development programs for innovative educators.

1. Teachers who are implementing innovation should develop communication support structures that allow them to resolve the eventual contradictions that result from change efforts in their work activity setting. In this study the teachers that were able to identify problems prior to and during implementation and were able subsequently to communicate and problem-solve successfully were able to resolve contradictions and increase their effectiveness (Russell & Schneiderheinze, 2005). Those teachers who did not identify contradictions or who did not communicate these problems within their local context were unable to resolve them and did not implement the online problem-based unit as successfully. Online professional development programs for innovative educators should include dialogs concerning potential problems and build support systems that educators need to resolve eventual problems.
2. Innovative teachers implementing online units designed to develop advanced learning processes in their students can have primary contradictions between their inert or unidentified beliefs about learning and the processes required for practical implementation of the mediational tools that they bring into their classroom in order to meet their goals. Teachers beliefs about the advanced learning processes that new tools, especially advanced technologies, are meant to potentially develop should be identified prior to the implementation of the tools and should be reviewed throughout the process in order to identify any contradictions that can decrease their effectiveness. Teachers' online professional development programs should include a reflective component that helps them identify their basic beliefs about teaching and learning in order to identify possible contradictions between the innovative tools and their goals.
3. Online professional development programs should identify the teacher's level of previous collaboration and innovation and mentor each innovative educator with other innovators at or above this level. This type of mentoring is important at all levels of innovation as teachers need to dialog with someone who has implemented similar reform at or above their level of innovation This is especially important if the teachers do not have support for innovation in their local contexts as the online forum replaces those needed collaborations and is the only support for the implementation of the innovation.

An online professional model for educators should raise teachers' awareness of their inherent beliefs about the new technologies they are using and the opportunities for advanced learning offered by collaborative tools, help them identify potential technological and instructional issues that may arise as a result of implementing new technologies, and allow them to collaborate productively and in timely forums with other innovative educators. Innovative educators have a need for a defined support system in their professional development programs. However, all educators are constantly responding to changes in their classrooms whether implemented by choice or by mandate. Any of the best practice goals identified as a result of this study would be useful to educators as they respond to their highly fluid and complex profession.

The process of studying teachers through a systemic and contextual lens of varying granularity can result in understandings that are not possible through other theoretical constructs. The benefit of this type of coherent practical understanding of how innovators implement advanced technologies is to facilitate the design of effective online professional development programs for educators striving to create and successfully implement innovative learning environments so their students can realize the potential of using advanced technologies in preparation for productive citizenship in technologically-advanced societies.

Acknowledgment

The author collaborated with Art Schneiderheinze, PhD in order to design and implement the study.

References

Barab, S. A., Hay, K. E., & Yamagata-Lynch, L. C. (2001). Constructing networks of activity: An in-situ research methodology. *The Journal of the Learning Sciences, 10*(1&2), 63-112.

Bereiter, C. (2002). *Education and mind in the knowledge age.* NJ: Lawrence Erlbaum Associates.

Bruner, J. (1990). *Acts of meaning.* Cambridge, MA: Harvard University Press.

Cole, M., & Engeström, Y. (1993). A cultural-historical approach to distributed cognition. In G. Salomon (Ed.), *Distributed cognition: Psychological and educational considerations.* (pp. 1-46). Cambridge, MA: Cambridge University Press.

eMINTS home page. (n.d.). Retrieved on April 15, 2001, from http://missouri.emints.org

Engeström, Y. (1987). *Learning by expanding: An activity-theoretical approach to developmental research.* Helsinki: Orienta-Konsultit.

Engeström, Y., Miettinen, R., & Punamaki, R. (Eds.). (1999). *Perspectives on activity theory.* Cambridge, UK: Cambridge University Press.

Fraenkel, J. R., & Wallen, N. E. (1996). *How to design and evaluate research in education.* NY: McGraw-Hill.

Il'enkov, E. V. (1977). *Dialectical logic: Essays in its history and theory.* Moscow: Progress.

Laffey, J., Musser, D., & Espinosa, L. (2000). Shadow netWorkspace™ Learning Systems Project. In J. Kinshuk, & T. Okamoto (Eds.), *Proceedings of the International Workshop on Advanced Learning Technologies* (pp. 188-189). Los Alamitos, CA: IEEE Computer Society Press.

Rogers, E. M. (1995). *Diffusion of innovations* (4th ed.). NY: The Free Press.

Russell, D. (2004). Paradigm shift: A case study of innovation in an educational setting. *International Journal of Instructional Technology & Distance Learning, 1*(12). 19-36.

Russell, D., & Schneiderheinze, A. (2005). Understanding innovation in education using Activity Theory. *Educational Technology & Society, 8*(1), 38-53

Schoenfeld, A. (1999). Looking towards the 21st century: Challenges of educational theory and practice. *Educational Researchers, 28*(7), 4-14.

Vygotsky, L. S. (1978). *Mind in society: The development of higher psychological processes.* Cambridge, MA: Harvard University Press.

Wertsch, J. (1998). *Mind as action.* NY: Oxford University Press.

Wertsch, J., Minick, N., & Arns, F. (1999). The creation of context in joint problem solving. In B. Rogoff & J. Lave (Eds.), *Everyday cognition: Development in social context* (pp. 151-171). Cambridge, MA: Harvard University Press.

Chapter IX

VIPER: Evaluation of an Integrated Group VoiceIP Software Application for Teaching and Learning in Higher Education

John Beaumont-Kerridge, University of Luton Business School, UK

Abstract

Recent developments producing new Internet conferencing (IC) and multipoint desktop conferencing (MDC) systems have emerged, which may supersede text-based and audio/video conferencing (AVC) software. The newer IC or MDC systems also integrate interactive tools and have the advantage of operating at a fraction of the cost when compared to AVC systems. Communication by face to face methods are important within the learning process, but can online methods that incorporate sound, video, and integrated online tools be as effective? AVC systems within higher education (HE) have been available for some time although the quality of such approaches, however, has been open to question. This chapter evaluates an exploratory study of one MDC application, "Voice Café," in a higher education, business school setting. For commercial distinctiveness, the academic application of this software was called "VIPER" (voice Internet protocol extended reach). Consideration is given to the software itself in terms of its features, pedagogic aspects, and how students and faculty viewed its use.

Introduction

Recent developments producing new Internet conferencing (IC) and multipoint desktop conferencing (MDC) systems have emerged over and above the text-based discussion and audio/video conferencing (AVC) software. The major differences of the newer IC or MDC systems are the integrated use of interactive tools and their advantage of operating at a fraction of the cost when compared to the AVC systems. Communication by face-to-face methods is important within the learning process, but can online software that incorporates sound and video and interactive tools be as effective? AVC systems within higher education (HE) have been available for some time. The quality of such approaches, however, has been open to question when compared to face-to-face methods (Knipe & Lee, 2002). Compatibility issues exist between competing AVC commercial providers, which have limited deployment, they are relatively expensive, and disagreement has also been voiced about how AVC should be used (Laurillard, 1993; Mason, 1998).

Easy access to education is not available for everyone. As a result, pressure is upon teaching providers to develop different methods of communication to extend the "reach" from an institution to students. Computer conferencing using text-based systems is widely used within online courses although learners and tutors have noted problems (Cartwright, 2000; Harasim, 1997; Salmon, 2000).

This chapter evaluates an exploratory study of an MDC application, "voice café," in a higher education, business school setting. For commercial distinctiveness, the academic application of this software was called "VIPER" (voice Internet protocol extended reach). Consideration is given to the software itself in terms of its features, pedagogic aspects, and how students and faculty viewed its use.

Voice Café and VIPER

The business school became aware of the voice café software at the beginning of 2004. It was initially evaluated as a useful means of improving communication for staff, students, and between partner institutions. It was initially applied to the overseas MBA program. Because of the "newness" of this software and the alacrity of HE providers to search out new methods of communication, it was decided to call the academic application of this software "VIPER," short for voice Internet protocol extended reach. Figure 1 shows a screen shot of the VIPER, which has the following features:

1. Voice to voice capability over analogue telephone modem: For a participant to speak, similar to a "walkie talkie" participants depress the F9 or ctrl button continuously for others to be heard. Either speakers or headphones can be used with a microphone needed for speech. Important, however, was the feature that communications took place over an ordinary telephone line and a broadband connection was not needed, helpful for connections in many parts of the world do not have the advantages of broadband. The minimum requirement for the software was 33kb, which is well below the normal

analogue telephone connection speed of about 40- 50kb, although in some countries speeds as low as 26k were recorded.

2. **Up to 25 synchronous connections:** The version used provided up to 25 simultaneous connections, although up to 500+ are possible. One connection could be one person, a group in front of one computer, or a computer in a lecture theatre. Where there was more than one person, a suitable screen or projector was needed, as well as speakers and a "moderator" to control the computer to allow for a full dialogue to take place.
3. **Browser capability with "follow me" functions:** The ability to combine voice and browser capability proved to be a most powerful feature. Not only could Web sites be accessed, but also materials for presentation within discussion could be viewed. The PowerPoint™ "publish and save as Web page" function proved to be most useful because of its ease converting PPT files to HTML files, which also provided an index within the conversion process.
4. **"Hands Up" functions:** Due to the absence of a video of the student, the tutor is not able to "see" if a student wishes to ask a question. The hands up facility is activated by the student using the right mouse button over the participants icon and the five options of (a) ask a question, (b) make a statement, (c) thumbs up image, (d) thumbs down image, or (e) never mind. The last function enables the user to reset this feature. Activating this provides a small icon for each of the items (a) to (d), which is viewable by all. There is also an overview screen that lists who is waiting to ask a question or make a statement, and a sum total of "thumbs up" or "thumbs down."
5. **Text chat, group and private:** Two text chat facilities are available, group and individual. The former allows all participants to see the posted messages, which can be saved in either a text or HTML format. The individual messaging allows only the participant and tutor to see the message.
6. **Interactive whiteboard:** This tool was interactive for all participants with a standard palette for the variety of drawing tools available. One interesting feature was the ability to "capture" a browser image for interactive use with students. In addition, as would be expected with software such as this, browser compatible images could be loaded from the desktop.
7. **Tutor video out:** Albeit a frame rate of some 24 frames per second, only one image is available of the tutor and this all participants can see. The default size of the image is 150x150 pixels, although this can be enlarged. The minimal video capability was, however, one of the reasons for the very low bandwidth requirement. This was essential for operation in some parts of the world where it was known that only analogue telephone over poor standard lines would be available. In addition, it was noted early on that once the video had been set up, and a tutor's image was available, it could then be paused further decreasing the bandwidth requirement.
8. **Installation and network requirements:** The voice café software operates on the client PC via a "plug in" on Internet Explorer™ v6.0 or later browser software. It requires a PC with at least a Pentium III equivalent, appropriate memory, hard drive, mic, and headphones or speakers. Functionally it worked via servers in the U.S. and Australia. Installation took about three minutes on a broadband connection, but 30 minutes on a dialup. This was, however, a once only operation unless the software was updated, which was automatically sensed by the installed program. Setup in the

home environment did not generally meet with problems unless the PC specification was below specification. Setup in an office or college environment, however, was more problematic due to the need for firewall ports required opening (9500 to 9509 outgoing traffic only). The major difficulty under these circumstances was being able to contact the appropriate member of staff. In almost all instances, once the network member of staff was contacted any communications' problems were resolved in a matter of minutes. What often caused the delays, often days or weeks, was the difficulty of contacting the member of the network staff.

9. **256 bit security encryption:** Previous experience by voice café designers were commercial considerations of confidentiality and outsiders "listening in" to conversations and documents under consideration. Although not tested, the software boasts this high level of security. The only drawback with this, however, was the inability to enter and show in the browser Web sites that required a username and password for access.
10. **Management functions:** The moderator has mute, boot, and banish functions if needed. Userful also was the ability to use multiple usernames and passwords, that is, one cohort could be assigned one username and password. This enabled a much easier management of student and staff access.

Pedagogic Considerations

Early models of learning suggested the "extended classroom" as a good design for online teaching and learning. VIPER would certainly enable this, either in the form of "one to

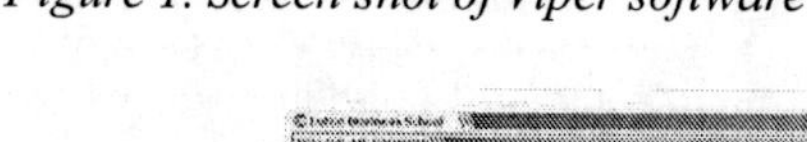

Figure 1. Screen shot of Viper software

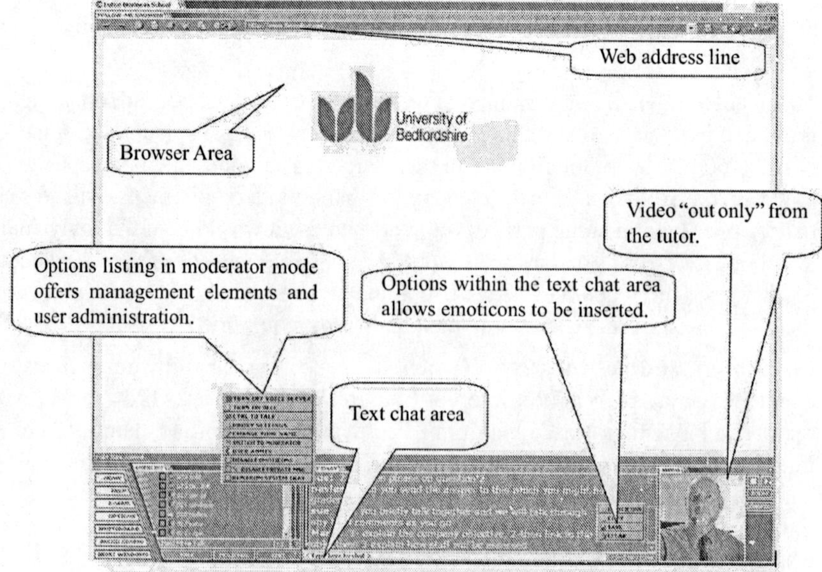

many" or "many to many" with respect to tutors and students. Criticism exists, however, that online tutors and instructors come to the new medium from traditional backgrounds with skills that do not translate well (Schieman, Taere, & McLaren, 1992), an issue, which is still reported (Salmon, 2003). This is mostly based, however, on text-based online learning models and this MDC application. Because VIPER incorporates voice and basic IT skills, may need a shorter learning curve and as a result such difficulties may not arise. Even so, the online environment is dynamic with developments in design continually being added to the knowledge base of this domain. Laurillard's important work in 1993 has been re-evaluated, and this original taxonomy cannot easily be applied to group work (Britain & Liber, 1999). Indeed, Laurillard (2000) herself has added more in the light of recent developments. It is perhaps as a result of this and the variety of online tools available within the "blended suite" that a single framework for teaching and learning to which a majority can subscribe as best practice has yet to emerge. This exploratory evaluation of the VIPER is therefore set against participant experience, observation, and interactivity.

Evaluation of VIPER

These were conducted with three student groups and faculty:

1. Six selected undergraduate business studies students.
2. A dissertation support group.
3. An MBA student group.
4. Faculty staff.

Selected Marketing and Business Undergraduate Students

Of six students, four were connected via computers that were "on campus," whilst the remaining two were connected via external connections to the University. Of particular interest were set up issues, learning curves of participants, and techniques of verbal discussion online. The two sessions began with the tutor outlining a topic and then inviting discussion. The set up and installation phase went well without event for all of the students. Anticipated firewall problems did not arise, and all equipment and software functioned appropriately. As a consequence, the use of the software was reliable.

Initially, students and the tutor engaged only in verbal discussion, and in the first session text chat used only very occasionally while a participant was talking. In the second session, however, particularly the students who considered themselves IT literate used the text function much more extensively. At one stage the tutor did ask the students to stop using the text function since they were using it to organize a forthcoming social function. This did appear to be similar to a face-to-face session where the tutor was asking the students in the "back row" to be quiet!

There are a number of tools in the VIPER suite available to both participants and tutor. It was not unexpected that only the voice, text and browsing functions were used but these were, toward the end of the second session all were used extensively. When asked, after the sessions had been completed, participants reported that they found the software acceptable, but two of the six stated that they would prefer face-to-face lectures. One commented:

I would not like to study in this way, being on my own in front of a computer. I would miss my friends.

Participants in the demonstration classes reported the software was "interesting." The quality of sound was reported as being acceptable. There was a request, however, by some "to slow down," since speaking quickly prevented comprehension. This appeared to be overcome in the first instance by asking participants to speak relatively carefully, but was not noted as an issue in later sessions. The sessions were deemed by the students and staff, however, as being successful, with the lectures having been conducted successfully.

Dissertation Student Group

This postgraduate group was completing their MSc in business related studies, and two were abroad for the data gathering exercise (Germany and India). Initial meetings were held face-to-face to begin the study process and resolve issues of subject matter and research directions. The set up of the software was straight forward and uneventful for all of the students. This was unexpected since all participants reported a mistrust of IT in general, reporting critical failures at some stage in their academic lives. The dissertation was a major academic stage, and seemed to heighten their lack of confidence in IT.

Regular meetings were arranged, at which it was intended that all participants would login at a set time. Students produced Word™ documents for discussion, for example literature reviews, questionnaires, and the group and tutor would discuss issues that arose. The tutor printed the Word™ document in an Adobe Acrobat™ format, and then placed them on a Web site so they could be accessed by the software and viewed by all in the group. In one instance, while the group was actively engaged, the student who was in India e-mailed a document (draft questionnaire), which the tutor converted "on the fly" and uploaded to a Web site for group discussion. It was noted that adequate IT skills on the part of the tutor are needed for this, not least the ability to "multitask" while the discussions are ongoing. After the sessions were completed, participants reported that they found the software relatively straightforward to use, and had the convenience of saving travel time. One participant stated:

I found VIPER to be really good for preparation, but for the really difficult issues that I did not understand, I really needed to meet my tutor to talk things through. It was frustrating, and I really needed to be in front of my tutor. (Student 9)

While the students were in the data collection phase, face-to-face contact was not possible. Although this might be preferable, learning objectives were achieved using VIPER. This student achieved good grades without the face-to-face communication, but none the less felt the need for this type of support and viewed VIPER methods for deep learning, secondary.

A similar result found by Katz and Yablon (2003), where no significant differences in grade performance between Internet and traditional lecture based courses were reported, but attitudinal differences, however, was identified where students preferred off-line methods.

MBA Student Group

Twenty-two participants were involved in learning and teaching situation, and 12 were selected for the evaluation on a random basis. Although this study concentrated upon the use of VIPER, other in course tools and techniques were also being used. These included face-to-face teaching, Blackboard™ virtual learning environment, and bespoke CD-ROM materials. The students on the MBA course met for an induction session at the beginning of the course. The intention was to create a better environment for socialization processes to take place rather than using online communication methods.

Those who considered themselves IT competent found no problems with the set up or use of the software. The following statement typified this for one such participant:

Good. Simple to use and a good way to hold tutorials. I have also found it excellent for our study group to use weekly to keep in touch.

One student, due to work commitment was posted to Saudi Arabia during the course. He was able to set up his laptop from his hotel room and participate as effectively as others within sessions. Although positive statements were received about the software and its use, comments of problems in this category are interesting and provide a different perspective:

Examples of problems reported were:

1. **A problematic Internet service provider (ISP), (blocked port access):** This was resolved by IT support by informing the student to request the ISP provider of the appropriate instructions.
2. **A PC well below the required and notified specification:** Overcome by the student purchasing a computer that was a reasonably new specification and not seven years old.
3. **Smooth functioning not occurring at peak periods due to a "free" ISP provider:** Resolved by the student "upgrading" to a paid service.
4. **Some individuals reported difficulties with audio settings:** This last aspect was resolved by providing a "set up routine," which students undertook when first logging into the system. This appeared in later sessions to resolve the problems.

Both moderated and un-moderated meetings were observed, and this provided an important collaborative mechanism for students. From these groups VIPER was reported as being very helpful for students to "stay in touch," and the level of academic use for the collaborative work varied from complex assignment oriented to social conversations. Better learning independence is noted as one of the higher order skills of learning sometimes characterized by the preference by students for un-moderated meetings to challenge the given "norms" (Salmon, 2000). Students appeared to require a need to develop "online" meeting skills, however, when they met through VIPER, which improved over time. Conversations were more relaxed in later meetings, with almost no problems being reported.

Where moderated group meetings were organized with tutors with no set agenda, requests were made for more information relating to assessment and other issues, for example, housekeeping matters such as the "font size" and "layout" of documents to be submitted. Both faculty and students felt that questions such as these improved the face-to-face meetings because much of the "trivia, but necessary trivia" had been resolved leaving the physical meetings to more important matters on the course. Students also considered this to be valuable, and saved considerably on travel time.

The Faculty Perspective

Salmon (2000) emphasizes that the skills of the moderator are paramount in the success of an online course. Theoretically, the basic use of the system should not impede the communication of the group and tutor. This appeared to be the case within the MBA group. One tutor commented:

...It has improved my listening and understanding skills of what a student was doing. Sometimes there would be a silence, and at first I was trying to work out what was going on. Then I began to realize the difference between when the student was thinking and when they were writing down notes. It enabled me to be more effective about who to draw into discussion and when there appeared to be some delay. It is a different kind of skill. (Tutor 1)

In addition to audio from the perspective of interaction and the available online tools, VIPER appeared to provide subtle additional aspects of communication.

...The communication was surprisingly active. It was not just all one way, it engaged many senses, and I had all my things around me, which I could quickly refer to. I was able to set myself up because they could not see. (Tutor 3)

This tutor went on to say:

...One soon learnt to bring the students in by asking questions, searching questions. Some students cannot bear to have a silence; others can so noting those who had not answered and bringing them in later.

More extensive use of the system was made following requests from some of the students. Observations of the seven tutors involved provided the following main usages of the system, and can be grouped under three headings: (a) voice only with hands up indicator, (b) voice only with hands up indicator plus Web browsing, (c) voice only with hands up indicator, Web browsing plus the use of the whiteboard.

Level I: Voice Only and Hands Up Indicator

Tutors and students engaged in conversations about topics, using the hands up indicator for dichotomous questions of the group. Often this was used to bring contributions together to redirect the flow of a discussion, a technique described by Salmon (2000) as "weaving." There was a perception by the tutors that Level I use was straightforward and easy enough after the set up procedures were complete. The text chat facility appeared to be used very rapidly within all sessions, contained questions, brief replies, clarity, or confirmation of issues between participants while the session was progressing. It was a main supporting communications channel supporting the voice discussion. It also served as a tangible record post meeting via a "copy of text" function.

Level II: Voice, Hands Up Indicator and Web-Based Materials

The browser capability enabled Web-based materials to be presented in conjunction with the other tools. The materials were either Web sites relevant to the topic or learning materials prepared for the Web specifically for the session, normally PowerPoint™ files saved in an HTML Web format or pdf files. One tutor demonstrated the dynamic use of the system:

We were discussing an assignment case study that was due, and one of the students mentioned that because they were at work did not have the material with them. The assignment was converted to a pdf document on the fly, posted to a Web site, and then used in the discussions. (Tutor 6)

The VIPER system operates by sending the Web address to participants, and thereby providing the same image to all those connected within that session. One obvious advantage of this method is the saving of bandwidth. Some equivalent systems send an "image" to connected participants. This can require a high bandwidth due to the file size of the images being sent.

Level III: Voice, Hands Up Indicator, and Web-Based Materials Plus the Whiteboard

The whiteboard "background Web browser capture" capability means documents and diagrams can be presented for participants to interact as a part of the discussion using the integrated tools. Students were requested to "mark" or "write text" on the images to elicit participant viewpoints pre, post, and during discussion. The same group and tutor also used the "capture browser" function to create an image of the assignment upon which all participants could put questions and comments for discussion.

...It was interesting; I could go through the issues in a much more interesting way. It was much more interactive than in class. (Tutor 4)

On an operational level, significant variations existed. In terms of the skills ability of tutors, some required very little guidance, while others needed considerable support both prior to, during, and post sessions. Tutors as individuals it would appear will need to go through a learning curve process if this type of system is to be used within teaching and learning. As a result, depending upon the ICT of the individual tutors varying levels of support will be required, an issue reported by other studies (Garrison, 1998; Salmon, 2000, 2003).

An interesting aspect has arisen in the use of VIPER between tutors in distant geographic regions. International courses require much administration, management, and communication "staying behind" after sessions to discuss issues of management, quality, and pragmatic housekeeping issues. This does represent an important advantage over previous communications methods. These were prohibitive due to cost, or limiting since they were based on text-based systems, telephone, or face-to-face meetings.

Senior Management Perspective

The view of senior management focused upon the strategic advantages of the software:

VIPER currently provides a USP, a unique advantage, which is very difficult in today's HE market place. It enables personal teaching at a distance. It also gives us further reach in terms of target markets. It has enabled us to win two overseas contracts against other HE institutions, and has dragged us to the attention in front of others...I am surprised, however, that other Universities have not used this type of software more extensively. (Dean, University of Luton Business School)

One contract, for example, to provide the MBA with the British Council in India, was won in competition against a number of other Universities. Although the distance learning packages were all similar, the inclusion of VIPER was unique and provided the significant advantage. Other issues raised by faculty concerned how the software was going to develop, over time with suggestions of video to improve the "comfort" of communication although the mechanics of large student numbers may be problematic.

Summary

VIPER has shown itself to be a useful communications tool, for both students and tutors. It has currently given a unique advantage to the University of Luton Business School product portfolio enabling it to win contracts in competition with other Universities.

The technical issues surrounding its use were mostly straight forward, with the only problems appearing where some wanted to use the system from within a commercial network that had stringent firewall policies. These were overcome once the appropriate network staff were contacted and appropriate ports opened. The low bandwidth requirement also enabled VIPER to function where other, more demanding MDC software applications might not have been possible.

Overall, the general view of the students that have used the system was positive. This was particularly true of those who were distant geographically and needed to make contact on a regular or emergency basis. Students and faculty did need repetitive use to gain confidence and expertise in the use of VIPER. The system was used for a wide range of applications from important learning issues, very basic house keeping matters, to a social aspect of students keeping in regular contact with each other. Students as recipients of the teaching management approaches appear also to demand the highest level of interaction available, irrespective of the tutor capability or indeed perhaps the need of the subject matter. As a result, the student learning curve appeared to progress ahead of the faculty learning curve, which can be a source of stress for members of staff, with the consequence of training resource implications.

Staff also found VIPER useful, from the perspectives of teaching and learning as well as keeping good communications with staff in partnership colleges that were based abroad. Issues of pedagogic design were important in conjunction with the three levels of use of VIPER from voice only to full use of all tools and the interactive whiteboard. Good planning and preparation to provide the maximum benefit for the student experience also emerged as important from a tutor's perspective. As a result, VIPER would appear to offer another helpful communications platform to add to the blended mix of online tools that are available for teaching and learning in an HE, business school context.

References

Britain, S., & Liber, O. (1999). *A framework for pedagogical evaluation of virtual learning environments*. Report to JISC Technology Applications Program.

Cartwright, J. (2000). Lessons learned: Using asynchronous computer-mediated conferencing to facilitate group discussion. *Journal of Nursing Education, 39*(2), 87-90.

Garrison, D., (1998). Distance education for traditional universities: Part-time professional learning. *Journal of Distance Education, 13*(2), 74-78.

Harasim, L. M. (1997). *Interacting in hyperspace: Developing collaborative learning environments on the WWW.* Retrieved October 1, 2005, from http://www.worldbank.org/html/fpd/technet/mdf/edi-trng/har1.htm

Katz, J., & Yablon, B. (2003). Online university learning: Cognitive and affective perspectives. *Campus Wide Information Systems, 20*(2), 48-54.

Knipe, D., & Lee, M. (2002). The quality of teaching and learning via videoconferencing. *British Journal of Educational Technology, 33*(3), 301-311.

Laurillard, D. (1993). *Rethinking university teaching: A framework for the effective use of educational technology.* London: Routledge.

Laurillard, D. (2000). *Keynote presentation, Alt-C 2000 Conference, Umist.* Retrieved December 20, 2003, from http://www2.umist.ac.uk/isd/lwt/altc/programme/keynote.htm#laurillard

Mason, R. (1998). *Globalising education: Trends and applications.* London: Routledge.

Salmon, G. (2000). *E-moderating: The key to teaching and learning online.* London: Kogan Page.

Salmon, G. (2003). *E-moderating: The key to teaching and learning online* (2nd ed). London: Kogan Page.

Schieman, E., Taere, S., & McLaren, J. (1992). Towards a course development model for graduate level distance education. *Journal of Distance Education, 7*(2), 51-65.

Chapter X

Investigating Patterns of Cognitive and Interactive Acts in an Online Student Cooperative Program

Lucio Teles, University of Brasilia, Brazil

Nancy Johnston, Simon Fraser University, Canada

Abstract

Student co-op programs are being increasingly developed to enhance employability skills of college and university students. While most of these programs are taught face-to-face, some universities and colleges are now offering co-op programs online. This article investigates the implementation of a pilot online co-op program, the Bridging Online (BOL) Program, at Simon Fraser University, in Burnaby, BC, Canada. A research methodology, based on transcript analysis of participants' messages and interviews, was used to address the research questions. Participants in the pilot project found the online version to be a valuable tool to support co-op students in learning and developing employability skills, including problem defining and solving, planning and goal setting, improved interpersonal communication skills and self assessment, and peer feedback skills.

Introduction

As our society is transformed into a knowledge-based economy, higher education institutions are exploring ways of ensuring students have knowledge and skills needed for the workplace of the new economy. Many universities have implemented "co-op programs" to help students develop employability skills through experiential learning in workplace settings. Students alternate periods of full-time school with periods of paid work as they complete their degrees.

While it is clear that co-op programs play an important role in the development of students' employability skills, a systematic and comprehensive understanding of the learning that takes place in these programs is an ongoing challenge (Johnston, 1996) and is complicated by the fact that valid and reliable data collection is often difficult to obtain. The challenge is further complicated by the emergence of innovative approaches to cooperative education. In particular, the relatively recent introduction of Web-based programs that provide online training and knowledge to co-op students represents a departure from traditional-based programs where the instruction is provided in a brick and mortar environment. As such, what we know about learning in a traditional environment may or may not translate to online programs. If we are to further our understanding of the nature and effectiveness of cooperative education programs, additional research is needed in this emerging area. The purpose of this study, therefore, is to investigate the online teaching of employability skills through a qualitative analysis of a program that was developed and implemented at Simon Fraser University (SFU).

We begin with a brief review of prior research in the area of online cooperative education programs. From here, we introduce the Bridging Online (BOL) Program and describe its background and general features. We then present the research questions, describe the method used in the study, and present the results. We conclude with a series of recommendations for the development and implementation of online programs. Post-script describing changes that were made in response to the results of this study is also presented.

Review of Research in Online Co-Op Education

Some initial research has been undertaken with online programs to support co-op students. For example, Northeastern University (in Boston) launched a pilot project for 86 electrical and computer engineering freshmen and sophomores who started their first co-op experience at one of 53 employment work sites across 10 states. The Internet was used to provide students with structured learning assignments during the work period. Students communicated via e-mail with their co-op coordinators and with their classmates through a computer conferencing system. Findings show that students reinforced work skills and work processes and developed insights into engineering fields and trends (Canale & Duwart, 1999).

The University of Victoria (in Victoria, British Columbia, Canada) developed a curriculum to prepare students for their first work term. The curriculum included 10 modules on topics such as market trends, self-assessment, résumés, and cover letters. The curriculum was then placed online and was accessible by students as a self-paced model to learn the curriculum. An evaluation found that the program met all curriculum objectives: it was generic, yet customizable to meet specific program needs; it was not paper-dependent; it could be easily updated; it had a consistent structure; it was based on students' self-directed learning and was not program or resource dependent; and it resulted in logical measurable outcomes that enabled the evaluation of student learning (McRae, 1999).

SFU developed a skills transfer focused curriculum in co-operative education to help students understand employability skills. The program was originally developed for face-to-face delivery and two years later was converted for online delivery (Johnston, 2002). Unlike the co-op employment preparation programs previously described, Simon Fraser University's Bridging Online Program has a different focus. The student handbook for the BOL Program describes the program focus as follows: "[BOL will] help you see how all your experiences, formal and informal, can contribute to your learning and enhance your performance. The program helps you better understand your existing skills, as well as how to develop and mobilize new ones" (p. 3). Also, some of the studies published in the literature, such as the one conducted in Northeastern University's Co-op program, took place when students were already in the workplace. The Bridging Online Program, however, is offered before students enter into the workplace.

Background: The First Version of the Co-Op Bridging Program

The Simon Fraser University Co-op Bridging Program was created in 2000 and has been offered to students and practitioners of co-op education throughout British Columbia. The program has steadily gained recognition since its inception when it was offered four times to a total of approximately 500 students.

The objective of the program is to help students "identify and use their skills and knowledge beyond those places where they were learned. Specifically, the program focuses on helping the student use what he or she has learned in school effectively in the workplace and vice versa" (see Student Handbook and Learning Guide—Bridging Online Program—p. 7). Students apply for various co-op positions offered by employers and, if successful, they work there for four to eight month terms. Students return to their academic studies after completion of the working semester. This cycle may be repeated three to four times over the students' academic career.

The Bridging curriculum developed in 2000 consisted of four modules: Skills Transfer, Personal Management, Effective Communication, and Workplace 101. The Skills Transfer module prepared students to better understand their skills and how to transfer them between school and work. The Personal Management module addressed the role of self-assessment and self-direction in career planning. The Effective Communication module shared techniques for effective communication and offered general guidelines for preparation of cover letters, résumés, and interviews. The Workplace 101 focused on office etiquette and ethics, rights and responsibilities, and on how to succeed in the workplace.

Each of the four modules was originally offered in a two to three hour face-to-face workshop with a maximum of 25 students and taught by co-op staff. The Bridging Program had two full time co-op staff, which, in addition to teaching the workshops, also developed and monitored the work experiences of co-op students. Once students completed the Program they typically demonstrated more effective transition between the university and the workplace, that is, obtained interviews, received job offers.

Over the past several years, student demand for co-op has been growing steadily; however, resources for the continuation and enhancement of the Bridging Program did not grow accordingly. Co-op program staff was exploring other means by which they might offer the program to a greater number of students while maintaining its unique qualities. As well, staff worked to improve access, offering the material any time and any place students were available. There was also a desire to reduce instructor workload and spread the co-op intake period over a larger window of time, giving students increased access to the program and reducing peak load periods for staff.

From Traditional to Online: Transition from the Face-to-Face to the Online Version of the Bridging Program

As a result of these considerations, the four modules of the Co-op Student Program were reshaped and developed as an online pilot project with a variety of learning tasks, peer-to-peer online interaction, and a final face-to-face wrap-up session with an instructor. This new pilot version of the program was launched in November 2001 to test its quality and how selected students and staff members of the co-op program would receive it. Twenty-four participants in the pilot were staff members from the SFU co-op program, and 22 were students who volunteered to be involved in the pilot. The original four modules of the Bridging Program were redesigned for online delivery, each module lasting approximately one week, for a total of four weeks for the entire program.

The pilot project of the BOL program used only online activities to teach students transition skills for the workplace. Students utilized the WebCT conferencing system to partake in the program discussions. Online, students had the support of mentors (university co-op coordinator) and employer "experts," and peers. Instructors had a facilitative role and only accessed designated online areas (i.e., Facilitator's Office and Peer-to-Peer) to read and to respond to student messages.

Each online module included content, self-reflection exercises, portfolio activities, and Web resources to be explored by participants. Students were expected to actively help and support each other online. Each of the four modules of the BOL Program had three areas for online interactions and discussions: peer-to-peer conferences, a facilitator's office, and an 'ask an expert' forum. The peer-to-peer conference was designed as a discussion area for reflections on specific tasks assigned throughout the module and to provide peer feedback and support. The ask an expert area provided students with options to gather information from people who were already in the work force, as well as some of the graduates of the co-op program. The student portfolio was designed as a repository for assignments and discussion between each student and the module facilitator, but due to technical problems it was cancelled during the program offering. The facilitator's office was an open discussion area for all students to deal with questions regarding assignments, to make comments, and to clarify issues with the facilitator.

As students completed the program they were expected to have become more confident self-directed learners, to acquire an understanding of their skills and how to transfer them across various contexts, and to have created a personal portfolio consisting of a résumé, cover letter, interview preparation materials, and self-assessment examples.

Development and Implementation of the BOL Program

A spin-off company of the Simon Fraser University, TELEStraining Inc., was hired to develop the content for the BOL program. TELEStraining Inc assigned three employees to attend the workshops the BOL instructors were teaching. They recorded and transcribed the presentations done by BOL instructors and used the material to generate the content for the modules. Once the content was generated, it was split into small units or modules and animations, tests, readings, examples, and references were included. The online version of the program was then generated and tested with a group of students and BOL instructors.

For the technical implementation of the BOL program, the Academic Computing Services (ACS) group, in charge of SFU's campus computing network, was contacted. They offered to implement the BOL program using a learning management system (LMS) used at Simon Fraser University, WebCT.

The Need for Research into the Teaching of Employability Skills Online

While there have been many studies conducted on the delivery of online courses, few studies have been conducted on the use of this delivery approach to teach employability skills to co-op students. Employability skills' training involves a unique combination of formal, non-formal, and informal education. Students learn to investigate their own past experiences for both formal and informal skill development and position these for a future employer. At the same time they have to learn—improve—their presentation skills including résumé development and how to prepare for, and conduct interviews with potential employers.

In BOL, these skills had to be developed through study, peer-to-peer interaction, and support from mentors. But can this model applied in an online environment effectively support the development of these skills? To test this hypothesis we have to investigate whether students taking such an online program interact with their online peers, to study the nature of this interaction and at the same time obtain student facilitators' views about the effectiveness of the online program to support the development of employability skills.

Research Questions

The objective of this preliminary investigation was to determine whether an online version of the Bridging Co-op Program could help students achieve the co-op program objectives. In the present study, the following research questions were investigated:

- How do participants in the Bridging Online Program perceive the implementation of an online version of Bridging Program to teach employability skills?
- Which patterns of cognitive and interactive acts were developed in the Bridging Online Program online?

Data collection was conducted after participants completed the four-week pilot program in November 2001.

Methodology

To investigate the research questions, a methodology consisting of three steps was developed, consisting of: (1) content analysis of conference transcripts to identify interaction patterns and types of cognitive and interactive activities taking place in the online environment; (2) organization of focus groups with selected participants; and (3) interview with selected co-op staff members.

In order to increase the reliability of the findings, the study utilized a multi-method approach to data collection and analysis. Data analysis, in the form of conference transcripts of participant messaging, provided information concerning the nature of participant learning and the types of interaction that occurred in the program and of participants' views of their experience based on focus groups and interviews. Focus group and interview data were analyzed using content analysis methodology (Weber, 1985) and online interaction of participants (Harasim, Hiltz, Teles, & Turoff, 1995). Through content analysis and participants' interaction of the messages the nature of the online discussion can be studied and patterns of communication identified. Conference transcripts were analyzed according to a methodology of discourse analysis developed by Harasim and Bakardjeva (2002).

According to these researchers, participant utterances in online educational conferences can be classified as either cognitive speech acts or interactive speech acts, or both. Cognitive speech acts operate on the subject matter of a discussion and serve such functions as clarifying, summarizing, and analyzing information, supporting the learning process. Interactive speech acts serve to establish relationships among conference participants. Acknowledgement, support, and the disclosure of personal information are examples of interactive speech acts.

Table 1. BOL coding scheme

Cognitive Acts			
Category	**Code**	**Category**	**Code**
1. Identifying problem	IPc	1. Support asking 2. Support giving	SAi SGi
2. Exemplifying problem	EPc	3. Encouragement	ENi
3. Introducing related problem	RPc	4. Acknowledgement	ACi
4. Linking problems	LPc	5. Building on	BOi
5. Analyzing problem	ANc	6. Negotiation	NEi
6. New perspective to problem	NPc	7. Partial agreement	PAi
7. Defining concept	DCc	8. Disagreement	DIi
8. Providing information	PIc	9. Challenge	CHi
9. Arguing position	APc	10. Personal info/reflection	PRi
10. Providing evidence to justify position	JPc	11. Revealing personal feelings	PFi
11. Comparing positions	CPc	12. Personal address	ADi
12. Questioning position	QPc	13. Coordination	COi
13. Opposing position	OPc	14. Metainteraction	MIi
14. Metacognitive act	MAc	15. Phatic communication	PCi
15. Drawing conclusion	CDc	16. Self-introduction 17. Greeting	SIi GRi
16. Offering solution	OSc	18. Closure 19. Jokes	CLi JOi
17. Challenging conclusion/ solution	CCc	20. Symbolic Icons 21. Technical comments	ICi TCi

In the present study, the researchers were also interested in both the cognitive and interactive nature of participant discourse. A slightly modified version of the Harasim and Bakardjieva (2002) taxonomy was utilized to analyze conference transcripts.

Table 1 shows the various categories of cognitive and interactive acts used for transcript analysis.

Transcript Analysis

Transcript analysis is an innovative research methodology and is based on the text-based analysis of messages exchanged in computer conferencing systems. Two graduate research assistants who had prior transcript coding experience conducted transcript analysis of all participant messages independently. Analysis of the messages was conducted for two groups of participants: staff and students.

A modified version of the consensual qualitative research (CQR) methodology was also used (Hill, Thompson, & Williams, 1997) to enhance reliability in coding messages. At each step in the data analysis procedure, the researchers met to clarify their understanding of the coding methodology. They then proceeded to code the data independently and followed up with one another to ensure that they were accurately applying the coding scheme. In utilizing this approach, the researchers achieved a percent agreement of more than 80% for all of the conference modules.

Focus Groups with Selected Participants

Focus groups with available participants were conducted at the end of the Bridging Online Program to provide additional program evaluation data. Participants were asked to respond to eight questions and discuss their own views and experience of the BOL Program.

Results and Discussion

Both the nature of the program (i.e., that of being a pilot project) and of the participants themselves impacted the results as we discuss below. For this pilot project, participants began the program in the first week of November 2001 and were to complete it sequentially by the end of that month: a period of four weeks. Each of the four modules of the program was to be completed in one week.

Participation for both staff and students, however, diminished over the course of the four-week program. Due to technical problems experienced with the connection to the Portfolio server, access to it ceased during the delivery of the BOL program. As revealed by data collected in the focus group discussions, participants, particularly staff members, became too busy with their own work and could not continue to participate as they did at the outset. Also, as participants were aware of the pilot nature of the project, they did not feel as committed to completing all the work as if they were taking the program on a regular basis.

Table 2. Number of messages by module

	Module 1	Module 2	Module 3	Module 4	Portfolio	Total
Staff	100	38	13	0	19	170
Student	72	19	14	27	23	155
Total	172	57	27	27	42	325

Figure 1. Patterns of cognitive acts for staff and student participants

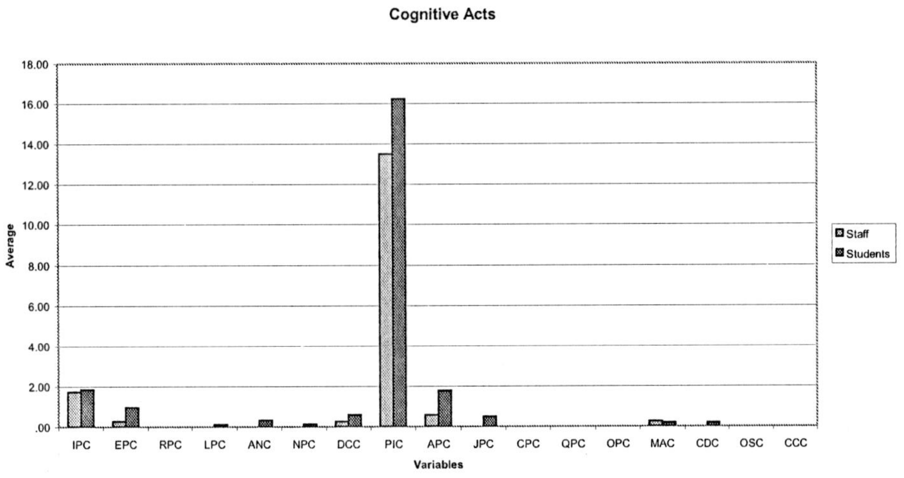

Figure 2. Patterns of interactive acts for staff and student participants

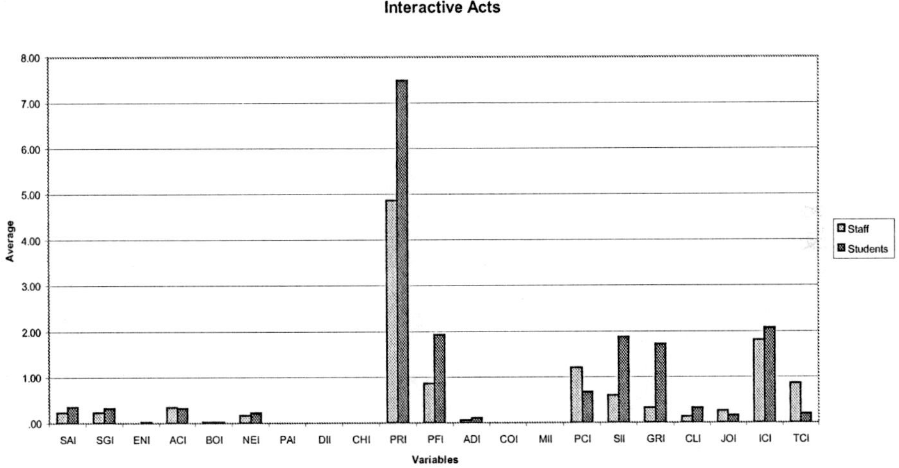

We analyzed the online conference data for both staff and student participants. Table 2 shows the number of messages, for both staff and students. When data from all of the other program modules were combined, staff participants submitted, on average, 3.55 messages.

Figures 1 and 2 provide a graphic representation of the patterns of cognitive and interactive acts for both staff and student participants.

Overall, these findings suggest that participants who submitted more messages in each of the modules, also tended to provide more factual information (PIC) in response to facilitator questions or conference tasks, personal information and/or reflections (PRI), indications of their feelings (PFI), use more symbolic icons (ICI) and identify themselves in their messages (SII).

Focus Group Data

After participants completed the BOL Program, a focus group of participants was organized to evaluate the program. Their comments are summarized here.

Question 1: Based on your experience in taking the first offering of the BOL Program, do you believe that the instructional approach used in the program supports the achievement of the goals of the SFU Co-op Program?

Most participants believed that the instructional approach did support the goals of the SFU co-op program. One participant noted, in addition, that it helped students to become "smart e-workers." Another participant felt that the content was more valuable than the delivery mechanism. A third participant noted that the self-based learning approach was beneficial along with the peer-to-peer forums and the 24/7 availability of the program.

Question 2: Do you find that the user interface facilitates navigation?

Focus group participants indicated that the BOL Program was, for the most part, easy to navigate. Some participants indicated that the font type used on some screens (San-Serif) should be changed to an easier-to-read font type.

Question 3: How do you perceive the benefits and disadvantages of the online version of the BOL Program compared to the face-to-face version?

The benefits of BOL, as noted by the participants, include the following: the program is self-paced and provides technical and academic support; it is accessible anytime; it is convenient for student schedules; greater learning opportunities are afforded through the online discussions; it helps to overcome traditional barriers to participation such as shyness.

The disadvantages of the program include the following: some people may learn best from an instructor in a face-to-face environment; there is no incentive to complete the exercises or read the materials if one is pressed for time; clarification and feedback may be better received in a face-to-face environment; this form of instruction takes some time to get used to.

Question 4: Has BOL taught you to transfer skills from the university to the workplace?

Each participant indicated that BOL had taught him or her to transfer skills from the university to the workplace. Two students noted, in addition, that their understanding of skills transfer was greatly enhanced after completing the program. Another student commented that the online interaction with the program moderators was very beneficial in this respect.

Question 5: Do you have any additional comments that might help to improve the BOL Program?

One student felt there should be more opportunities for peer-to-peer conversations, but that, overall, it was "a great pilot course and [s/he] would recommend others to take it." Another student indicated that it was difficult to keep up with all of the conference messages. This student suggested setting up the conferences as closed newsgroups that can be accessed via e-mail. A third student suggested that more information should be provided in the module focusing on the rights and responsibilities of both employees and employers. A fourth student commented that the success of the BOL Program would depend, largely, on the quality of the online moderators.

Conclusion

Based on data analysis, participants of the BOL Program have found the online program to be a valuable tool to support co-op students in learning and developing employability skills. Most participants stated that the program helped them in developing various skills, including problem defining and solving, planning and goal setting, improved interpersonal communication skills, and self-assessment and peer feedback skills.

Participants in the BOL Pilot Project, while benefiting from the program content and the self-directed learning approach afforded by the online system, tended not to engage in direct interaction with one another. Direct interaction among the participants (i.e., where they engaged in direct conversation with one another) occurred on fewer than 10 occasions. There were, however, many more instances of indirect interaction, where participants referred to the contents of another's message or provided some indication of agreement with a message writer. Each of the program modules was structured in such a way as to require participants to complete a number of tasks. As it turned out, participants spent much of their online time completing only what was asked of them. In this case, perhaps the perceived inflexibility of the program modules as well as time constraints discouraged more direct peer-to-peer interaction. Figure1 tends to support these observations.

It is apparent that much of the cognitive act activity involved providing information (PIC), in other words, providing factual information in response to facilitator or participant comments or queries. Most of interactive moves activity centered on providing personal information or reflections (PRI), providing some indication of one's feelings and, to a lesser extent, providing information unrelated to the program module (PCI), identifying oneself in one's messages (SII), offering words of greeting or appreciation to participants (GRI), using various symbolic icons (ICI), and asking a variety of technical questions (TCI).

Some participants also mentioned that they see some disadvantages in the offering of the BOL program as compared to the face-to-face format. Some of the perceived disadvantages include the fact that some students may learn best from an instructor in a face-to-face environment; there is no incentive to complete exercises or read the materials if one is pressed for time; clarification and feedback may be better received in a face-to-face environment; and this online form of instruction may take some time to get used to.

Overall, however, participants seem to support the viability the BOL Program as an effective and valuable tool for identifying and developing employability skills.

Recommendations

Several recommendations were made regarding the packaging of the program. It was felt that the BOL program was too long and too content heavy. As well, facilitators found the workload fairly high, especially in providing online feedback.

There were also a number of technical problems that arose with the BOL Pilot, as some participants could not logon to the program, while others could not access their Learner Portfolio area. This caused some frustration for some participants in the beginning, but the technical difficulties were eventually resolved. Participants recommended that technical support should constantly be provided to BOL students.

The Learner Portfolio was created as an online folder where students could place some of the materials produced during the course of the program, such as their personal résumé to be reviewed by a BOL facilitator. As it was accessible only by the student and the instructor, it implies a substantive amount of work for the facilitator having to logon to each of the participants' learner portfolios. Participants in the pilot suggested a different format be found for the portfolio. In the BOL version offered in September 2002, the learner portfolio has been eliminated from the online version and is now part of the face-to-face review meeting with the BOL facilitator.

As the Ask an Expert discussion was not available in the pilot project, participants emphasized the importance of that discussion area when the program is implemented. In the Ask an Expert area, employers, alumni, or co-op staff offer support and mentorship to BOL students.

A final recommendation in this preliminary review of the pilot program is that the "Student Handbook" of the BOL Program was perceived to be a valuable resource and should be made available in both hard copy and online.

Post Script

Since this initial research was conducted, the Bridging Online program at SFU has undergone some significant changes in response to both the pilot study feedback, and an opportunity to partner with the SFU e-learning and Innovation Centre (eLINC). Major changes are outlined next along with an update on BOL developments and further research. As of September 2003, over 1,300 students have participated in the BOL program at SFU.

The following changes to the Bridging Online Program have been made based upon initial pilot feedback reported in this chapter.

Feedback: The course was too long and too content heavy.

Change: The four-week course was separated into two, two-week-long modules. The first (BOL I) is required as part of the application to co-op. BOL I content includes Skills Transfer and Effective Communications, including the development of a résumé and cover letter and interview preparation. The second module, BOL II, focuses on Personal Management, Self-Direction, Our Portfolio, and Workplace 101 (ethics, first day on the job, rights and responsibilities, etc.). BOL II must be completed prior to the student's first work term.

Feedback: The load for moderators/facilitators was too high.

Change: Facilitators no longer provide personal feedback on student résumés and cover letters. Rather, students are directed to produce a draft using the course content and feedback to related questions from peers and the expert. This draft is included in their portfolio and presented in a face-to-face meeting with a co-op coordinator once they are accepted to co-op.

Feedback: Technical issues related to hosting the online portfolio resulted in minimal use of this function.

Change: Students now are encouraged to store their portfolio items on their own file space and create a hard copy version that they submit to coordinators as part of the acceptance criteria. Efforts are being made to address the online portfolio issue.

Feedback: Some participants, mainly staff that were less Internet accustomed, wanted a hard copy of the course.

Change: Produce a one-year supply of courseware, handed out to students upon application to co-op. We are currently investigating the option of having a current version of the course available to past students.

Feedback: There is a need for more peer-to-peer interaction.

Change: Re-tooled the Review and Reflection exercises to enhance greater interaction (e.g. instructed students to respond to two other student posts, directed students to ask for peer feedback, etc.).

A comprehensive review of the new BOL II and I was conducted in the summer 2003 surveying over 1,000 students, course facilitators, and employers. The results of this research were compiled and served as a basis for even more detailed revisions and course refinement. Currently the SFU co-op program is developing a series of follow-up "On Demand" employability-related modules, which will reside in the SFU Online Co-op Learning Community (launched in fall 2004), available for students to access when, and wherever, they need them. Topics include: Workplace Trends You Need to Know, Interview Skills to Get Your Dream Job, How to Exceed Employer Expectations, Print and Electronic Career Portfolios, Effective Networking With Potential Employers, Corporate Governance and Social Responsibility/Ethics, and Consulting, Contracting, and Pitching Proposals. These will be short, un-moderated modules containing current topical information, with many links to related sites as well as video-streaming and discussion areas.

References

Canale, R., & Duwart, E. (1999). Internet based reflective learning for cooperative education students during co-op work periods. *Journal of Cooperative Education*, *34*(2), 25-34.

Harasim, L., & Bakardjeva, M. (2002). The discourse of online learning: Cognitive and interactive dimensions. *TeleLearning Research Handbook.* School of Communications, Simon Fraser University.

Harasim, L., Hiltz, R., Teles, L., & Turoff. (1995). *Learning networks: A field guide to teaching and learning online.* Cambridge, MA: MIT Press.

Hill, C., Thompson, B., & Williams, E. (1997). A guide to conducting consensual qualitative research. *The Counselling Psychologist*, *25*(4), 517-572.

Johnston, N. (1996). *The nature of learning in cooperative education in the applied sciences.* Unpublished master's theses, Simon Fraser University, Vancouver, British Columbia, Canada.

Johnston, N. (2002). Bridging online: A WebCT-based co-op curriculum. *Presentation at the CAFCE National Conference,* Ottawa, August 13, 2002.

Section II

Cases on Blended Online Learning Systems

Chapter XI

Learning Sport Management through Interaction with the Real World

Alistair Inglis, Victoria University, Australia

Matthew Nicholson, La Trobe University, Australia

Clare Hanlon, Victoria University, Australia

Abstract

The development of a course in sport administration in which case studies form the basis of the learning activities is described. The case studies are based on a variety of documents and resources provided by eight sport organizations. The documents and resources are supplied to students on CD-ROM. Students interact online but also meet weekly face-to-face. As a result, these real-world examples have increased students' motivation and improved student learning outcomes.

Introduction

The fact that this book has been put together as a set of case studies points to the educational value that case studies are recognized as having. It is particularly appropriate, therefore, that at least one of the case studies should illustrate the use of the case model in an e-learning context. This chapter describes the development of a course in sport administration that uses case studies to introduce students to some of the management practices used in sports organizations.

The case study is a common method in social science research. Its value is seen to be that it provides rich data that permits a much deeper understanding of a situation than is possible with more traditional quantitative methods. The same characteristics that make use of the case study a valuable method in social science research also make it a valuable method in teaching and learning although its use in teaching and learning is much less widespread. Its history, nevertheless, goes back a lot further than many people realize. The case method was first introduced into teaching in the Harvard Law School in the late 1800s (Merseth, 1991). It was subsequently taken up in business and in medicine. In recent times, it has also been taken into engineering (Raju & Sanker, 1999), biology, and teacher education. However, the method can be applied to almost any discipline that is practiced within a real world context.

The case study allows the student to internalize the realities of situations and develop much deeper understandings of them, and to see relationships manifested in real life. From a pedagogical perspective, case studies offer the advantages of allowing problems to be explored in real-world contexts and situations to be explored from multiple perspectives.

Case studies are useful not just because they enable students to link theory to practice but also because they allow the student to acquire tacit knowledge (Polanyi, 1967) of the situation. The student is able to develop their understanding of the situation from their pre-conceptual awareness. Kreber (2001) analyzed the use of case studies in terms of Kolb's learning model (Kolb, 1984) and argued that case studies have the potential to combine concrete experiences, abstract conceptualization, internal reflection, and active experimentation. Depending on how the case method is used, case studies are also able to facilitate the development of key generic capabilities such as information gathering and analysis and problem solving. They may also be used to develop teamwork and leadership. In health sciences, engineering, and biology, the case is generally presented as a scenario accompanied by a statement of the issue, and the student is required to come up with some solution. However, the case method can involve more complex scenarios.

Problem-based learning is a specialized form of case-based learning in which learning is structured around collaborative work aimed at solving a series of authentic complex problems of increasing difficulty (Boud & Feletti, 1997; Schmit, 1993). The major difference between this and more general case-based learning is the use of problems to provide access to a deeper understanding of the case. The problem-based learning approach has been employed extensively in medical education (Barrow & Tamblyn, 1980). The University of Maastricht in The Netherlands has implemented problem-based learning on a whole-of-institution basis. Various attempts have been made to implement models of problem-based learning online. This approach is termed "distributed problem-based learning." Various attempts have been made to develop models for engaging in problem-based learning, generally referred to as "distributed problem-based learning" (Lehtinen, 2002).

Victoria University is a dual-sector university providing higher education and technical and further education to approximately 50,000 students at 11 campuses throughout Melbourne's inner city and western suburbs. The university is not a major distance education provider, although it does offer some courses by distance education. The way in which the university mainly sees itself using online learning is to support mixed mode teaching, that is, teaching in which learning online is combined with face-to-face interaction. Use of mixed-mode teaching allows the extent of face-to-face contact to be reduced somewhat while still allowing students the opportunity for face-to-face interaction. This use of online learning recognizes the university's multi-campus nature. The value of having many campuses is that it enables students to study locally. However, the potential difficulty is that staff move between campuses to teach, often the same course, to a different cohort of students. Use of online learning has the potential to make a major contribution to enabling staff to manage interaction and work routines.

Over recent years, Victoria University has mounted a grant program that provides funding for innovation in teaching: the Curriculum Innovation Grant Program. The university grant scheme was introduced to support strategically important curriculum change within the university. In particular, the grant scheme was concerned with making learning more innovative and flexible.

E-Learning Program

The course that is the case for this case study, *Sport Administration Foundations*, is offered as part of the Sport Administration program at Victoria University. Victoria University is one of three providers of undergraduate programs in sport administration and management education in the state of Victoria in Australia. The provision of sport management related education in Australia is a relatively recent development. The oldest course is not yet 20 years old. As a discipline, sport studies in general and sport management in particular alternate between emulating older and more established disciplines and their teaching styles and developing new and innovative teaching methods that are appropriate to dynamic and changing sport and business environments.

The Sport Administration program has approximately 300 undergraduate students across four-year levels. Students entering the program have come directly from high school, have completed a course at a technical and further education college which allows them to articulate into the degree program, or have been employed (depending on the number of years, the student might qualify as mature-age) and are returning to study. Students entering the course directly from high school are typically in the top 30% of their cohort. All students entering the program have good oral and written communication skills and are proficient in the use of computers and basic software. Students who successfully complete the program may find employment in organizations that vary greatly in size, complexity, context, and orientation, from the Australian Football League, the premier professional sport league, to thousands of local and regional associations and clubs.

In 2002-2003, Sport Administration teaching staff received a Curriculum Innovation Grant to redevelop *Sport Administration Foundations,* a core first-year course within the Sport Administration program. The course is designed to introduce students to four aspects of management within a sport specific context: strategic planning, organizational structure, stakeholders, and human resource management. The redevelopment of this course had several objectives: (1) to increase the flexibility of delivery so that the course was easier to deliver across two geographically-separated campuses; (2) to decrease delivery costs, taking into account the fact that the course is delivered across two campuses; (3) to integrate the teaching of the theoretical and practical components of the course more effectively; (4) to improve student learning outcomes; and (5) to enhance the motivation of the students by aligning the learning process with the work environment students would encounter after graduation.

Academic Issues

The revised course, in which e-learning is now a major feature, is based on a series of case studies from real sporting organizations. Rather than passively attend lectures and participate in tutorial discussions by answering "set" questions, students in the revised course access a range of case study material from the organizations being studied, as well as supplementary theoretical material. They use this material to examine the ways in which sport organizations engage in specific management processes such as developing a vision statement or designing an orientation and induction process for their employees.

In taking the course, students follow a six phase learning process for each of the four core management areas. First, students are introduced to the case study information and theoretical foundations of a topic, such as strategic planning, via a face-to-face session. One such session is conducted for each management area. Second, students access the case study material provided to them on CD-ROM. This material includes a range of sport organization documents and material, such as strategic plans, annual reports, and a short video interview with a key person. In phase two, students also access key readings that illustrate the core theoretical principles underpinning the core management areas. Third, students develop a basic statement of principles for each of the major topics that they are able to illustrate from the real-world examples. For example, in the case of the topic, "Vision Statements," the student completes the reading associated with vision statements, interacts with the relevant case study material, and then develops a statement that clearly illustrates what a vision statement is, what would constitute an effective one, and how a poorly written statement could be improved. Fourth, students use their statement of principles and knowledge gained from the case studies to engage in face-to-face workshop discussions, in which core principles are refined and confirmed. Fifth, as a group, and as part of the face-to-face workshop, students use the case study resources to generalize about the core principles of the topic and develop a common statement of principles. Sixth and finally, in a subgroup of the larger workshop groups, students use the common statement of principles to write, for example, a vision statement for a fictional sport organization. This sixth phase is conducted via asynchronous online discussion.

Administrative Issues

Because the materials used in this course included video clips as well as a substantial body of material in the form of PDF files, many of which included graphics, they were provided to students on a CD-ROM. The materials could have been distributed online via WebCT. However, providing them on CD-ROM eliminated the problem of excessive download times along with the attendant cost in cases where students are relying on a dial-up rather than a broadband connection. Providing the materials on CD-ROM also allowed them to be reproduced at the highest resolution.

Eight national, state, and local sport organizations were invited to contribute case study material. These organizations ranged from the national Australian Football League to the local Yarraville Cricket Club. All sport organizations that were invited to participate did so. A meeting was held with each organization. In the meeting, documents related to the organization's strategic plan, organizational structures, and human management practices were collected from the organization. It was explained that the materials would be used to complement teaching of the theory of sport management. The meeting was also used to record an interview with one of the managers in each organization for inclusion on the CD-ROM.

The importance of limiting download times was increased by the fact that at the Sunbury Campus where one of the workshop groups was based, the timetable had been arranged so that most students needed to be on campus two or three days a week and were therefore much more reliant on use of online connections than they would have been had they been studying on-campus five days a week.

The university has adopted WebCT as its centrally supported platform for online delivery. The version of WebCT that the university currently uses is Campus Edition 4.1.

In the case of this particular project, all staff teaching the course were involved in its development, and as a result the staff development needs were mainly met during the development phase. However, the Curriculum Innovation Program provided for instructional design support for the project, something that is not generally available to staff teaching online.

Program Evaluation

The *Sport Administrations Foundations* course was evaluated using Victoria University's "Student Evaluation of Subject" questionnaire, that is available at Victoria University for evaluation of all its courses. In this questionnaire, students are asked 10 standard questions related to the delivery of the course, as well as two open-ended questions about those aspects of the course the students found most and least helpful/stimulating.

In response to the open-ended question asking which aspects were most helpful/stimulating, students answered:

- "The concept of developing your own hypothetical organization;"
- "Knowledge of the inside of sporting clubs;"

- "Learning about behind the scenes of an organization and how everyone's role at a club is important;"
- "Real life situation for the project;"
- "Readings on disk;"
- "The CD-ROM, with all the required reading, was very helpful. It saved a lot of time, and also gave a variety of examples;"
- "Building an organization;"
- "Learning about a sporting organization was worthwhile;"
- "Applying the principles by creating our own fictional organization;"
- "Working in groups made me a person that now can effectively communicate with people."

The open-ended question asked students to indicate which aspects of the course they found least helpful. This yielded answers that showed that students were still critical of some aspects of the course. In particular, some students complained that although the CD-ROM was significantly less expensive than a textbook, they found that some of the readings were difficult to read off the screen. What they were referring to was the quality of the page image. In revising a course such as this, it is important that any digital or e-learning resources are as professionally produced as possible. It is likely that as Internet databases become more widespread, in terms of content and usage, original PDFs will be able to be obtained, thus increasing quality and minimizing student complaints.

Students clearly grasped the relevance of the course to the sport industry. Incorporating case studies resulted in students actively contributing to workshop discussions and debates and actively participating in teamwork activities. Students were required to read articles on the CD-ROM prior to a workshop so that they could answer questions asked by the tutor. The outcome of this requirement was that students were eager to express their opinions on the article, on related issues, and on the relevance to the case study, prior to question time. When a question was asked of a student, others wanted to extend or debate the points raised. The extent of this student contribution was not expected. There was no need to change or adapt the course because of this increased communication and collaboration. Rather, the willingness of students to contribute enhanced the quality of discussion and assessment that were already built into the course. As these were first year students in a first semester course, their interaction increased their confidence. Their increased confidence then supported their studies in later courses that required student interaction.

Networking and Collaboration

In general, the sport industry is willing to engage in collaborative activities that benefit students in terms of increasing their knowledge of management practices within sport organizations. As a result of incorporating the case studies into the course, the number of students requesting field placements in these organizations increased, and the number of graduating students accepted into the organizations also increased.

In addition to the collaboration that occurred between the industry and the University, cross-campus collaboration also occurred. The course, *Sport Administration Foundations*, was delivered across two university campuses, but the topics and content taught on the two campuses were not aligned. The Curriculum Innovation Grant Program provided an opportunity to strengthen the relationship and flexibility between the cross-campus course lecturers, agree on common topics and content, and thereby decrease delivery costs. The resulting outcomes were stronger teaching and learning practices, incorporation of real-world case studies, and increased student satisfaction.

Policy Implications

The course has had less impact on other courses within the Sport Administration program at higher year levels. This probably is accounted for by the fact that the costs involved in the design and development stage of this project were met from centrally provided funds, rather than being met at the departmental level. Staff teaching at higher levels within the program have not received any financial support to adopt or adapt the approach used throughout this project. The Sport Administration program as a whole has, however, adopted the use of CD-ROMs to deliver resources and materials across a range of courses at all year levels. This development has proved a welcome departure from traditional "reading packs," and staff and student feedback has been overwhelmingly positive. The CD-ROM format enables students to access course materials off-line, which enables them to save resources if they are studying from home and not accessing the computer facilities on-campus. At a base level, the amount of information available to students has also increased via the CD-ROM, while the cost of accessing the materials has decreased.

Victoria University is committed to work-integrated learning and to strengthening connections between the University and its communities. However, more robust institutional structures will need to be activated for the development of case study CD-ROMs to be adopted more widely within the University. While this project was developed with the aid of an internal grant, most course teams do not have access to such funds. Neither do they have access to the types of support that in this instance the grant funds were used to provide.

Development of resource materials for teaching online is a costly activity. The major revision of *Sport Administration Foundations* that has been described here was made possible by the funds received through the Curriculum Innovation Grant Program. However, most course teams do not have access to funds for course revision. The amount of time that teams can devote to course development on a year-to-year basis is quite limited. To extend the program, the University will need to develop and expand the Curriculum Innovation Grant Program.

Sustainability and Conclusion

It is well known that the major cost of course revision is the cost of the staff time involved in undertaking the design, development, and production of the learning materials. The Curriculum Innovation Grant covered most of the cost of the staff time in this instance. The recurrent costs involved in delivering the course following renewal have not been greatly different from the costs of delivering the course in its previous form. The CD-ROM is sold to students at a price set to recover the cost of pressing and distribution. Readings that exceeded the University's licence to distribute to students were placed in the library for them to read. The overwhelming response from students to the provision of resource materials on CD-ROM rather than requiring them to purchase textbooks, search the literature, and scan the Web for possible case studies has been positive. Students considered the CD-ROM to be inexpensive and found the materials to be easily accessible in that form.

Two years have passed since the introduction of this set of case studies. The readings and case studies have been updated, and new case studies have been added. Whether it will be possible to continue relying on the goodwill of sport organizations for sourcing case studies remains to be seen. The information required to construct a worthwhile and engaging case study that enables students to develop a complex picture of an organization may be of a sensitive nature, and if this is the case, the organization may be reluctant to participate.

Given that sport is a highly commercialized field and that the intellectual property represented by contents of strategic planning documents may be considered a valuable commodity, it may be necessary in the future to structure the relationships with sport organizations as commercial partnerships.

The approach could be extended to other courses and programs through central allocation of funding. This in turn would be likely to yield additional benefits, including closer links with industry and greater community engagement, both strategic priorities of the university.

Lessons Learned

1. If funding is available to develop the case studies, use some of this for hiring of an assistant to produce the resource materials and recording of videos.

Compilation of the materials for a case study CD-ROM requires a lot of organization. Responsibility for overseeing the production tasks is best put in the hands of a project officer rather than left for teaching staff, who are already likely to be heavily loaded, to organize.

2. Leave sufficient time ahead of when the course is being offered to contact participating organizations, gather resources, and conduct interviews.

It is easy to underestimate the amount of time required to obtain agreement from organizations to participate in a project like this and then to assemble and prepare resources. Completing these tasks requires forward planning.

3. Leave a month for compilation of documents onto the CD-ROM.

Compiling a CD-ROM is tedious and time consuming. If the task is rushed, mistakes are likely to be made that will then require even more time to rectify.

4. Leave at least one month for testing of the CD-ROM.

The CD-ROM needs to work flawlessly. To be certain that it will, all aspects of the structure of the information on the disk need to be checked.

5. Compile the case study materials so that they can be easily updated.

The currency of documents used in a case study will diminish with time. It is important to design the CD-ROM containing the case study materials so that documents can be replaced with a minimum of effort.

6. Plan for a two-year renewal cycle for case studies.

Case studies themselves can become less relevant with changes in the work environment. It is therefore prudent to plan to replace one or more of the case studies every couple of years.

7. For a case study mixed-mode unit to work, part of the curriculum must focus on development of teamwork and communication skills.

For students to work collaboratively it is likely that they will need some additional skills in teamwork and communication. Opportunities should be built into the structure of the course for students to acquire these skills.

8. Start with an orientation session in a computer laboratory.

Students need to be confident that they understand the structure of the course and can use the resources provided to support it. Scheduling an orientation session at the start of the course allows students to resolve any uncertainties they may have.

9. Do not expect large organizations to be keen to serve as cases.

Larger organizations have more information of a type that is required for a case study but are also more reluctant to make it public. The experience of our lack of success in involving large organizations has led us to consider that a way of pursuing creation of resource materials for this type of model in the future may be through entry into commercial partnerships.

10. If you are approaching small organizations, start with a much larger pool of organizations than you need to include.

Small organizations are quite willing to serve as cases but often do not have the documents needed for a suitable case study.

Best Practices

For instructors wanting to use case studies in their online teaching, the following three practices are especially recommended, in order of their importance:

1. Engage students fully within e-learning environments by integrating the study of theoretical concepts with real-world scenarios.
2. Combine theory with practice by using a sequence of (a) individual self-study of documents and resources belonging to real-world cases, (b) large group discussion of theoretical and practical issues, and (c) collaborative small group creation of fictional organizations.
3. Engage students and encourage them to study the case in detail by including a variety of activities on the CD-ROM. A range of core and supplementary documents and multimedia resources must complement theoretical readings that introduce students to the core concepts.

References

Barr, R., & Tagg, J. (1995). From teaching to learning: A new paradigm for undergraduate education. *Change, 27*(6), 12-25.

Barrow, H. S., & Tamblyn, R. M. (1980). *Problem-based learning: An approach to medical education.* New York: Springer.

Bennett, G. (2002). Web-based instruction in sport management. *Sport Management Review, 5*(1), 45-68.

Boud, D., & Feletti, G. (1997). *The challenge of problem-based learning.* London: Kogan Page.

Kolb, D. A. (1984). *Experiential learning.* Englewood Cliffs, NJ: Prentice-Hall.

Kreber, C. (2001). Learning experientially through case studies? A conceptual analysis. *Teaching in Higher Education, 6*(2), 217-228.

Lehtinen, E. (2002). Developing models for distributed problem-based learning: Theoretical and methodological reflection. *Distance Education, 22*(1), 109-117.

Merseth, K. (1991). The early history of case-based instruction: Insights for teacher education today. *Journal of Teacher Education, 42*(4), 243-249.

Polanyi, M. (1967). *The Tacit Dimension*. New York: Anchor Books.

Raju, P. K., & Sanker, C. S. (1999). Teaching real-world issues through case studies. *Journal of Engineering Education, 88*(4), 501-508.

Schmidt, H. G. (1993). Problem-based learning: An introduction. *Instructional Science, 22*(4), 247-250.

Chapter XII

Experimentation and Challenge: Online Criminology at the University of Bologna

Raffaella Sette, University of Bologna, Italy

Abstract

The online course on criminological topics carried out in an undergraduate course for "Security and Social Control Operators" (Faculty of Political Science "Ruffilli," University of Bologna) represented a real challenge for three different reasons: (1) it was inserted in the syllabus of a three-year undergraduate course that was the first university course in Italy intended for the training of operators to carry out an activity that calls for being able to manage modern investigative, security, and control strategies; (2) it dealt with the teaching of criminology, and it is useful to emphasise that, in Italy, criminology has a difficult time freeing itself from similar disciplines (legal medicine, criminal law, sociology, psychology), even while knowing that it has to maintain a good relationship with them; and (3) it dealt with one of the first online courses activated at the Faculty "Ruffilli." The case study describes and critically analyzes the implementation of the online criminology course.

Introduction

In Italy, there are 79 schools between state-recognized universities and institutes of higher education of which 53.2% are small (fewer than 15,000 students), 35.4% medium-large (between 15,000 and 60,000 students), and 11.4% large (more than 60,000 students) (Liscia, 2004). University studies have been reorganized on the basis of Ministerial Decree No. 509 of 3/11/1999 ("Ruling attributed to the regulations concerning the didactic autonomy of universities"), which has brought about some notable changes with respect to the past:

1. A different organization of degrees: the achievement of a degree (triennial or first level) is foreseen with which one can enter the work world or continue studying toward a biennial specialized degree or do further study through a first level Master's degree. A specialized degree insures advanced level preparation for the exercise of high level professional activities in specific areas. Subsequently, education can continue with a second level master's degree or PhD.
2. A system based on credits, which are the unit of measurement of the overall involvement of a student.
3. A greater impulse for diverse typologies of didactic activity, such as, for example, stages, laboratories, group work, practice, seminars, and also e-learning.

Therefore, an additional milestone was reached with a decree on telecommunication universities on April 17, 2003, signed by the Ministry for Education, University and Research and by the Ministry for Innovation and Technology, which also regulates the institution of the Open University.

The author's triennial experience as the head of an online course in criminology at the University of Bologna, Faculty of Political Science "Ruffilli" was embedded within the limits of this scenario of intellectual, reform, and experimental ferment at various levels. It is important to specify that the University of Bologna is defined as a large university; in fact, according to the statistics reported in the University Yearbook for the academic year 2001-2002, there were 102,856 students enrolled. In regards to the online course of criminology in particular, we dealt with a laboratory-type educational activity provided for in the first level degree course in "Security and Social Control Operators" and which, following an oral final exam, awarded three credits to the student. The online course, which the author organized and ran for three academic years (from 2001-2002 to 2003-2004), as the teacher responsible and the e-tutor, was certainly both an experimental activity, new for the degree course into which it was inserted, and a permanent educational offer given that, until the moment of complete deactivation of the entire degree course, it was regularly inserted into the activities provided for in the syllabus. It is also important to point out that the online criminology course assigned to me represented one of the first initiatives of this type in the panorama of Italian academics in regards to criminological science.

E-Learning Program

The configuration of the first level degree in "Security and Social Control Operators" was also planned on the basis of research carried out for several years by the team of the University of Bologna (Balloni, Bisi, & Sette, 1998; Bisi, 1999; Sette, 1998, 1999). From this research, it emerged that criminology, as an autonomous discipline, is very diffuse in universities around the world while, in Italy, it suffers from identity crisis (Balloni, 2000). In fact, this degree course, based prevalently on subjects linked to criminological sciences, was the first of its kind in Italy and, therefore, represented a challenge to render the autonomy of criminology and its utilization in the professional preparation of security and social control operators more and more current, oriented toward prevention, the repression of forms of conventional, and non-conventional forms of criminality, and capable of planning programs for the protection and support of victims (Balloni & Sette, 2000).

Within this cultural, scientific, and didactic scenario, the online criminology course has taken shape as a significant piece of the overall mosaic of the educational curriculum of the students having, as its fundamental objective, that of acquiring the necessary capability of carrying out an activity that presupposes knowing how to manage advanced investigative, control and security strategies oriented toward the analysis of criminal phenomena and the prevention of criminality, bearing in mind the necessity of contributing to the well-being of the population by contributing to the growth of the quality of life.

In fact, in the current social context, characterized by change and vulnerability, security and social control operators have to be equipped with adequate methodological instruments and have to be put into condition to improve their professionalism in a continuous way, imposing education as a process that passes from an initial starting-up phase to continuous learning that leads to constant growth (Bisi & Sette, 2004; Sette, 2003).

With regard to the needs of the professional education of security and social control operators cited previously, given that the evolution of the role of these operators requires them to work in concert with the population and to resolve the problems that undermine the security of citizens from the point of view of the operative model of community policing, such a didactic environment represents an ideal place for the attainment of these educational goals since it allows students to work in groups and it encourages the refining of some capacities such as, for example, those of organization and mediation (Sette, 2004).

Therefore, the online course provides for the study of subjects considered fundamental for reaching some of the educational objectives reported previously such as, for example, the analysis of some types of criminality through the study of "classic" authors, the in-depth study of various aspects of juvenile criminality, or the prevention of the victimization and support of the victims, through study methodologies and innovative research.

Academic Issues

The planning of the online course was divided into two closely correlated macro-phases: the real didactic project and the project of the architecture of communication functional for the development and the management of the educational activities programmed (Trentin, 2001). In regards to the educational project, on the basis of the constructivist approach to e-learning, the educational modality of the online course was based on the collection and integration of purely constructivist methodologies of "digital didactics" with those of face-to-face education that are made up of a mix of blended education (Ferri, 2003). In particular, one is dealing with a form of constructivism particularly attentive to social implications, essentially Vygotskian in nature. In summary, three principal concepts characterize it: (1) knowledge is a product of active construction of the subject; (2) it is anchored in a concrete context; (3) it is carried out using particular forms of collaboration and social negotiation (Jonassen, 1994).

On the level of educational planning, therefore, it is necessary that the attention is focused on the preparation of a "learning community" (Calvani & Rotta, 2000) and, for this reason, the online course placed discussion in the Web forum at the center of the educational activity (online collaboration) (this will be specified in detail later).

The blended solution, in such sense, is made up of a synergetic and flexible mix of different modalities and different systems of education realized in an integrated and customized way where online and face-to-face reinforce each other reciprocally (Liscia, 2004).

In particular, the methodological solution adopted is that which, in the literature, is defined as integrated or collaborative typology in which the values of the "virtual class" and the collaboration assume a central role (Rotta & Ranieri, 2005). The contents of the course are fluid and dynamic, and this implies that these are also co-constructed and negotiated through interaction between the participants and with the e-tutor (who assumes the role of a moderator and organizer of a learning community). The basic idea on which approaches of this type are based is that learning consists in the formation of a constructive dialogue and social negotiation of the meanings, and it is for this reason that notable importance was given to analysis of the interactions that were produced in the virtual class (as is described later in the section on "Networking and Collaboration").

In fact, the following are part of the didactic platform: (a) a single face-to-face lesson at the beginning of the course, (b) online collaboration, (c) resources available on the Internet, and (d) teacher-tutor online and face-to-face.

a. **Face-to-face lesson:** Contrary to the traditional educational point of view, the network is always available; on the network, you overcome traditional time-slots, and there is no fixed schedule (Amatiste & Quagliata, 2004). Therefore, in the online course in question, only one face-to-face lesson was held, preliminary and preparatory to subsequent activity during which the course was presented from the point of view of the CMC (Computer Mediated Communication), analyzing the technical elements of the software platform and managing some organizational aspects relative to deadlines, to the distribution of work within a typical week, to the operative modalities of collective work, to the rules of netiquette and the verification of learning. The face-to face lesson also had the aim of sharing the educational objectives of the course and formulating an "educational pact" with the students (Trentin, 2001) and began with a discussion of the contents and the modalities of fruition of the course and which concluded with a final evaluation of the meeting (distribution of a questionnaire to the participants).

b. **Online collaboration:** Included in this "space" are all the activities that the virtual learning community realizes and that support collaborative learning. These activities are separated into: (1) thematic discussions; (2) working in groups; (3) research and exchange of information. In the area of thematic discussions, by means of a Web forum, the students make suggestions and exchange ideas and opinions about the subject under discussion ("Topic"), which are decided on by the teacher/tutor during the planning phase of the didactics. The Web forum is, therefore, to be considered like a virtual learning space in which one verifies the active and knowledgeable participation of learners in the learning community (Calvani & Rotta, 2000). In the forums, the students, by means of a minimum number of interventions established by the e-tutor, make proposals, exchange ideas and opinions relative to the topic, which is the object of the discussion. In this virtual sphere of discussion and collaborative learning, moderators (the teacher-tutor) introduced the subject and moderated the debates. In particular, the prime mover is the student who assumes the job of pointing out the principal topics, which are the object of the discussion and suggesting hints useful for reflection. As e-tutor, the author was responsible for stimulating and moderating the forum by means of the following types of interventions (Rotta & Ranieri, 2005): (1) interventions to remedy the discussion, oriented to bringing the discussion back to acceptable lines in those cases in which the contributions of the students showed uncertainties or tended to go off-course; (2) hints for reflection or interventions that invited them to think about what they were discussing; (3) stimuli for in-depth discussion, giving them further questions, materials, and integrative information; (4) interventions in order to accelerate the discussion, that is, strategic suggestions for going ahead in moments of impasse.

Each debate then presupposes a final activity carried out by the summarizing leader, that is, by a student who, on the basis of the contributions furnished by the students in the Web forum, prepared a final paper, which assumes the form of the examination paper like real collaborative work. In regards to group work, the students collaborate among themselves (each group composed of about 10 people) to realize autonomous projects on themes suggested by the teacher-tutor. Finally, in the area of researching information, using the Internet, the students have the possibility of searching for information related to the themes to be studied. The reports had to be accompanied by a logical synthesis of the content of the sites found and, furthermore, they had to dwell on the motivations, which were the basis of their choice. With this set of collaborative activity on the Internet, we would like, therefore, to propose a mental model. The space of intervention and discussion is part of the perceptive and cognitive field of the student, being realized as a mental place inside of which and through which information fluctuates, organized in malleable forms yet anchored and logically ordered according to a concept of flow/hierarchy, making the collection of many diversified notions easy (Pravettoni, 2002).

c. **Resources available on the Internet:** The technological platform used, NiceNet, available free on the Internet (www.nicenet.org), constitutes the interface for the entire course. It is user-friendly, and it is organized conceptually like a physical place; therefore, it is possible to associate the different activities with a "space" in which to carry them out. The virtual places activated are: a space for carrying out discussions asynchronously ("conferencing"); a virtual "library" ("link sharing") where the students report the references to the online material linked to the subjects of the course; a space to file documents and the work of the students ("documents"); an agenda with appointments and deadlines ("class schedule"); a space for internal personal mail ("personal messages"); and a space for a virtual class list ("class members").

d. **Teacher-tutor online and face-to-face:** The role of the teacher-tutor during the online activities was, for the most part, that of observing and, if necessary, stimulating the groups and the correct carrying out of the collaborative work. The teacher, therefore, needs to be aware of the rhythm, like the conductor of an orchestra, and have a sharp eye, like a film director; the teacher has to pick up the movements that the learning community carries out and interpret their needs and expectations, so as to immediately come up with an adequate intervention for each eventuality. Finally, almost inversely, you have to be able to accept the impossibility of having total control and the eventuality of letting a consistent part of the process slip away since, if a community is formed, it often has an uncontrollable evolution and its own rules (Innocenzi, 2004). To this end, when it was necessary, the resources of personal e-mail or face-to-face meetings during the hours the teacher received (more than once a week during the semester of the course) were also used to correct or modify the pathway of the process.

Administrative Issues

In regards to the project of the architecture of communication, the choice of the telematic service appropriate for supporting the educational activity was oriented toward an e-learning platform that put at our disposal a series of practical aspects calibrated on the necessity of a long-distance student (access to educational materials and the possibility of interpersonal communication) and that was based on the metaphor of traditional educational environment (the classroom).

Of all the software available, NiceNet was chosen because, on an equal level of functionality with respect to other platforms, (1) it was a free resource; (2) it was user-friendly and, therefore, did not require special computer ability to use it; (3) it offered guarantees of stability in time (in the three years of activation, every online course took place during an academic semester for about three months); (4) it put technology at the disposal of the virtual class, which permits the definition of subjects to discuss and the opening of a Web forum on each of them, the definition of a calendar of deadlines, which is also published on the homepage of the site, the exchange of messages so that they are visible to the entire class or part of it, the possibility of sharing files of various types, and the sharing of network resource links.

Therefore, NiceNet software was chosen because it facilitates discussion and the development of subjects, furnishing the students with the possibility of verifying that their own intervention is posted under the right topic and, in answering the intervention of a colleague, of clicking on the "reply" command in order to render the debate a "threaded discussion forum" (Bates, 2003).

From a graphic point of view, the NiceNet graphic of the virtual class appears as in Figure 1.

Finally, from the point of view of the visibility of the course outside the class, NiceNet software allows protection of the virtual space by assigning a username and password to each student. The reasons for opting for the "closure" of the site to those not in the virtual class were of substantially two types: (1) protection of the password is a way of controlling

Figure 1. NiceNet screen shot

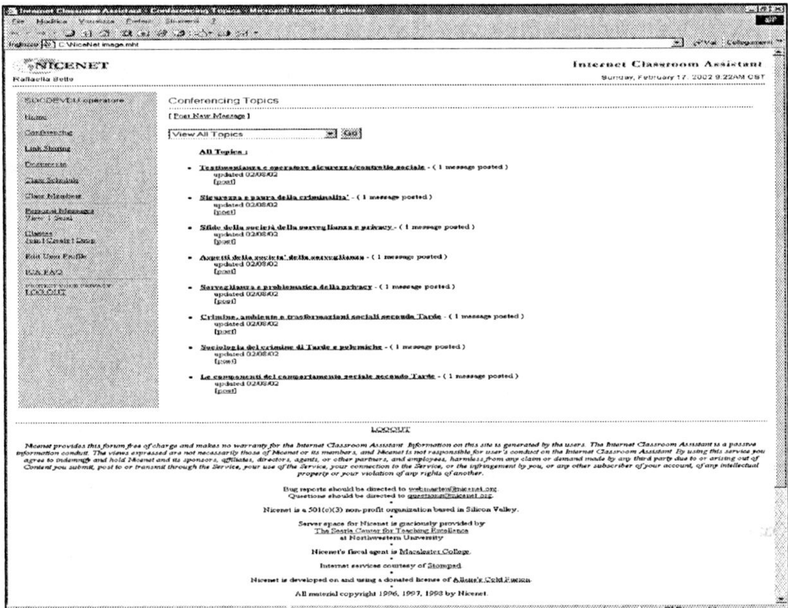

the number of students and to ensure, therefore, that only those who have the right can accede to the course and (2) the aspect of the protection of confidentiality, which is equally important.

This closure also permits the elimination of the problems relative to the intellectual property rights of the material and products used.

In the three years of activation, the courses represented an obligatory activity for the students and were attended by a high number of students (157 in the academic year 2001-2002, 131 in 2002-2003, and 130 in 2003-2004). Given the high number of students to manage, for practical reasons, every year the students were divided into two groups, each of which gained access to the NiceNet technological platform with a different course code.

Program Evaluation

There are two aspects to discuss in particular on this vast subject: (1) evaluation of the activities carried out by the students on the part of the teacher and (2) evaluation of the students relative to the course (content, didactic methods, organizational and technical aspects, merits, and defects).

The first aspect refers to "evaluation of profit," to all those operations traditionally carried out by the teacher with regard to the activities of the students; these can be distinguished into summative evaluation and formative evaluation (Calvani & Rotta, 2000).

Summative evaluation of profit is a type of evaluation that is carried out at the end of the learning activity while the traditional one consists in giving grades and, in that sense, our obligations consisted of fixing exam sessions, according to Article 16 of the Didactic Regulation of the University of Bologna, to be carried out face-to-face, with the aim of assigning a grade to the student, expressed in thirtieths, which also allowed them to get the credits linked to the educational activity.

Dealing with a course carried out online, certainly based on individual study but, for the most part, founded on discussions and retrieval of information from the Internet and collaborative work, here one has to particularly deal with the formative evaluation of profit, which is dynamic and indicative and which consists in the analysis of the contents of the messages that are exchanged on the Web forum and from which it is possible to obtain information on the students, their method of learning, and on the strategies that they use in dealing with problematic situations. In summary, this type of evaluation is based on the assumption that each message has a particular meaning, both as a single contribution and in relation to those of the other participants, and that analysis of the contents of this messaging is based on distinct levels of in-depth study: "what was said" regarding the contents of the discussion, "how it was said," "what was the process and the strategies adopted in dealing with the contents," "how each single message was linked to the others/or generated others" (Trentin, 2001).

We asked ourselves about the opportunity of evaluating the participation in the online discussion forums and the author believes that, to this end, we need to reflect on epistemological questions and also examine the results expected from the learning (Bates, 2003).

Even though we are dealing with an activity, which is expensive in terms of time, considering the pros and cons carefully, it was an opportunity to evaluate the students in the context of their interventions in the online forums. In order to do this, on the basis of the previously cited theoretical considerations, a quantitative criteria (the obligation of each student was that of intervening at least once a week on each topic of discussion) and qualitative parameters (i.e., in terms of fairness, the pertinence of the themes dealt with, command of the subject, consistency, modification of the contents, and lexical properties) were fixed. When the evaluation was carried out, the results were communicated to each student by e-mail, specifying the availability of the course coordinator for a face-to-face meeting to discuss it.

The author believes that the students wish to obtain immediate gratification from what they do, and this is a motive for assigning grades for their online participation. Furthermore, "the main goals of the course are to teach students online participation skills, collaborative learning skills, or academic discourse" (Bates, 2003, p. 35), and, therefore, this is an additional motivation, which induced us to evaluate the interventions in the online discussion.

At the end of each one, a questionnaire-based survey was conducted amongst students in terms of "evaluation as a monitoring of the process" (Calvani & Rotta, 2000). Overall, these online courses have been received with favor and interest on the part of the students, and, using multivariate analysis called multiple correspondence analysis, three profiles of students defined as "traditionalists," "diplomats," and "innovators" could be outlined. In summary (for an in-depth view of the results of the questionnaire, see Sette, 2004), the variables used for the analysis are:

1. An indicator that synthesizes, with a numeric value, the overall judgements on the quality of the educational activity of the online course as perceived by the students (from a minimum value of 4 in the case in which the content of the course was not at all interesting, the didactic methods were not at all efficacious, the quality of organization was insufficient, and the NiceNet site was difficult to use, to a maximum value of 16, which was the opposite: the content was very interesting, the didactic methods were efficacious, the quality of organization was good, and the NiceNet site was very easy to use). Therefore, the overall quality of the online educational activity can be insufficient (if the indicator is not greater than 9), sufficient (if the indicator has a value of 10 or 11), fairly good (if between 12 and 14), and good (if 15 or 16);
2. A variable relative to the opinion of the students on the percentage to assign to each of the two types of didactics (online and face-to-face with the sum of the two values having to total 100%) for a hypothetical degree course;
3. A variable with which to indicate the eventual practice of a profession, other than that of a student.

In particular, the profile of *traditionalists*, very few, includes those subjects who are only students, who prefer face-to-face didactics, and who evaluated the online educational experience in which they participated as sufficient (in the years 2001-2002 and 2003-2004) and fairly good (in the year 2002-2003). The *diplomats* are those students who practice a profession that has nothing to do with security, investigation, or social control, who do not express a real preference for one of the two forms of didactics (online or face-to-face), putting them on the same plane, and who regard the quality of the online activity offered to be fairly good. Finally, the *innovators* project themselves with optimism toward new things; in a future degree course, they would like the didactics to be online for the most part. Furthermore, they judged the course in which they participated to be good, and, besides being a student, they practice a profession linked to security, investigation, or social control (Sette, 2004). In brief, what emerges is a strong link between the type of student and the type of teaching preferred; the full-time student evidently thinks that one of the precise tasks of his or her own role is to follow the lessons requiring physical presence, while the worker-student considers alternating moments requiring physical presence with online activities profitable or prefers, for the most part, to experience new teaching methods.

As far as the oral exam, which signals the end of the course, is concerned, for example, some held that the large amount of work required was not proportional to the number of credits they received while others perceived it as a "just yardstick" for determining the student's contribution in terms of work. In other terms, this last opinion is based on the fact that the final face-to-face exam with the teacher furnishes the possibility of giving merit to the majority of those who really worked seriously on the online activities and not, instead, to those who took advantage either of the virtual identity or some possibilities offered by the Internet to easily find material so that they could simply transcribe into order to discharge their obligation of taking part in the discussions without working.

It can be said that this latter behavior of plagiarism by some students has been perceived, obviously, as an offence both on the part of the teacher-tutor (who, at various times, punished such an attitude by assigning a new intervention or by assigning negative grades) and on the part of all the other students who intended to work for their educational growth from some positive aspects of their modality of learning and did not want, instead, to only record "instrumental" behavior.

Networking and Collaboration

The "group" has always existed, and, in this sense, it is reassuring to think that the Greeks and Romans utilized groups. The work group, as has been noted, is a certain number of people who know each other, who recognize each other, who have an objective to reach, and who live the sentiment of belonging (Ambrosini, 2001).

In spite of the unquestionable advantages that independence from the space-time restraints offered by e-learning can involve, it is exactly on the side of the relocation of the relationship that a part of the literature has pointed out the critical state of a learning process using the computer. Physical distance can certainly constitute an unknown for the learning relationship; nevertheless, one wonders if the problem can be reduced to overcoming the physical isolation produced by geographical distance and what does the value of physical absence have on the net (Rotta & Ranieri, 2005). An answer to these questions focuses attention on the fact that, from a learning point of view, it is necessary not so much to replace what is physically absent (geographical distance) but, rather, it is necessary "to circulate signs of face-to-face" (Jacquinot, 2000). One of the greatest challenges of e-learning is exactly that of putting into action devices through which the e-student can have the sense of face-to-face understanding in a pedagogical sense or rather can perceive the existence of intercession, which guides him or her in overcoming difficulties, supports him or her emotionally, and helps him or her in the process of learning, construction, and negotiation with his or her conscience (Rotta & Ranieri, 2005).

In this sense, interaction in an online group can be more or less facilitated by an adequate use of telematic instruments. In fact, for example, as an e-tutor, the author often turned to the mailing list to solicit participation, to offer extemporaneous stimuli, which could rekindle interest for the discussion going on, or to send "service communications" that had to be quickly acknowledged by everyone. Instead, we took advantage of the Web forum when, during the collaborative activity of discussion, we wanted to share reflections, co-construct argumentation, or modify books and study materials in a collaborative way.

In this sense, we found it interesting to analyze the interactions, which were produced in the virtual class of one of the last courses, activated, both from a quantitative and a qualitative point of view, taking as a point of empirical reference.

In order to analyze the interactions in the virtual classes, on the inventory of other research that emphasized the efficacy of this instrument for these types of study internally to the virtual community of learning (Mazzoni & Bertolasi, 2005), we utilized social network analysis, which adopts a quantitative-relational approach given that it considers the actors (in this case, the students) and their actions (in this case, the messages exchanged during the discussion in the Web forum) from the point of view of interdependence, linked by relationships that constitute the means for transferring the "flows" or material and immaterial resources (Wasserman & Faust, 1994).

Online discussion was subdivided into two phases (each one relative to two topics of different discussions, established during the planning of the didactics): (1) the victim of a crime and the study of cases based on the particular link that unites the victim and the criminal; (2) socio-criminological aspects of juvenile gypsy deviance in Italy and juvenile justice and, with reference to the quantitative aspect, the following values emerged after analysis:

1st phase: number of students = 73; total number of messages = 129; number of messages per student = 1.77.

2nd phase: number of students = 70; total number of messages = 93; number of messages per student = 1.33.

Following this, we tried to determine the quality of the interaction by using specific analysis of the content of the messages, starting from the study of the reference of each message to the preceding ones, with the aim of defining a map that would graphically demonstrate the links and connections between one message and another, furnishing a sort of "measurement" of the level of interaction inside the virtual class.

In brief, in the first phase, 47 students out of 73 (64% of the total), with various crossed messages of postponement, constituted a network in which the figure of the prime mover was not the center of the interactions. Therefore, probably more than as a point of reference, the prime mover was the one who had the job of opening the discussion within an established date. Instead, in the second phase, it was seen that 36 students out of 70 (51% of the total) constituted a network in which the prime mover was one of the most important points of reference for the discussion.

It can therefore be seen how, in the passage from the first to the second phase of the discussion, a qualitative change of the level of these interactions also corresponds to a quantitative decrease of the interactions: the data, in fact, indicates the increase, in the second phase, of the number of those students who, though having sent one or more messages, did not have an answer or who did not try to activate reciprocal relationships with other students (sending them a message or answering their message) but reported only toward the entire community. Therefore, in the first phase, the discussion is formed apart from the social dynamics that would have been able to be in relatively hierarchy around the role of the leader; the links of the net became more embedded, and the virtual class that this network depicts is equipped with its own propulsive force; in the second phase, instead, this happened in a lesser way even if, in the capacity of tutor, they took part, more than previously, in order to try to stimulate more complex and articulated reactions.

This change can be analyzed from different aspects. The first phase was accompanied by the element of curiosity toward new things, which stimulated active participation; the first phase also provided for discussion on case studies relative to different situations of being victimized by a crime, which perhaps stimulated the interest of the participants even more because it permitted, in Dewey fashion, the construction of a circular flow between theory and practice that allowed creating knowledge in view of a specific objective to be reached, and, finally perhaps, in the second phase, the "end-of-semester exhaustion" factor played an important role.

Sustainability and Conclusion

Literature on the subject of e-learning emphasizes that, on the subject of sustainability and quality of the educational offering, it is to be hoped that, behind an online course, there is an articulate staff composed of at least a teacher, tutors in an adequate number for the number of students and personnel for technical-logistical support (Khan, 2005). It has also been suggested that, in the phase of preliminary planning, in order to verify sustainability, it is necessary to answer the following three questions (Rotta & Ranieri, 2005): (1) How many e-tutors are necessary for the educational project that one intends to carry out? (2) How is it possible to calculate with relative accuracy, the obligation that will be asked of each e-tutor in relation to the assignments that will be assigned? (3) How to calculate the cost of an e-tutor in order to avoid both excess and waste?

In our experience, it was not possible to carry out all these evaluations, and as we carried out the role of teacher-tutor alone, it was very difficult from the point of view of managing the workload and bringing to completion the complex, but truly stimulating, assignment of technical, organizational, social, and conceptual nature.

From a pedagogical point of view of an online activity, we believe that, thanks to this modality, if used strategically for specific objectives, one is capable of educating an individual by helping with the memorization of ideas, actively working them out and sharing them with others to have information, to understand that to have it, it is necessary to give (constancy of presence in the area, sense of social responsibility), and that to give it, it is necessary to have it and to find it (stimulus for research, observation, and analysis), in a virtual cycle of common and personal enrichment (Pravettoni, 2002).

Furthermore, since the idea of instituting telematic universities is new for Italy, we believe that e-learning is fundamental in order to furnish the students with the possibility of personalizing the educational pathways as well as allowing them to take advantage of university instruction as lifelong learning and also reaching the sector of the population that would otherwise not have the possibility of participating.

Finally, from the point of view of the students, we hope that they did not appreciate only the utilitarian side of the online activity (anytime and anywhere learning) but that they become more and more capable of identifying its potentiality to be used cyclically in the course of their professional life.

Lessons Learned

1. It is necessary to put aside the myth of the inexpensiveness of e-learning because it is a system that requires enormous highly competent human resource abilities. In fact,

we had to take courses of specialization in order to learn how to carry out the role of an e-tutor, and, in the three academic years of the activation of the online courses in criminology, due to the lack of additional economic resources, our didactic obligation was notably superior to that which it would have been if the criminology courses had been of the traditional face-to-face type, also due to the high number of participants. On this subject, Rowntree holds that, "And yet, economic constraints being what they are, tutors are likely to be pressured to accept higher student:tutor ratios. Tutors in organizations that have adopted resource-based or distance learning are already complaining about their increased workload. They are often rewarded for their ingenuity in finding ways of teaching students at a distance by being given more students to teach on campus. And this can easily push the support of their distant students into their own time" (Rowntree, 1999).

2. It is necessary to make the academic environment understand that an online course is not necessarily "series B" teaching just as a traditional face-to-face lesson is not necessarily "series A" teaching. Literature on this subject confirms the perceptions we have from our experience of teacher/e-tutor; in regards to e-learning, in Italy, above all in the academic world, the idea according to which it is something structurally inferior to face-to-face teaching, which is considered the optimal reference mark, is still widespread (Calvani & Rotta, 2000), even if the 2003 law on telematic universities is certainly contributing to a change in the cultural climate.
3. The tasks of the e-learning teachers have to reckon with a larger number of variables, part of which is new (organizational tasks, structural tasks, social tasks).
4. It is necessary to change the way in which the progress of the student is measured: evaluations, to be carried out during the course and not only at the conclusion of the learning process, in which the quality of the interaction and the capacity of elaborating the collaborative products are also measured.
5. E-learning is capable of responding to the capacity of comprehension and learning of each student with an adequate rhythm.
6. The virtual class furnishes the possibility of raising the minimum level of active participation with respect to traditional classes.
7. From a psychological point of view, the virtual class offers the opportunity of keeping the anxiety levels of the participants low given that there is less direct comparison with the others.
8. Masking the identity of the students can cause forms of lack of commitment or, worse, the substitution of people in the carrying out of the activities.
9. Group online work can present problematic aspects given that each activity inevitably undergoes a certain delay, therefore, a wait that can also be frustrating. To get around the fact that, in this way, it is more difficult to make decisions, it is necessary to wait for some groups to remove themselves from the online environment and meet face-to-face for discussion.
10. Even running the risk of increasing the workload of the teacher, it is important to organize face-to-face "debriefing" meetings with small groups of students, at least at the end of the first phases of collaborative activity online in order to discuss what had

happened online and in order to improve organizational and communicative strategies.

Best Practices

1. Make a clear agreement with the person responsible for assigning the online didactic activity about the technical support and human resources requirements in order not to run the risk of underestimating and of being underestimated, perhaps playing down, the experience of online teaching. "We cannot realistically promote such learner-centered computer conferencing as a new, low-cost, mass medium" (Rowntree, 1999).
2. Distribute an evaluation questionnaire to the students, even during the course, because, from the point of view of the students, this makes them feel like social actors participating in the learning process and, from the point of view of the teacher, this allows the merits and the defects of the online activity to emerge and the gathering of data on aspects that eventually need to be modified.
3. Availability of communication and meetings with the students and speed in trying to gather, as far as possible, their requests. In our opinion, the "virtual presence" should not be transformed into "real distance" in the e-learning course.

References

Amatiste, S., & Quagliata, A. (2004). Uno sguardo d'assieme, fra teoria e tecnica. In R. Maragliano (Ed.), *Pedagogie dell'e-learning* (pp. 3-41). Roma-Bari: Laterza.

Ambrosini, M. (2001). Gruppi di lavoro online e gruppi di lavoro "reali." *Risorse Umane in Azienda, 82*(12), 6-8.

Balloni, A., Bisi, R., & Sette, R. (1998). La didattica in criminologia: L'evoluzione di una disciplina e l'esigenza di una professionalità. *Rassegna Italiana di Criminologia, 1*(9), 23-53.

Balloni, A. (2000). Criminalità, scienze criminologiche e prospettive future. In A. Balloni & R. Sette (Eds.), *Didattica in criminologia applicata. Formazione degli operatori della sicurezza e del controllo sociale*. Bologna: Clueb.

Balloni, A., & Sette, R. (Eds.). (2000). *Didattica in criminologia applicata. Formazione degli operatori della sicurezza e del controllo sociale*. Bologna: Clueb.

Bates, A. W. (2003). Supporting online learning. *Asian Journal of Distance Education, 1*(1), 20-38.

Bisi, R. (1998). (Ed.). *Criminology teachings from theory to professional training.* Bologna: Clueb.

Bisi, R. (1999). Teaching and professional training in criminology. *European Journal of Crime, Criminal Law and Criminal Justice, 7*(2), 103-129.

Bisi, R., & Sette, R. (2004). Trasformazioni sociali e nuove esigenze di formazione professionale. In A. Febbrajo, M. Raiteri, & A. La Spina (Eds.), *Cultura giuridica e politiche pubbliche in Italia* (pp. 207-222). Milano: Giuffrè.

Calvani, A., & Rotta, M. (2000). *Fare formazione in Internet.* Trento: Erikson.

Draves, W. (2000). *Teaching online.* River Falls: LERN Books.

Ferri, P. (2003). Click, s'impara?. In R. C. D. Nacamulli (Ed.), *La formazione il cemento e la rete* (pp. 47-72). Milano: Etas.

Innocenzi, S. (2004). Essere docente online. In R. Maragliano (Ed.), *Pedagogie dell'e-learning* (pp. 93-127). Roma-Bari: Laterza.

Jonassen, D. H. (1994, April). Thinking technology, toward a constructivistic design model. *Educational Technology, 34*, 34-37.

Khan, B. H. (2005). A comprehensive e-learning model. *Journal of E-Learning and Knowledge Society, 1*(1), 33-44.

Liscia, R. (Ed.). (2004). *E-learning. Stato dell'arte e prospettive di sviluppo.* Milano: Apogeo.

Mazzoni, E., & Bertolasi, S. (2005). La Social Network Analysis (SNA) applicata alle comunità virtuali per l'apprendimento: Analisi strutturale delle interazioni all'interno dei Web forum. *Journal of E-Learning and Knowledge Society, 1*(2), 243-257.

Pravettoni, G. (2002). *Web psychology.* Milano: Guerini Editore.

Rotta, M., & Ranieri, M. (2005). *E-tutor: Identità e competenze. Un profilo professionale per l'e-learning.* Trento: Erikson.

Rowntree, D. (1999). *The tutor's role in teaching via computer conferencing.* Retrieved June 17, 2004, from http://www-iet.open.ac.uk/pp/D.G.F.Rowntree/derek.html

Sette, R. (1998). Courses in criminology in different parts of the world. In R. Bisi (Ed.), *Criminology teachings from theory topProfessional training* (pp. 24-47). Bologna: Clueb.

Sette, R. (1999). *L'insegnamento della criminologia nelle Università e in altre istituzioni: Rapporto di ricerca.* Bologna: Clueb.

Sette, R. (2000). L'attività seminariale nell'ambito del corso di diploma universitario per operatore della sicurezza e del controllo sociale. In A. Balloni & R. Sette (Eds.), *Didattica in criminologia applicata. Formazione degli operatori della sicurezza e del controllo sociale* (pp. 105-126). Bologna: Clueb.

Sette, R. (2003). La preparazione professionale degli operatori della sicurezza e del controllo sociale. In E. Rezzara (Ed.), *Globalizzazione della criminalità* (pp. 117-128). Vicenza: Edizioni Rezzara.

Sette, R. (2004, October). Criminology online: An Italian experience. *European Journal of Open and Distance Learning, 2*, 1-13.

Trentin, G. (2001). *Dalla formazione a distanza all'apprendimento in rete.* Milano: FrancoAngeli.

Wasserman, S., & Faust, K. (1994). *Social network analysis. Methods and applications.* Cambridge, MA: Cambridge University Press.

Chapter XIII

Learning Computer Science over the Web: The ViSCoS Odyssey

Jarkko Suhonen, University of Joensuu, Finland

Erkki Sutinen, University of Joensuu, Finland

Abstract

Most of Finland's landmass consists of vast, sparsely populated rural areas. Even though there are high school students in these areas who are interested in computer science (CS), and especially in programming, the educational institutions that they attend in these rural areas cannot offer them more advanced levels of CS studies. To meet this need, the Department of Computer Science of the University of Joensuu, Finland, has devised for such students an e-learning program called ViSCoS (Virtual Studies of Computer Science). This program enables ViSCoS students to study first-year university-level computer science courses through the medium of the Web. A total of 109 students completed the ViSCoS program between the years 2000-2005. The designers of the program concomitantly created a number of digital learning environments that supports ViSCoS learning and teaching activities. The FOrma*tive* DEvelopment Method *(FODEM), an action research-oriented design method used in the ViSCoS program, has enabled gradual development in the program.*

Introduction

The *ViSCoS* (Virtual Studies of Computer Science) e-learning program enables students who would otherwise not have any opportunity to engage in advanced computer science studies to study first-year university-level computer science courses over the Web (ViSCoS, 2005). The ViSCoS curriculum is divided into three main areas: (1) *the preliminaries of information and communication technology (ICT), (2) the basics of programming with Java, and (3) an introduction to computer science* (Haataja, Suhonen, Sutinen, & Torvinen, 2001). ViSCoS courses require about 600 hours of study (which is equivalent to 25 credit points in the European Credit Transfer System [ECTS]). The courses are undertaken in three half-year semesters. The whole program is designed for completion over one-and-a-half years (Torvinen, 2004).

There were three main reasons why a program such as this was urgently needed. Firstly, many high schools in Finland could not offer university-level ICT studies in spite of the fact that there were students who wanted to study ICT (but most especially programming). Secondly, the Department of Computer Science at the University of Joensuu needed some means of identifying and recruiting talented high school CS students. This was important also from the industrial point of view. Thirdly, the ViSCoS program would serve as a kind of research laboratory for the development of new educational technology solutions for online learning, especially within our own research group (http://cs.joensuu.fi/edtech).

ViSCoS studies became available for the first time in September 2000. The ViSCoS program was the first of its kind in Finland, and the content of the course was entirely original. The course made use of online technologies that made it possible for students to study from their homes or from partner institutions, which were usually schools. This was a distinguishing feature of the ViSCoS program from the beginning: it was designed as an option for students who were prevented by their physical circumstances from studying in person at the university. At first, ViSCoS was offered only to high school students (between the ages of 16 and 18) who lived in the vicinity of Joensuu. Later the program was extended to other parts of Finland. ViSCoS has been offered by the Continuing Education Centre (CEC) of the University of Joensuu since 2004. Now adult students may also enroll for ViSCoS. The entire program costs 250 euros for high school students and 350 euros for other students.

ViSCoS E-Learning Program

An average of 100 students per year enrolled for ViSCoS between 2000 and 2005. One hundred and nine students completed the program during this period. If a student passes the program with sufficiently high marks (i.e., grade 3 out of 5), she or he qualifies for entry into Joensuu University as a computer science major. This makes it possible for high school students who started their university studies through the ViSCoS program to complete their university degree earlier than they would otherwise have been able to do. Almost all the graduates of the ViSCoS program qualified for a direct entry to the university. When students who have graduated from ViSCoS enter the university in Joensuu, they are eligible to go straight into the second year of computer science degree program. Table 1 shows how

Table 1. The number of students in the ViSCoS program in 2000-2005

Years of enrollment	2000	2001	2002	2003	2004	2005
Number of students who enrolled	89	184	156	94	101	72
Graduated	22	42	14	16	15	- **)
Continuing at the university ***)	10	3	6	- *)	- *)	- **)

Note:
* *Some of these students will apply to the university in the fall of 2006. Details not available.*
** *These students were still studying at the time of writing.*
*** *Some students have applied to university although they have completed only parts of ViSCoS.*

Table 2. Content and schedule of ViSCoS courses

Course	Content	Schedule
Introduction to ICT and Computing	Introduction to ICT and computing. Practical skills required for using word processing and spreadsheet applications; the basics of Unix	Semester 1
Programming I	Algorithmic thinking. Basic structures of programming with Java	Semester 1
Programming II	Introduction to object-oriented programming (objects, classes, inheritance)	Semester 2
Hardware, Computer Architecture, and Operating Systems	An overview of the architecture of computers, parsers, system software, and databases	Semester 2
Programming Project	Software design, implementation, testing, and documenting	Semesters 2 and 3
Introduction to the Ethics of Computing	General understanding in the ethics of computing	Semester 3
Discrete Structures	Introduction to mathematical concepts and tools useful for a computer scientist, such as logical reasoning, set theory, induction, and basics of probability calculus	Semester 3
Research Fields of Computer Science	Introduction to a selection of research fields in computer science	Semester 3

many students started and graduated from the program between 2000 and 2005. The last row shows the number of ViSCoS students who elected to continue their studies at the Department of Computer Science in University of Joensuu.

While placing a strong emphasis on programming skills, the curriculum of ViSCoS program strikes a balance between the theoretical and practical aspects of computer science studies. On the one hand, students need to achieve a mastery of theory so that they will be in a position to continue their studies. On the other hand, the practical skills will equip students to become professionals in the field of ICT. Table 2 summarizes the content and schedule of ViSCoS courses.

Academic Issues

ViSCoS courses are currently run with an open source Moodle learning platform. Moodle includes the basic learning management system activities such as discussion forums, calendars, management of assignments, and distribution of the learning materials. The learning content in the ViSCoS courses consists of both printed material (such as course books) and digital learning materials. This was done so that the printed material could be linked to an activating digital learning environment on the Web. The digital learning materials include theory, exercises, activating examples, and visualizations in the form of animations. Four kinds of learning methods have been utilized in ViSCoS courses. They are assignment-based courses, collaborative study, essays, and project work.

The digital learning materials in the *assignment-based courses* are divided into between 6 and 12 learning units. Each learning unit covers a one- to two-week period of time during the course. Each unit consists of:

- learning content (theory, examples, exercises);
- optional warm-up exercises; and
- 4-6 assignments.

In the assignment-based section of the course, students undertake a number of diverse, mainly individually accomplished, learning assignments. The course will normally require a student to complete a third from a total of between 40 and 50 assignments. These assignments are distributed among the learning units and are tightly linked to the learning content. All submitted assignments are evaluated by instructors from the university, and returned to students with constructive feedback. The assignments are designed to motivate students by getting them to offer solutions to relevant and even open-ended problems. The purpose behind this is to ignite student interest so that the excercises support meaningful learning. When they learn keyboard programming, for example, students are asked to create an applet that moves a figure inside the drawing area. In the assignment-based section of the course, students' learning outcomes are evaluated by means of a written examination.

Visually appealing game-like examples and assignments were created especially for the programming courses. Animations, event-driven and mouse programming were used to motivate students to learn the necessary theory. An approach that gives priority to visuals is extensively used for teaching object-oriented programming. The assignments at the beginning of the Programming II course are thus mainly programming tasks of graphically oriented applets (Kareinen, Suhonen, & Sutinen, 2001).

In the *collaborative study* part of the ViSCoS program, two to six students combine to undertake a short study. Such short studies are circumscribed investigations into given topics. There are no ready-made learning materials for these short studies. Students have to use the Internet and the library without assistance to find the information that they need. Examples of topics chosen for a study in the Research Fields of Computer Science course include MPEG-4 compression technique, OpenGL, digital portfolios, and usability engineering. Both instructors and peers assess each study. Students are also required to write individual *essays* on set topics. In the Introduction to the Ethics of Computing course, for example, students use the essay format to ponder and analyze the ethical implications of problems that arise in ICT development. *Project work* is also used. In the Programming Project course, for example, students design, implement, test, and document small applications either individually or in pairs. One of goals of the course is to familiarize students with a small-scale software development. Typical project topics relate to small applet-based games.

ViSCoS students are supported both by digital learning materials and by digital learning tools. Three digital learning tools—Jeliot 3, Ethicsar, and LEAP—were either created to support ViSCoS students or else the ViSCoS context played an important part in the development of the tool. The Jeliot 3 visualization tool has been extensively used to support the learning of programming. Jeliot 3 visualizes the execution of Java programs by showing the current state of the program (e.g., methods, variables, and objects) as well as animations of the expression evaluations (Moreno, Myller, Sutinen, & Ben-Ari, 2004). ViSCoS students use Jeliot 3 mainly in their assignments. Students have also been instructed to use the Jeliot 3 tool when they encounter difficulties in programming courses. Figure 1 shows a snapshot of the Jeliot 3 interface.

Ethicsar—a Web-based ethical argumentation tool—was developed for the Introduction to the Ethics of Computing component of the course where it supports collaborative discussion and the analysis of ethical problems (Jetsu, Meisalo, Myller, & Sutinen, 2004). Ethicsar translates interactions (such as the analyses and comments that students make about the ethical opinions of their peers) into visual analogues or metaphors. This program also allows instructors to enter new ethical cases into its database. Students work out their own answers to the problems posed by the cases, and they use a drawing line to present their ethical arguments. They can also add their own cases. The software enables students and instructors to obtain an overall view of how discussions and different opinions evolved during the course. Figure 2 shows a snapshot from the interface of Ethicsar.

The LEAP (*LEA*rning -rocess companion) digital learning tool was developed to support

Figure 1. Jeliot 3 visualization environment

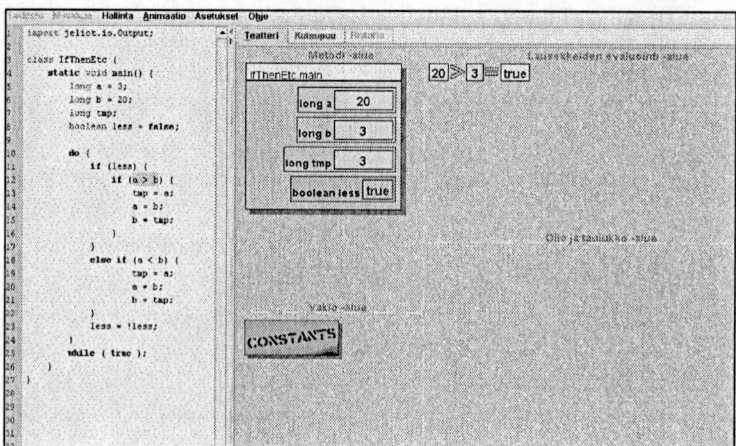

Figure 2. Ethicsar digital learning tool

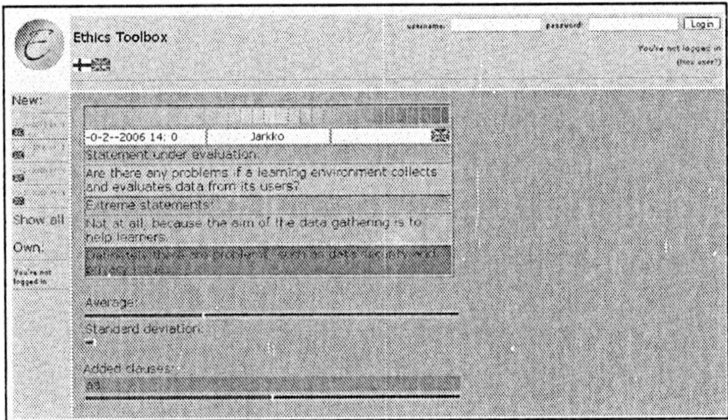

the management of the software project in the Programming Project course (Suhonen & Sutinen, 2002). LEAP is a Web-based tool whose two main functions are digital learning portfolio and creative problem management support. LEAP offers students a way of managing their project and of reflecting on their learning. Creative problem management support offers activities for students to process their problems during the project.

Administrative Issues

Between 2000 and 2003, the ViSCoS program was run as a pilot project. It was financed mainly by the Department of Computer Science and the Eastern Finland Virtual University (EFVU) project, a sub-project of Finnish Virtual University (funded by the Finnish Ministry of Education) (Torvinen, 2004). In the beginning, students were not asked to pay for their involvement in the ViSCoS program. By 2004, the department could no longer finance free study, and by 2003 EFVU could also not continue to do so. This meant that a new source of funding was needed. An agreement was reached with the Continuing Education Centre (CEC) at the university in terms of which ViSCoS studies were allowed to continue. And so study fees were introduced in 2004. The present situation is that the CEC is currently responsible for all practical arrangements (student administration, examinations, etc.) while ViSCoS staff administers courses and provides student support. ViSCoS studies are currently financed both by CEC and by the department. The ViSCoS project obtains funding from the CEC in terms of a formula that takes the number of finished courses by a student into account. The department has given an undertaking to pay the salary of one person working for the project.

While the ViSCoS staffs are mainly master's students and other postgraduates, preference is given to students who are studying to become teachers of ICT. Some members of the department have also been seconded to the program. New staffs do not receive any official training. They are expected to learn their duties on the job. The following human resources have been used to develop, organize, and run the ViSCoS program.

- **Instructors** work online at the university. They are responsible for running the courses. The main duty of instructors is to assess and provide feedback for student assignments. Instructors also answer students' questions by e-mail and through discussion forums.
- **Material designers**, who are often also instructors, produce digital learning materials for the courses. High school students have also designed materials for the programming courses.
- **Researchers** plan and organize the research activities of ViSCoS. They are not regularly involved in the running of the program.
- **Project workers** are undergraduate students who have implemented some parts of digital learning materials for courses. Project workers receive credits toward their master's degrees in lieu of payment for their work.
- **Tutor teachers** work in partner institutions and provide whatever local support students might need. Although tutor teachers are not responsible for arranging the courses and are not necessarily even domain experts, it is their responsibility to encourage and counsel students whenever necessary. Tutor teachers can also choose whatever working methods and timetables they personally prefer at their local level. Some tutor teachers from partner institutions, for example, organize regular meetings with their students. And while some partner institutions pay their tutor teachers some kind of compensation for their services, they are not obligated to do so. Tutor teachers are recruited mainly from the ranks of local ICT teachers in their own areas.

Instructors and material designers are the only people the university hires directly for the program. These include both full-time and half-time (50% time worked) workers. Table 3 summarizes the number of full-time and part-time workers who took part in the program between 2000 and 2005. The four numbered rows in the table represent four identifiable periods or phases in the ViSCoS program.

- **Period 1:** The design and implementation phase of the first courses (May-August 2000).
- **Period 2:** In this period, the first group of students began to study. In the meanwhile, design and implementation of course activities continued to take place (September 2000-August 2001).
- **Period 3:** New students continue to be enrolled in the fall of every university year. In the meanwhile, changes to course structure and content continue to be effected (September 2001-August 2004).
- **Period 4:** ViSCoS studies become available through CEC (September 2004-December 2005).

As seen in Table 3, an average of three personal months per a calendar month has been used in developing and running the program. It should be noted that Table 3 includes only those persons who were officially hired and paid to work in ViSCoS program. Other members of staff in the department performed some of the tasks required to keep the program running,

Table 3. Number of staff working in the ViSCoS program

Period	Length (months)	Full-time working months	Half-time working months	Total working months in period	Total number of personal months per calendar month
1	4	12	2	13	**3.2**
2	12	36	8	40	**3.3**
3	36	84	24	96	**2.7**
4	15	30	15	37.5	**2.5**

such as project management. At the present time, the cost of keeping the ViSCoS program running is approximately 54 000-60 000 EUR per. If the number of students increases, running costs will also increase. Any further updates and future development of the program will also increase costs.

Program Evaluation

The action research oriented method—the FODEM (*FO*rmative *DE*velopment *M*ethod) approach (Suhonen, 2005; Suhonen & Sutinen, 2005)—was used to develop the ViSCoS program. Continuous evaluation of course arrangements, digital learning materials, and the structure of the program have all contributed to the progressive development of the ViSCoS program. The first versions of the program courses were tested in 2000 and 2001. While these first courses were running, feedback was collected from all stakeholders. Their experiences were then evaluated in several studies that used a formative evaluation scheme. A number of different methods such as questionnaires, interviews, log files, the analysis of examinations and submitted exercises, and the analysis of student and tutor feedback were all incorporated in the evaluation of the day-to-day progress of ViSCoS courses. This research focused ultimately on trying to discover the reasons why students experienced learning difficulties. Our first evaluations indicated that it was the programming courses that students found most difficult. This tended to be confirmed by the fact that the drop-out rate was greatest in programming-related courses. Clearly, it was the Programming Project course that students found most challenging.

Evaluations of these early experiences resulted in modifications to the ViSCoS program. The initial focus of the courses was changed, and two courses were merged into one. Course structures were also modified in a way that permitted more resources to be devoted to those areas in which students experienced the greatest difficulty. Extra examples and exercises were devised and included in such courses. Feedback provided by students was used in this way to modify the curriculum and provide more effective support in those sectors of the program that students found most problematic. Thus, for example, the number of learning units in the Programming I course was increased from 10 to 12 weeks, and more support was offered in the programming courses because these were the ones (as mentioned previously) that students found most daunting. Optional exercises and easier examples were also devised to make challenging topics such as arrays, loops, and methods more accessible. For the same reason, developers also created extra Flash animations and interactive applets.

A decision was also taken to make the dropout phenomenon the primary focus of formative evaluation efforts. The aim of this formative evaluation research was, firstly, to investigate the reasons why students dropped out of the program, and, secondly, to consider how teaching practices and digital learning environments could be improved so that the dropout problem might be alleviated. Several studies of this phenomenon were undertaken between 2000 and 2004 (Meisalo, Sutinen, & Torvinen, 2002, 2003; Torvinen, 2004). The most recent study, for example, focused on analyzing the profile of the assignments in terms of their difficulty (Meisalo, Sutinen, & Torvinen, 2004). The premise on which this research was based was that real improvements to the courses would ameliorate the dropout problem because these two factors exist in a dynamic relation. New information about the dropout phenomenon was therefore used to effect adjustments to the courses themselves. In addition, such adjustments to course design and presentation enabled us to investigate which solutions were most effective in decreasing the dropout rate among students. The students told us that the main reasons why they dropped out devolved on lack of time, difficult exercises, and failure in examinations. Many students also felt that it was inherently difficult to study independently. They felt that they needed more support for the most difficult topics in programming (these included arrays, methods, applets, and animations). The dropout research also incidentally revealed that the dropout rates in ViSCoS were on a similar level to those experienced in other distance learning contexts. The dropout rate in the ViSCoS program ranges from zero up to 43%, depending on the course (Torvinen, 2004). Pölönen's (2005) research revealed that that those students who submitted assignments were more likely to continue their studies than those who did not. She concluded from this that more support of the kind that will help them to complete their assignments successfully needs to be given to ViSCoS students.

Table 4 summarizes the research and development (R&D) outputs of the ViSCoS program. ViSCoS research may be divided into three main areas: (1) pedagogical (evaluation of digital learning environments, the dropout phenomenon), (2) technical (the development of digital learning tools), (3) design method (the FODEM approach). *Publication* in the table below means an article published in an academic journal, a book, or conference proceedings. A *thesis* in this table means a thesis for a master's degree or a licentiate, and a *dissertation*

Table 4. Research and development outputs in the ViSCoS program (situation in December, 2005)

		R&D category		
		Publication	Dissertation or thesis	Prototype
R&D focus	Pedagogical	17	4	–
	Technical	12	3	2
	Design method	2	1	–
	Total	*31*	*8*	*2*

means a doctoral dissertation. A *prototype* is a software product that was designed for use in a ViSCoS course.

Policy Implications

ViSCoS began as a pilot program in the department. From the very beginning, the ViSCoS courses were slightly different from the regular courses offered by the department, and there was little if any collaboration between ViSCoS instructors and other members of staff in the department. The piloting part of the program lasted for about four years. But because interest in and demand for the ViSCoS continued to grow from year to year, it eventually became clear that ViSCoS would be a sustainable e-learning program and that there was scope for expanding this program beyond its original high school focus and context.

What has happened over the years that the ViSCoS has been active is that regular departmental courses and ViSCoS courses have slowly started to merge. One of the first signs of this convergence of interests was when the department, following the example set by ViSCoS, adopted Java as its principal programming language. This is but one example of how an e-learning program can act as an agent of change for the regular curriculum. There have also been discussions about the possibility of merging the department's contact teaching courses and ViSCoS courses. This would give the university's campus students more flexibility in their choice of first-year courses.

ViSCoS has also served as a "spin-off" project to other e-learning programs. IMPDET (http://www.impdet.org) is, for example, an e-learning program for PhD postgraduates who are studying educational technology in the Department of Computer Science at the University of Joensuu. These IMPDET courses are offered online to students all over the world. Similar online master's programs in educational technology and computer science education are being planned for the future.

Lessons Learned

The following section summarizes our main experiences in developing and running ViSCoS courses.

1. That a formative development process in the creation of e-learning programs is of vital importance. When resources are limited, the best strategy for survival is to improve course materials and teaching practices in accordance with feedback received from the user (students). The most important feedback in this context concerns what did *not* work well.
2. That a trade-off must be affected between solid design procedures and fast development. Solid design requires investments and longer periods of development. On the other hand, fast development means that the program will be developed within a

shorter period of time. Fast development also means that the program's structure can be more easily modified.

3. That a commitment to the program needs to be made by the host institution. The commitment and interest of the host institution in matters of support and in constructive criticism of the online programs is vital for successful outcomes.
4. That authentic learning community should be created. If one wishes to obtain commitment from students to a program, it is necessary to create an authentic and vibrant learning community in which students are constantly encouraged to take part in all activities, including the design and development of digital learning materials and tools.
5. That the best possible support and feedback should at all times be offered to individual students in the online learning situation. All feedback offered to students should be accurate, personal, constructive, and encouraging.
6. That support efforts in any online learning situation are dependent on the availability of resources. If the resources are limited, technical solutions should be utilized to fill the gap.
7. The accurate identification of a program's limitations and deficiencies is critical for the ultimate development of the program. Such limitations and deficiencies need to be addressed in the development of digital learning materials and tools.
8. Digital learning materials are not in themselves either adequate or sufficient for addressing the whole range of student needs and problems. Digital learning tools should nevertheless be utilized to help students to process their learning.
9. That one should always be prepared for surprises and unexpected results. Such an example from the ViSCoS program is that although the number of dropouts in individual courses decreased during the development of the courses, the number of graduated students has remained more or less the same.

Best Practices

Three best practices from the ViSCoS program that could be emulated by others are:

- *A formative development of the online learning program with extensive research orientation.* The creation of new applications to support learners. A gradual development of the courses and digital learning environments.
- *The light design of the courses.* Digital learning materials focus on the most important aspects of courses. Easy updating and modification of materials is possible.
- *Personal support rendered in response to individual feedback.* Regular constructive feedback enhances other forms of support in the courses.

Conclusion

We can evaluate the success of the ViSCoS program by examining its initial statements of purpose. Firstly, the program ViSCoS has proved that it is a sustainable method of studying CS over the Web. Interest in the program has grown throughout the years that the project has been in existence. Over 100 students have completed the program, most of them while studying at high school. The ViSCoS program has also proved to be a most valuable research platform. Several academic publications and theses have been based on ViSCoS program research. New digital learning tools have also been evolved to meet the needs of the ViSCoS program. Table 2 shows that the problem of how to persuade ViSCoS students to continue their studies in the organizing department remains unsolved. Although almost all of the graduated students are entitled to direct entry into the university, most of them did not enroll for studies in the organizing institute. This is one of the main challenges faced by the ViSCoS program in the future.

One of the original aims of the ViSCoS program was to attract more students from throughout Finland to study at the University of Joensuu. At the moment, however, most of the students still come from the eastern part of Finland. Although the number of students enrolling in the program is satisfactory, there is still room for more students. Plans are also in hand to expand the ViSCoS project beyond its original intentions. Firstly, the ViSCoS program could be expanded to other cultural contexts such as those in developing countries. In this regard, initial steps have already been taken to provide ViSCoS programming courses in Tanzania. The first programming course in English is already partly implemented. Secondly, a ViSCoS Mobile platform has been created that permits ViSCoS program learners to use mobile devices for study purposes (Myller, Laine, & Suhonen, 2005).

References

Haataja, A., Suhonen, J., Sutinen, E., & Torvinen, S. (2001). High school students learning computer science over the Web. *Interactive Multimedia Electronic Journal of Computer-Enhanced Learning (IMEJ)*, *3*(2). Retrieved March 10, 2006, from http://imej.wfu.edu/articles/2001/2/04/index.asp

Jetsu, I., Meisalo, V., Myller, N., & Sutinen, E. (2004). Ethical argumentation with Ethicsar. In P. Kommers, P. Isaías, & M. B. Nunes (Eds.), *Proceedings of the IADIS International Conference on Web Based Communities* (pp. 255-261). Lisbon, Portugal: IADIS Press.

Kareinen, A., Suhonen, J., & Sutinen, E. (2001). Graphical and event-driven approach to teach introductory programming. *Informatika, 38*(2), 25-38.

Meisalo, V., Sutinen, E., & Torvinen, S. (2002). How to improve the virtual programming course? *Proceedings of the 32nd ASEE/IEEE Frontiers in Education Conference (FIE2002)*. Boston. Retrieved March 10, 2006, from http://fie.engrng.pitt.edu/fie2002/papers/1180.pdf

Meisalo, V., Sutinen, E., & Torvinen, S. (2003). Choosing appropriate methods for evaluating and improving the learning process in distance programming courses. *Proceedings of the 33rd ASEE/IEEE Frontiers in Education Conference (FIE2003)*. Boulder, CO. Retrieved March 10, 2006, from http://fie.engrng.pitt.edu/fie2003/papers/1553.pdf

Meisalo, V., Sutinen, E., & Torvinen, S. (2004). Classification of exercises in a virtual programming course. *Proceedings of the 34th Frontiers in Education Conference (FIE2004)*. Savannah, GA. Retrieved March 10, 2006, from http://fie.engrng.pitt.edu/fie2004/papers/1296.pdf

Moreno, A., Myller, N., Sutinen, E., & Ben-Ari, M. (2004). Visualizing programs with Jeliot 3. In M. F. Costabile (Ed.), *Proceedings of the International Working Conference on Advanced Visual Interfaces (AVI2004)* (pp. 373-376). New York: ACM Press.

Myller, N., Laine, T., & Suhonen, J. (2005). ViSCoS Mobile: Learning computer science on the road. In *Proceedings of the Fifth Koli Calling Conference on Computer Science Education (Koli Calling 2005),* Koli, Finland (pp. 183-184). Turku, Finland: TUCS Publication No. 41.

Pölönen, P. (2005). *Ohjelmoinnin verkkokurssin ohjaaminen—Case ViSCoS (Counseling measures in an online programming course, Case ViSCoS).* Retrieved March 10, 2006, from ftp://cs.joensuu.fi/pub/Theses/2005_MSc_Polonen_Pirkko.pdf

Suhonen, J. (2005). *A formative development method for digital learning environments in sparse learning communities*. Doctoral dissertation, Department of Computer Science, University of Joensuu, Finland. Retrieved March 10, 2006, from http://joypub.joensuu.fi/publications/dissertations/suhonen_learning/suhonen.pdf

Suhonen, J., & Sutinen, E. (2002). Creative problem management in Web-tutored programming projects. In Kinshuk, R. Lewis, K. Akamori, R. Kemp, T. Okamoto, L. Henderson, et al. (Eds.), *Proceedings of the International Conference on Computers in Education (ICCE 2002)* (pp. 557-558). Los Alamitos, CA: IEEE Computer Society.

Suhonen, J., & Sutinen, E. (2005). FODEM: A formative method for developing digital learning environments in sparse learning communities. In P. Goodyear, D. G. Sampson, D. J.-T. Yang, Kinshuk, T. Okamoto, R. Hartley, et al. (Eds.), *Proceedings of the 5th IEEE International Conference on Advanced Learning Technologies (ICALT2005)*. Kaohsiung, Taiwan (pp. 447-451). (An extended version of the article will appear in the *Journal of Educational Technology & Society* in 2006). Los Alamitos, CA: IEEE Computer Society.

Torvinen, S. (2004). *Aspects of the evaluation and improvement process in an online programming course—Case: The ViSCoS program*. Unpublished licentiate thesis, Department of Computer Science, University of Joensuu, Finland. Retrieved March 10, 2006, from ftp://cs.joensuu.fi/pub/PhLic/2004_PhLic_Torvinen_Sirpa.pdf

ViSCoS. (2005). *Virtual Studies of Computer Science.* Retrieved March 10, 2006, from http://cs.joensuu.fi/viscos

Chapter XIV

Fiji Implements Blended E-Learning as Appropriate Flexible Learning

Elspeth McKay,
RMIT University School of Business Information Technology, Australia

Abstract

This chapter describes a learning environment that implements a learning design that promotes an adaptive approach toward e-learning. A theoretical model describes the interactive components of an e-learning environment. This model can be used as a designing tool for implementing an effective framework to support the social aspects of human-computer interaction. It discusses the institutional and national context of the e-learning program offered by a school in Fiji that is accredited by the International Baccalaureate Organization. A zoom-lens approach is taken by the year-5 classroom teacher to encourage her students' experiential learning. However, alternative instructional strategies are required when the Internet becomes unstable. This means extra activities are required that do not involve computers. Some of these tasks are self-reflection diary entries that produce added interest for the students as they prepare for their presentations at the school assemblies.

Introduction

There can be no doubt that interest in learning has shifted from an insular approach to school-based education to participation in a global knowledge-sharing environment. As a result, we have reached a turning point in the design and development of multimodal courseware. There are already many collaborative relationships between industry and academic institutions providing research with excellent models upon which to work.

This chapter proposes a learning systems designing model through efficient and effective human-computer interaction that articulates the complexity of the e-learning delivery environment for both novice and experienced Web-resource developers (McKay, 2005). Not all people around the globe have access to stable Web-based learning centers. This chapter will show how alternative resources are utilized to provide appropriate flexible delivery to isolated communities. The range of technological aids currently under review will involve radio, interactive television, CD-ROM resources, and paper-based materials. This case study is offered to describe flexible delivery of an educational program underway for Pacific Islanders.

Readers will see that the *Method of Delivery Transfer Agent* (learning facilitator) can direct the *Instructional Conditions* (learner characteristics and instructional format) according to the results of specific *Learner Characteristics* (cognitive style) and learning *Event Conditions* (complexity of processing the learning material), and the *Measurable Instructional Outcomes* (cognitive performance). Due to the overall problems associated with unstable Internet connections, which interfere with effective human-computer interaction (Preece, 2002), alternate learning resources can be kept ready for implementation when access becomes impossible.

Therefore, directions for choice of *Instructional Format* (e.g., purely textual resources, radio, interactive television sessions, CD-ROMs) can be given by the *Method of Delivery*

Figure 1. Learning systems designing model: Effective human-computer interaction

Transfer Agent (face-to-face, radio/television broadcasting, and other asynchronous mechanisms that involve information and communications technologies) (McKay & Martin, 2002). Consequently this Learning systems design model (Figure 1) serves as a robust instructional design framework or learning systems' design tool to facilitate discussion on how to ensure that flexible learning resources are appropriate.

When describing flexible learning, one assumes there is an intention for the effective reuse of instructional resources. This reuse may be classified in many different ways, for example, participation time (global time-zones), location (home, school, or office), or learning/instructional context (content and delivery mode). However, as this chapter will demonstrate, the tendency to assume the *one size fits all* approach to e-learning delivery mode is cumbersome, ineffective, and not appropriate for many isolated communities of learners. Often isolated communities value educational resources that improve a range of social development issues such as youth group management and development, working with communities, conflict resolution, and basic computer literacy for the facilitators. To illustrate how a successful blended e-learning instructional strategy can be implemented in a remote region, we have chosen the Republic of Fiji Islands located in the South Pacific.

The Fiji economy over the past decade has seen both good and bad times. There is great potential in this region, with diverse natural resources, and a large labor force. Fiji's central position in the South Pacific provides the opportunity for a very successful tourism industry. However, years of under achievement and a monopolistic communications infrastructure have caused rising business costs and inefficiencies of service in the telephone and information technology. Tourism has become the country's largest source of foreign income. In the past, sugar was traditionally the largest export product, accounting for a quarter of the country's foreign exchange that supported over 20,000 farmers and their families.

Institutional and National Context of the Learning Program

In theory, all local Fijian government-funded schools are mixed-race. However, these schools are often of one race only in rural areas where the population is unbalanced. A contrast also arises from the differences between the villages or countryside and town centers. For instance, in the villages it is a subsistence life, and the school is often a single room with just one teacher doing his or her best with 20 pupils of varying scholastic levels. Moreover, in the towns, classes are larger with the teacher having to cope with 50 children at a time. Overall, Fiji has 700 primary schools and almost 150 secondary schools.

There are a dozen or so private boarding schools around the islands, mostly on the east coast of Viti Levu around Suva and on the island of Ovalau. Often the schooling is arranged for boys except for the Adi Cakabau School, which is about half an hour inland from Suva. Two international schools have recently been established in the country, both of which are accredited by the International Baccalaureate Organization—one in Suva, which takes children up to the age of 16, and the other in Nadi taking children to the age of 14. Fees are charged for these schools; they are affordable by only a few locals and expatriate families.

There are four schools of higher education in Fiji. The Fiji-based University of the South Pacific has its campus in Suva and is financed by the 12 countries of the region. There are 2,500 full-time students, with double this number studying in distance or extension mode through local centers in the various neighbouring countries. Other learning institutes include the Fiji School of Medicine and the Fiji Institute of Technology. They are all based in Suva, and the Teachers College is based in Lautoka on the western side of Viti Levu.

The International School in Nadi, Fiji has 280 students (http://www.isn.school.fj/). The school is located on the main island of Viti Levu in Nadi District, between the Nadi International Airport and Nadi Town. Nadi is located on the western side of Viti Levu and is the main tourist area featuring major international hotels and resorts. Since its inception in 1992, this school has served the Nadi and Latoka communities to provide families with effective and quality educational programs that fully engage students with their learning. The school takes pride in celebrating religious and cultural events. This is an important step toward intercultural tolerance and understanding in an international school. Special days are celebrated at an assembly involving the whole school. There are cultural performances and speeches, and opportunities to dress in a variety of costumes. These multi-cultural events are usually held in the Junior Primary Assembly.

Brief Description of Organization Offering the Program

Due to the expectations from parents for a more enhanced learning environment than the generic curriculum on offer in the local Fijian school system, in 2004 the school was authorized for the International Baccalaureate Primary Years Program and the Middle Years Program. As such, the school's curriculum is different from the local Fijian education system, where one class will be required to cover many ages and grades. From January 2002, the school began implementing programs offered by the International Baccalaureate Organization. This organization provides the curriculum and assessment development, teacher training and information seminars, electronic networking, and other educational services to more than 1,000 participating schools in nearly 100 countries around the world (http://occ.ibo.org). This online curriculum center is recognized as a program of academic excellence, emphasizing cultural awareness, development of the whole person, and contemporary relevance. Community service is an important requirement of students at all levels of the programs. There are no external examinations in the Middle and Primary Years Programs. Certificates for special achievements are presented at the school assemblies. This educational context is therefore in striking contrast to the educational resources available in the village or local schools.

- **Primary school:** At the international school at Nadi, the primary school assembly is held every second week. Different classes take responsibility for assembly performances. In keeping with the holistic approach to education, parents and visitors are most welcome. School assemblies may involve singing the national anthem, and celebrating birthdays. Children may present their work or perform dance or drama.
- **Middle school:** These assemblies often have a curriculum focus, or involve guest speakers, community service, or other areas of educational interest; they take place in one of the middle school classrooms.
- **School library:** Primary school children visit the library at least once a week as a class. In addition, students are also encouraged to visit individually during the second

half of lunchtime (an understandable advantage to attract children to keep out of the tropical heat). Children may borrow books by following the library procedures. There is a limit of one book at a time for classes 1-3; however, students from class 4 and higher may borrow more than one.

- **Computer room:** All classes have access to the computer room. There are 30 networked computers with Internet access. In addition to class time, senior students may purchase Internet time at Fiji$10 per term. Students may use the computer rooms during the morning and lunchtime breaks. By striking contrast, in the local Fijian schools, there are practically no computer facilities for staff and students.

Mandate for E-Learning Initiative

- **The Primary Years Program:** This is an international curriculum framework designed for all children between the ages of 3 and 12 years. It combines the best research and practice from a range of national systems with a wealth of knowledge and experience from international schools to create a relevant and engaging educational program. The Primary Years Program offers an inquiry-based approach to teaching and learning, incorporating guidelines on student learning styles, teaching methodologies, and assessment strategies. Aims of the Primary Years Program are expressed in a series of desirable attributes and dispositions that characterize successful students. They involve a propensity for communicating well, risk-taking, knowledge acquisition, demonstrating a caring attitude, open-minded inquiry, well-balanced, and reflective thought.
- **The Middle Years Program:** The Middle Years Program is designed for students aged between 11 and 16 years. It is a complete and coherent program that provides a framework of academic challenge and life skills appropriate to this stage of adolescence. Subjects include Language A (English), Language B (French), Humanities, Sciences, Mathematics, Arts, Physical Education, and Technology [www.ibo.org].

E-Learning Program

The e-learning program involves a range of instructional resources at the school, including various forms of written material, in both electronic and non-electronic media. The school offers the International Baccalaureate Organization's Primary Years Program, which is structured around organizing themes (who we are, where we are in place and time, how we express ourselves, how the world works, how we organize ourselves, and sharing the planet). These themes are integral across the learning disciplines of science, social study, and technology. This chapter will concentrate on the Sharing the Planet organizing theme, to explain how the Year 5 classroom activities of the International School Nadi may differ from other learning environments for pupils of similar ages in other locations. In particular the teaching strategies are designed to create the experiential learning environment for exploring the rights and obligations involved in the global nature of sharing the finite water resources.

During the second half of 2004, the year 5 and 6 teachers prepared an evaluation of existing learning resources. They conducted brainstorming sessions to ensure they could innovate experiential sessions that would ignite the children's fascination for exploring their world. Because sharing the finite resources of water is especially important in Fiji, it soon became evident that the teachers could devise an educational program that would involve their pupils in investigating this strategic knowledge base. Therefore, it was decided that the learning program should initiate awareness in the pupils of the impact of water sharing with other communities to emphasize the relationships within and between other people and other living things. The planned inquiry into water resources included these topics:

- Where does our water come from?
- How do we use water?
- How much water do we use?
- What happens to the used water?

In the year 5 classroom the pupils are encouraged to think about the broader theme of "Sharing the Planet" to create the context for explaining that our planet has limited resources that are unevenly distributed. This type of instructional strategy follows the zoom-lens approach of the elaboration theory. Subject matter studied through an elaboration model takes the pupil on a journey of discovery that is similar to studying a picture through a zoom-lens on a movie camera (Reigeluth, 1983). In this scenario, pupils can commence their investigation with a wide-angle view, allowing them to see the major parts of the picture with the major relationships among the important parts, without disclosing too much detail.
Two different types of activities commence this learning journey:

- A thesaurus is used by the year 5 teacher to familiarize her pupils with the terminology relating to our planet's finite resources and language of the discipline; a secondary benefit is to develop investigative skills through the thesaurus. Pupils need to complete a table that conveys what they know, what they want to know, and what they have learned. These tables are collected by the teacher and kept for reflective discussions on the pupils' understanding and learning outcomes later.
- A series of (tuning in) activities are implemented to encourage pupils to generate their own set of questions on the topic. One example of this activity was a year 5 and 6 tour and camp. Pupils traveled with their teachers from Nadi to Suva, to stay at a mountain lodge in Suva. This journey takes two hours by bus, traveling around the main island of Viti Levu. The location of the camp was chosen because it was located close to a large stone quarry filled with water. This quarry is high in the mountains overlooking Suva. An additional feature for the pupils to understand on this tour was the effect of the unfavorable weather, which often occurs in Suva due to closeness of the high mountains. During a recent storm, quarry vehicles were unable to escape the sudden deluge of water. Pupils could observe the trucks and earth-moving equipment that were submerged deep within the quarry. The lodge, which has a very good pumping system, uses the water from this artificial lake for guest consumption. Pupils were able to see the various methods of community water treatment. For instance the differences

between chemical purification for drinking and the notion of grey-water, which is a term used to describe the run-off water from kitchen sinks and bathrooms.

Moreover, museum trips also involve the pupils in their discovery of water storage processes. The subsequent reflection this time involved a series of questionnaires and knowledge rubrics that included knowledge gained during the tours, attitudes about water resources, and trans-disciplinary skills (social, thinking, communication, self-management, and research skills). Back in the classroom students are given time to write up their questions of what they want to know. The whole class evaluates each response sheet and classifies different questions according to these criteria:

- **Form:** What is it like?
- **Function:** How does it work?
- **Causation:** Why is it like this?
- **Change:** How is it changing?
- **Connection:** How is it connected?
- **Perspective:** What are the point of views?
- **Responsibility:** What is our responsibility?
- **Reflection:** How do we know?

The teacher reviews the question clarifications to initiate five activities that involve the pupils in finding answers to their questions. The instructional resources range from keyword searching on the internet and library. To encourage group participation and decision making collaboration amongst the pupils, the following media are invoked by the teacher:

- Audio/visual tapes (CD and DVD are usually not available).
- Appropriate library books when available (currently resources in Fiji are limited).
- Online computer laboratory sessions (or working standalone when the server is down, which sadly happens often with power fluctuations and heavy load).
- Visiting speakers invited to come into the school to talk about the learning topics.
- Sharing of experiential learning knowledge in student lead conference forums held during the school assemblies. Pupils are invited to share their learning outcomes with the rest of the school and also their parents. These activities often involve the pupils in drama, light humor performances, songs, and poem readings.

- **Objectives of the program:** The instructional strategies adopt an interdisciplinary approach to ensure the understanding of the relationships between the Program of Planned Inquiry learning streams (language of other disciplines, science, social studies, and technology). Special needs teachers are employed by the school to monitor pupils' progress.

- **Entry requirements:** Due to the multi-cultural nature of the pupil cohort, this school places a special emphasis on developing English as a second language. To this effect, the International Baccalaureate Organization's (Primary Year Program) standards are observed at the school to provide a comprehensive set of objective criteria against which the school determines a pupil's educational level. They also fulfill the requirements that articulate the pupils' self-study activities. Finally, these criteria are vital for program evaluation.

Academic Issues

The instructional design principles adopted by the year 5 teacher involves a blended pedagogical model to ensure an appropriate and flexible learning environment. At times the learning outcomes require both traditional face-to-face learning/instruction as well as collaborative classroom activities. This blended e-learning approach to the instructional strategies can be seen in the learning systems designing model (McKay, 2005). Drawing on this model each component can be identified, studied by the teacher, and refined for classroom practice. For instance, the *Method of Delivery Transfer Agent* directs the *Instructional Conditions* according to the results of the *Learner Characteristics.*

In our international Fijian school example, the cultural orientation and knowledge development level of each pupil is always an important factor for consideration. While the classroom teacher must evaluate the relationship between the *Learning Event Conditions* (this is the complexity of cognitive processing required by the learning material), and the *Measurable Instructional Outcomes,* which define the knowledge/experiential awareness the class-room teacher deems desirable for each topic. Moreover, the Learning Systems Designing Model reveals that the directions for choice of *Instructional Format* are given by the *Method of Delivery Transfer Agent* (or learner), as described by McKay (2005). Therefore, blending the instructional format (textual, graphical, audio) or delivery mechanisms (books, radio, TV, computers) is vital to keep pupils engaged in their learning when implementing e-learning environments.

In the case of the year 5 classroom at the International School Nadi, the teacher must assume a watchful eye on how successful the pupils are at achieving the expected instructional outcomes. For instance pupils need to show that they know where our water comes from. The Self-Reflection Profile sheets (written responses) and Classroom Wall Diaries (graphical representations) reveal the pupils experiential knowledge development. When the response is weak, the classroom teacher may revisit the instructional event from a different perspective.

The school's computer laboratory is equipped with 30 networked machines. The teacher needs to be ready to initiate alternative instructional strategies to manage the learning environment when the server is unavailable. Unfortunately this unpredictable server downtime is a constant challenge for both the pupils and teacher alike. However, when it becomes necessary, they adopt a positive attitude to the technological misbehavior and find various ways to further ignite their imagination through alternative resources like talking with older family members to learn from them, watching what happens in the villages nearby, listening to radio programs, watching TV, visiting the library, or reading newspapers. To this end, the Encarta Kids reference library and Story Weaver software applications offer the pupils a comprehensive set of computerized tools they can access on the computers when the Internet is not available. Creative writing is encouraged with an emphasis on the pictorial aspects of the multi-media that underpins these packages. These programs promote self-directed learning through pupils constructing their own learning activities (Jonassen, Meyers, & McKillop, 1996).

From time to time teachers and technology assistants attend international workshops run by the International Baccalaureate Organization. This is where they learn how to teach Internet skills to children. The focus of these staff development activities is primarily designed to facilitate the use of electronic tools that will achieve successful instructional outcomes back at school. At this point in time, open source or commercially produced virtual learning environments are not appropriate for schools in Fiji due to the difficulties they face with systems' support.

There are several assessment and evaluation practices implemented for the year 5 children. Children are not expected to undertake written tests. Instead, the teachers determine when the children have gained knowledge and skills in their classroom through a series of activities that include group participation in school assembly performances:

- Role play skits
- PowerPoint presentations

Administrative Issues

The technical infrastructure required by the program draws heavily on the inventiveness of the classroom teacher to initiate a student-led instructional environment. Because of this, the year 5 teacher relies on strategies that have emerged through her own educational journey. This means family influences play an important part of the instructional design installed in the classroom.

Copyright ownership and intellectual property issues rely on the generous nature of the International Baccalaureate Organization and their propensity for the sharing of resources. Primarily this collaboration is achieved through the Online Curriculum Center's Web site, http://occ.ibo.org.

Quality assurance and standards' policies, including learning objects, meta-data, and learning design (McKay & Martin 2006), are evaluated by the senior teaching staff in conjunction with each classroom teacher. Moreover, an Executive Committee consisting of a Primary Syndicate Leader (year 3) and the Upper Primary Syndicate Leader (years 5 and 6) meets regularly with classroom teachers and senior teachers. The school's executive principal is also available for classroom observation and consultation.

Program Evaluation

The Primary Years Program standards provide the set of objective criteria against which both the school and the International Baccalaureate Organization measure success in the implementation of the Primary Years Program. It is important to note that all the criteria provided are requirements and not just suggestions, including:

- **Standard A1:** There is close alignment between the educational beliefs and values of the school and those of the Primary Years Program.
- **Standard A2:** The school promotes an international mindedness on the part of the adults and the children in the school community.
- **Standard B1:** The governing body of the school has made a formal decision to adopt the Primary Years Program and continues to support it.
- **Standard B2:** The school management is fully committed to the continuous implementation and further development of the program.
- **Standard C:** There is a comprehensive, coherent, written curriculum.
- **Standard D:** The school has implemented a school-wide system through which teachers plan and reflect in collaborative teams.
- **Standard E:** Teachers use a range and balance of teaching strategies that are selected appropriately to meet particular learning purposes.
- **Standard F1:** There is an agreed school-wide approach to the assessment of student learning that recognizes that the fundamental purpose of assessment is to acknowledge student learning.
- **Standard F2:** There is an agreed school-wide approach to the recording and reporting of assessment data.
- **Standard G:** Students learn how to choose to act and how to reflect on their action, which contributes to the well-being of the self, the community, and the environment.
- **Standard H:** In the final year of the program in the school, students will engage in a problem-solving project culminating in the Primary Years Program exhibition.

Opinions of school stakeholders are sought through the School Board of Trustees. The School Board consists of teacher representatives and various school administrative officers to deal with a range of initiatives including the School Constitution and Strategic Business Plans, as well as the overall authorization by the International Baccalaureate for the Middle Years Program and Primary Years Program.

Network and Collaboration

A collaborative relationship exists between the International School in Suva (located on the Eastern side Viti Levu, which is the main island of Fiji) and the International School Nadi (on the Western side). This means that economies of scale improve the quality of the experiential learning offered in both places. For example, the Training Workshops are located in Suva with teachers traveling from Nadi, while the tuning in tours and camps offer a change of pace and location for pupils on both sides of Viti Levu.

Policy Implications

The high level of trust placed in the classroom teachers evidences an important feature of the school principal's influence upon the policy development. To achieve this, the principal encourages the newer teachers to implement innovative instructional classroom climates. This means there is a continual recognition by the school principal for their professional judgment on selection of creative activities in the classroom.

Lessons Learned

Positive experiences that flow from the Primary Years Program conducted at the International School Nadi include:

1. Pupils develop high levels of self-awareness of their learning skills.
2. Attributes of collaborative learning develops in the earlier school years.
3. Teachers recognize when pupils require remedial instructional strategies.
4. Non-English speaking pupils improve their second language skill development.
5. Innovative instructional strategies can be replicated by other teachers.
6. Appropriate blended e-learning instructional strategies are necessary to cope with technological downtimes.
7. Enjoyment for life-long learning is regarded as a natural human potential.

Negative experiences that flow from the Primary Years Program conducted at the International School Nadi include:

1. The emphasis on electronic courseware tools requires substantial infrastructure.
2. The International School Baccalaureate can only be offered for a relatively small number of pupils.

3. Traveling away from Fiji to participate in teacher development schemes is limited.
4. Continuous technology problems limit the range of programs implemented via the Internet.

Best Practice

Three actions/practices (in order of priority) that should be emulated by others include:

1. English language programs.
2. Learning methodologies for encouraging playful mathematics learning.
3. Encourage a broader learning environment

It is highly desirable that this list be transferred to the local Fijian school environment, where resources for self-directed experiential learning especially involving human-computer interaction are somewhat limited. Opportunity for English language development is weak, due to a lack of opportunities in the village communities to exchange knowledge and experience with people speaking fluent English. Moreover, mathematics is taught with traditional means, through out dated textbooks. Unfortunately, due to the isolated nature of most village communities, a view of the broader community is not as easily implemented.

Finally, the reporting of this case study on the Fijian International School at Nadi, forms part of a much larger project that is evaluating appropriate human-computer interaction in a blended approach to e-learning instructional resources for accessible education and lifelong learning in other communities of learning in the broader region of the South Pacific Islands to include Cook, Samoa, Tahiti, Tonga, and Hawaii.

Acknowledgments

Aseri Fong—5th grade classroom teacher; Mrs. Joan Wilisoni—school principal; Mrs. Rosi Uluiviti—coordinator; International School Nadi.

References

Jonassen, D. H., Meyers, J. M., & McKillop, A. M. (1996). From constructivism to constructionism: Learning with hypermedia/multimedia rather than from it. In B. G. Wilson (Ed.), *Constructivist learning environments: Case studies in instructional design* (pp. 93-106). NJ: Educational Technology Publications.

McKay, E. (2005). Cognitive skill capabilities in Web-based educational systems. In S. Mishra & R. C. Sharma (Eds.), *Interactive multimedia in education and training* (pp. 213-248). Hershey, PA: Idea Group Publishing.

McKay, E., & Martin, B. (2002). The scope of e-learning: Expanded horizons for life-long learning. In *Conference Informing Science 2002 + IT Education: Where Parallels Intersect* (pp. 1017-1029). Cork, Ireland: Mercer Press/Marino Books.

McKay, E., & Martin, J. (in press). Multidisciplinary collaboration to unravel expert knowledge: Designing for effective human-computer interaction. In M. Keppel (Ed.), *Instructional design: Case studies in communities of practice*. Hershey, PA: Information Science Publishing.

Preece, J. (2002). *Interaction design: Beyond human-computer interaction*. New York: John Wiley & Sons.

Reigeluth, C. M. (1983). Meaningfulness and instruction: Relating what is being learned to what a student knows. *Instructional Science, 12*, 197-218.

Chapter XV

Project-Based Learning in Chemical Engineering Education Using Distance Education Tools

Katia Tannous, State University of Campinas, Brazil

Abstract

This chapter will exhibit the experience of applying project-based learning in different subject matter, identifying and comprehending the efficiency of this teaching methodology from an analysis of the activities undertaken. The subjects focused on were transport phenomena and unit operations in chemical processes. The methodology of project-based learning is to associate concepts acquired during classes and integrate them with other subjects in order to integrate the parts into the whole. It develops a variety of skills in addition to technical ones, such as cooperation, communication, involvement, knowledge construction, decision making, and problem solving. All these skills being supported by the use of distance education tools. The creation of the subjects in a virtual environment sustains student materials previously required for project development. It also monitors student activity (access by frequency statistics), and facilitates communication. The motivation and interactivity aspects have been shown to be positive with students and professors systematically involved in the constructive evolution of both individual and group knowledge.

Introduction

Learning is a search for meaning, which requires understanding of the whole framework in order to relate the parts of the context. Therefore, the learning process focuses on the three primary levels leading to learning, which consist of data, information, and knowledge. The data are considered to be raw facts and when processed become information. The information is meaningful data and when refined leads to knowledge. In order to teach well, one must understand the relationship between these elements as being the path to learning in order to develop mental models that students use to understand the world and the assumptions that support these models. Learning is inherently inter-disciplinary where the students understand and construct their own meanings based on the knowledge base they have acquired.

The chemical engineering course is still a fragmented degree where the student has only one opportunity to integrate all the practical and theoretical concepts learned in five years. The course subject known as chemical projects has been the object of the association and integration of all these concepts, but such a degree requires extensive work in practical applications.

Since 2001, project-based learning has been implemented in several subjects of the undergraduate and graduate chemical engineering courses at Unicamp. The objective has been to initiate students' motivation and to continually maintain their interest in courses, so as to acquire a successful learning process. This chapter will present these experiences in different subjects, identifying the efficiency of this methodology.

Literature Review

As a literature review of learning theories illustrates, there are many labels being used to describe these methodologies. The main learning theories that influenced traditional and distance education during the 20th century were behaviorism, cognitivism, and constructivism. From these theories, some tendencies with different perspectives defended by theorists and researchers were discovered.

Behaviorism is characterized by directed instruction, where the results are reflections of the observations of human behavior, controlled by exams. Planning follows segmentation of the contents into short sequences, so that the subject matter is learned in a gradual way, step by step. It is an approach that does not promote the learning process for students, as only the professor relates the information and knowledge deciding when, how, and what to teach. The effect leads to interaction between student-student and student-professor being weak due to the learning process being understood by only one party and the other members not knowing "why" the knowledge requires relations in a general context (Forrester & Jantzie, 2003; Rodrigues, Melo, Ferreira, Pinho, & Pereira, n.d.).

The theory of cognitivism is centered on the pedagogical activity of the professor, who considers learning as a mental process involving the information with the memory path for a long time. The previous knowledge of the student and his or her constructive sense both have a determinate role in the whole learning process. This line also considers technology as a partner in the learning process, and suggests a series of strategies for planning and implementing online courses (Doolittle, 2002).

Constructivism is linked to cognitive and social constructivism. Constructivism is recognized as a unique learning theory in itself. It may, however, be associated with cognitive psychology, because as a theory of learning it focuses on the learner's ability to mentally construct meaning into their own environment and to create their own learning. As a teaching practice it is associated with different degrees of non-directed learning (Forrester & Jantzie, 2003).

Courses with subjacent constructivist theories must allow the students to learn from the base contents, to be stimulated to research complementary sources and to construct his or her knowledge. The student develops a non-linear path dictated by his or her own interests, and must decide *what* and *when* to learn in an active and interactive process.

All these theories are applied in academia because the students are still passive. Our observation is that more and more students do not understand the learning process and make mistakes, confusing the transmission of information with knowledge. In sequence, we present some pedagogical methodologies applied to the engineering courses based on the principles of the constructivist theory. A few experiences with cases of chemical engineering were found in the literature, and can be compared with this work.

Inquiry-Based Learning

This teaching approach is derived from the work of Dewey (theory of inquiry), who suggests applying the principles of scientific research. It is basically different from traditional teaching, in which the professor prepares didactic material for the students. In the inquiry-based learning approach, students look for data in order to deal with a problem, plan their work, and create a synthesis of the information extracted from a range of resources. Also, after their interest has been aroused the students become involved, and are encouraged to define the problem, propose hypotheses, carry out the project/experiment, search for answers and explanations, analyze and interpret the final data, draw conclusions, and make decisions connected with the subject researched (Frank, Lavy, & Elata, 2003; Tamir, 1990).

Project-Based Learning

Project-based learning (PBL) is a method of instruction that emphasizes learning activities that are student-centered, interdisciplinary, and integrated with real-life world issues. In the Buck Institute for Education (BIE) vocabulary ("project based," n.d.), project-based learning is a general term describing an instructional method that uses projects as the central focus of instruction in a variety of subjects (*Project Based Learning Handbook*, n.d.). Often, projects emerge out of an authentic context, address controversial or significant issues in the community, and unfold in unexpected ways.

Thomas (2000) also tried to define this approach, and emphasized that in the PBL environment students are, in fact, investigating solutions to a problem. They build their own knowledge by active learning, interacting with the environment as suggested by the constructivist approach, working independently, or collaborating in teams, while the professor directs and guides them as they make real products.

Okelo (2001) cites eight features of project-based learning, as follows:

1. It engages students in the real world, where the students can select and define issues or problems that are meaningful to them;
2. It requires students to use inquiry, research planning skills, critical thinking, and problem-solving skills as they complete the project;
3. It requires students to learn and apply content-specific skills and knowledge in a variety of contexts as they work on the project;
4. It provides opportunities for students to learn and practice interpersonal skills as they work in cooperative teams and with adults in workplaces or in the community;
5. It gives students practice in using the array of skills needed for their adult lives and careers;
6. It expects outcomes with respect to accomplishments and learning;
7. It incorporates reflection activities, leading the students to think critically about their experiences and to link them with specific learning standards; and
8. It presents a product that demonstrates learning and is assessed (students decide upon the criteria).

Also, it is important to observe the advantages for the professors. Krajeik, Czemiak, and Berger (as cited in Frank, Lavy, & Elata, 2003) suggest three possible advantages for them:

a. The professor may find the work enjoyable, interesting, and motivating, since teaching will vary constantly as he/she explores new projects with each new group of students;
b. In project-based teaching, the professor continually receives new ideas, thus becoming a life long learner; and
c. Classroom management is simplified because the students are interested and involved.

Problem-Based Learning

Okelo (2001) defines the difference between project-based learning and problem-based learning as processes that are deliberately designed to require students to learn content-specific knowledge and problem-solving skills.

For problem-based learning (PBL), BIE designs realistic scenarios and role-plays to lead students along a carefully planned path toward a set of prescribed outcomes (*Project Based Learning Handbook*, n.d.). A project must be rooted in standard contents and allow for student-centered inquiry into a meaningful question (Okelo, 2001).

Some science and engineering educators are attracted to the ideals of problem-based learning and how current "methodologies of experience" express them. Following Walls and Rogers (as cited in Simões, Relvas, & Moreira, 2004), "Problem-based learning reorients education from the dominance of the professor," provides knowledge for the autonomy of student encounters with the conditions of "knowing," with learning processes and with circumstances that require and build knowledge and skill. It reorients education in a paradigm that is more fluid, circuitous, and permeable. One danger for problem-based learning enthusiasts is that while the "teaching paradigm" may have yielded to a new "learning paradigm," gaps may exist between their pedagogical views and their practice.

Teaching Objective

Motivating students is certainly a stimulating and challenging problem, always present in teaching activities. In fact, it is not easy to motivate students (Davenport, 2000; Green, 1998). Many factors are involved, such as non-stimulating subjects, knowledge transmitted essentially by oral expositions, professor-student relationship, and student and professor social problems.

Additional dilemmas can certainly be related to the teaching methodologies. It is certainly not a rule, but a very high percentage of lecturers teaching technological subjects at universities had no kind of pedagogical preparation or formation, a problem being successively ignored. However, this can be minimized if stimulating, diverse types of activity based on real professional contexts are implemented.

The courses were designed to help students meet the following objectives: develop scientific thinking and technical competence to resolve engineering and industrial design problems; promote individual capacities for the analysis and critical interpretation of case studies; develop aptness for good quality and rigorous scientific research work; develop planned working methodologies; develop innovative and creative attitudes; develop and stimulate cooperative and responsible attitudes.

Engineering education programs must provide students with extensive hands-on experience, a comprehensive experience in teamwork and technical communication, and the opportunity to exercise and develop their creativity (Simões, Relvas, & Moreira, 2004).

Pedagogical Project

In the educational context, Boutinet (as cited in Tannous & Ropoli, 2005) presents different nomenclatures, sometimes applied in a disorganized manner, as synonymous: a number of examples highlighting this point include educational project, consulting project, educational and cultural activities project, formation project, and pedagogical project. According to the author, the confusion around the terms is from the elucidation failure about the meaning of educational project, pedagogical project, school project, pedagogy of project, and formation project.

The pedagogical project follows the regulations defined in the educational project and guaranteed by a higher institution, which supervises different systems. It is defined by four essential parameters: the pedagogical negotiation, the articulation between different learning projects, the determination of objectives, the duration, and the evaluation. It is important to remark that the structure of chemical engineering curriculum is still centered on applying the contents in a fragmented manner and solving problems according to the criteria of each subject. The integration of these modules has been implemented only in a chemical process design subject, but yet the contents of each course have been studied and questioned intensively in order to enhance the whole educational context. Once the subjects studied in the curriculum are moving relatively it will enable a progressive approach to project-based learning and hence a standardized vision for students to progress in their learning process (Tannous & Ropoli, 2005).

In our work, we have applied these parameters as a base to orient the chemical engineering courses in the following way:

Pedagogical negotiation allows for a diagnosis of the pedagogical situation, considering student acquisition and the program requirements. It also allows the students to express themselves and make questions about their own difficulties in comprehending the situation of process learning. This negotiation is only partial with the professor's intention predominating over the students. The design could be related to the programmatic contents in the classroom.

The articulation between different learning projects of the professor and the students renders concrete pedagogical projects. The interferences and adjustments could be determined by negotiation. This allows for reflection and for corrective and modifying actions of the perspectives chosen. This articulation can occur between subjects offered in different semesters.

The determination of objectives must emerge from the developmental process of the pedagogical project by way of negotiation. This negotiation can occur between the professor and his or her students, considering the whole developmental process, the time registers, the pedagogical methods, the techniques used, and the possibilities for action and carrying out of the project. In this process the student or group of students develop their own technical knowledge and computer programs to carry out practical projects, making these available for the other students.

The duration of the work is an essential factor to conduct pedagogical projects. The period should neither be too short, putting at risk the quality of the project, nor too long, which could become impracticable. The duration of a pedagogical project is linked to the time limit required to make the contents available and learner availability.

The evaluation must include the whole developmental process of the pedagogical project. It can be considered as an indicator for the intermediate and final evaluations. The final result of the evaluations can represent the effective involvement in the whole learning process, with a definition of the objectives and the steps to be taken, participation in the activities, and the evaluation process.

Chemical Engineering Subject Design Considerations

The complete undergraduate course of chemical engineering at Unicamp has 10 semesters, in a day course, and 11 semesters in an evening course. The critical factors in the learning process are lost during these semesters due to the fact that in some courses the information is being disseminated in a unidirectional manner with minimal to no time for reflecting on the whole context. To acquire knowledge means to understand and aggregate all the fundamental concepts in order to observe the big picture, relative to each student's time requirements.

The graduate course, Master of Science and Doctorate, the chemical engineering at Unicamp has four and eight semesters, respectively. The students follow the compulsory subject, but the professors have more autonomy and flexibility to teach.

So we remark that the project-based learning (PBL) could be applied no matter what semester or degree in the chemical engineering courses. Then, since 2001 the PBL concept was implemented in different subjects of these courses. This section presents some examples of chemical engineering subjects, applying project-based learning to undergraduate (Transport Phenomena and Unit Operations I) and graduate (Fundamentals and Applications of Fluidization, Momentum Transfer and Particulate Systems) engineering subjects in the School of Chemical Engineering at the State University of Campinas (Brazil). As each subject has his or her own specificities, we chose the Unit Operations I subject to show the methodology and strategy idealized. It is important to remark that all subjects are taught in a hybrid approach where the traditional manner of student/professor attendance is complemented with the use of a distance education environment (WebCT and TelEduc) to enable more flexibility and interaction in the learning process between students and professor. The use of distance learning tools is widely used in undergraduate evening courses and for students that have restricted time constraints for being in a physical classroom environment (graduate students).

Course Organization

The discipline Unit Operations I was presented to participants through the software TelEduc. The programmatic contents of subject Unit Operations I involve pumps and compressors, solid particles dynamics, flow and porous media, filtration, sedimentation, and solid particles transport. It provides links to several options: general information on the subject matter (program, bibliography, evaluation) and the professor; chronogram of the course through periodically updated agendas; course notes with videos, animations, and simulators; activities; communication tool using electronic mail; area available for each individual or group participant (portfolio); and student profiles.

The TelEduc software makes it possible to monitor the access frequency of the students within the whole home page and the interaction between them and the professor (Figure 4). The home page login access is restricted to the students registered in those subjects.

Methodology Applied

The proposed methodology encompasses three steps: technical knowledge, interaction, and collaboration and decision-making.

Technical knowledge: At this step the acquired knowledge and abilities (computational or not) were evaluated. All the projects developed were based on basic concepts and their applications, where the students should design adequate equipment for the process chosen. As an example we cited the subject Unit Operations I, applying the knowledge acquired in the subjects Applications of Materials in Chemical Engineering and Technical-Economic Analysis (Tannous & Ropoli, 2005). Figure 1 shows the schemes adopted to construct the projects.

Figure 2 shows the list of activities (projects) available using the TelEduc Software and relevant information for each project.

Figure 3 shows the scheme of a fluidized bed dryer (Fluidized Bed System). The activity involves concepts concerning compressors, distributor plate, fixed and fluidized bed, cyclones, and fluid flow through the pipes.

Interaction: The interaction and interactivity among students is assessed during the course. Motivation is observed through of involvement with the project developments. The tools used in this step are the e-mail and portfolio, and the login records. The lectures provided ground for discussions about the course content to strengthen the acquired knowledge, to develop the communication among participants and professor, as well as to help to assess the participation of each member in the projects. The projects were chosen by the students and carried out in groups of four or five students.

Figure 1. Scheme of the PBL with different subjects

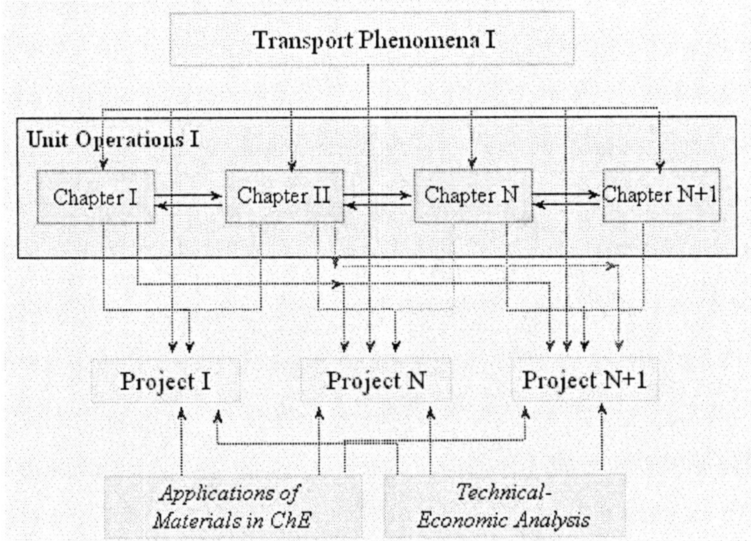

Figure 2. List of activities available using the TelEduc Software

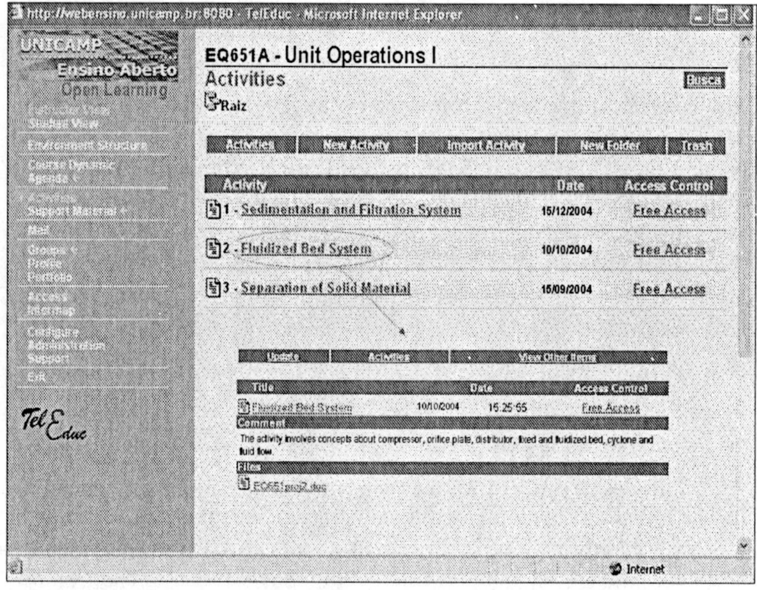

Figure 3. Unit of a fluidized bed dryer

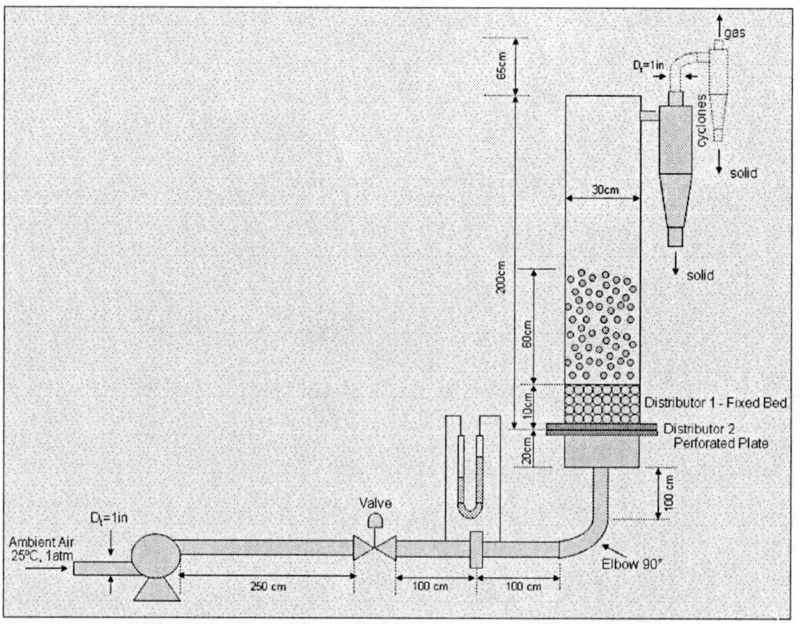

Collaboration and decision making: To assess these features it is taken into account the students' contributions and suggestions to solve the projects. The students are mainly evaluated for their participation in the interactive projects.

Results and Discussions

The evaluation of the methodology has the objective to analyze their adaptation in undergraduate learning in the chemical engineering course. In this item we present some results about the professor and student evaluations about the TelEduc and PBL methodology.

Student Profiles

The Unit Operations I is taught in the sixth and seventh semester for day and evening courses, respectively. This subject approaches specific operations of the chemical process involving solid-fluid associated with functionality and design of equipments. The project-based learning was applied in three consecutive semesters.

The general profile of the students of day course was characterized by 95% of students without contract of employment and evening course, with up to 50% of students working 40 hours per week. Only 15% of the students taking university entrance examinations for evening courses are employed in a permanent job. After approval, the student searches for an internship and "Scientific Initiation" starting his or her own professional activities.

Analysis of Software

The students found it easy to deal with the software TelEduc as well as to find information from the source. The disposable tools in the software were associated with the methodology applied. The students applied initiative in the use of distance learning tools in order to try to cooperate and collaborate on issues discussed in the sessions. The course home pages were accessed from the university, work place, and home, and mostly during the evenings. Students accessed the home page once or twice a week. The students used it mostly to access the course didactic materials and activities. Nevertheless, the interaction between students, professor, and teaching assistant was limited because all of them were in integral time at the university.

Analysis of the New Methodology

The experience of PBL allowed us to identify and comprehend the efficiency of this learning methodology. The aspects of motivation and interactivity during the subjects exhibit a positive direction where the students and professors are systematically growing (i.e., building their own knowledge, individually and in a group).

Figure 4. Intermap of TelEduc

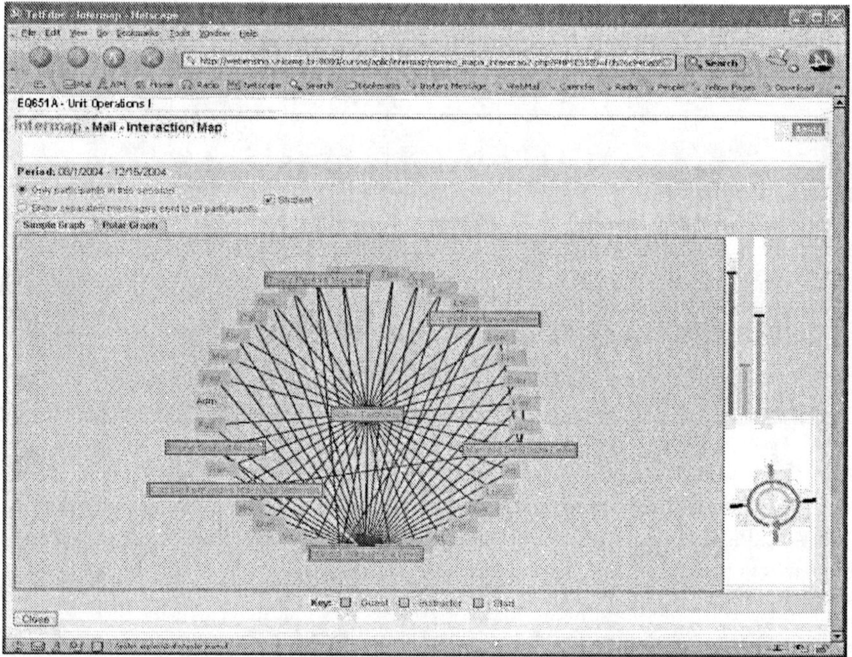

The student's involvement in the interactive process is evaluated in the course. As indicators of analysis, the motivation, creativity, and decision making of students must be observed. The interactivity is associated in the evolution process and course dynamics. Through the evolution process, students can be observed from being passive to active in their pursuit of the learning process. The tool that was applied the most was e-mail, and it was used by the evening course. Although from a technical perspective it should be noted that the discussions were uninformative. We observe from the records that for most of the part it is the professor and teaching assistant sending messages for the students. Figure 4 shows the e-mail Internet where one can see the interactions between the professor, teaching assistant, and students. The utilization of TelEduc tools must be better applied allowing the students to integrate the technical knowledge with interactivity. Nevertheless, the students are still in a passive position.

But according to student opinions, this option was considered to be a good initiative, with 89% of approval, and the suggestion was made to extend it to other subjects.

Comparison between the Subjects Applying PBL

Tables 1 and 2 show the undergraduate and graduate subjects where project-based learning was used, operating in different semesters (Tannous, 2003, 2004; Tannous & Donida, 2003; Tannous, Rodrigues, & Fernandes, 2002; Tannous & Ropoli, 2005).

Table 1. Undergraduate subjects taught using project-based learning

Subjects	Motivation and Objective	Student Profile	Software	Methodology	Results
Transport Phenomena I	First complex theoretical subject of the chemical engineering course involving mass, momentum, and energy balances, applied to different fluid flow. Application of the simulators with a friendly interface of two independent modules (head-loss and boundary layer) as project-based learning.	The student ages are around 20 years old and are characterized by day and evening courses The day course has 95% of students with free time and the evening course has 50% employees working 40 hours per week.	WebCT	After orientation from the professor, each student group simulated a specific process.	The students had more time to make a critical analysis of the results and to be more conclusive. Suggested the more frequent implementation of computer classes in the chemical engineering subjects.
Unit Operations I	Study of the operational principles and equipment dimensioning for the different chemical processes. To develop project-based learning interacting with all the concepts of the different subjects.		TelEduc	The methodology was based on technical knowledge, interaction, collaboration, and decision making.	Better comprehension of the concepts and application in real chemical processes. Greater motivation and interactivity between the students and professors.

The undergraduate subjects (Table 1) are taught to third year chemical engineering students and the graduate subjects (Table 2) to MS and PhD students. The student profiles were distinct according to the different characteristics and objectives of the regular students (academia) and professionals from industry. We noted that the graduate students had more interaction and involvement with the projects than the undergraduate students did. The professional experience of the students gave them the opportunity to extend their knowledge and make exchanges with other students.

The subjects were adapted to make use of the distance education environment, allowing easy access to the contents taught in the classroom, promoting a better interaction amongst the participants.

Table 2. Graduate subjects taught using project-based learning

Subjects	Motivation and Objective	Student Profile	Software	Methodology	Results
Momentum Transfer	Compulsory subject for graduate students. Theoretical subject matter involving concepts of stationary and transient flows, boundary layer, and turbulent flow. To promote activities developed in class with major information diffusion and major contact with the students and professor.	There are two different profiles: regular students with 23-25 years old and special students (in general engineers) with 27-40 years old. The last one is registered as a distinct classification from the regular graduate students.	WebCT and TelEduc	Each group of students carried out a part of the project as a function of their own profiles, developing technical and scientific abilities. One group was responsible for integration of the project.	The constructivist approach adjusted the development of a piece of software (learning oriented object) divided into two parts: theoretical and mathematical approaches (analytical and numerical development).
Fundamentals and Applications of Fluidization	The subject deals with chemical processes in the pharmaceutical, food, and petrochemical industries, using fluidized beds. Most of the bibliography is from periodicals. To make didactic material available, to promote major contact between professor and students, and to apply project-based learning, integrating all the concepts obtained from the different subjects.	There are two different profiles: regular students with 23-25 years old and special students (in general engineers) with 27-40 years old. The last one is registered as a distinct classification from the regular graduate students.	WebCT	The methodology was based on three levels: technical knowledge (elaboration of integrated projects, self-evaluation, chat, and discussion) interaction and collaboration, and decision-making. Project development could be individual or in groups of students.	Interest in the new methodology and learning of technological tools; flexibility of access to the course contents; use of Internet to facilitate access to information; stimulus and motivation promoted by the professors in the learning process; individual learning process but allowing for effective discussions; passivity of students. The possibility of simultaneously carrying out professional activities with time flexibility was remarked on.

Table 2. continued

Particulate Systems	Theoretical and practical subject dealing with industrial chemical processes, involving: Solid-Fluid Dynamics; Porous Media Flow; Filtration; Fluidized Bed; Transport of Solids; Sedimentation. Application of project-based learning using small-scale projects.	There are two different profiles: regular students with 23-25 years old and special students (in general engineers) with 27-40 years old. The last one is registered as a distinct classification from the regular graduate students.	TelEduc	After orientation by the professor, each group of students chose one specific process and developed their own project.	Facility of access to the course contents; elaboration of specific projects involving interactions with the contents; more responsibility with respect to their own knowledge.

Conclusion

Constructivism is a theory concerning learning and knowledge that suggests that the human being is an active learner who constructs his or her own knowledge on experience and on efforts to give meaning to that experience.

Project-based learning presents significant advantages with respect to other conventional methods and has been the subject of various papers in journals of engineering education. The experience gained over the last five years has produced an effective know-how in the engineering and methodological designs.

The chemical engineering curricula continues to be centered on the contents developed by the professor. The compartmental organization of the contents has been intensively questioned. New proposals and experiences can be found in curricula centered on inquiry-based learning, project-based learning, and problem-based learning, amongst others.

The aspects of motivation and interactivity observed in all subjects were shown to be positive, with both students and professors being systematically involved in constructivist evolution, obtaining individual and group knowledge. To participate in the project, the students became involved in an educational experience in the integration of the search for knowledge with existing practices. The students stopped being mere novices in the contents of the knowledge area and became more conscious, reflective, and participative.

In addition, the professor could also find the work enjoyable, interesting, and motivating, since the teaching task varied constantly as they explored new projects with each new group of students. In project-based learning, the professor continually receives new ideas, thus becoming a lifelong learner, and classroom management is simplified, because when students are interested and involved, there are likely to be fewer disciplinary problems.

The creation of subjects in the distance education environment (WebCT and TelEduc) allowed for the complementary and support student material to be made available for the development of all the projects. In general, class attendance became a more dynamic learning process, and student participation could be followed by using the statistics of subject access frequency and by communication between the professors and students.

According to student opinion, they considered a good initiative and suggested to extend it to other subjects.

Acknowledgments

The author gratefully acknowledges the contribution of many students, TAs, and professors who were involved in these subjects and projects, and the positive acceptance of the chemical engineering students at Unicamp. The author also wishes to thank CAPES and FAEP/UNICAMP for their financial support.

References

Davenport, D. (2000). Experience using a project-based approach in an introductory programming course. *IEEE Transactions on Education, 43*(4), 443-448.

Doolittle, P. E. (2002). *Online teaching and learning strategies: An experimental exploration of teaching, learning, and technology*. 3rd Annual Irish Educational Technology User's Conference, Carlow. Retrieved May 16-17, 2005, from http://edpsychserver.ed.vt.edu/workshops/edtech2002/pdf/online.pdf

Forrester, D., & Jantzie, N. (2003, March 21). *Learning theories*. Retrieved July 19, 2005, from http://www.ucalgary.ca/~gnjantzi/learning_theories.htm

Frank, M., Lavy, I., & Elata, D. (2003). Implementing the project-based learning approach. *International Journal of Technology and Design Education, 13*, 273-288.

Green, A. M. (1998). *Project-based learning: Moving students toward meaningful learning*. Washington, DC. Office of Educational Research and Improvement (ERIC Document Reproduction Service N° ED422466).

Okelo, L. (2001, August 29). *Project-based learning*. Retrieved August 2, 2005, from http://www.iearn.org/pbl

Project based learning handbook. (n.d.). Buck Institute for Education (BIE). Retrieved July 22, 2005, from http://www.bie.org/pbl/pblhandbook/foreword.php

Rodrigues, J., Melo, R., Ferreira, S., Pinho, S., & Pereira, T. (n.d.). *Formation online: A view about the importance of conception and implementation of courses of distance education.* Retrieved July 19, 2005, from http://www.apevt.pt/c12.htm

Simões, J. A., Relvas, C., & Moreira, R. (2004). Project-based teaching-learning computer-aided engineering tools. *European Journal of Engineering Education, 29*(1), 147-161.

Tamir, P. (1990). Considering the role of invitations to inquiry in science teaching and professor education. *Journal of Science Professor Education, 1*(3), 41-45.

Tannous, K., Rodrigues, S., & Fernandes, F. A. (2002). *Utilization of computational of software directing learning of fluid mechanics.* XXX Brazilian Congress in Engineering Education, September 22-25. Piracicaba, Brazil.

Tannous, K. (2003). *Mejoría en calidad de la enseñanza de ingeniería: Transformación de comportamiento entre docente y discente.* Engineering Education in the World of No Frontiers-ICECE2003, March 16-19, Santos, Brazil.

Tannous, K. (2004). Interactive learning in engineering education. In S. Mishra & R. C. Sharma (Eds.), *Interactive multimedia in education and training* (pp. 289-305). Hershey, PA: Idea Group Publishing.

Tannous, K., & Donida, M. W. (2003). Evaluation of e-learning engineering graduate courses. *TechKnowLogia—International Journal of Technologies for the Advancement of Knowledge and Learning, 5*(1). Retrieved August 25, 2005, from http://www.techknowlogia.org

Tannous, K., & Ropoli, E. A. (2005). Project-based learning pedagogical proposal in the chemical engineering courses. In R. M. Barbosa (Ed.), *Virtual environment learning* (pp. 85-100). Porto Alegre, Brazil: Artmed.

Thomas, J. W. (2000, March). A *review of research on project-based learning.* Retrieved August 24, 2005, from http://www.bie.org/tmp/research/researchreviewPBL.pdf

Chapter XVI

The "Pastoral" in Virtual Space: A Tale of Two Systems and How E-Learning Practitioners Re-Make Them

Mary Griffiths, University of Waikato, New Zealand

Michael Griffiths, Independent Researcher, New Zealand

Abstract

Two online undergraduate media and communications projects, one in Australia (1999-2003), and the second from New Zealand (2004-2005), are analyzed and compared in this chapter. Written by two flexible-learning practitioners, the case study gives the background and contexts of the two projects. We describe how we developed intercultural, pastoral pedagogies suited to contrasting "internationalized" cohorts, despite trends in new "market-driven" universities. The framework used is Michel Foucault's "pastoral" power, as modelled by Ian Hunter in studies of the milieu of the face-to-face English classroom, and the agency of the teacher in constructing self-reflexive subjectivities (Hunter, 1996). The development of valuable intercultural skills in the student depends in part on the composition of the "internationalized" student groups themselves, and on their and their teacher's awareness of the formative nature of the software being used. Learning software has the potential to mediate conduct, the choice of what kind of relationships ensue rests with the e-practitioner.

Internationalization Contexts

In a Western university era driven by the massification of educational opportunities, and the privatization of costs caused by a general downturn in state spending on education, many universities in the Australasian region have turned to the global education market in order to survive. Moves toward user-pays education and an emphasis on business-models, as opposed to fully-funded state education and notions of "the public good," are slowly changing the traditional relationships between universities, their academics, and students, and altering the range of activities in on-campus classrooms, or off-shore locations of study. Pedagogy is changing to meet the changing composition of cohorts. Over the six years of this comparative study, universities in Australia and New Zealand have become nodes in a globalizing system of communities of learning and communication exchanges. A recent *Economist* report shows mainstream financial journalism's representation of the phenomenon of international trade in learning:

Several countries—most notably Australia and New Zealand—are trying to turn education into an export industry. (The brains business, 2005)

It quotes 2002 OECD figures showing that foreign students comprise 10% of all Australian students. The feature of "internationalization," which we focus on here, is our experience of developing e-learning strategies in two institutions for the growth in media and communications students under these conditions. Since the mid-1990s, Australian and New Zealand universities have adopted educational technology for most aspects of knowledge and human resource management. Administrators, academics, and students are now subject to an assemblage of new technology services discourses garnered from e-domains outside the academy such as e-commerce with its emphasis on choice and value for money, which has impacted on international student recruitment, and e-government with its emphasis on client services, cost-effectiveness, and transparency, which, along with high student numbers, is altering traditional "pastoral" relationships between academics and their students. This climate brings with it new habits of thought for all concerned: not all productive of the conditions of knowledge seeking, for its own sake. Institutional audits of student "competencies" now emphasize those involved in retrieval and management of vast information resources, as well as particular content acquisition and mastery. E-systems, adopted for information delivery and communication across university libraries, teaching departments, bureaucracies, and university campuses, have become routine. Examples include staff intranets, narrowcast student networks, digital libraries, and external links to partnerships with community and industry, and online enrollment and course delivery. From a teacher's perspective, the choice of digital platforms and communication protocols is shaped initially by institutional bureaucracies prioritizing their fiscal remit. Dependency on soft funding means that universities aim to reach as many cohorts as possible, as cheaply as possible (see Mazzarol & Hosie [1996] for an early discussion of Australian dependency). As well, even those campuses, which primarily serve on-campus students, use e-learning packages for content delivery in an effort to streamline the management of large numbers.

Institutional decisions about e-learning packages can be made without considering the longer-term constitutive effects on students' learning of those packages. Crucial differences between potentially quite different learning outcomes are sometimes not taken into account in platform adoption. Even though extensive staff training programs may be provided by an institution, our own experience shows that these tend to be general and instrumentalist, and are more concerned with developing technological and virtual class management skills in the teacher, rather than with explorations of the specific kinds of deep learning opportunities offered if the pedagogy drives the technology uptake, rather than the other way around.

The internationalized class itself can offer opportunities to push the technology to deliver opportunities for even geographically distanced cohorts to learn more than content. Just as being in a face-to-face multi-national classroom can provide the opportunities for intercultural literacies' learning, so can online learning communities. In a globalizing world, intercultural literacies—the routine ability to be aware of and understand different perspectives—are important for studies of representation and mediation, but they also form the kind of learning that Schank (2002) calls "really important knowledge"—"the things that enable students to do things and perform and behave in their daily lives." These literacies are of particular use for media and communications students. Hunter's ideas about the pastoral classroom proved useful as we were thinking through the relations of power and the technologies to hand when teaching internationalized cohorts. Hunter, following Foucault's governmental notion of self-discipline, argues that the "English studies" classroom with its emphasis on reading techniques and writing protocols is the pastoral apparatus where the civic attributes of self-reflection can be taught. These are useful ones for democratic participation and, in the case of this chapter, for intercultural learning. The concept not only helps the student's acquisition of Schank's "really important knowledge," but produces, in the academic, an e-practitioner who starts to use online spaces and their different protocols as pastoral milieu. The virtual spaces of e-learning, whether they are online lectures, mail lists, chat forums, personal folders, resource banks or "public" exhibitions of student work, become a series of interlocking pastoral milieu in which the student's work is on display and in which the work of others can be used as models of conduct. These milieus, whether they are the "public" discussion forums or the private portfolios for an individual's writing, can help produce the attributes of self-reflexivity. The following comparisons aim to show how the e-practitioners concerned worked to adapt their pastoral aims to different institutional conditions. The case studies are a few years apart, and represent the writers' developmental approach to e-pedagogy, as e-learning technologies and institutional readiness develop over time.

Two Learning Programs

Monash's *Redremex*: Convergences of Communities and Information Flows

The first case involves undergraduate writing courses in an international communications program at a regional distance campus of what would become, following national education reforms in the 1990s, the largest university in Australia. Midway though 1998, staff in the communications department began to experiment with converging online components of flexible education to meet the needs of a newly expanded metropolitan-based institution with a number of smaller outer-metropolitan satellite campuses, one in Malaysia (and later South Africa) and an educational partnership in Singapore. The main issue was the continuing management of the communication program's rapid internationalization—of places of delivery, student cohorts, and curriculum. At the start of amalgamations and internationalization, the longer term questions of shared university-wide praxis, quality assurance with its emphasis on benchmarking against set standards, and university branding (to be discussed in the "program evaluation" section)—all of which were to result in the decision to streamline and standardize the university's online software—were not seen as pressing ones. The expansion of the international programs directly affected only a small group of communications staff. Pedagogic dilemmas rapidly arose for these distance practitioners as their student cohorts diversified culturally, becoming more and more geographically distanced from the local point of course delivery, and exhibiting different kinds of prior, culturally-specific educational trainings and expectations. The new off-shore student groups in Malaysia and Singapore were ethnically Chinese in the majority, trained in different media reading protocols and had, in most cases, none of the shared cultural capital on which the media course had been built for Australian student cohorts. What, academics asked, now constituted their "shared teaching and learning space?" Staff noted an increase in e-mails from individual students about the Western-oriented print course materials, as well as ones that focussed on the personal difficulties of study isolation. Students were increasingly noting a lack of what they perceived as a "community" of learning. Many of the e-mails had the same theme: the study independence and stamina that they acquired in completing an undergraduate degree (sometimes over six to eight years) did not facilitate their acquisition of other study competencies, such as the ability to see one's achievement in relation to that of a group, the social aspects of sharing with others, including teachers. Despite the *self-evaluation* exercises in the print study materials, there was a perceived lack of multi-layered, "deep learning" arising from the interaction and dynamics of face-to-face classroom situations. They wanted to understand and take on the attributes of "being a student," "being a writer," through contact, and "the conduct" of learning in relation to others studying at the Australian university. The "pastoral" issue raised required a pedagogic response. Given the constraints experienced in balancing two modes of delivery (on-campus and off-campus), teaching staff knew it needed to be time-efficient, in keeping with the distance learning expectations that equitable protocols be found to establish equivalence of experience for both sets of students. What was presenting was a "governmental" problem of the kind Foucault calls the "conduct of conduct." Staff decided on a custom-made holistic approach to the writing major, and all student groups. *redremex*, a portal Web site, was initiated when three staff applied for a teaching innovation grant (TIF) of $A5000 to develop an integrated approach to teaching a sequence of six papers, across a varied and geographically separated student cohort. Australian on-campus students, off-shore students around the world, discrete on-campus groups in Singapore and Malaysia were all to be supported by print materials, the latter also with locally-based staff. The university had not yet adopted nor endorsed proprietary software, so the online design field seemed open for experimentation, creative solutions, and the development of learning tools, particularly by those with "distance" or flexible experience. The local Gippsland campus multimedia group from the Centre for Learning and Teaching (CeLTS) proved to be excellent and generous project partners, providing in kind at least twice the TIF-funded deliverables for the project. The attempted "solution" was an attractive portal Web site with five public "exhibition spaces" for students and other writers to publish their work; and associated course e-mail groups run through *yahoo* (*inside-forum* for the whole writing major, and *mtxt* and *auw* for specific subjects). It was a custom-designed, inter-departmental project, where there were regular meetings between multimedia staff, the administrative officer responsible for finessing the legal and regulatory matters with the university bureaucracy, and the academic staff who were to be editors and online moderators. Overall designing the site converged and maximized diverse staff resources, student cohorts, and the curriculum.

These aims were in keeping with (what were then emerging, but are now familiar) trends in contemporary Internet culture: the convergence and integration of multiple communication flows in a portal with a number of functionalities. Co-editing protocols (what are now called "wiki") were to be part of the portal, as the first design called for multiple editors to be included in collaborative tasks. The fifth exhibition, "Landscapes, Memories" was designed to generate stories about place, and home, from contributors. The e-mail groups were set up as a compulsory component of the assessment. Students identified themselves and their locations. The idea was that the geography and mixed cultures of the class were to be transparent and a learning resource from the beginning.

Waikato's "Paperless Paper"

The second case derives from an on-campus course with large international enrollments at the small regional University of Waikato, New Zealand. An instructor (with *redremex* experience) taught a "paperless" paper to a combined on-campus second-year media research methods class, comprising students from both arts and management faculties, putting an existing institutional e-learning platform to new uses. Waikato educational software is a customized class management tool called *classforum*. The "media studies" core studies cohorts are made up of up to 60% mainland Chinese students, in addition to Kiwis and a small number of other international students. The significant issues raised by internationalization are different from those arising in the Australian example. Some Waikato on-campus groups are bifurcated along faculty and ethnic lines. They are sharing F2F learning spaces such as lecture halls, library and tutorial rooms, as well as the virtual spaces of *classforum*. Unlike the Monash student cohorts situated in home countries, Waikato international students are living in the host country, speaking English in an immersive way often for the first time, and dealing with the challenges of life off-line in a small regional NZ city. They tend to be digitally confident and possess up-to-date hardware.

Unlike the bottom-up design focus adopted for the dispersed groups addressed by *redremex*, the approach to this Waikato cohort differed in that ease of communication across two faculties needed to be emphasized. The international students from management often adopted Western names while in New Zealand—in some cases, a student might select a different one each year—creating identification problems for their teachers until the online mode was adopted. Another reason for moving the on-campus class online was to improve intercultural conduct and communication skills across the whole cohort. By requiring group work online, written submissions, collaborative editing tasks, and peer assessment of some work, the instructor aimed not only to demonstrate the research uses of an intranet through simulations, but the strength of intercultural learning about mediation and representation. Media research traditions were demonstrated to differ, according to the two main cultures represented by the student cohort. This was useful in challenging any latent Western orientalism, and notions of "objectivity." In both the *redremex* case and the *paperless paper*, the e-learning technology was adopted to serve wider aims than "content delivery."

Academic Issues

mtxt and *auw* through Redremex

The academic issues were: how to integrate the online delivery of the two courses chosen for the *redremex* pilot, *Media Text: Practices* and *Audiences* and *Authorship and Writing*, especially for Malaysian and Singaporean cohorts. All students already received print materials: a course guide and reader. The main challenge was finding a way to use *yahoogroups*, in a way that the university would endorse, for a series of themed discussions. The online groups were named after the titles of the papers *mtxt* and *auw*. The groups were set up to help share knowledge relevant to the courses, and develop awareness of cultural perspectives, particularly recognition of the specific material factors that shape audience beliefs and practices in different countries. The pilot run of the mail groups was beginning in troubled times: lecturers needed to be quickly informed about, and able to moderate the multi-ethnic, multi-polity discussion of sensitive issues (e.g., gender issues, 9/11, terrorism, when non-Western media coverage from "minority home" countries such as Muslim Malaysia impacted on "host country" majority class discussions). Students could access, through the yahoo Web site, a passworded "educational" online community, or choose to receive a "daily digest" of messages. Instructors favored the latter approach as it acted as a quotidian reminder of discipline and commitment in learning. Students were required to join in discussions and were assessed on two self-chosen submissions to the international discussions. They also wrote their own self-reflexive evaluation of this aspect of the program for *Media Text: Practices, Audiences*. In all pedagogic decisions about course design and use of *yahoogroups*, the idea of making the techniques of learning transparent and shared was uppermost. If media discussions went "off target" or were inappropriately expressed, the re-setting of boundaries quickly occurred—spontaneously students became moderators of each other's conduct.

Classforum, University of Waikato, 2004-2005

In contrast to designing a set of e-spaces to meet student needs, using an institution's software package means a different kind of adaptation to technology. *Media and Society 2: Media Research* is a core paper in the communications degree where students learn research methods (basic media research terms, quantitative and qualitative methodologies, research praxis, regulatory environments, ethics, data collation and handling, and professional issues). The two faculties involved in the degree—arts and management—have different instruction styles and thus there are significant issues for lecturing staff in meeting and adjusting to student assumptions. Media production students in both faculties, aiming at professional entry into industry, either on the artistic side or in public relations, generally believe that creative work (such as video production, brand development, and scriptwriting) is more important and satisfying than "critical work." Marketing students were well trained in using intranets; arts students were not.

In *Media Research*, students worked from the beginning in groups of four to design a media research project, from the "getting started" phase, through annotated literature searches, to research design, and then to the submission of an ethics application for a fully worked out research proposal. In this undergraduate course, they do not proceed to fieldwork. As a result, simulated research activities must maintain interest and motivation. This is where the online environment can be very productive in providing no-fail learning for the whole cohort as drafts of projects were posted and commented on. Multicultural groups were encouraged: people learned each other's names and strengths quickly, and clarifications of instructions were easier online, especially for non-native speakers of English. Media research is culturally and nationally shaped, so many unshared assumptions came under scrutiny, as students compared their hypotheses online. One example of this was the familiar (in the West) "media effects" debate on children's viewing of violence on television. Despite being warned about the difficulty and controversial nature of the topic (Google returns millions of entries on this kind of research) a group of international students chose it, and defended their hypothesis about the connections between watching violent programs, children's unacceptable behavior, and strict state censorship of viewing. The peer commentary became a way of discussing cultural and national differences. Research traditions are as mediated by culture as are technology uses.

In 2004, all but one piece of assessment was to be submitted online, and marked and returned online by tutors using Microsoft Word's "track-changes" option. A "paperless paper" helped arts on-campus students begin to feel at home with online protocols. It provided greater efficiencies in the group facilitation tools offered by *classforum*, such as "folders," "discussions," "polls," "live mail," and "wiki." The self-naming of the 2004 groups inspired team loyalty. Hunter found that the protocols of writing in the face-to-face classroom helped develop subjectivity; this also occurs online as writing tasks go on under a particular rubric. The cooperative nature of learning was a key objective: media work generally, and media research specifically, is often conducted in project teams. The instructor's aim was to simulate as many of the "real" events of research design and development through the use of the online facility, thus deliberately developing digital literacies as a component of undergraduate research competencies. A modified online assessment submission was adopted in 2005, after it was clear that some arts students were finding it hard to adapt to some online protocols.

Student polls were used during the course as formative tools, to assess satisfaction with group work and with the e-learning framework. On the 2005 run of the paper, the instructor addressed the student lack of digital literacy, by working from the "steps of learning" approach through Salmon's "e-tivities" (*All thing,* 2005; Salmon, 2002) and allowing each tutor and group restricted freedom to change names or functions. The 2005 course began with developing the social aspects of the course online, with a no-fail hurdle requirement to "spark" motivation and begin online capacity building. The "hurdle" and diagnostic assignment worth 10% ensured that all students committed to accessing and using the online environment. Although a Mandarin-speaking tutor helped the international students, and the services of the Teaching and Learning Development Unit were used, it quickly became clear which students needed additional English language instruction. The discussion fora, while only used intermittently, were designed for less social and purposeful interactions between groups. Assessment of student satisfaction took place through the usual course assessment procedures of a template offering a series of questions relating to course evaluation, and satisfaction with lecturing and tutoring staff. It was regarded as a well organized and useful paper.

Administrative Issues

Redremex: Aiming for High Interoperability; Operational Hitches

The Monash campus has a 20-year institutional history of print-supported delivery of distance study, and of high school and alternative mature age entry paths. There was (and, at the time of writing, still is) a distance education print publishing unit, with long-established, developed writing protocols mutually derived from the work of staff (both academic and support) and students, and with a series of annual print production routines in place. They have since proceeded to customized software. Normalized teaching and learning expectations result from this history of layered annual learning and the research and design work of a specialized branch of academic support workers. Discrete genres of study material emerged, which everyone then learned to handle: the endorsed template of a study guide, the length and constituent parts of a course reader, and the student assessment schedules. Everyday ways of "doing things" are set in place; and the print technologies give rise to "technologies of the self," such as reflective reading, note-taking, and self-check tasks. Moving to a virtual e-learning environment challenges all these. A number of administrative protocols needed to be worked out in the design of a university-auspiced Web site: the internal contractual arrangements with multimedia design staff, the privacy policy with the university solicitor, the intellectual property issues, the branding demands of the university. Being allowed to use an outside provider for the e-mail groups was less a matter of enlightened support from the administration, and more a matter of having insider technology developers who were themselves keen early adopters, with enthusiastic managers interested in the research and development process. Elsewhere in the university, the argument that "real," outsider, and more flexible mail-list practices were better for media students than the existing clunky institutional application, was accepted. Probably this was because online literacies were not widespread at the time. *Yahoogroup* software meant that the lecturer had to manually construct each course group using *yahoo* protocols of member subscription invitation, passwords, and two modes of reading student messages commentary (Web and e-mail "daily digests"). Student unfamiliarity with online list discussions meant that moderation often included the deletion of long message trails. The intellectual property issues were handled eventually by marketing arm decree (by institutional branding) by the time the Web site was functional and an attractive commodity with functionalities that could be adapted for general use (for example, online mechanisms for student submissions). There was no online support apart from that offered by the yahoo moderators' list. There was no specific evaluation tool for the whole package apart from the regular flexible student evaluation pro-formas from the Centre for Learning and Teaching, which use generic questions to assess student satisfaction.

Classforum: Low Interoperability = Time Inefficient

In Waikato, there was no need to work from the ground up in constructing a series of public or private online environments and communities. The e-learning tool is already developed and so are the interactive protocols, even if, as we discovered, they were not well understood by students on the first run of the paper. The first difficulty encountered was that the university-run student database, Jasper, did not talk back to *classforum* databases in very sophisticated ways. This meant that, for a large class of 155, the instructor had manually to add the usernames of all students into online tutorial groups, working from students' handwritten notes. The tutors (who had been given host status) also were so enthusiastic about the platform's possibilities, that they added multiple different functionalities to their tutorial groups' space in 2004, thus contributing—for the very best of reasons—to the general difficulties in managing the online environment from the point of view of equity for all students. Nevertheless the live e-mail, interactive student feedback, and polling functions were useful ways of working with the class, and "governing" the remainder of the processes of learning. A support person from ECTUS, the outsourced provider, helped trouble-shoot and helped with the training of lecturers and students. Teaching staffs are regularly allowed to give feedback to ECTUS on desirable future functionalities, and the provider has recently won a prestigious ComputerWorld Excellence Award ("Virtual classroom," 2005) for interactive multimedia. Interoperability of metadata has been improved in 2005, with the Jasper database now supplying overall student subscriptions and withdrawals automatically. This now places Waikato's support for academic adopters at less of an ad hoc, experimental stage of e-learning development.

Program Evaluations: Comparison

As the deeper issues caused by Monash's institutional amalgamation and expansion emerged, a centrist—rather than devolved or distributed—model of policy and governance became the preferred option for managing the teaching programs. This impacted eventually on the e-learning choices made for teachers at an institutional level, and challenged early-adopters of e-learning technologies: individual practitioners lost autonomy as the university moved to university-wide models. Eventually, the university adopted *WebCT* and then *Vista* as its online support software, discouraging individual uses of other proprietary software or *opensource* technologies. The need to "govern" disparate cultures over the whole university meant that academics' pedagogic and pastoral individualism was gradually subsumed by university training schemes, and by branded platforms and auspiced technology.

Despite the fact that the *redremex* Web site became a point of institutional discussion and interest, its aesthetics were admired, and it was considered appropriate for "Creative Writing" papers, it stood outside of institutional priorities. Design team members (both academics and technology designers) were invited to "best practice" workshops to discuss the design and pedagogic imperatives (Griffiths, 2003), but specific components of *redremex* development ran into difficulties as code had to be re-written for the customized site in the submission and collaborative editing area. Multimedia designers tend to be headhunted, and move on, causing delays and rewriting tasks. "Branding" the site by the university has meant that the academics and designers who have moved on from Monash have "lost" mutually held intellectual property. The schedule of production milestones kept CeLTS multimedia commitment high, as it did with academic staff, but the intellectual property problem did not emerge until later in the site's development. The *redremex* portal never became the "access point" for all writing students that its initiators imagined. There are a few submissions in the first exhibition, "Glow." On the other hand, the *yahoo* e-mail discussion groups in two writing subjects were successfully operated over three years. The online traffic was substantial (over 500 considered messages—initiating discussion and replying—in *mtxt* and 278 in *auw*). Student feedback across the whole multi-site cohort was positive about the experience of being in the multicultural student online community: *mtxt*. In *Media Text: Practices and Audiences* the aspects of the course most commented on were the sanctioned access to an informed, contested, but civil space where intercultural perspectives could be experienced on questions of significance in a globalized world. In particular, learning to "talk" about 9/11 across Christian and Muslim worlds was cited as having a high value. In *Authorship and Writing*, the instructor used a sophisticated FAQ approach to unpacking theoretical and critical questions for students with varying levels of English skills.

In contrast, *Media Research* at Waikato using *classforum* fulfilled the course objective of being an almost "paperless paper" on its 2004 run, but the high (and baseless) assumptions of teaching staff about some students' digital literacies meant that the usual "unruliness" of the Web emerged as a contentious issue. New online users with a new package to learn as well as the content heavy course struggled in the first three weeks. A lack of netiqette, the challenge to familiar on-campus ways of interacting, and the group assessments combined made the first run very difficult. Sometimes submissions were inappropriately expressed, and an intervention had to be made by the course leader. One instructor spent 200 hours in moderating and facilitating the online management of a class of 155 because, despite detailed instructions, some students posted "private" work in "public" spaces, disadvantaging themselves (because their work was downloaded by others) and class managers. Yet student feedback on the online polls, on perceptions of online group work, and of its "deep learning" potential, was very positive. In 2005, the online component of the paper was reduced, the online expectations and protocols were established early, and the class ran more successfully. Acceptance of the value of learning "knowledge worker" skills through *classforum* by colleagues teaching at first-year has meant that improvements in motivation and competency have been noticeable in the second-year cohort. The civic and cultural issues of learning in a mixed cohort have been shaped up in a pastoral way explicitly by class instructors—who recommend that students chose group partners from another culture; and that differences in approaches to media be discussed (for example, censorship, free press, and state controls as opposed to public interest institutions).

Networking and Collaboration: Comparison

Both projects required networking and collaboration by staff and students. The creative writing portal, *redremex*, was a team project from start to finish: the continued involvement of the immediate TIF group of three, the Web and graphic designers in multimedia and their managers, the lecturers and tutors off-shore who taught the subjects, the editors who volunteered their help was high. One of the most satisfying experiences in the project was its collaborative and developmental nature. It became a research project, and an experimental site for praxis for all involved. This openness of attitude was even true of the tenor of negotiations in the "branding" exercise. Although it was seen as an unnecessary commodification of a joint effort by the teaching academics, this did not affect commitment.

The networking involved in the *classforum* example was mainly with tutors and ECTUS staff, in the early stages of the 2004 run, and then it was a matter of readjustment, building drafting and collaborative editing into the group assessment tasks in smoother ways, in the 2005 run. Networking at the student level began in 2005, as the first group assignment was posted in "public space," and while these are un-graded drafts, they act as models of the work which is going on elsewhere in the cohort. Students began to exchange Internet resources suitable for each project, aspects of collaboration that are far more haphazard and unnoticed in F2F environments.

Policy Implications: Comparison

The unresolved policy implication raised by *redremex* is the issue of intellectual property. Collective creative efforts (especially those that involve a good deal of pro bono work over years on the part of all concerned), need to be recognized by an educational institution with a more flexible copyright response than the traditional one of institutional "branding." The "creative commons" or "copyleft" approaches to intellectual property are more of an unbundling of user and producer rights and, were institutions to take either of these more enlightened ways of dealing with collective endeavours, there would be more e-learning innovation. The strength of this argument is confirmed in the world of *open source*. There is still an argument to be made about using, and putting together, elements of what is freely available on the Web, rather than directing limited resources into the replication of proprietary software.

The issues raised by *Media Research* on *classforum* are quite different: the large numbers of international students find the weekly posting of lecture PowerPoints, the Q&A folder, the tutorial spaces, live mail, and the polls increases their ability to study in another language. In addition, their names and pictures, and the resources they post broaden and deepen the learning experience of Kiwi students. Just "recognizing the influence your own culture has on the way you view yourself" and "expanding your knowledge of the ways of other cultures" is a valuable addition to the discrete learning objectives of this research methods paper (see Wiley [n.d.] on reusable digital learning objects, pp. 1-35). Existing online environments, properly handled, can be very good resources for NZ university teachers with large on-campus international groups: a lot of no-fail learning and questioning can go on without any of the potential loss of face experienced in F2F contexts.

Sustainability and Conclusion

redremex has been inactive since February 2004, as members of the academic staff have moved institutions. To continue to develop it would have required a major re-design after *yahoogroups* were no longer supported in line with centralized decisions about online delivery through WebCT and Vista. It might still be possible to run it as a publishing space, but IP issues remain unresolved, although as suggested previously, they could be handled by the adoption of different IP protocols.

Classforum, or another e-learning application, is sure to continue to be developed by Waikato. E-learning is too valuable to on-campus learning and teaching, and to dovetailing with the development of business applications, to be dropped. Every practitioner of e-learning uses communication practices online that have implicit values and assumptions (see Blaker & Nafstad, 2004). It is worth doing away (in virtual environments) with what Hunter calls "anxieties" about exerting professional choices in F2F classrooms. Students are also learning what the e-learning package readies them to learn—code is socially constructive. Ethical interventions in the designs of e-learning applications will need to be ongoing, according to the cohort's needs, trainings, and cultures. Teaching intercultural literacies and civic behavior can be done without ever mentioning the word "democracy." One can break down a number of cultural barriers in any international student cohort. As one student of *mtxt* wrote, "'one of the most interesting aspects was the contributions of people of different cultural backgrounds; this served to highlight the importance of cultural literacy as it applies to this unit."

Lessons Learned

1. Designing for "deep learning" online enhances one's understanding of the formative potential of technology and changes one's pedagogy.
2. Conduct online is replicated. Students in multicultural cohorts are learning many things implicitly at the same time that they are learning subject content. The e-practitioner makes the choice between using technology as a tool, or formatively.
3. It is essential to understand institutional policy and protocols, and to be able to explain yourself and your project at regular intervals to all institutional stakeholders.
4. A thorough costing and resource feasibility study is essential, if one is developing anything outside of routine online institutional practices. We did not estimate staff time adequately for either project.
5. A flexible intellectual property strategy should be agreed with the institution before beginning developmental collaborative work.

6. Time training online tutors in order to optimize understanding and uptake is essential. Student familiarity with online protocols cannot be assumed. Class representatives should be helped to understand the "invisible work" of online pedagogic design.
7. Moderation techniques are the key to productive online discussions. Publish e-rules, and do not intervene too early in online debates.
8. Digital literacy skills need to be upgraded regularly; this includes policies on privacy.
9. Relevant and useful software, and new practices, exist outside the academy.
10. Intellectual traditions are culturally constructed. The international composition of student cohorts is a learning resource.

Best Practices

1. Student feedback suggests that providing the pastoral spaces to develop cultural literacies has worked. Online learning can be no-fail learning about another culture; so designing for integrated virtual learning helps bring important (if temporary) communities of learning into being.
2. Designing for multiple interactions online (both public and private) helps produce digital literacies. The course assessment needs to bring students online quickly and effectively, and requires a range of group and individual tasks.
3. All student cohorts, in themselves, are a resource for learning. Learning objectives may be specific, but each community itself provides opportunities to acquire, in addition to course content, "really important knowledge."

References

All things in moderation. (2005). Retrieved 10 September, 2005, from http://www.atimod.com/index.shtm

Blaker, R. M., & Nafstad, H. E. (2004). Towards a definition of communication encompassing ethical dimensions. *Ethical Space: The International Journal of Communication Ethics, 1*(4), 13-17.

Classforum. (2004, 2005). http://classforum.waikato.ac.nz/

Griffiths, M. (2003). redremex: Moderating creative writing and learning cultural literacies. *Student-centred online learning*. Retrieved from http://www.monash.edu.au/groups/hepcit/Presentations/2003/

Griffiths, M., Thornby, C., & Griffiths, M. (1999-2003). *redremex*. Retrieved throughout 1999-2005, from http://www.redremex.monash.edu.au/

Hunter, I. (1996a). Is English an emancipatory discipline? *Australian Humanities Review.* Retrieved from http://www.lib.latrobe.edu.au/AHR/archive/Issue-April-1996/Hunter.html

Hunter, I. (1996b). Four anxieties about English. *Southern Review: Literary and Interdisciplinary Essays, 29*(1), 4-18.

Jandt, F. E. (1998). *Intercultural communication.* Thousand Oaks, CA and London: Sage.

Mazzarol, T., & Hosie, P. (1996). Exporting Australian higher education: Future strategies in a maturing market. *Quality Assurance in Education, 4*(1), 37-50. Retrieved October 10, 2005, from http://www.emeraldinsight.com/Insight/ViewContentServlet?Filename=/published/emeraldfulltextarticle/pdf/1200040106.pdf

mtxt@yahoogroups.com.au. Archives for Griffiths, M. *Media Text: Practices, Audiences* (2001-2003)

Salmon, G. (2002). *E-tivities: The key to active online learning.* London: Kogan Page.

Schank, R. (2002). *Designing world-class e-learning.* New York: McGraw-Hill.

The brains business: A survey of higher education. (2005). *The Economist,* (September 10-16), 1-22.

Wiley, D. (n.d.). *Connecting learning objects to instructional design theory: A definition, a metaphor, and a taxonomy,* 1-35. Retrieved December, 2005, from http://www.e-strategy.ubc.ca/news/update0303/030312-wiley_442.html

Chapter XVII

Using Scenario-Based Learning for E-Learning in Vocational Education

K. C. Chu, Hong Kong Institute of Vocational Education (Tsing Yi), Hong Kong

Abstract

A multimedia Web-based scenario-learning package is prepared for the students of an engineering course. This learning package is to simulate a scenario, which is close to the students' learning or future working environment. Using up-to-date information and multimedia technology, it can simulate issues and conditions similar to those encountered in the real world. Students can virtually experience how the actual working environment should be. They can also take this opportunity to study how different equipment are interconnected together and signals flowing between different units. Students can use this virtual environment to understand deeper about the operation and the theory behind. Further explanation will be displayed in a hierarchical way to suit different backgrounds of students. This online scenario-based learning package is to let all students have a chance to virtually immerse in a scenario to enhance their learning and knowledge. Preliminary study shows that this scenario-based learning is well accepted by students and is worth further study.

Introduction

Multimedia technology can make a transformation of the nature of teaching/learning from reception to engagement, from classroom to real world, from isolation to interconnection, and from exclusive access to a global campus. Online teaching or learning can provide a variety of interactions that include interactive techniques used to present each concept; interactive exercises that help learners integrate multiple concepts; interactive simulations that challenge learners with decision-making situations encountered in the real world; and interactive games to increase retention and provide motivation for learning (Whelan, 1997). Web-based teaching is proved to make remote learning easier, more convenient, and encouraging interactive learning and feedback (Chu, Urbanik, Yip, & Cheung, 1999). Also, computer or Internet access is so well suited to produce a discovery learning environment, which involves a lot of interactivity, feedback, and challenge.

Professional development is now recognized as an important feature in the education of engineering. However, classroom teaching mainly provides student concepts of rules, theorems, and devices. Many employers are finding that graduates are too narrowly based and in practice need to accept wider training (Harris & Bramhall, 1999). Students should learn to apply that knowledge practically through problem solving and design exercise (Chan, 1997). With the help of advanced multimedia technology, it will make learning easier and much more attractive when those exercises are put into the computer or accessed through Internet (Ching, Poon, & McNaught, 2004; Chu, 2004).

In fact, increasing time for practical work will equip students with more useful knowledge for their future career (Ko et al., 2000). Engineering is found upon a variety of rules, theorems, and devices that must be understood by the student and which involve primarily knowledge-based learning; but students must also learn to apply that knowledge practically through problem solving and design exercise (Chu, 1999; Ericksen & Kim, 1998). This provides a good reason to support remote-access practical work for Web-based teaching systems. Another objective of the Web-based laboratory is to provide hands-on lab activities to enhance online courses. A study at East Carolina University found that virtual laboratories help students to understand the concept and theory of those online courses (Yang, 1999). Virtual laboratories are particularly useful when some experiment involves equipment that may cause harmful effects to human beings. The laser virtual laboratory developed by the physics department of Dalhousie University shows how to perform a real time dangerous laser laboratory with the help of commanding equipment through the Internet (Paton, 1999).

The aim of the Department of Engineering of Hong Kong Institute of Vocational Education (Tsing Yi) is to educate and train students with basic knowledge and useful practical skills for their future career (Leung, 1999). Many consultancy works and cooperation have been made with the industry. Such linkage with industry is very valuable to both educational institutions and the society. This can provide more chances for educational institutions to understand the needs of industry and in turn provide students more job opportunities. Virtual laboratories are good to achieve the purpose of practical knowledge transfer but much better if students can actually get involved with some jobs in an environment similar to their future career (Harris & Bramhall, 1999). However, it is impossible for all students to have a chance to engage with suitable companies and work for a short period of time. In this study, an online scenario-based learning package, which can be accessed either in the computer or through the Internet, is prepared for an engineering course. This idea is similar to the integrated studies delivered by the use of "ghost company" at Sheffield Hallam University and Glasgow Caledonian University (Harris & Bramhall, 1999). Those ghost companies provide a framework for a product development scenario, which integrates the various disciplines of the course within a simulated industrial environment.

Scenario-Based Learning (SBL)

Traditional course delivery is vocationally inefficient (Leung, 1999). That is why there is a growing interest across all education sectors in the use of SBL. The impetus comes from a desire by educators and allied professionals alike, to help adult learners bridge theoretical knowledge of a subject/discipline area with "real-life" professional practice (Errington, 2003). The most common kinds of scenarios are (Errington, 2003):

- **Skills-based scenarios:** Students have opportunities to acquire and demonstrate certain abilities, understandings, and skills;
- **Problem-based scenarios:** Students are presented with a scenario that has a dilemma or problem to solve. More emphasis is placed on the problem-solving process than on reaching one solution;
- **Issues-based scenarios:** Students seek out knowledge and explore vested interests surrounding an issue, make a stand, and justify choices;
- **Speculative-based scenarios:** Students are given information, upon which to speculate, behavior, assumptions, and/or outcomes of human actions.

Scenarios can be applied across all discipline areas. SBL is ideal for scenario-creating novices, and for more experienced practitioners wishing to develop their ideas and teaching options.

Another SBL case is to develop personal and professional developments that are essential for the vocational education of an engineer. A scenario based on a "ghost company" that has been successfully used to develop these skills in students (Harris & Bramhall, 1999). This fictitious company provided a vehicle both for developing communication skills as well as for integrating the various disciplines. The scenario finally provides a framework for a product development within a simulated industrial environment.

SBL also provides the chance for a virtual hands-on training environment to expose students to the realities of working in a complex and diverse construction project environment (Kazi & Charoenngam, 1999). Virtual scenarios are created to simulate real life construction activities and to engage the students into the dynamics of decision making through information exchange and communication devices.

Current Work on SBL

Engineering is a fast growing industry, and it becomes impossible to buy every piece of advance equipment to train the student. This SBL learning package is to simulate a scenario that is close to the students' future working area (Figure 1). Using up-to-date information and multimedia technology, it can simulate issues and conditions similar to those encountered in the field.

It will prepare students for difficulties that can occur by allowing them to perform realistic investigations at virtual site using preferred test equipment. Troubleshooting these simulated problems will result in a saving of time and money at actual site. Students can also virtually walk around and realize how the actual working environment should be. They can also take this opportunity to study how different equipment can be interconnected together and how to operate that equipment. If students find it interesting to study a particular equipment or product in the simulated environment, they can just virtually touch that equipment or product by clicking it using the mouse. The selected item (e.g., digital clock in Figure 1) will be enlarged, and hierarchical information will be provided step-by-step as requested. Figure 2 shows the internal view of a digital clock after selected in this simulated environment.

Students can use this virtual SBL environment to understand deeper about the operation and the theory behind it. They can also have the chance to discover the composition of any equipment or product simply by selecting the object on the screen (Figure 3). In this case, students can understand the internal structures, study different printed circuit boards, and what electronic components are used inside the digital clock without disassembling a real one.

If students would like to know the theories behind different parts of a digital clock, further explanation will be displayed in a hierarchical way to suit different backgrounds of students. Figure 4 shows the block diagram of the electronic part of the digital clock.

Further knowledge of a particular electronic circuit can be displayed if students click into that part (Figure 5).

Figure 1. Scenario for working area

Figure 2. Internal view of a digital clock

Figure 3. Counter circuit in the digital clock

The next stage is to study the integrated circuit used for that part of the digital clock (Figure 6).

Animation of logic design such as using programmable logic devices (PLDs) is also given to enhance students' understanding of the design. An example is shown in Figure 7a where immediate result of logic outputs will be calculated once users burn the fuse of input logic array of the PLD (Figure 7b).

Students can use this hierarchical information to gain the practical knowledge that they like to explore.

Figure 4. Block diagram of digital clock

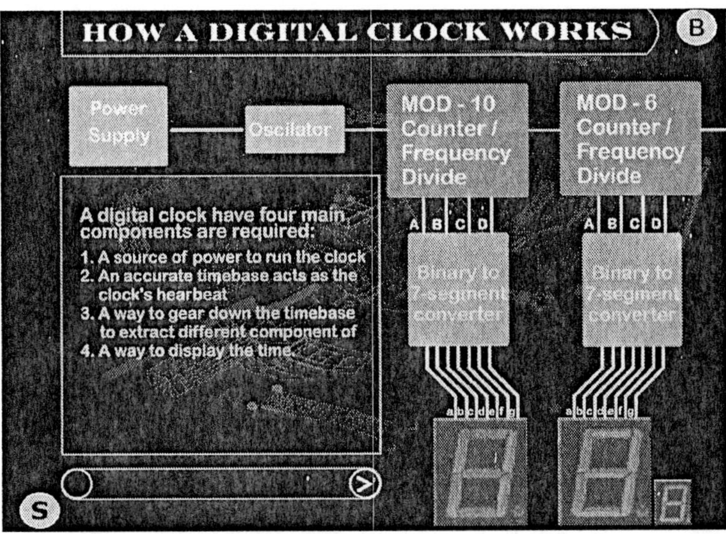

Figure 5. Electronic circuit of a digital clock

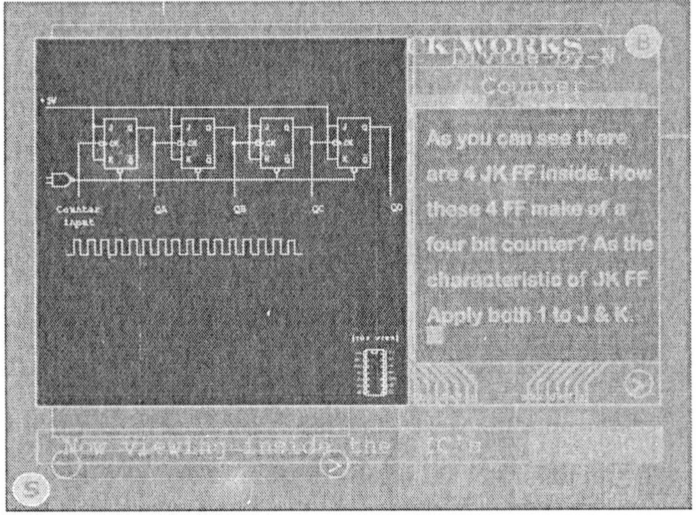

Figure 6. Integrated circuit used in digital clock

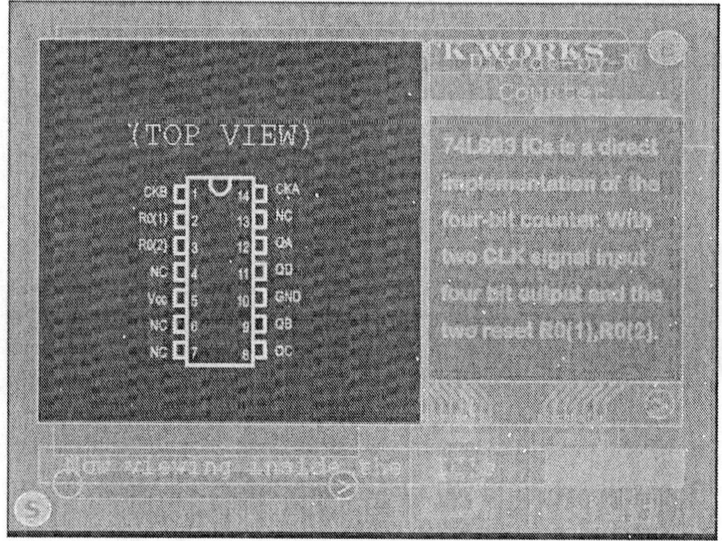

This SBL system can be used in any time, any location, and any pace. Actually, this SBL is included in a learning package where it uses different learning media to stimulate student's interest to learn. There are five sections in this learning package:

- Logic room
- Overviews
- Group discussion
- Information search
- Contact us

Logic room section contains an interactive movie, which simulates an environment closed to the students' future working area. Using up-to-date information and multimedia technology, it can simulate issues and conditions similar to those encountered in the field. Students can virtually walk around and realize how the actual working environment should be. They can also take this opportunity to study how different equipment can be interconnected together and how to operate that equipment. Figure 8 shows how students can discover the composition of any equipment or product simply by selecting the object on the screen.

For the *overview section*, students can use another interactive animation to enhance their learning in the class. Practical exercises are given to students to generate more interest and ensure deep understanding. Figure 9 shows a movie that contains a step-by-step description of a binary number change to decimal; students can interactively input the number and the conversion will be immediately displayed.

Figure 7a. Animation of PLD before burning fuses

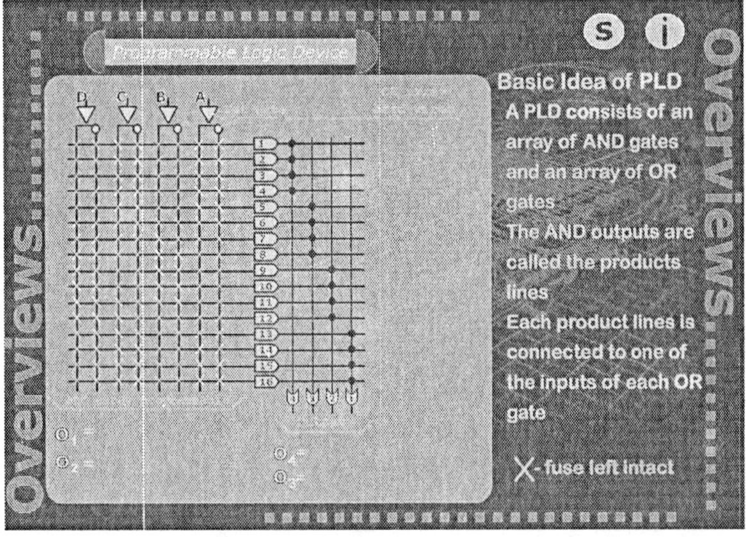

Figure 7b. Animation of PLD after burning fuses

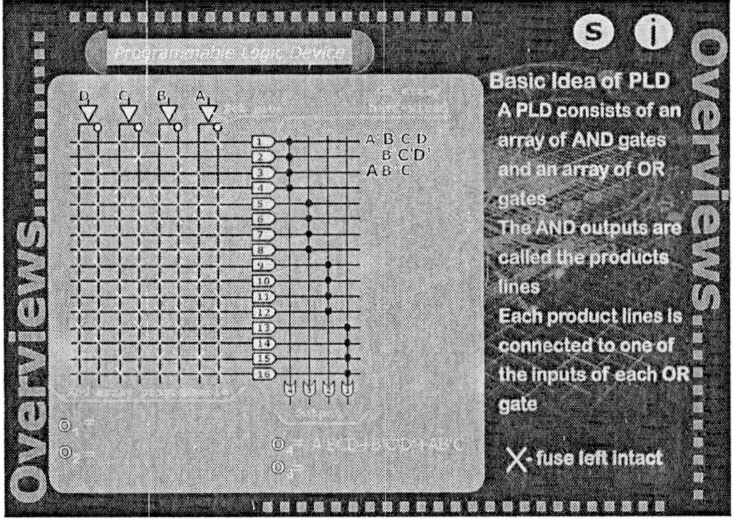

Figure 8. Composition of equipment or product

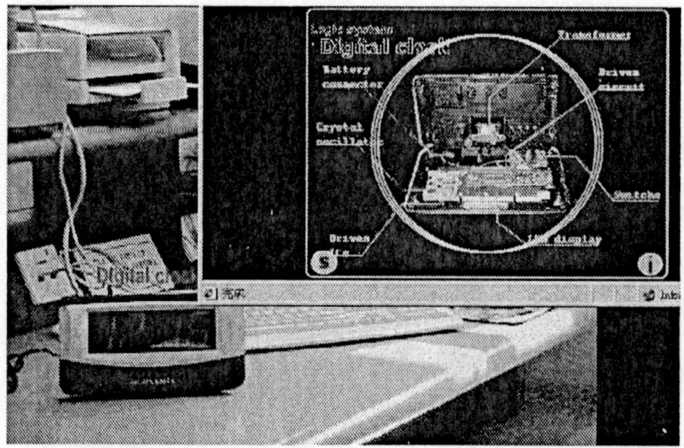

Figure 9. Interactive exercise for number conversion

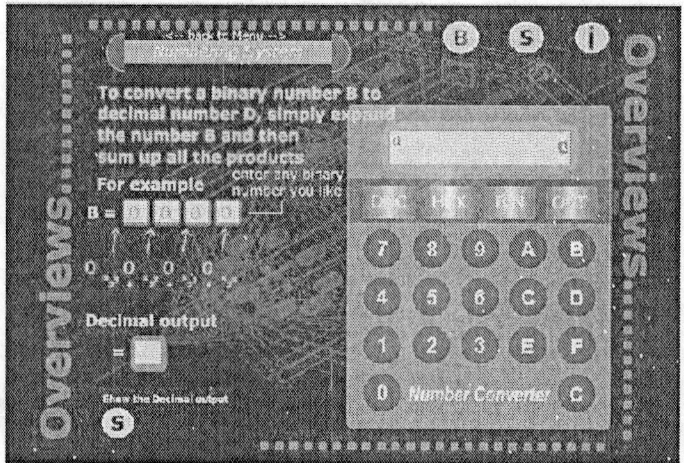

The *group discussion section* provides an online discussion area for students, and it is divided into two parts:

- Logic forum
- Chat room

The logic forums set up an information exchange channel to the students. They can post their own message through this forum, which act as the function of message board and FAQ. Figure 10 shows the structure of this logic forum.

Figure 10. Structure of logic forum

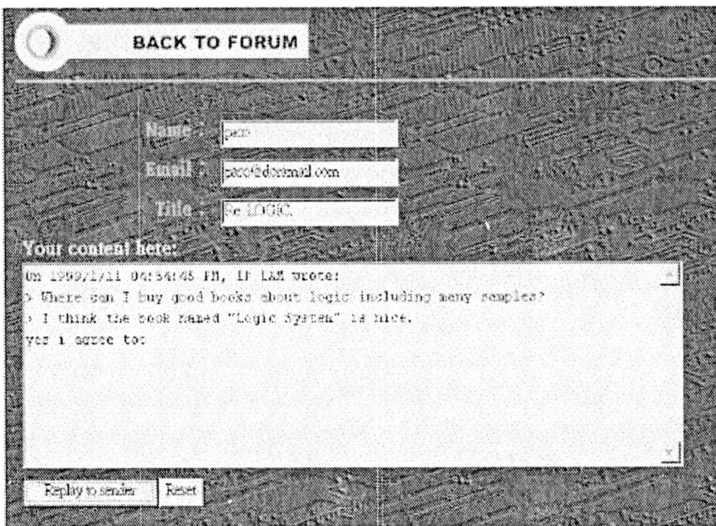

The students can get a real time talk with each other through the chat room (Figure 11). When the users login to the chat room, their information (e.g., user name and e-mail address) is collected. After that, students can enter to the chat room for real time talk.

The *information search section* consists of a built in search engine. Students just key in the word that they would like to search, and the search engine (Figure 12) will find out any matched information from the database. Students can use this section to search any documentation that they like to read.

The *contact us section* contains two parts: guest book and voice mail. Students can write down any comment or question in the guest book or they can send a voice mail on this section. Figure 13 shows the outlook of the guest book where voice mail is active on the top.

Development of this SBL Program

As a non-research institution, it is hard to get budget for educational research. After the idea was formed, two higher diploma students found this SBL title interesting, and this SBL program became their final year project. These two students used nearly one year to write various programs with the help of Frontpage, Dreamweaver, Flash, and so forth. At the beginning of the development, feedback from colleagues and students after using this SBL gave much valuable advice to modify this SBL program before the final version was formed.

Actually, when the first version of this SBL program was prepared and introduced in a college senior management meeting, it was well accepted and encouraged to develop such kind of e-learning materials to support students to learn better in another way. A later version was then promoted to colleagues' level through internal seminars. After that, two more SBL

Figure 11. Structure of chat room

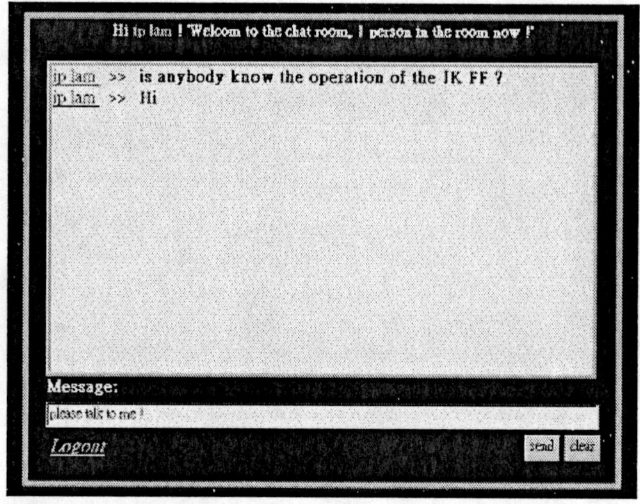

Figure 12. Information search

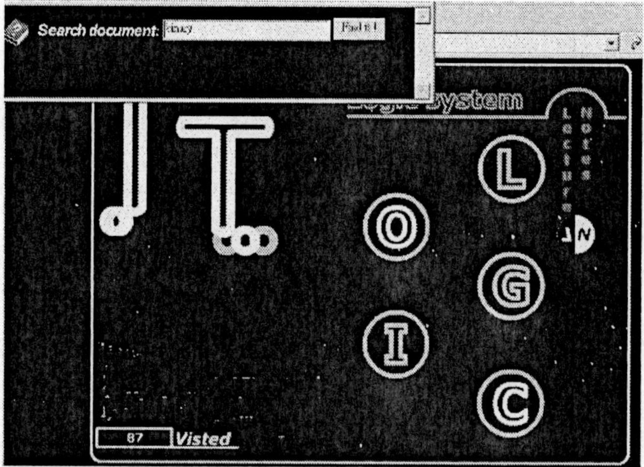

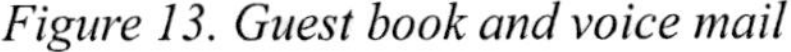

Figure 13. Guest book and voice mail

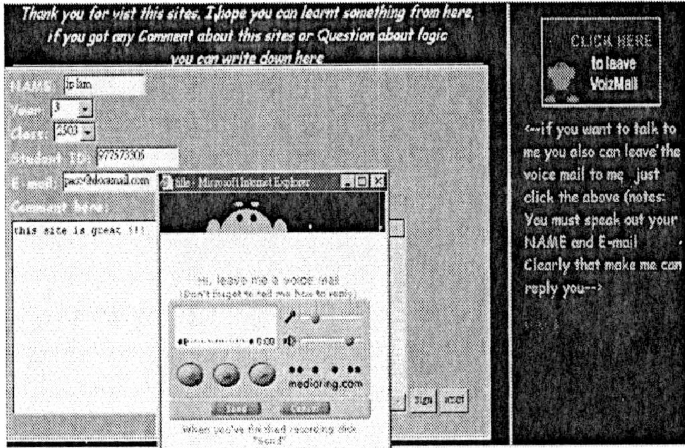

packages were started with the help of full time and part time final year students in the next academic year. The results were also presented in some international conferences.

Due to the success of these SBL programs, an e-learning group was set up in the college level, and some posts were created to help and promote e-learning to benefit students to learn in a better and more flexible way.

Method of Study

This SBL package needs to be evaluated to determine whether it is achieving its designed aims and finding rooms for improvement. Through the action learning process, the design of this SBL package can be continuously modified to suit the requirement of student learning and employment needs.

The subjects were year one engineering students (N = 80) studying in the Hong Kong Institution of Vocational Education (Tsing Yi). Most of them were Form 5 graduates. None of them have experience of this innovative way of e-learning. They were separated into groups of 20 and performed this SBL in a laboratory environment for three hours. They could freely discuss the SBL with their classmates as well as the instructor.

In order to assess students' view of this SBL, questionnaires were immediately given to these year one engineering students after their first experience of this package in the laboratory environment. The questionnaire aimed to investigate students' views toward existing functions of the learning package, about learning using SBL, user interface, the needs of students in this SBL, and comparison of SBL with teaching in the classroom. Eight students were randomly selected and interviewed to probe further their views toward this SBL.

Students' Feedback

All the students gave positive feedback to this SBL package. Most of them (89%) felt interested in learning through SBL. Some students (66%) even found that it is easier to learn theories via SBL:

I like this learning package because the animation can let us visualize the effect or result, which helps us a lot to understand some difficult concepts and signal flows that are hard to be understood by just reading textbooks.

Actually, many students (83%) were encouraged to learn this subject due to the attractive animation used in this SBL:

It is attractive, and my feeling is that it looks like playing instead of learning. I like to learn in this way.

However, more than half (63%) of students do not agree that SBL can replace normal classroom teaching. An interviewee reported that SBL could only increase their practical knowledge, and especially it can simulate how a real electronic product works. SBL is not so easy to replace the discussion and real interaction in the traditional classroom.

Another drawback of using SBL is that it depends on student's initiative to learn. Some students can stay in front of the computer for hours but others hate to do so.

The human interface is an important factor for success of a Web-based learning. Students reported that they do not like this package simply because the color matching of the Web page is not so good or diagrams are not so attractive.

For the improvement of this learning package, many students suggest having more animation (89%), video (83%), interactive elements (83%), and sound effect (80%) added into the content. Also, they do not like Web pages filled with words. They only accept small amounts of text in print form only. Even better is that a game is included to allow them playing and learning at the same time.

Other improvements are to provide chat room for discussion and add some quizzes (80%) or exercise (94%) at the end of the learning package to help them to check how much they understand the knowledge provided.

Conclusion

This scenario-based learning package is mainly used to support teaching and does not mean to replace activities inside classroom. The main objective is to let all students have the chance to virtually immerse in a scenario to enhance their learning, review knowledge on request, and hopefully improve their practical sense. Preliminary study shows that this scenario-based learning is well accepted by students and is worth further study.

Although this SBL package has freedom to execute different courses of action, creativity that restructure the basic exercise is not encouraged. Another issue for further improvement is to include reality of function so that actions that participants taking at a later stage depend partly on their response of earlier actions.

Similar SBL is developed on computer hardware learning and mobile phone construction learning. Future development of this SBL will integrate other teaching materials and place on an e-book. Users can freely choose linkage to basic knowledge, online exercise, virtual laboratory, and SBL.

Acknowledgments

The author would like to thank Lam Ip and Jay Leung for their help in developing the SBL packages for this study. Appreciation is also given to Queendy Lam for her continuous support and verification of this chapter.

References

Chan, C. C. (1997, October). The role of engineers and the challenges of engineering education. *Asia Engineer*, 28-29.

Ching, H. S., Poon, P. W. T., & McNaught, C. (2004). Virtual workshops of distance learning practising what we preach. *Journal of Distance Education Technologies*, *2*(1), 2-5.

Chu, K. C. (1999, July). *What are the benefits of virtual laboratory on student learning?* Paper presented at the HERDSA Annual International Conference, Melbourne, Australia.

Chu, K. C. (2004). Using virtual instrument to develop a real time Web-based laboratory. *Journal of Distance Education Technologies*, *2*(1), 18-30.

Chu, K. C., Urbanik, N., Yip, S. Y., & Cheung, T. W. (1999). The benefit of virtual teaching to engineering education. *International Journal of Engineering Education, 15*(5), 334-338.

Ericksen, L., & Kim, E. (1998). *Projects for the Internet.* Reading, MA: Addison-Welsey.

Errington, E. P. (2003). *Developing scenario-based learning: Practical insights for tertiary educators.* Australia: Dunmore Press.

Harris, R. G., & Bramhall, M. D. (1999). The development of professional skills using a product development scenario. *Engineering Science and Educational Journal*, October, 215-219.

Kazi, A. S., & Charoenngam, C. (1999, June). *Construction communication simulation through virtual set-up environment and information technology*. Paper presented at the ASEE Annual Conference, Charlotte, VA.

Ko, C. C., Chen, B. M., Chen, S. H., Ramakrishnan, V., Chen, R., Hu, S. Y., et al. (2000). A large-scale Web-based virtual oscilloscope laboratory experiment.*Engineering Science and Education Journal*, *2*(9), 69-76.

Leung, D. (1999, January). *Some issues in the implementation of vocational education.* Paper presented at the 2nd Joint Conference of SCUT and IVE(TY), Hong Kong.

Paton, B. (1999). *Sensors, transducers and labVIEW.* Upper Saddle River, NJ: Prentice-Hall.

Whelan, P. F. (1997, October). Remote access to continuing engineering education (RACeE). *Engineering Science and Education Journal, 6*(10), 205-211.

Yang, B. (1999, June). *Virtual lab: Bring the hands-on activity to online courses.* Paper presented at the American Society for Engineering Education Annual Conference, Charlotte, NC.

Chapter XVIII

An E-Workshop Model for Teacher Training

Yan Hanbing, East China Normal University, Shanghai, China

Zhu Zhiting, East China Normal University, Shanghai, China

Abstract

In China, teacher training plays a very important role for the improvement of education. E-learning, as a new and effective life-long learning method, plays an increasingly important role in teacher training. It is well known that teacher training and e-learning are all open and developing domains. So, the integration of two domains will certainly bring about many new problems. The case focuses on how does the e-workshop model, which is designed specially for teacher training by the Distance Education College of East of China Normal University find a way to solve the problems. By way of analyzing the successful factors of e-workshop model and following the problem clues of the above-mentioned two domains, this chapter shows the corresponding solutions.

Background

In China, teacher training plays a very important role for the improvement of education. In order to meet the requirement of education reform, the Ministry of Education has conducted several five-year training plans for whole in-service teachers in the recent two decades. Taking the (2003-2007) training plan as an example, the Ministry of Education has instituted the following tasks:

1. Organize and implement 1,000 rural back-bone-teachers' training
2. Organize and implement one million primary and middle school teachers' training
3. Support 2,000 primary and middle school teachers to meet the standard of teachers' educational levels.
4. Implement 1,000 back-bone-teachers' (except rural teachers) training.

Based on the whole training plan, the educational bureaus of provinces or cities will take corresponding training measures. Most educational bureaus ask their primary and middle school teachers (PMST) to get certain training credit hours. For example, such a five-year teacher training has been implemented three times (within 15 years), and a new five-year training plan is just on the road.

In the face of the massive and routine PMST training, the training content needs to be updated often, and trainers' competence needs to be improved often too. It can be said easily that the present PMST training is bringing pressure to bear on the local training centers. As a result, former closed PMST training systems (the Ministry of Education-local educational bureaus-local training centers) have been broken to open one—normal universities and teacher research institutes become an important part in PMST training. At the same time, the former simplex training model becomes multiform. E-learning, as a new and effective life-long learning method, plays an increasingly important role in PMST training (China Education News, 2005; MOE, 2002). With such background, the e-workshop model, which is designed specially for PMST training by the Distance Education College of East China Normal University, had its start in July 2003.

Profile of E-Workshop Model

In order to give readers an overall impression of the e-workshop model, we introduce several key elements of the model next (Yan, 2004):

- **Goal:** To make PMSTs' learning activity and instructional activity changed, so that they can meet the requirements of educational reform.
- **Tenet:** Based on e-learning, PMST-center, active-learning, and active-research.
- **Workshop content:** Problem-oriented or task-oriented, the workshop aims to support PMSTs to solve the problems they may encounter in their professional development; in the training process, learning content would be dynamically updated.
- **Form:** Face to face at key stages (for example, the first day of e-workshop), online at other times (BBS, audio classroom, blog, product-sharing system, e-mail).

- **Evaluation:** Performance evaluation.
- **Environment:** Working environment and online environment.
- **Platform:** http://jsjy.dec.ecnu.edu.cn.
- **Achievement:** Since July 2003, 3,328 PMSTs (from JinShan District, Nanhui District, SongJiang District, PuTuo District, Jia Xing City, SuZhou City, and so on) have participated in the teacher training in the form of E-Workshop model. According to the statistic results from online questionnaires (see the following graph, 3,178 available questionnaires), e-workshop model is quite welcomed.

It is well known that teacher training and e-learning are all open and developing domains. So, the integration of two domains is expected to bring about many new problems. In this case, how does the e-workshop model find a way to solve the problems? By way of analyzing the successful factors of e-workshop model and following the problem clues of the previously mentioned two domains, this chapter shows the corresponding solutions.

Problem Clues of Teacher Education and Solutions

Although massive and routine teacher training has laid a solid foundation for the development of China's education, there are still some commonly recognized problems that need solving as soon as possible.

Problem 1: Time Conflict between Working and Training

Problem: Along with the deepening of teacher training, the training model trend is to be more and more experience-oriented and process-oriented rather than originally knowledge-oriented and result-oriented. Such a trend leads to comparatively longer training time than before, however, more training time, less working time. PMSTs' time conflict between working and training becomes more and more severe.

Solution: Relying on the most outstanding advantage of Web-based learning, that is *no limit on time and space*, e-workshop model solves this problem by organizing face-to-face interaction at key stages and online at other times. For example, if a PMST chooses to take training with the e-workshop model, he or she only needs to take part in one-day face-to-face training at the very beginning of the e-workshop in an appointed place; at other times, he or she can learn synchronously or asynchronously in his or her own working or living environment through an e-workshop platform.

... We used to take training in ShangHai Educational Institute before. At that time, traffic was so bad that we had to spend three to four hours on the road. Really wasteful! Nowadays, e-learning comes into being; we can receive professor's direction at our own home and enjoy the discussion with craft brothers. How could I image these before? So convenient, so efficient...

Post by JinKang, JinShan District, Shanghai

Problem 2: Lack of High Quality Learning Resources

Problem: In China, teacher training centers used to shoulder the most responsibilities of teacher training independently. However, their training pressures are increasing gradually owing to the climbing training requirement. Therefore, more and more training centers are changing their usual practice and beginning to look for powerful training resources from key normal universities.

Solution: In order to achieve high quality online learning resources, Distance Education College has held several public contests among the staff of East China Normal University. All the entrants have to reach two standards required. First of all, they should have rich experience in primary and middle school instruction or educational reform so that they can understand PMSTs requirement and provide them with valuable guidance. Secondly, they should submit well-chosen training materials developed by themselves. The training materials should not only take PMSTs' former knowledge and experience into consideration, but also be PMSTs-centered. In order to meet the requirement, many professors rebuild the learning outlines of their research results. As a result, several excellent training resources come into being. These training resources are just the main clues of e-workshops.

Since I took part in the e-workshop, I have listened to some talks of three modules. These talks are really persuasive; I like to clap my hands for them! I am a fresh teacher with only two years experience, know little about education research, and have few chances to listen to such high level talks. Thanks to the CD, now I can listen repeatedly...

Post by ZhouPing, Nanhui District, Shanghai

Problem 3: Weak Relationship between Training and Working

Problem: On the one hand, many training courses cannot satisfy PMSTs' learning demand owning to their weak pertinence to PMSTs' work. On the other hand, the fact that training credit hours have great influence on working qualification makes PMSTs take training seriously. The irrelevance between training and working, without doubt, greatly affects PMSTs' learning enthusiasm. According to the result of an online questionnaire of NanHui participants before e-workshop, we got the graph in Figure 1. It reveals that 44% of participants take part in the e-workshop only to increase their credit hours, and that 11% participant to obey their school's arrangement.

Figure 1. Training needs

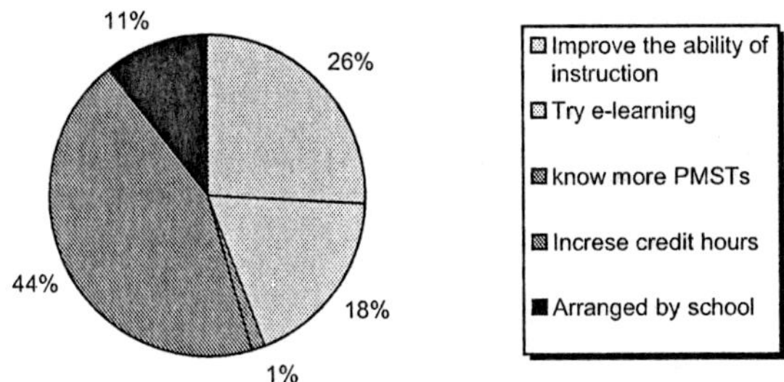

Table 1. The late performance requirement of some e-workshops

Name of e-workshop	*The late performance requirement*
Instructional Design with IT-support	You need to design a unit plan according to the unit in your own class. The unit plan should meet the following requirements: 1. Theme, grade, subject, task (goal), learning (instructional) process, supporting materials, evaluation tools included. 2. IT-supported. The unit plan will be evaluated from suitability, relativity, rationality, feasibility, and innovation.
Educational Research of Primary and Middle Schools	Please compose a research project based on the selected instructional topic.
Instructional Media Art Design	Please design a PPT, a Flash, or a Web site to support your instruction. The evaluation will pay equal attention to the art effect and the instructional effect of the product. You need to hand in the product with a paper that analyzes your designing method from instructional and art factors.

Solution: Besides high quality and feasible online training materials, the e-workshop model adopts performance evaluation to solve the problem. According to the goal of the e-workshop, participants will be asked to create some products, unit plans, papers, and experiment reports that are closely related to their own work, and therefore, training is integrated into participants' working. Table 1 shows the late performance requirement of some e-workshops (Yan, 2005).

Problem 4: Traditional Training Ideas Couldn't Give Enough Guidance to PMSTs

Problem: The global educational reform has called on student-centered and process-oriented instruction for quite a long time. Regrettably, so many teacher trainings still stay on the traditional training stage that takes lectures as the main methods of the training. PMSTs can know the "what" and "why" question, but it is difficult to answer the "how to do" question.

Solution: Master teachers are propellants in e-workshops. They aim at creating a self-learning environment for participants by case studies, question inquiring, communication, and self-evaluation. Besides training material learning (by CD or online), participants will make use of the following to communicate, and to share opinions:

- **BBS:** Is the main device for participants' communication and discussion. Master teachers will bring forward e-workshop topics and develop meaningful discussion by effective organization.
- **Update resources:** Master teachers can upload new, fresh content by this device, so that the content of the workshop is still in an updating status.
- **Product sharing:** Master teachers can easily set *Share* on some participants' performance products, so that others can view and evaluate them.

Besides these devices, there are some other means on the platform specially to create the online campus culture. We will introduce them later.

It is noticeable that participants' Web-based communication skills have been improved a lot through such experience-oriented and process-oriented learning. Figure 2 shows the comparing results of participants' self-evaluation before and after training with regard to their *Web-based communication skill.*

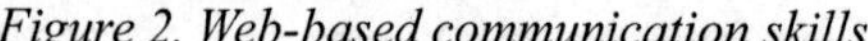

Figure 2. Web-based communication skills

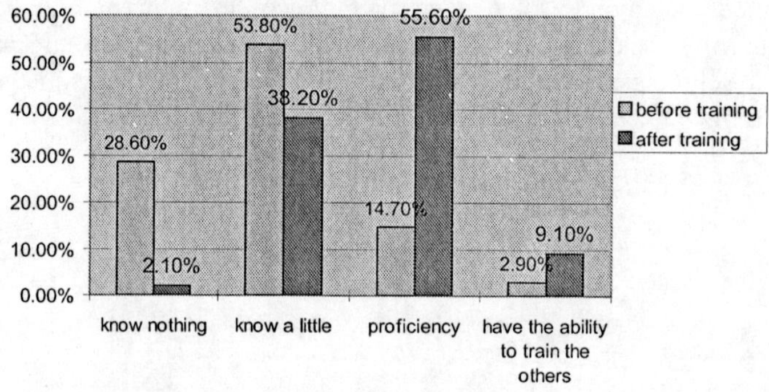

Before training, I always tried to find my schoolmates and chatted with them by QQ only if I was online. But after I participated in the training, I would log on the e-workshop homepage only if I am online. It feels like BBS is my heart homestead when I enter our BBS. I enjoy the feeling to drink the soul soup boiled by all participants.

Post by JinLing, JinShan District, ShangHai

Problem Clues of Web-Based Learning and Solutions

Network will not effectively support learning if users have no deep felt understanding of its advantages and disadvantages. In other words, if we cannot make use of network correctly, things will go contrary to our wishes. Now come the problem clues of Web-based learning and corresponding solutions of the e-workshop model.

Problem 1: Master Teachers' Online Instructional Skills Need to Improve

Problem: A master teacher's psychology, teaching method, and information quality are crucial factors for an e-workshop's success. Since e-learning is a comparatively new domain, many master-teachers have no experience of e-learning.

Table 2. Rubic for master teacher

Evaluation Criteria	Description	Point Scale
Face to face instruction	Finish the desired work earnestly, on time.	10
Online-chat	Preside over the chatting; guide the participants to discuss instructional themes on time.	20
Management of e-portfolio	The management of e-portfolio clearly aligns with the requirement of Distance Education College. The contents of finished e-portfolio are enriched and available.	20
BBS	Organize topic-discussion on BBS at least three times. Browse and answer participants' questions or comments at least twice per week.	30
Student evaluation	According to the online questionnaire, the master teacher's credit scale=20*support percent (%).	20

Figure 3. Sketch map of e-portfolio

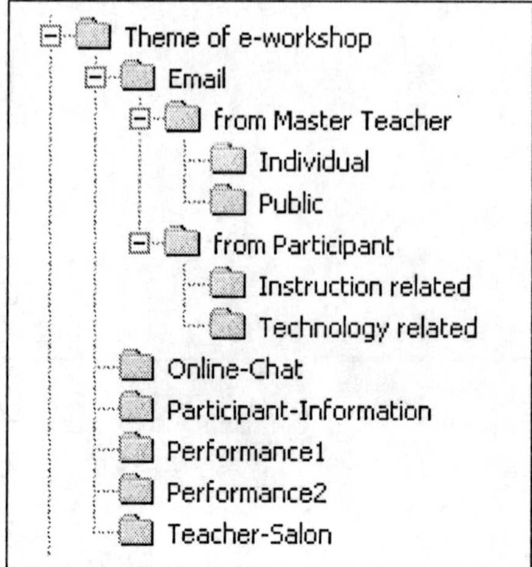

Solution: In the process of the preparation for e-workshops, master teachers are considered as learners first. Therefore, a series of learning scaffolds are provided for their better e-instruction, including examples, templates, case studies, e-portfolio, rubric, and so on. Simultaneously, all the master teachers should get together to prepare for the coming e-workshops by learning, communication, and sharing.

Rubric for Master Teacher: Rubric for master teacher settles the evaluation criteria from several aspects. Based on the rule of Evaluation Priority, the rubric will be shown to the master teacher before the start of e-workshop, so that the master teacher can align to it consciously in the process.

E-Portfolio

In order to facilitate the management of participants' work, the organizers of Distance Education College prepare a structured e-portfolio for each master teacher (see Figure 3). In each folder, there is corresponding information or template. For example, there are a *Teacher-e-Salon Application Form* and *Teacher-e-Salon Introduction* in the *Teacher-Salon* folder; there are a *participants' information* and *address list* in the *Participant-Information* folder; there are *online-chat recording templates* in the *Online-Chat* folder, and so on. The practice proves that structured e-portfolio plays a very important role in supporting master teachers' work. In addition, e-portfolio provides valuable resources for later e-workshop on the same topic.

Problem 2: PMSTs' Online Learning Habits Need Cultivating

Problem: PMSTs are accustomed to being trained face to face. Based on this situation, online learning is too new to adapt for them.

Solution: The important solution is to provide transparent guidance for PMSTs so that participants can understand learning goal, learning evaluation, and learning processes clearly before the e-workshop kicks off.

The first letter to participants: Each participant will receive a letter from a master teacher before e-workshop kicks off. This letter will answer some questions clearly such as, "How to become an excellent participant in an e-workshop?" or "How about the evaluation of e-workshop?"

Figure 4 shows part of a letter from the master teacher of the *Instructional Flash Design* e-workshop.

Figure 4. First letter to students

Dear friends:

...

The evaluation of the e-workshop will switch to score according to your performance:

1. The total scores are 100, including participating status (30), the first task (30), and the last task (40).
2. We will decide the participating status by three aspects, including face-to-face lecture, online questionnaire, and BBS.
   (1) Face-to-face lecture: 5 scores. You need to participate in the lecture all the time.
   (2) Online questionnaire: 5 scores. You need to fill in a certain online questionnaire separately before and after the e-workshop.
   (3) BBS 20 scores. You are expected to have a meaningful and active discussion on BBS. The scores will convert from EXPERIENCE COST on BBS. (Note: EXPERIENCE COST is counted by the platform automatically. Let us pay attention to the counting rule: post a discussion, +1; delete a discussion, -1; if the discussion is very excellent, then I will set ELITE sign on it, ELITE discussion, +5).
3. The first task is a periodic flash production. You need to use Flash software to ...
4. The last task is a courseware for your own instruction, ...

......

Figure 5. Common agreement for e-workshop

As a participant of the e-workshop, I guarantee:

- Browse the platform of e-workshop (http://jsjy.dec.ecnu.edu.cn) at least twice per week. Pay attention to bulletin board.
- Participate in the e-workshop actively; keep on self-reflecting and integrating the learning into my working.
- Participate in the online-chat on time, not late, no early-leave. Put forward my point of view actively; evaluate other participants' performance and give suggestions earnestly. If possible, I will provide corresponding reference for the others.
- During the e-workshop, I promise to respect other participants' opinions. If there is objection, we will try to come to an understanding by discussion rather than escape from it.
- Browse BBS at least twice per week. Put forward my point of view actively. Never post the words that have no relation to this e-workshop. Firmly reject uncivilized, reactive saying.
- Make the best of blogs to develop my educational narration; visit and comment on other participants' educational narration frequently; never give sarcastic and provocative comments to the others.
- Accomplish all the learning tasks serious-mindedly, and upload them to the platform on time.
- Develop self-evaluation, peer evaluation earnestly and seriously.
- If there is criticism or suggestion, I will post it to the master teacher initiatively rather than keep silence or complain.

Common Agreement for E-Workshop

Common agreement aims at presenting the quality-expectation for participants of the e-workshop, such as initiative, creative, confident, cooperative, earnest, and so on (Figure 5).

Learning Process Manual

During each e-workshop, the master teacher will design a set of learning activities. At the *face-to-face* time, all the participants will get a *learning process manual*. By the learning process manual, participants know main stages of the workshop, such as the time period and introduction of discussion, product upload, audio-chat, and so on. By the learning process manual, participants know what they should prepare before each stage. By the learning process manual, participants can adjust their learning rhythm easily. At the same time, participants can inquire an *online learning process manual* at any moment.

Problem 3: Online Learning Culture Needs Creating

Problem: It is repeatedly noted that rich campus culture exerts great influence upon one's development besides teachers' instruction. The creation of online campus culture gives e-workshop model a meaningful challenge.

Solution: Creating online campus culture by different titles, so that participants have more chances to exchange ideas with many instructional experts and virtual schoolfellows. Also, they can get more information and resources from those titles. Some of these are:

1. **Wisdom community** (*http://jsjy.dec.ecnu.edu.cn/community/index.asp*)

Many instructional experts, excellent teachers, and Educational PhDs "live in" here. Participants of any e-workshop have the right to visit them and post questions to them. By doing so, they find a way to exchange ideas with originally strange experts. Also, they can share the newest articles and instructional cases uploaded by those "Wisdom Community Man."

2. **Web sites Treasure** (*http://jsjy.dec.ecnu.edu.cn/web/index.asp*)

This is a dynamic Web site collection including many useful and high-quality educational Web sites. Sorted by subjects, this title facilitates participants to search information. In addition, there is an online entrance to encourage participants to recommend more useful educational Web sites for better sharing.

3. **E-Schoolroom** (*http://jsjy.dec.ecnu.edu.cn/lecture/index.asp*)

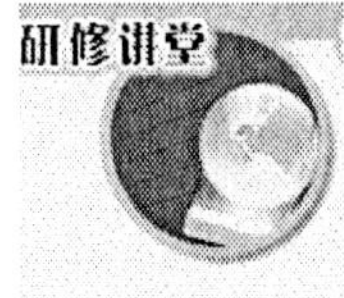

Many public online lectures and teacher-e-salons are held here. Participants discuss with experts in audio-chatting rooms at the same time, or can listen to the recording of the lecture at a different time. If a participant has an interest in some educational topics, he or she can apply for the host of teacher-e-salon, then explore these topics with other participants who share the same interest with him or her on a scheduled time in audio-chatting room.

4. **Educational Narration** (*http://jsjy.dec.ecnu.edu.cn/project/mylog/index.asp*)

Each participant can get his or her own word space here. The space supports the participant to deliver his or her understanding and explanation of education in a narrative way. Participants analyze and reflect on the meaningful and valuable instructional stories, and at the same time share the analysis and reflection with the other participants.

Problem 4: Participants' Technology Level Needs Improving

Problem: Most of participants feel afraid that their technology level cannot meet the requirement of e-learning.

Solution: The e-workshop model depends on mature learning support services. The whole learning support services include friendly and easy-operated platform, clear and detailed platform manual, a special e-workshop for technology practice, face-to-face platform training, Flash online learning guidance, FAQ, *Answer you in 24 hours* title, and hot line service.

Take training through the Web? It sounds so mysterious! I heard of the Web a long time ago, but as an old man and a computer stranger, I still take it as a faraway thing. It is really a surprise that I meet the Web in 2005! Not only do I meet the Web, know WEB, but I also love the Web. Ha-ha, that is the Web, not offish, not strange. It is so charming!

Post by Shen Shangyong, Nanhui District, Shanghai

Conclusion

Although there are many problems that still exist in distance education due to lack of experiences and other reasons, various levels of governments, educational institutes, and schools in China have considered the importance of e-learning in teachers' training, which is transferring or will transfer to all kinds of powerful implements to empower teachers with e-learning. We are confident that the e-workshop model will become more and more mature and effective.

Acknowledgment

These authors are thankful to Ms. Luo Hongwei for her assistance with the writing of this article.

References

MOE. (1999). *Decree No. 7 of MOE: Rules of Teachers' Continuing Education.* Retrieved September 16, 2005, from http://www.moe.edu.cn/edoas/website18/level3.jsp?tablename=743&infoid=5945

MOE. (2002). *Proposal for promoting the construction of teachers' e-education.* Retrieved February 4, 2006, from http://www.moe.edu.cn/jsduiwu/jspeiyang/35.htm

MOE. (2002). *2003-2007 Training plan for whole in-service teachers.* Retrieved December 25, 2005, from http://www.fltrp.com/newsdetail.cfm?iCntno=4638

China Education News. (07/31/2005). *Ten thousand teachers access online training in Sinkiang.* Retrieved December 25, 2005, from http://www.moe.edu/cn/edoas/website18/info15331.htm

Yan, H. B. (2004). E-workshop comes into being. *China Audio-Visual Education*, 11.

Yan, H. B. (2005). The research and practice of performance evaluation of e-learning. *China Audio-Visual Education*, 9.

Section III

Cases on Resource-Based Online Learning Systems

Chapter XIX

Creating a Multimedia Instructional Product for Medical School Students

Mitchell Weisburgh, Academic Business Advisors, LLC, USA

Abstract

Because most medical school textbooks do not adequately address pain management, the American Academy of Pain Medicine wanted to create TOP MED, an online textbook that would address this need for different specialties and which also could be used as a textbook for the Introduction to Pain Management course. This online textbook would cover 11 topics and consist of the latest findings from the most renowned experts in the different disciplines of pain medicine. This case study is a description of the process of designing and producing the online textbook.

Introduction

The American Academy of Pain Medicine (AAPM) is the medical specialty society representing physicians practicing in the field of pain medicine. Because most medical school textbooks do not adequately address pain management, the academy wanted to create TOP MED, an online textbook that would address this need for different specialties and which also could be used as a textbook for the Introduction to Pain Management course. This online textbook would cover 11 topics and consist of the latest findings from the most renowned experts in the different disciplines of pain medicine.

This case study is a description of the process of designing and producing the online textbook, including how we determined what to cover and how we involved the subject matter experts and translated their content into interactive, entertaining learning segments.

E-Learning Program

The academy had created reference materials online, and they published articles, but this was their first program that was designed for teaching medical professionals. One requirement was that the program have similar production values to television; they did not want something that looked like PowerPoint slides; they did not want talking heads; and they did not want just video. SmartPros, Inc. developed TOP MED for the American Academy of Pain Medicine. The author served as the instructional designer and overall project manager.

Academic and Administrative Issues

The academy wanted TOP MED to be an online textbook, not an online class. The typical use would be, say, in a course on pediatrics. When the professor wanted to cover pediatric pain, the students would turn to TOP MED to find out the different ways the children felt pain, how to assess pain in children, how children react differently to drugs, and how pain affects children's, and their family's, lives.

The academy also wanted there to be an assessment at the end of each section so that the professor and the students could determine knowledge acquisition.

The use of video created an interesting problem. The client wanted the course to look as if the video was full screen, but bandwidth considerations prevented the use of full-screen video. One solution could have been to find or build a proprietary solution to serve and access the video. Another could have downloaded the video onto student machines during off-hours. We wanted a more standardized and immediate solution, so we took advantage of a feature in Flash that allowed us to blend video into a Flash animation. We built a virtual "set," which blended in with the video to give the appearance of full screen video without the huge bandwidth requirements.

As a textbook for medical school students, TOP MED has to be authoritative, drawing scientific content from experts. We needed people at the top of their field, individuals who were either conducting or utilizing the latest research. Then we needed to distill and transform their knowledge into lessons for individuals who might become general practitioners, not necessarily pain specialists or researchers.

But if we just wanted to present content, we could have produced a book, audiotape, or video. We wanted to benefit from the unique advantages of a Web-based instructional system, using high quality video, student interaction, assessment and feedback, flexible navigation, tracking, and reporting.

The client wanted the actual lessons to primarily be delivered via video, but they were adamant that the content not be delivered as talking heads with bullet points. They wanted the material to look like full screen video. This is problematic over Internet protocols, because, to be of reasonable production quality, video requires significant bandwidth. We were able to solve this problem by using video embedded in Flash animations. By blending the video in with a digital set, we minimized the size of the video, but the set looked like the video was full screen.

We decided on 12 units, which could later be expanded:

1. Introduction
2. Neurobiology of pain
3. Neuropathic pain
4. Analgesics: NSAIDs and COXIBs
5. Analgesics: Opioids and Adjuvants
6. Patient evaluation
7. Acute and postoperative pain
8. Musculoskeletal pain
9. Cancer pain and palliative care
10. Pediatric pain
11. Misuse and abuse of pain medications
12. Race, culture, and ethnicity in pain management

The rationale for sequencing the modules was that we would begin with an introduction to TOP MED and a review of how pain is perceived in the medical community and the population as a whole. The next two units are on how the body reacts to pain and painful stimuli. The two units on analgesics focus on the common medical treatments for pain. Evaluation is necessary for any manifestation of pain. Then the next series of units focus on different common causes and the corresponding treatment for pain. The last two units focus on particular aspects of pain management, which go across all types of pain symptoms and treatments. We started by designing and producing two units: neurobiology of pain and pediatric pain.

Our original goal was that each module should last about a half hour. This was based on initial guidance from the advisory board. We planned the following sections for each module:

1. Introduction: what this topic includes and why it is important.
2. Series of four to eight lessons, each consisting of:
   - 2.1. Introduction to the lesson
   - 2.2. Video lecture with animated, text, and graphic aids
   - 2.3. Summary
   - 2.4. One to three questions, problems, or exercises
   - 2.5. Possible links to supplementary material
3. Conclusion of the topic
   - 3.1. Animated summary of the whole topic with voice
   - 3.2. Quiz of 10 to 20 questions
     - 3.2.1. Each question will have an explanation of how the correct question was arrived at and what learning material was represented
     - 3.2.2. Student responses will be tracked
4. Extra materials
   - 4.1. Printable files of all textual and graphical content
   - 4.2. Glossary with definitions of key terms
   - 4.3. Index of all key topics

Figure 1. Phases in TOP MED development

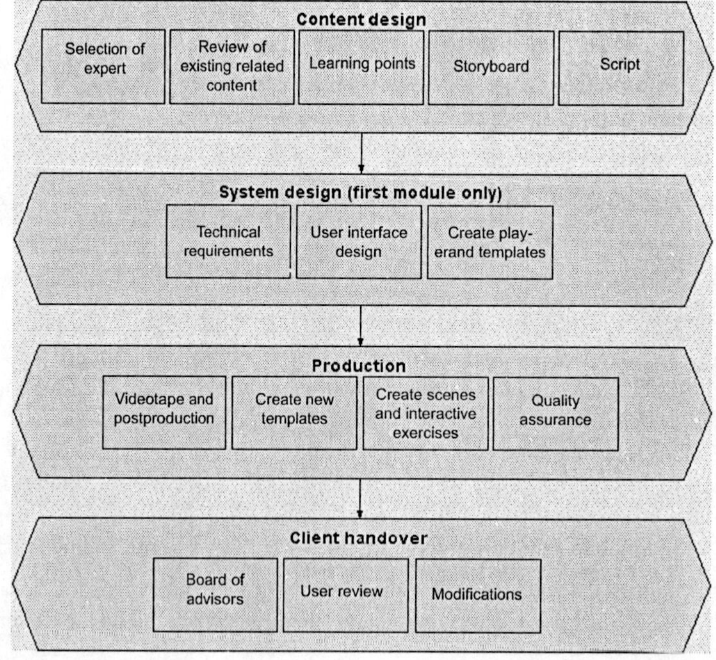

Subsequently we decided that the end of module quiz would have a question bank of 30 questions, and that students would get a random sampling of 10 questions each time one took a quiz. Additionally, we combined the index and glossary into a searchable *glindex* that both defines key terms and links to content in the modules.

Our project plan divided our work into four phases. For all modules, there would be a content design phase, a production phase, and a client handover phase. On the first module, we would also perform a system design phase, which would include prototypes that used material from the first module. Figure 1 shows the steps in each phase. The balance of this article will detail how each phase was carried out.

Content Design

Selection of Expert

For this project, the experts were chosen by the client, generally some of the best-known people in the field of pain medicine. In addition to the expert, there was an overall medical editor, who chaired the group that wrote the original federal guidelines on the treatment of pain.

Review of Existing Related Content

AAPM was able to provide videotapes of many of the experts teaching these topics, or at least lecture notes. These videos were generally from 45 minutes to 90 minutes long. The experts also provided copies of materials that they used when they lectured.

Very few of the materials had the production values we needed. There were minimal graphs, grainy unlabeled photographs, and, with one exception, rudimentary animations. But often the content was extremely relevant leading us to conclude that we would have graphic artists recreate and animate graphics and charts.

Learning Points

This phase of development produced an interim and then a final learning points document. The interim document contained a series of learning points with questions for the medical expert, while the final document was used to produce the storyboard.

The instructional designer (ID) first transcribed any video lectures and then outlined the concepts that were covered. There were two key tests for content: (a) would a doctor knowing this information do a better job with a patient (relevance), and (b) if a person did not already know the information, was the way it was presented sufficiently clear to learn from (clarity).

In terms of relevance, if the ID was certain that the information would not help a general practitioner, it was not used. If it was clear from the materials how it was helpful for a doctor, it was included. If there was a question, the information was tagged so that it could be reviewed with the expert. Sometimes the instructional designer could research the topic.

For example, there were concepts that were backed up with intricate descriptions of scientific research. While the concept itself was useful, and the research would have been necessary for people going into pain research, the detailed research explanations were excised from the learning point document, pending approval from one of the content experts.

In terms of clarity, if the explanation was sufficient, it was copied into the learning points. If it was not clear, the subject was researched and/or tagged for discussion with the expert. For example, the following point from the neurobiology of pain module is important to the material and would be understood by those who were already familiar with the topic. But we deemed it too erudite for an introduction to pain management textbook:

There is NMDA receptor-mediated central sensitization that amplifies the input coming both from the injured tissue and also the unharmed tissue surrounding the area of injury.

This statement would be tagged for a more expansive explanation. So that you can see the contrast, refer to Example A for this explanation as it appears in the final script.

And while this text would never make it into a Stephen King best seller, it is something that a second year medical student should be able to understand.

Finally, items were grouped into general topics or sections; all technical terms were defined in footnotes; and a request was made for clinical examples.

The interim learning points document thus had:

- A list of topics that had been covered in lectures or in any additional research.
- Points tagged with, "how is this useful to a doctor?" Or, "why should someone learn this?"
- Other points tagged with, "how else can this be explained?"
- Terms that were tagged with definitions were questioned as, "is an explicit definition necessary in the lecture, or can it just be defined in the glossary?"
- For each topic or section, there was a question, "can you provide a patient history that will illustrate some of the points in this section?"

Once the interim learning points document was assembled, the ID met with the expert face to face. This meeting tended to take about four hours to review all of the questions.

Armed with the answers to the questions and the case studies, the ID would then assemble the final learning point document and submit it to the expert for review. Generally, a one-hour phone meeting was sufficient to review and approve this document.

It also became evident very early on that, for the topics contained in the TOP MED course, modules were going to be 45 to 60 minutes long, not 30 minutes. The learning point documents (Figure 2) tended to run about 20 pages of 12-point font.

Example A.

How does central sensitization occur?

Glutamate appears to play a key role. Glutamate is an amino acid released in excitatory synapses. It affects several types of receptors, both in the spinal cord and in the brain. One of these receptors can be labeled with an artificial reagent, N-methyl D-aspartate (NMDA). That receptor is therefore termed the NMDA receptor.

The NMDA receptor has binding sites for the neurotransmitter glutamate and several other substances that modulate its activity, including glycine, zinc, and various polyamines.

We know that two things have to happen for activation of the NMDA receptor in the spinal cord.

First is the firing of the nociceptor, which causes depolarization and ion flux across its cell membrane, which in turn causes the release of glutamate into the synapse. Prolonged firing by C-fiber nociceptors causes release of glutamate.

Second is the binding of glutamate to the postsynaptic NMDA receptor—keeping in mind that other chemicals also bind and may have additional roles.

Activation of NMDA receptors causes the spinal cord neuron to become more responsive or sensitive to all of its inputs.

Figure 2. Sample learning points page

·Causes and implications of cancer pain¶

·Neurology¶

Pain is nociceptive, neuropathic, or both; many cancer patients have a mixture of both¶

Nociceptive¶

Bone invasion by tumor can be one of the most severe pains associated with metastatic disease.¶

Infiltration and occlusion of blood vessels can cause ischemia[2] and pain, after which neuropathic pain may be persistent.¶

Obstruction of a hollow viscous can lead to visceral pain syndromes, which can be quite severe.¶

Swelling of a structure invested by fascia or periosteum can be very painful.¶

Necrosis and/or infection of cancerous tissues, with inflammation and ulceration, are tumor-specific pain.¶

Post-chemotherapy and radiation therapy syndromes are very common, even when a patient is in remission or has been cured.¶

Any persistent pain syndrome can lead to sensitization and so-called "wind up" of the central nervous, leading to a chronic neuropathic pain state (see TOP MED module on Neurobiology)¶

Neuropathic¶

Compression or infiltration of nerves, nerve roots or spinal cord is a potent stimulus for acute or persistent neuropathic pain¶

Concomitant neurological disease, e.g., diabetic neuropathy, post-herpetic

Storyboard

We decided based on the length of the material that we needed to have more than one presenter for each module. We fixed on an intro/review person, an explanatory person, and the medical expert. We also learned that we generally needed to change speakers every minute or so, although a few segments, as long as three minutes, could still maintain interest.

The storyboard document was produced in PowerPoint. The slide showed a stick figure of the actor along with any bullet points or graphics that were going to be displayed, and the speaker notes contained a copy of the learning points that were going to be covered in that scene. If a learning point could be diagrammed, then there would sometimes be a full screen animation along with a voice-over instead of a video.

If there was going to be a graphic, chart, or animation, the ID would create a "wire-frame" from which a graphic artist could work. At the end of each section there were general instructions for an interactive exercise to be completed by the student, generally some type of drag and drop problem. The storyboard was then reviewed with the medical editor. This was also generally a three-hour meeting. The medical editor would typically point out places where the medical expert needed to make his/her sources more explicit, needed more updated references, or, in a few cases, where recent data had modified the assertions.

The comments and storyboard were then reviewed by the medical expert and passed back to the ID. The ID created a final storyboard (Figure 3), which was then reviewed one more time by the editor and medical expert.

Script

The scriptwriting is in three stages. A scriptwriter writes the script. It goes through a review process with the medical editor and instructional designer. Blocking and animation instructions are added. For this project, we used a scriptwriter who had written video scripts for pharmaceutical companies. He provided a fresh perspective to the material. The scriptwriter also wrote any bullets that would appear on the screen and completed the end of section exercises. We determined that there should be some bullet or some change to the screen every 5 to 10 seconds in order to maintain interest.

The script (Figure 4) was then reviewed by the instructional designer and then the medical editor, and then the production team added animation, bullet, and stage instructions.

System Design

Technical Requirements

There were three broad areas that needed to be defined for TOP MED: (1) the player that would be able to display something that looked like nearly full screen video over the In-

Figure 3. Sample of storyboard page

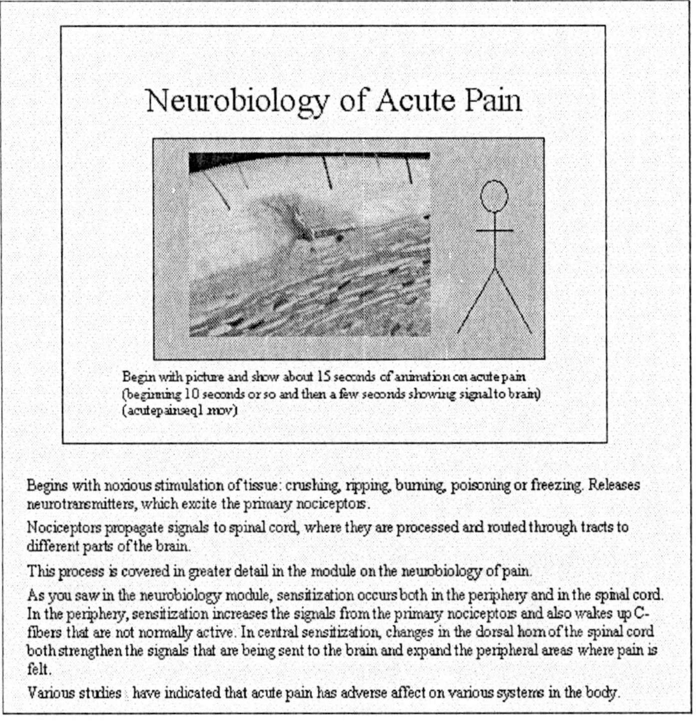

Neurobiology of Acute Pain

Begin with picture and show about 15 seconds of animation on acute pain (beginning 10 seconds or so and then a few seconds showing signal to brain) (acutepainseq1.mov)

Begins with noxious stimulation of tissue: crushing, ripping, burning, poisoning or freezing. Releases neurotransmitters, which excite the primary nociceptors.

Nociceptors propagate signals to spinal cord, where they are processed and routed through tracts to different parts of the brain.

This process is covered in greater detail in the module on the neurobiology of pain.

As you saw in the neurobiology module, sensitization occurs both in the periphery and in the spinal cord. In the periphery, sensitization increases the signals from the primary nociceptors and also wakes up C-fibers that are not normally active. In central sensitization, changes in the dorsal horn of the spinal cord both strengthen the signals that are being sent to the brain and expand the peripheral areas where pain is felt.

Various studies have indicated that acute pain has adverse affect on various systems in the body.

Figure 4. Script sample

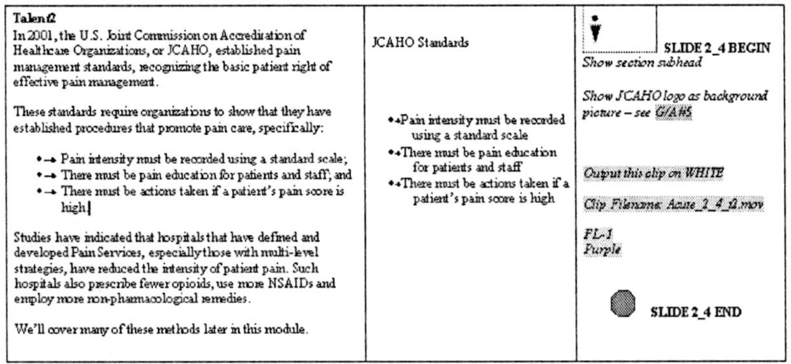

Take n2 In 2001, the U.S. Joint Commission on Accreditation of Healthcare Organizations, or JCAHO, established pain management standards, recognizing the basic patient right of effective pain management. These standards require organizations to show that they have established procedures that promote pain care, specifically: • Pain intensity must be recorded using a standard scale; • There must be pain education for patients and staff; and • There must be actions taken if a patient's pain score is high Studies have indicated that hospitals that have defined and developed Pain Services, especially those with multi-level strategies, have reduced the intensity of patient pain. Such hospitals also prescribe fewer opioids, use more NSAIDs and employ more non-pharmacological remedies. We'll cover many of these methods later in this module.	JCAHO Standards • Pain intensity must be recorded using a standard scale • There must be pain education for patients and staff • There must be actions taken if a patient's pain score is high	**SLIDE 2_4 BEGIN** *Show section subhead* *Show JCAHO logo as background picture – see G/A#5* *Output this clip on WHITE* *Clip Filename: Acute_2_4_t2.mov* *FL-1* *Purple* **SLIDE 2_4 END**

ternet; (2) the features of the learning management system (LMS) that would be used for student registration, tracking, and reporting; and (3) the hosting to meet response time and security requirements.

We knew that we would not be able to send a 600x800 pixel, 15 frames per second video over the Internet. It would be too large, requiring too much bandwidth on both the hosting and the user side. On the other hand, we knew that the end product needed a high production value; students and professors would want something comparable to what they see on television. We also knew that the target audience would have access to high-speed Web access, using advanced desktop and laptop computers.

Our conclusion was to use Flash Video. We would tape all segments on a chroma-key background and then blend the video image into the rest of the Flash stage in order to give the appearance of full screen video, cutting the bandwidth requirements by over 75%. Of course, it sounds simpler than it is; but the SmartPros Interactive staff was able to work out all the glitches and make the process relatively straightforward.

The lesson player also needed to be SCORM compliant so that the lessons could be easily ported to different LMSs. We also knew we were going to work with the SmartPros LMS: the Professional Education Center (PEC). The LMS gave us the capabilities to interface with the Flash player, register students, track student progress, provide end of module quizzes, and create custom reports for medical schools and for the AAPM. We needed to define the specific information that needed to be sent back and forth between the LMS and the player and also to specify the key data that the AAPM wanted to maintain.

Hosting presented an interesting conundrum. Between the U.S. and Canada there are over 140 medical schools. What if all the medical schools were using the program and 16,000 medical students needed to access lessons or answer questions at the same time? What would we need for hosting? On the other hand, since we would be starting off with just a few schools for the first semester, why should the client pay for excess capacity that they were not using? On the other hand, the number of students could change rapidly, in as little as a few weeks and with little advance notice.

For us, one of the strong attractions to the SmartPros PEC was that it was already serving hundreds of thousands of users, with bandwidth, processing, and storage to accommodate spikes in demand. If we started with just a few schools and the numbers of students increased by a factor of five three months in a row, it would not be a significant jump in the demands faced by the overall system.

User Interface Design

The user interface design involved both the LMS and the lesson player. For each, we first defined the types of operations a student was likely to perform. From the LMS, a student would need to register, logon, go to a specific module, take a test for a specific module, view results from previous tests, and view descriptions of the different modules. The priority for the LMS was to make these as easy as possible and keep the screen as simple as possible.

A student would be looking at a particular module from the player. From within that module, a student would want to continue, go to a particular section, fast forward or backward, pause, turn off the sound, take a quiz, see results for the previous quiz, look up a word, find where a topic is covered, and go back to the LMS.

We wanted to make these tasks simple; we wanted a unified color scheme and slide layout, but with a few different options to maintain interest. We initially brainstormed the different ways that the features could work and how they would relate to each other. A graphic designer then created screen layouts for five different looks, which were discussed with the client and sample users. Once we had narrowed the look down to two, we created working prototypes using the materials from the first module. These were again discussed with the same groups, and we ended up with our final look and feel.

Player and Template Creation

In order to allow for multiple developers to work on the material, we created the Flash player. All navigation and media controls were built into this player. Inside the player, there was a stage area. The player was designed to run each scene on that stage. The scene developer thus only had to worry about the specific content that was going to be deployed in that scene.

We then created different digital set templates for the different types of scenes: Introduction, Summary, Activity, person on left, person on right. The scene developer would receive a flash video file (flv file), a list of animation elements and/or bullets, and background photographs. The job of the developer was to assemble these source materials and choreograph them with the video. Figure 5 is a sample of the player with a digital set running.

Figure 5. Sample player view

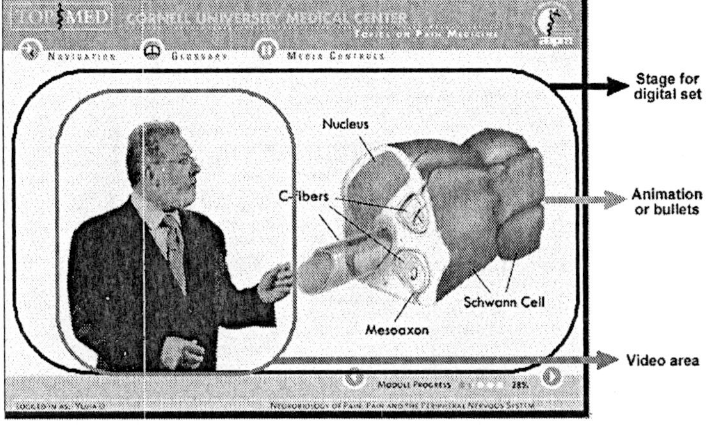

Production

Videotape and Post Production

Videotaping was performed in a green room with a teleprompter on the main video camera. Before each scene the actor would be coached on how to enter the frame, when to gesture, and where to stand.

With the medical experts, our challenge was to get them to relax and move freely in front of the camera. With the actors, it was pronunciation of medical terms like parenterally, NSAID, and allodynia. We found that one-hour of video required about one and one half days of shooting. The good takes were then transferred to flash video files and the sound was normalized.

Create New Templates

As we progressed with additional modules, we found we periodically needed to add to the number of templates, for example, person starting on left moving to right, person starting on right moving to left, and voice over with animation were all added to the original templates.

Create New Scenes and Exercises

We created a styles document and sample scenes that were given to the developers along with the templates and objects that were relevant to them. Before development started we had a kickoff meeting to discuss the purpose and audience of TOP MED, the story for that particular module, the graphics, bullets, and animations for each scene, and how to use the style document and templates.

Quality Assurance

There were two initial rounds of quality assurance for each module, with four individuals going through each scene. For the third round, the medical editor and two representatives of AAPM also participated in the review. The status of all suggestions and findings was maintained in a database that was accessible to all of the QA staff. The project manager was responsible for discussing each finding with the QA individual(s) who found it, verifying it, and then ensuring that the developer understood the changes.

Client Handover

Board of Advisors Review

In February 2005, the board of directors of the American Academy of Pain Medicine viewed the first two modules, and the result was very well received. In fact, one of the directors mentioned that this would be a good prototype for the way medical textbooks should be produced. The general comments were that the length of the modules was appropriate, the content was current, relevant, and focused, and the presentation would maintain the interest of the target student.

User Review

There have been quite a few doctors, residents, and students who have viewed the material. More formal review with medical school classes is also planned.

Modifications

There were three main changes that were requested from our initial feedback. First, since the first impression is going to be from the introduction to each module, we needed to make the intro compelling, and we have added graphics and animations to the background of these sections.

Second, while we initially felt the washed out colors would reduce learner fatigue, the feedback was that we needed a brighter color scheme. We have increased the color contrast for the second and third modules. Third, the initial feedback on the second module was that we needed to add a few animations, which we have done. We also increased our use of animations in the second two modules.

Program Evaluation

A panel of medical experts evaluated all contents for accuracy, currency, and relevance before the program was created. Since the first modules were created, the program has not yet been fully evaluated. We have shown the program to doctors, nurses, and med school students. The feedback has been very positive, but we do have a punch list of changes, most of which are minor. Currently the academy is waiting for the next level of funding to conduct a full evaluation and complete the additional modules.

Networking and Collaboration

TOP MED was designed to be run asynchronously; there is no collaboration built into the program itself. Instead, it is designed as a tool to be used by a professor to provide content to students, with projects to be assigned by the professor as part of the class.

Policy Implications

The advisory board of the AAPM has indicated that they would like to provide more materials in this fashion and that the cost for creating this course was similar to the cost of developing a textbook with similar content. They feel that this style more closely addresses how the current generation of doctors will want to study.

Sustainability and Conclusion

TOP MED was designed in such a way that additional modules could be added. Because of the use of video, though, it will be difficult to edit existing modules should methods become obsolete; it is difficult to splice in a new video and have it look continuous.

By having the project sponsored, the AAPM is ensuring that there are no monetary hurdles for students to obtain the content. On the other hand, TOP MED is dependent on the ability of the AAPM to find partners who can afford the approximately $75,000 it takes to create each one-hour module.

Lessons Learned and Best Practices

We thought that the process of defining the content, developing scripts, building in interactivity, and then taping, developing, and editing worked very well. After watching the first two modules, we learned how to make additional transitions to keep the students' attention and the importance of frequent reviews, especially reviews that explain the content in a different manner that when it is first explained.

The three actions that can be identified as best practices are:

1. Determine the needs and content that is needed before doing any of the work. This means pulling the content from a variety of sources and having it checked by content experts.

2. Develop a script with stage and animation instructions before any videotaping or animation development. It is very valuable to have these instructions reviewed by people experienced in animation and video to make sure that what you have envisioned will maintain the interest of the audience and to see if there are alternatives that might be lower cost but just as effective.
3. Flash was a great tool to work with, but you do need experts in Flash, and you need to build in four to five quality assurance rounds. You need to test to see if the product functions and also if it works for the intended audience.

Chapter XX

Hard Fun: A Case Study on a Community Problem Solving Learning Resource

Colette Wanless-Sobel, Inver Hills Community College, USA

Abstract

Current pedagogical theory promotes deep learning environments in online instruction as well as authenticity. This chapter discusses the pedagogical framework, academic issues and logistics of a deep learning resource that is "hard fun," to use a phrase of Seymour Papert, because it challenges and immerses students in real life learning environments through community problem solving. Success of the learning resource is largely due to the intrinsic motivation and cognitive engagement afforded through civic engagement, allowing students to pursue personally relevant knowledge in familiar milieus, their residential communities. Technology plays a role in increasing intellectual self-esteem and digital literacy by allowing students the opportunity to become bloggers and Web publishers.

{Hard fun} is expressed in many different ways, all of which all boil down to the conclusion that everyone likes hard challenging things to do. But they have to be the right things matched to the individual and to the culture of the times. These rapidly changing times challenge educators to find areas of work that are hard in the right way: they must connect with the {students} and also with the areas of knowledge, skills and (don't let us forget) ethics adults will need for the future world.

Seymour Papert, Founder, MIT Media Lab

Introduction

Current theory in online instructional design promotes the benefits of inclusive and constructivist pedagogy that centers on students, benefits a broad range of learning styles, and focuses on critical thinking and knowledge assembly, including digital literacy, cross cultural literacy, and fluency in multiple media (Carr & Ledwith, 2000; Dede, 2005; Lemke, 1998; McLoughlin, 2001; Taylor, 2001; Tierney & Damarin, 1998; UDI Fact Sheet, 2005; Weigel, 2001). Accordingly, e-learning environments must be more than information repositories; instead they need to be reconfigured as electronic "teaching theaters" that provide depth education through use of the semantic Web, multimedia, and real world applications (Berners-Lee, Hendler, & Lassila, 2001; Billinghurst, Kato, & Poupyrev, 2001; Chandler, 1995; Knemeyer, 2005; Lee & Owens, 2000; Web-based Education Commission, 2000; Weigel, 2001). Some theorists go so far as to say online instructional units should be works of art in terms of the intricacy of design and the transforming educational experience afforded to learners (Ceraulo, 2003). This position may seem far-fetched; however, the concept of learning resources (LR) and learning objects (LOs) as works of art is currently realized through academic ventures such as Project Merlot (http://www.merlot.org/Home.po), one of several repositories where instructors can find material to enrich online learning. For one example of an intricate, artistic, and pedagogically rich LR, see Andreja Kuluncic's *Distributive Justice Interactive Web Site* (http://www.distributive-justice.com/).

To this list of pedagogical do's, I also add one more, the variable of "fun," which should not be taken to mean catering to novelty or taking the substance out of learning but creating for students passionate engagement—"flow" (Csikszentmihalyi, 1990), with online learning (Ceraulo, 2003; Papert, 2002). Seymour Papert, founder and professor *emeritus*, MIT's Media Lab, has written extensively about fun as a necessary component of learning (Papert, 2002; Papert, 1952-2002).

It is within the theoretical contexts of constructivism, inclusivism, digital-multimedia fluency, and fun discussed previously that, I designed an online community problem solving LR for two introductory level semester length English classes at Inver Hills Community College, Inver Grove Heights, Minnesota, United States. (Access the learning resource online at http://loproblemsolving.blogspot.com/.) The two classes, "Writing and Research Skills" and "Research Writing in the Disciplines," are foundational courses for the Associate of Arts degree, including paraprofessional degrees on campus, such as Emergency Health Services (paramedic training). Competency areas for the classes include critical thinking, research, and college level writing with focus on essay writing. As the LR designer and instructor, I added the competencies of digital and multimedia literacy through blog creation and civic engagement through participatory inquiry (Heron & Reason, 1997) in each student's residential community. The LR is designed for online and hybrid instruction and is applicable to on-site instruction as well.

This essay shares the pedagogical alchemy of a community problem solving LR whose "hard fun" design immerses and challenges students in the learning experience as researchers, community activists, writers, multimedia artists, editors, and Web publishers. This case study is not intended as a pedagogical recipe or even a best practice; instead it offers colleagues the community problem solving teaching experience as a pedagogical smorgasbord to sample for their own course designs.

Institutional and Student Frameworks for the LR

Innovation in online education is a priority at Inver Hills Community College (hereafter, "Inver Hills"), an accredited institution for online instruction located in an eastern suburb of the Twin Cities in Minnesota, where I teach part time. Inver Hills supports faculty efforts in online course development through grant money, technology support, laptop computer allocation, and continuing education (CTL, 2004).

The community problem solving LR is designed to meet the diverse interests and goals of the student population at Inver Hills, who is required to fulfill distribution requirements in English composition. Students who enroll in "Writing and Research Skills" and "Research Writing Across the Disciplines" range in age from 16 on up and comprise a diverse demographic: high school students; two-year college students; paraprofessional students; four year degree candidates; displaced workers; women with children; and life-long learners. African Americans, Asian Americans, and Mexican Americans often comprise the student body, as do recent émigrés from Africa, Russia, and the Ukraine, among others. Despite the ranges in age, ethnicity, and circumstance, most students hold down full time jobs and have busy lives outside of school. Many of them are parents. Another common denominator among the diverse student body is apathy, boredom, and dread toward English composition, typically viewed as a necessary evil distribution requirement. The community problem solving LR is designed to revive enthusiasm and intellectual engagement in the composition classroom. This motivational aspect will be discussed more fully later.

Computing and CMS with the LR

Computing is central to the community problem solving learning resource. However, it is computing for keyboarding, blogging, and knowledge construction using the Internet. The community problem solving itself does not require the use of a course management system (CMS); however, because the LR is designed for online and hybrid courses, we utilize a CMS as an assignment repository—first WebCT and now, currently, Desire to Learn (D2L).

We designed the LR assuming students possess little prior knowledge of the CMS or online class instruction. Accordingly, there is no prerequisite computer skill required for the classes I teach or the community problem solving LR. In the first few weeks of a semester term, emphasis is placed on orientation to the CMS environment and building computer confidence using the Internet. Computer access is not generally an issue, as most students at Inver Hills own personal computers; however, computers are also available for use in the technology lab on campus and also at community libraries around the Twin Cities. Technical support for students and the CMS platform is provided by technology services on campus, and there is a CMS trouble-shooting hotline maintained by Minnesota State Colleges and Universities (MNSCU), a consortium of 32 institutions, including 25 two-year colleges and seven state universities. (The system is separate from the University of Minnesota.) As the facilitator of learning, I also provide technical support for the class, especially in terms of the blogging platform and multimedia utilities. No special materials for the LR are needed; no cost is incurred.

The Pedagogical Framework of the LR

Because structure-content-delivery-service-outcomes of the LR are all interconnected (MacDonald & Thompson, 2005), I shall weave the pedagogical framework discussion with each of these LO threads, while focusing on the pedagogy.

Nine instructional events, based on Robert Gagne's events of instruction, are contained in the LR: gaining learners' attention and interest; informing learners about the learning objectives; stimulating recall; providing content; providing guidance, relevance, and organization; eliciting learning objectives by demonstrating them; providing feedback on performance; assessing performance through feedback and reinforcement; and enhancing retention and transfer to other contexts (Gagne, 1985; Gagne, Briggs, & Wager, 1992).

The community problem solving LR is experiential and active learning augmented with work on the Internet and blog creation. LR's tasks are substantive, requiring significant investment of time (five to six weeks) and intellectual resources. Learners can be uniquely identified; content can be specifically personalized; and multiple forms of intelligence are accommodated. Interdisciplinary and cross-disciplinary perspectives are encouraged. Solitary, collaborative, and interpersonal learning activities are interspersed throughout the LR. Learning activities entail learning through self-direction; goal setting; problem identification and creative solution through aggressive inquiry, community collaboration, and primary research; self-testing and metacognition; peer review; and blogging. Realizing students accustomed to teacher-centered modes of instruction may have difficulty in changing dependent learning habits and that problems can arise if students are not self-motivated, the setting for the LR is each student's residential community, which offers a safe and familiar learning environment to pursue the independent and challenging tasks required.

The LR is comprised of three main "cumulative constructivism" activities (Bruner, 1962), whereby learning and discovery are organized: community problem solving; blog creation and content management; and Web publishing. I shall provide the skeletal frame for each of these activities to provide inroads to various pedagogical issues.

Task Orientation

The community problem solving LR uses a "minimalist" approach (Carroll, 1990), meaning its composition is task oriented. Accordingly, it does not ask students to find and read what "experts" say about their community problems, nor does it ask them to read for theoretical background on the problems. Instead, "non-expert" students start immediately on realistic problem solving tasks and primary research in their residential communities. Passive activity, such as reading, especially conceptual, theoretical reading, is kept to a minimum for the entire LR. Academic and professional knowledge is not privileged over knowledge production in other sites, namely, the residential communities (Gibbons, Limoges, Nowotny, Schwartzman, Scott, & Trow, 1994). The pedagogical implication here is not that conceptual models should not be explicitly facilitated, but they should be postponed. My roles in all this are keeping students on the tasks; leaving them room for reflection; not impeding students' serendipitous and experimental learning strategies; and providing a theoretical center for learning.

Mining for Knowledge

To return to the three components of the LR, using Richard Paul and Linda Elder's text *Critical Thinking*: *Tools for Taking Charge of Your Learning and Your Life* (2002), which students read for scaffolding in critical thinking earlier in the term, students are instructed to consider real life problems in their residential communities, and select one to focus on for the next five to six weeks. Instructing students to think of community problems in terms of community *needs* is helpful to students, who then conduct needs analyses and assessments in their communities. The needs and problems students identify in their communities cover all areas of social and civic life. Some examples include the need for…a sexual and reproductive health clinic; a stop sign at an intersection; a battered women's/men's shelter; a youth recreation center; an alternative community newspaper/newsletter; affordable mass transit in the suburbs; a neighborhood crime watch; a humane shelter for other creatures besides dogs and cats; rent control; a safe-house for gay, lesbian, and transgender youth; and a skate-board arena.

Once students identify their community problems, they then apply a critical thinking rubric designed to analyze all the components of the problems and suggest possible solutions. The rubric has a meta-cognitive focus. (*Meta-cognition* here refers to students' self-curious and self-critical thought processes assumed to be crucial for the selection and implementation of complex problem-solving strategies.) The rubric also mines for students' intuitive knowledge or internal tacit knowledge on the community problem. Tentative solutions and creations are acceptable for the purpose of the assignment.

In the next step, students begin a three-part primary research investigation using the rubric created, although the rubric is also negotiable. In the first part, students are directed to conduct primary research (participation-observation) on the problems in their neighborhoods, which entails keeping research logs. Essentially, this phase of the primary research rubric instructs students to look with new eyes at the commonsensical and normal ways in their communities, and analyze the conversations and written languages used to explain the community problems, although prior knowledge and experience of the problem can be used to inform their investigations. The second phase of primary research entails conducting interviews with two city officials or citizens who have jurisdiction or responsibility for the community problems and who can offer possible solutions. Focus here is on drafting interview questions to yield substantive interview content. The third phase of primary research involves research on the Internet, ranging from databases, Web sites, forums, podcasts, wikis, blogs, forums, and screencasts relating to the community problem. Here the focus is in familiarizing students with primary sources available on the Internet as well as informatic literacy (Lemke, 1998), whereby students learn to locate and evaluate sources. Once the primary research is completed, students then do some background reading in secondary sources they locate and evaluate on their community problems, which may entail theoretical reading, depending on students' interests and the problems themselves. A 7 to 10 page synthesis on the community problem solving process and the research process is the end result.

Blogging for Knowledge

The second component of the LR is blog construction with *Blogger.com* (http://www.blogger.com/start), a free blogging platform created by Pyra Labs, located in San Francisco, California, in 1999 and now owned by Google.com. Although there are several free blog platforms available (Blog Software Comparison Chart, 2005), I utilize Blogger.com for several reasons. First, Blogger.com is a robust platform that can accommodate blogging novices as well as experts. Without any knowledge of HTML or Java programming, Blogger.com users can add audio, video, digital photos, commenting, and trackbacks (Taylor, 2005). Second, Blogger.com has a user-friendly and intuitive interface. For instance, Blogger.com provides a "Compose Mode," which is also known as a WYSIWYG (what-you-see-is-what-you-get) editor, in the text editor section. The WYSIWYG editor essentially allows bloggers to compose on a screen similar to a word processor, although it is arguable that the vague visual clues of the WYSIWYG editor are not sufficient to enable the user to fully utilize this sophisticated software tool (Glasersfeld, 1995). In my experience, however, both as blogger and as instructor, user trial and error with the WYSIWYG editor is highly successful.

User trial and error, a minimalist approach, is used for the entire blogging component of the LR. Students are instructed to start blogging without a formal introduction into blogging or the blog platform, although due to the attention political bloggers received during the last United States presidential election, most students have at least heard of blogs, even if they are not certain what they entail (Rice, 2003). The LR instructs students to login to Blogger.com and initiate their blog accounts and create their blog template, which takes all of 10 minutes. Once students are familiar with the blog platform and the *WYSIWYG* editor, which is usually less than one half hour, they then begin content management, which will include their problem solving report but also a multimedia presentation and appropriate hyperlinks.

The focus of the LR's blog component is students learning to use a blog platform and developing authoring skills using multimedia, requiring familiarity with multimedia semiotics (Lemke, 1998). The LR's multimedia-blog unit is not unsubstantial or superficial content filler or fluff. In the post-typographic world of the 21st century, knowledge construction is no longer logocentric, and the perceptual field is no longer just visual and linear, but spherical and acoustic (Glogowski, 2002; Lemke, 1998, p. 288). Students enter their community problem solving reports (usually linear text but not always) on their blogs; however, they also envision information (Tufte, 1990) and amplify knowledge about the problems using hyperlinks to relevant sources; video; news photos; their own digital photos and videos; advertising images; audio files; statistical charts and tables, including creative quantitative figures and graphs; and remix techniques applied to all media (Remix Culture, 2005). The polyphony of this multimedia creates rich and deep knowledge construction (Lemke, 1997).

All utilities the students use for the blogging multimedia are free: Hello.com, a digital photo management utility; Haloscan.com, a commenting and trackback (Taylor, 2005) system; Tag-Board.com, a facility that provides real-live discussion boards; AudioBlogger.com, an audio utility; and Bravenet.com, which allows bloggers to add blog extras, such as mini polls, site search, and chat rooms to their sites.

After content management of the blogs is completed, a peer review process takes place, based on a rubric designed to gauge primary research validity, generalizability, and reliability and as a way around students' "pathological politeness" (Garrison & Anderson, 2003) when providing peer feedback. Instructor review of the blogs also occurs at this juncture, and students make appropriate revisions.

Web Publishing for Authorship and Authenticity

The third component of the problem solving LR is Web publishing or the formal announcement of the blog projects' URLs to the entire class and to individuals and organizations in each student's community. The Web publishing component of the LR is put in the forefront at the very beginning to emphasize to students that they will not be "handing in" class work to me but instead will be sharing it with the class and their residential communities. The LR community problem solving research and blog productions are valuable products in their own right rather than just class projects. The polished blog projects are evidence of not only students' hard—yet fun—work, but also their apprenticeship in a complex intellectual project. Additionally, the blog showcase at the end of the LO unit allows students see how the community problem solving activities permit a range and diversity of outcomes open to multiple solutions of an original nature, rather than a single correct response obtained by the application of rules and procedures. Because students see varied practices in their class peers' blogs, they are also able to generalize the capabilities they acquired in the LR.

The Logistical Framework of the LR

As with any large endeavor, the execution or logistics of all the required tasks can seem daunting, especially as in the case of this community problem solving LR, where the project entails coordinating the efforts of 20-some students per class, without set content, who are thinking and working in many simultaneous segments; directing students' primary and secondary research, including community activism; and assisting students in learning a blog platform—all done online, too! Nevertheless, all of these tasks are manageable and enjoyable for all—students and instructor—as long as the instructor does some micro-managing before students begin the project. Essentially, what is involved is (1) breaking down a massive undertaking into manageable but flexible steps; (2) allowing students enough time and flexibility to perform the steps with the instructor acting as intellectual midwife; and (3) anticipating and correcting "technical difficulties."

Technical Difficulties

In general, I found Blogger.com is free of any technical difficulties. The same goes for Hello.com, the digital photo management utility, and AudioBlogger.com, the audio utility. Invariably, however, some student always contacts me, saying he or she is experiencing "technical" trouble. What a student terms as technical difficulty is usually his or her initial inability to understand and correctly utilize the features of the blog construction platform or the utilities. If indeed an actual technical difficulty arises, Blogger.com, Hello.com, and AudioBlogger.com offer members' forums where technical advice is provided.

When a student experiences "technical difficulty," the easiest way to handle this is for the student and the teacher to "sit down" together online, in front of their respective computer screens and go through the features of the blog platform, preferably while talking together on the phone. Once the student has orientation, the problem clears up. If the student is willing and able to meet on campus, the blog orientation can also be accomplished face to face in an office or computer lab. In the worse case scenario, where the student is unable to lay out the basic site (I have had one such case out of 100 plus students), I ask for the username and password and go in and construct the basic site, and then assist the student with hyperlinks and multimedia applications.

Often colleagues interested in pursuing blogging in the classroom ask how much technical expertise with Blogger.com should an instructor have in order to use blogging in a course. In answer, I can only share my experience:

When I first used Blogger.com in an online classroom, I had only been using the platform myself for about a month, and it was a slippery learning slope. Lack of proficiency was stressful and sometimes embarrassing; however, I soon discovered that I liked being on the slippery slope because it provided first-hand experience what my students would be experiencing, and because it forced me to value play and experimentation, two activities that are crucial to learning immersion in the LR, although I did not realize this until teaching the LR for one semester.

Academic Issues

Three academic issues are fundamental to the administration and success of the LR, all closely interconnected: instructor as expert learner; intellectual risk and play; and recalibrated assessment.

Instructor as Expert Learner

Constructivist learning theory promotes learning that is active, situated, and social (Levy, 2003); furthermore, for deep learning to take place, students need to be able to choose content (Ramsden, 1988). All of these conditions run contrary to the dominant learning paradigm, the curricular paradigm, where what students need to know, the order they need to learn to know it, and the classroom as *the* learning environment (Lemke, 1998) are all predetermined or laid out in sequence. The community problem solving LR, by its very nature, cannot be contained in a packaged learning module that provides students with a hierarchical sequence for obtaining knowledge, although the LR provides guidance by way of rubrics. Instead, with the LR, the learning environment is life itself: residential communities throughout the Twin Cities. Similarly, the traditional educational figure of authority, the instructor, recedes and is superseded by community authority figures and knowledge competency models in communities whom students encounter and talk with in the course of the LR and whom students use to measure the effectiveness of the instructor (Glogowski, 2002).

Intellectual Risk and Play

The importance of play for preschoolers is widely accepted; the importance of play for college students and adults sounds like New Age psychobabble. Despite this, I find "playful learning," which I define here as curiosity, discovery, novelty, risk-taking, trial and error, pretense, games, and other more complex adaptive activities, the most important pedagogical ingredient in the community problem solving LR for producing students' cognitive independence and social interdependence, two variables necessary for a deep learning experience (Garrison & Anderson, 2003). Play is also important because the intellectual work in the LR requires students to actively engage with the learning environment in non-scripted ways associated with play, while simultaneously being instructed to conduct themselves as serious researchers and community activists. Finally, playful ingredients of energy, imagination, and confidence are required of students in the face of unpredictable, complex, emergent learning environments—their residential communities. A playful stance allows students to maintain adaptability, vigor, and optimism while completing LR tasks that are uncertain, risky, and demanding.

Recalibrated Assessment

The importance of assessment in "shaping intentions" and in how students approach an educational experience (Garrison & Anderson, 2003; Ramsden, 1988) is well documented. Early on with the creation of the LR, I understood traditional assessment would not be useful for shaping student intentions. If I want students to take risks and venture into unknown intellectual territory, there cannot be grade penalties for "mistakes." Further consideration of assessment variables in the LR reveals even thornier issues. Let me briefly enumerate: (1) Although inaccurate prior knowledge and assumptions about community problems are identified and revised, meta-cognition is encouraged for revisiting and expanding previous knowledge building. The learning from this intellectual process is difficult to assess. (2) The tools of authentic assessment in the LR (research logs and blogs) are rich in content but lean in assessment quantification. (3) Likewise, performance on a test seems to be a poor indicator or measurement for students' construction of rich conceptual materials and problem solving tasks. (4) Because the LR is task-oriented, grading on a curve or absolute standard grading is also questionable. (5) If multiple intelligences (abstract, textual, visual, musical, social, and kinesthetic) are valued and encouraged for the LR—and they are—then there must be assessment tools to gauge these multiple intelligences. (6) Finally, the multimedia component of the LR necessarily calls for recalibrated assessment, as most assessment strategies are attuned to reading student papers or tests that conform to standardized formats. Writing in the LR, however, is sometimes structured in non-standard formats, even including reflexive and multi-voiced segments of text. In other words, because LR productions are no longer just typographical, linear, and homogeneous, there are whole new questions about standards of assessment.

For all these reasons, I decided to reevaluate and recalibrate my grading rubric for all tasks required in the LR, realizing colleagues will have varying degrees of accord and dissent regarding the assessment rubric I devised. This case study is not the intellectual venue to engage in the grading debate. What seems to lie at the heart of this issue is the question about the importance of competitive evaluation, and each instructor must come to his or her own position on this matter, as the debate reflects the wide range of beliefs educators hold about educational psychology and the nature of education.

To accomplish the LR assessment recalibration, I modified and tailored a preexisting rubric, "A Publishable Quality Rubric," from the *Leadership Institute Integrating Internet, Instruction and Curriculum Web Site* (http://www-ed.fnal.gov/trc/projects/rubric.html). Although I attempted to integrate assessment with major tasks in such a way as to reflect real world assessment rather than assessment removed from the tasks, I did not completely succeed. The rubric I designed is far from seamless, and not all assessment issues for the LR are resolved. Points rather than grades were assigned for each criterion with extensive and substantive comments. Emphasis was placed on process and revision. (See truncated version of the assessment rubric in Figure 1.)

Program Evaluation

For an LR to be successful, users must be the central consideration in the development and implementation of learning modules. Usability testing evaluates effectiveness by gauging learnability, ease-of-use, efficiency, and appeal (Evaluation Criteria, 2000). At this stage, I have not yet employed tools and techniques of usability testing to the LR. Identification of user success and user difficulties here is, therefore, based on my own observations and experiences facilitating the LO for three years.

Learning outcomes, evidenced by the LR tasks, specifically primary research, research logs, problem solving reports, and blogs, indicate students experience deep learning, higher order

Figure 1. Community problem solving learning activities rubric

Logistics/Knowledge Production/Digital Literacy 70%	Points Earned	Comments:
All key elements and activities of the project are covered in a substantive way:		
~Identification of stereotype, assumption, and tacit knowledge about "problems" in a community.		
~Problem identification/community needs analysis, using critical thinking, creative thinking, and lateral thinking.		
~Questions, concerns, issues, hypotheses, or problem-solving suggestions are developed that guide the problem solving.		
~Progress Report I Rubric completed. (Mechanism in place for instructor's assessment of student progress and also for student to assess his/her own learning.)		
~Primary research subjects identified and interview times set up.		
~Primary research is conducted thoroughly and rigorously; research log maintained diligently. Field work.		
~Professional and courteous behavior and communication maintained at all times with community problem stakeholders.		
~Thank you notes composed and mailed to interviewees.		
~Progress Report II Rubric completed.		
~Recursive/meta-cognitive thinking applied to community problem after primary research. Refinement of "solution."		
~More research, based on recursive reasoning about the problem, either primary or secondary, including theoretical material.		
~Progress Report III Rubric completed.		

Figure 1. continued

~Formal write-up of project. • The content is comprehensive, accurate, and professional in presentation. • The project develops a central theme or idea, directed toward the appropriate community audience. • The project is analytical and logical, and is fair and balanced in its arguments. • Major points are stated clearly; are supported by specific details, examples, or analysis; and are organized logically. • The "solution" is logical and feasible for the community, flows from the body of the paper, and reviews the major point. • MLA/APA citation etiquette observed. • MLA/APA bibliography format.		
~Blog/URL creation and blog design, including design decisions about project presentation.		
~Cut and paste project onto blog. Format.		
~Internet search for hyperlinks to enrich blog presentation and dialogue about the community		
~Internet search for multimedia to enrich presentation and foster dialogue.		
~Search for online utilities, such as Audioblogger.com, for blog enrichment.		
~Inclusion of student's own digital photos or media production for the blog presentation.		
~Progress Report IV Rubric completed.		
~Revision for diction/syntactic fluency.		
~Proofreading: usage, spelling, grammar, punctuation.		
~Peer feedback, using rubric with special focus on logical fallacies		
~Instructor feedback, using rubric, macro-perspective.		
~Revision after peer/instructor feedback.		
~Formal publication of blog URL by e-mail to class, instructor, and stakeholders in the community problem (e.g. mayor, community activist).		
~Progress Report V Rubric completed: Meta-cognitive self-evaluation of the community problem, using rubric.		

Figure 1. continued

Style, Clarity and Readability 15%	Points Earned	Comments:
The diction and tone appropriate to the project.		
Paragraph transitions are present and logical and maintain the flow throughout the paper.		
Writing is suitable for blog (paragraphs not too long).		
Sentences are complete, clear, and concise.		
Sentences are well-constructed, with consistently strong, varied sentences (syntactic fluency).		
Sentence transitions are present and maintain the flow of thought.		
Hyperlinks…		
~link to useful places/sites that provide needed information to enrich or supplement project.		
~link to places/sites that provide information or needed skill development for community problem solution (e.g., a site on "how-to" start a community food shelf).		
~link to datasets that are updated (if data involved).		
~link actively (links not broken).		
Multimedia includes…		
~audio-visual material that supplements and enhances the project; it is not filler.		
~adequate instructions for readers/users, if required.		
~proper citation.		
~consideration for graphic design of the blog and the text (e.g., enough white space).		
Mechanics 15%	Points Earned	Comments:
The project/blog, including the title page, reference page, tables, and appendices, follows MLA or APA guidelines for format.		
Citations of primary and secondary sources within the body of the project follow MLA/APA guidelines.		
The project is laid out in the electronic space with effective use of headings, font styles, and white space.		
Rules of grammar, usage, and punctuation are followed.		
Spelling is correct.		
Total 100 Percent	Points Earned	Comments:

thinking, critical thinking, or problem-solving skills, civic engagement, and digital literacy. There are also immeasurable learning outcomes in terms of class morale, personal empowerment, and self-esteem. As mentioned previously, the majority of students in my online and hybrid English composition classes is politely disengaged and expects to do grin-and-bear -it forced labor. The work entailed in the LR is a pleasant surprise for them, and, for the most part, students tackle the assignment with energy and enthusiasm. Indeed, although the workload for the LR is sometimes an issue, most students are challenged and engaged, especially in terms of conducting primary research in their residential communities, which allows them to develop immeasurable social, cultural, and intellectual capital. Moreover, the LR's authentic learning settings, students' residential communities, have the capability to motivate and encourage learner participation and provide motivation and perseverance with learning tasks that initially students view as stressful and cognitively dissonant. Finally, the blogging component of the LR adds a dimension not typically available to all students. Previously, only students with a background in Web page design could produce electronic displays and portfolios for assignments. Blogger.com now allows anyone to do so, as well as professionally showcase work to not only class peers and community members but also to family and friends. The skill sets and self-esteem developed from blogging encourages future ventures in computerized instruction, and digital knowledge construction.

Conclusion

The central lesson that informs and underpins every other recommendation to emerge from this case study is that course design and teaching methods are critical to deep learning success. At one level, this seems obvious, but it has profound implications for LR design. My experience with the community problem solving LR demonstrates the importance of tapping into the reservoir of material relevant to students' daily lives for course content. When instructional content and tasks tap the passions of learners and harness learners' intellectual and emotional energies, then learners have incentives to perform the hard work needed to tackle difficult material and acquire habits of self-discipline. Likewise, when instructional tasks require learners to master skills that are hard and challenging—skills that stretch their comfort zones, even to the point of cognitive dissonance, such as with creating and designing blogs and conducting primary research—"learners" acquire self-esteem and capabilities they can carry forward after the course unit ends. Finally, the fun factor of an LR should be considered for learners and instructor. If an LR design is pedagogically viable as a deep learning experience, students and instructor are immersed in the learning process, and this immersion provides the "fun" needed for initial perseverance with discomforting and unfamiliar tasks and the social lubricant for students and instructor to engage and interact in a nonhierarchical learning community. This "hard fun" is what constructivism is all about.

References

A Publishable Quality Rubric (2001). *Leadership Institute Integrating Internet, Instruction and Curriculum Web site.* Retrieved May 15, 2002, from http://www-ed.fnal.gov/trc/projects/rubric.html

AudioBlogger.com. http://audioblogger.com

Berners-Lee, T., Hendler, J., & Lassila, O. (2001). The Semantic Web. *Scientific America, 284*(5), 34-43.

Billinghurst, M., Kato, H., & Poupyrev, I. (2001). The magicbook: Moving seamlessly between reality and virtuality. *IEEE Computer Graphics and Applications, 21*(3), 6-8.

Blog Software Comparison Chart. (2005). *University of Southern California Annenberg Online Journalism Review,* July 14, 2005. Retrieved August 11, 2005, from http://www.ojr.org/ojr/images/blog_software_comparison.cfm

Bravenet.com Mini Polls. http://www.bravenet.com

Bruner, J. S. (1962). *On knowing: Essays for the left hand.* Cambridge, MA: Harvard University Press.

Carr, R., & Ledwith, F. (2000, February). Helping disadvantaged students. *Teaching at a Distance, 18*, 77-85.

Carroll, J. M. (1990). *The Nurnberg funnel: Designing minimalist instruction for practical computer skill.* Cambridge, MA: MIT Press.

Center for Teaching and Learning (CTL/MNSCU). (2004). *CTL grant guidelines, 2004-2005.* Retrieved from http://www.ctl.mnscu.edu/programs/grants/guidelines-05.htm

Ceraulo, S. C. (2003). Instructional design for flow in online teaching. *E-Learn Magazine.* Retrieved July 13, 2005, from http://elearnmag.org/subpage.cfm?section=tutorials&article=14-1

Chandler, D. (1995). *The act of writing: A media theory approach.* Aberystwyth: University of Wales.

Csikszentmihalyi, M. (1990). *Flow: The psychology of optimal experience.* New York: Harper Collins.

Dede, C. (2005). Planning for neomillennial learning styles. *Educause Quarterly, 28*(1). Retrieved August 2, 2005, from http://www.educause.edu/pub/eq/eqm05/eqm0511.asp?bhcp=1

E-Learning Leadership Team, Minnesota State Colleges and Universities, MNSCU. (2003). *E-learning initiatives overview.* Retrieved June 14, 2005, from http://www.academicaffairs.mnscu.edu/divisionhomepage/elearningproject/elearningmain1.htm

Evaluation criteria for peer reviews of MERLOT learning resources. (2000). *MERLOT.* Retrieved August 3, 2005, from http://taste.merlot.org/catalog/peer_review/eval_criteria.htm

Gagne, R. (1985). *The conditions of learning* (4th ed.). New York: Holt, Rinehart & Winston.

Gagne, R., Briggs, L., & Wager, W. (1992). *Principles of instructional design* (4th ed.). Fort Worth, TX: HBJ College Publishers.

Garrison, D. R., & Anderson, T. (2003). *E-learning in the 21st century.* London & New York: Routledge Falmer.

Gibbons, M., Limoges, C., Nowotny, H., Schwartzman, S., Scott, P., & Trow, M. (1994). *The new production of knowledge: The dynamics of science and research in contemporary societies.* London: Sage.

Glasersfeld, E. von. (1995). A constructivist approach to teaching. In L. P. Stee & J. Gale (Eds.), *Constructivism in education* (pp. 3-15). Hillsdale, NJ: Lawrence Erlbaum Associates.

Glogowski, K. (2002). *Knowledge-building in electronic environments.* Retrieved July 20, 2005, from http://home.oise.utoronto.ca/~kglogowski/enhance.html

Halocan.com. http://www.haloscan.com/

Hello.com. http://www.hello.com/index.php

Heron, J., & Reason, P. (1997). A participatory inquiry program. *Qualitative Inquiry, 3*(3), 274-294.

Knemeyer, D. (2005). Web design for all the senses: Innovating the Web experience. *Digital Web Magazine*, January 12, 2005. Retrieved January 13, 2005, from http://www.digital-web.com/articles/web_design_for_all_the_senses/

Kuluncic, A. (2001-2003). Distributive justice interactive Web site. *MERLOT.* Retrieved July 20, 2005, from http://www.distributive-justice.com/

Lee, W. W., & Owens, D. L. (2000). *Multi media-based instructional design: Computer-cased training, Web-based training, distance broadcast training.* Indianapolis: Jossey-Bass.

Lemke, J. L. (1997). Multiplying meaning: Visual and verbal semiotics in scientific text. In J. R. Martin & R. Veel (Eds.), *Reading science* (pp. 87-113). London: Routledge.

Lemke, J. L. (1998). Metamedia literacy: Transforming meanings and media. In D. Reinking, L. Labbo, M. McKenna, & R. Kiefer (Eds.), *The handbook of literacy and technology: Transformations in a post-typographic world* (pp. 283-301). Mahwah, NJ: Lawrence Erlbaum Associates Publishers.

Levy, P. (2003). A methodological framework for practice-based research in networked learning. *Instructional Science, 31*(1-2), 87-109.

MacDonald, C. J., & Thompson, T. L. (2005). Structure, content, delivery, service, and outcomes: Quality e-learning in higher education. *International Review of Research in Open and Distance Learning*, 6(2). Retrieved July 20, 2005, from http://www.irrodl.org/content/v6.2/macdonald-thompson.html

McLoughlin, C. (2001). Inclusivity and alignment: Principles of pedagogy, task and assessment design for effective cross-cultural online learning. *Distance Education, 22*(1), 7-29.

Monticeno, V. (2004). *Introduction to Internet terminology. Education and technology resources.* Retrieved August 13, 2005, from http://mason.gmu.edu/~montecin/netterms.htm

Papert, S. (2002). Hard fun. *Bangor Daily News*. Retrieved August 3, 2005, from http://www.papert.org/articles/HardFun.html

Papert, S. (1952-2002). *Works by Seymour Papert, PhD*. Retrieved August 12, 2005, from http://www.papert.org/works.html

Paul, R., & Elder, L. (2002). *Critical thinking: Tools for taking charge of your learning and your life*. Upper Saddle River, NJ: Pearson Prentice-Hall.

Ramsden, P. (1988). Context and strategy: Situational influences on learning. In R. R. Schmeck (Ed.), *Learning strategies and learning styles* (pp. 159-184). New York: Plenum.

Remix Culture. (2005). *wikipedia.* Retrieved August 9, 2005, from http://en.wikipedia.org/wiki/Remix_culture

Rice, A. (2003). The use of blogs in the 2004 presidential election. Campaignsonline.org. Retrieved August 2, 2005, from http://www.campaignsonline.org/reports/bLOg.pdf

Tag-board.com. http://www.tag-board.com/

Taylor, D. (2005). *What are Weblog trackbacks and why should I included them on my blog?* Ask Dave Taylor Web site. January 16, 2005. Retreived August 9, 2005, from http://www.askdavetayLOr.com/what_are_webLOg_trackbacks_and_why_should_i_include_them_on_my_bLOg.html

Taylor, J. (2001). The future of learning—learning for the future: Shaping the transition. *Open Praxis, 2*, 20-24. Retrieved August 25, 2006, from http://www.usq.edu.au/users/taylorj/publications_presentations/2001OpenPraxis.dc

Tierney, R., & Damarin, S. (1998). Technology as enfranchisement: Crisscrossing symbolic systems, paradigm shifts, and social-cultural considerations. In D. Reinking, L. Labbo, M. McKenna, & R. Kiefer (Eds.), *The handbook of literacy and technology: Transformations in a post-typograhic world* (pp. 253-268). Mahwah, NJ: Lawrence Erlbaum Associates Publishers.

Tufte, E. R. (1990*). Envisioning information*. Cheshire, CT: Graphics Press.

UDI Fact Sheet. (2005). *FacultyWare Web site*. http://www.facultyware.uconn.edu/home.cfm. Retrieved July 7, 2005, from http://www.facultyware.uconn.edu/files/UDI2_Fact_Sheet.pdf

Wanless-Sobel, C. (2005). *Community problem solving LO.* Retrieved August 13, 2005, from http://loproblemsolving.blogspot.com/

Web-based Education Commission. *The power of the Internet for learning.* Retrieved July 20, 2005, from http://www.hpcnet.org/webcommission

Weigel, Van B. (2001). *Deep learning for a digital age: Technology's untapped potential to enrich higher education.* Indianapolis: Jossey-Bass.

Chapter XXI

ESPORT Demonstration Project, Canada

Patrick J. Fahy, Athabasca University, Canada

Patrick Cummins, CEP Consulting, Canada

Abstract

This chapter describes the purpose, processes, and effects of an e-learning employment readiness system, ESPORT, currently being pilot tested in Canada. The essential skills portfolio (ESPORT) system is a facilitated and supported Internet-delivered system primarily intended for adults with a high school education or less, intended to assist users to choose an occupation, assess their enabling skills in respect to the chosen occupation, identify and (optionally) remedy skills gaps, and document in a résumé their abilities for prospective employers. While this e-learning project was not complete at this writing, this report describes the piloting process, and some already obvious conclusions regarding ESPORT's technologies, design, delivery, and support models, and training protocols. As anticipated, both the project's components and the evaluation design have changed, recognizing pressing issues requiring early attention, and responding to lessons learned.

Background

Workforce development is a priority of the Government of Canada, through the Department of Human Resources and Skills Development Canada (HRSDC). The evidence that Canada is approaching a workforce crisis is unambiguous: the workforce in many industries is aging, with a large cohort approaching retirement. In many sectors, worker and skills shortages are already occurring.

Two seminal policy papers, *Achieving Excellence* (Canada, Ministry of Industry, 2002), and *Knowledge Matters* (Canada, HRSDC, 2002), have grappled with the approaching crisis. Both advocate, as one solution with both social and economic dimensions, creative and flexible education and training programs to qualify populations now underrepresented in the workforce, including youth, aboriginal people, and immigrants.

Background to these policy papers is the study of *workplace essential skills* (ES), as perceived by employers and typically exhibited by employees. After wide discussion and debate (HRSDC, 2004a, 2004b), 10 essential employment skills clusters have been identified (Canada, HRSDC, 2005):

1. Document use
2. Writing
3. Oral communication
4. Problem solving
5. Decision making
6. Job task planning
7. Finding information
8. Computer use
9. Reading text
10. Numeracy

The interest of the federal government in ES identification efforts is intended both to help employers match job opportunities to suitable potential employees, and to simplify the job search process for clients of job-search and employment preparation programs. The latter objective is a priority because trainees often receive a stipend or unemployment benefits from the federal government to support them during job-search. Policies within HRSDC and among its clients have evolved regarding the role of technology in the training and search process, so that in recent discussion and planning the proposed use of e-learning strategies and technologies has been regarded favorably. The proviso in regard to technology is that potential users have adequate bandwidth, and that content, as much as is appropriate and economically feasible, be Canadian (Advisory Committee for Online Learning, 2001).

The ESPORT system is being evaluated by HRSDC to address especially the employment preparation needs of previously poorly served targeted populations in Canada. It is hoped that ESPORT, as it now exists or with modifications recommended by project evaluation data, can help large numbers of unemployed or marginally employed adults and young adults to re-explore their career options, using well designed applications of new technologies (Moore, 2004), including, especially because of its flexibility and adaptability (Kassop, 2003; Rovai & Barnum, 2003).

ESPORT

ESPORT (http://www.esportfolio.com/esport/) has been developed over the last several years as a tool for adolescents and adults with high school education or less. It is tied to the identified Canadian Essential Skills (noted previously and described further later), letting learners explore their interests in relation to a database of over 200 entry occupations (to increase as HRSDC adds more occupations to those already articulated).

ESPORT is interactive learning delivered via the Internet, and is thus a form of e-learning (Neal & Miller, 2005). Aldrich (2001) warns that terms risk losing their meaning if they stand for too many applications, or if too many terms are coined for a small number of applications. In this project, the term *online* learning was used more often than *e-learning,* but both referred to the same interactive and flexible qualities of the technology and the delivery system.

Internet-based delivery was chosen to maximize access, and minimize hardware, operating system, and general compatibility issues. Sitze (2001) argues that the term *e-learning* is actually synonymous with *online* learning, as both require computer resources to communicate with other users and to access support. Regardless of the terminology applied, the important aspects of ESPORT, shared with all e-learning technologies, are its flexible availability, its ability to address individual learner needs and preferences, and its capability to provide support-at-a-distance to users.

Support is provided in various forms. ESPORT users have online (e-mail and telephone) assistance in using the system's technologies. (Technical support is usually by e-mail response to inquiries, but real-time access via telephone is also available during business hours.) Clients of participating career counseling agencies also enjoy optional access to face-to-face human assistance, if they choose to request it. All users are served by ESPORT's knowledge management system that automatically keeps records and generates system-level and individual reports.

For the client, the focus of ESPORT is the development of an occupational *portfolio.* The portfolio comprises the results of an inventory of interests, a self-assessment of present skills related to profiles of various occupations the client is interested in, and, if the client is motivated sufficiently, a plan to enhance academic skills. The process of portfolio generation makes ESPORT a special form of e-learning, an *electronic performance support system* (EPSS): an "online job [aid] that guide users through a task as they're doing it" (Sitze, 2001, p. 6). Users of ESPORT generate the desired occupation-related portfolio, at the same time as they learn about the portfolio's contents and usefulness.

ESPORT portfolio development typically proceeds as follows:

1. **Interest inventory:** Users answer 50 questions about things they like to do and the ways they like to do work. At the conclusion, the program generates lists of occupations that match their interest patterns. This step may include prior interaction with a local counselor, if problems are anticipated or special needs are present; as an e-learning activity, clients access the inventory at their convenience, over the Internet. The decision to ask questions of or seek further guidance from a counselor is left to the user, but the technologies to facilitate the interaction as provided.
2. **Skills self-assessment:** In this step users assess their own academic and interpersonal skills, with the aid of job-related ESPORT materials. Any mismatches between the client's skills and the requirements of desired occupations are highlighted, and may later be addressed in counseling and/or in the client's learning plan.
3. **Occupational choice:** Based on capabilities, aptitudes, experience, and willingness to upgrade academic or skill deficiencies, the client chooses occupations to study further. HRSDC's detailed occupational profiles, and information detailing workplace conditions and realities, are available. The online nature of these resources assures they are current.
4. **Portfolio construction:** Using the profile of essential skills for occupations selected, users assess how their abilities or experience meet the requirements. The results become part of a résumé, highlighting present skills, experience, and career intentions, including any upgrading completed, in progress, or contemplated. ESPORT also generates a cover letter that the learner can modify and send with the résumé to a prospective employer.
5. **Learning plan:** If they wish, clients may work with a facilitator to develop a learning plan that addresses any deficient skill areas identified in their self-assessment. Available on-site learning resources include HRSDC's *Authentic Materials* (work-related documents around which facilitators can design learning activities), *Evaluating Academic Readiness for Apprenticeship Training* (EARAT) materials (worksheets employing workplace examples and scenarios), and PLATO™ online e-learning materials (http://www.plato.com/). The degree of instructor intervention in the learning plan is largely up to the client, consistent with basic e-learning principles.

Because self-assessment is part of the process, ESPORT demands that learners have the maturity and judgment to assess realistically their own career prospects. For assistance, learners have access, via ESPORT's communications technologies, to counseling and advice from local or remote sources. Additional skill, aptitude, and psychomotor testing may also be provided online, as needed.

Expected Project Outcomes

The ESPORT project planning framework anticipates a "(r)eplicable and scalable Internet deliverable model for employment-focused literacy programs in which participants, having selected goals based on interests and abilities, prepare for and obtain satisfactory employment." The framework calls for participatory evaluation, "allowing developers to rectify difficulties or inconsistencies in the software and management system," as well as to "document successful assessment and learning strategies" (CEP Consulting, 2004a).

Target Populations and Project Locations

The ESPORT pilot project sites that are the subject of this chapter are located in Cape Breton, in the northern portion of the eastern Canadian province of Nova Scotia, Vancouver, British Columbia, on Canada's west coast, and in Ottawa, Canada's capital. Each was chosen for different reasons.

"The Cape" is a physically beautiful but geographically remote region of Atlantic Canada, where unemployment rose with the closure of "smokestack" industries such as coal mining and steel making. Unemployment approached 30% in the 1990s, but by mid-2004 it had stabilized at about 16% (Hamm, 2004). In comparison, the Canadian unemployment rate at the same time was about 7% (Statistics Canada, 2005). Vancouver is the second largest Canadian city (after Toronto), with a metropolitan population of over 2 million. The need for employment services for aboriginals and youth in this city prompted its selection for the ESPORT project: according to the 2001 national census, 30% of aboriginal adults 25 years of age or older residing in Vancouver did not have a high school diploma, and the aboriginal adult unemployment rate in the city was 19.1% (Mendelson, 2004), while for all Canadians the rate was 6.8% (British Columbia, Ministry of Advanced Education, 2001; Statistics Canada, 2003). The Ottawa site, sponsored by the John Howard Society, serves the special employment-related needs of recently released inmates of federal and provincial penitentiaries (Masters, 1995).

Evaluation Planning

In order to achieve practical and useful evaluation products, the ESPORT project evaluation was designed to capture and disseminate results broadly. A four-stage *participatory action research* (PAR) model was employed, consisting of *reflection, planning, action,* and *observation* (Patton, 1975, 1982; Seymour-Rolls & Hughes, 1998). All participants were to engage in an ongoing process of identifying and thinking about problems or opportunities, developing and putting into operation plans of action, and then further observing and reflecting on the results, leading into another iteration of the cycle. Evaluation consultants managed the evaluation process by:

- Engaging participants (facilitators, managers, staff, learners, developers, and trainers) in the evaluation process.
- Helping participants to state their initial views, and their suggestions (*reflection*).
- Facilitating communications among project personnel.
- Producing notes and reports directed to people implementing the project.
- Monitoring progress toward addressing key questions and themes.

Various methods used to encourage interaction and reflection by project participants included:

- On-site (face-to-face) and online (telephone and e-mail) interaction.
- Surveys (questionnaires, opinionnaires).
- Direct on-site observations.
- Reports of analyses of records and documents.

This chapter is based upon the results of evaluation reports and observations.

Initial Findings

While the evaluation of the project was not complete as of this writing (late 2005), there are already findings on the effectiveness of some elements of project planning and implementation.

Initial facilitator training. The importance of initial training was reinforced by this project. Groups of facilitators (instructors) from the participating agencies received local ESPORT training, over three days. The workshops were designed to allow participants to learn about the project and the evaluation, practice using ESPORT's components, review the proposed evaluation process, and join in making future plans for the project (including the evaluation). Participants generated important questions they felt the project should strive to answer, including questions about participant training, preparation, and recruitment; the impact of the training processes and materials; the kind and quality of learner and facilitator interaction; program management and administration; interaction among program and project stakeholders; and technical performance and issues (including user support).

Revised facilitator training. After the first training sessions in Cape Breton and Vancouver, it was determined, through evaluation feedback and observations of trainee behavior, that facilitators were not acquiring or retaining the training adequately. The reason seemed to be that too much was being imparted, and not enough opportunity for practice was available. As a result, two modifications of the training were introduced in the John Howard Society training, in Ottawa, in November 2005. First, training on PLATO was not included, permitting focus on ESPORT, and reducing the cognitive load on the participants. Second, facilitators were encouraged to bring one of their clients with them to the training, so they could immediately apply their new ESPORT instructor skills. Clients took the training, too, and provided valuable feedback and input on the training process.

Readiness survey results. Shortly after the conclusion of training, when the facilitators had returned to their own centers, they received an online 15-item questionnaire, intended to determine their feelings of initial readiness for using ESPORT with learners. The results of the questionnaire for the Cape Breton and Vancouver sites are shown in Table 1.

On five of the items in Table 1, the two groups disagreed (at or near a liberal .10 level of significance, adopted, for this pilot project, to assure that salient findings would be detected).

Table 1. Trainee readiness (ranked from most to least agreement[1]) [Items in bold regarded as significant at the probability level shown]

Questionnaire item	Cape Breton		Vancouver		Total		t	p
	Mean	S.D.	Mean	S.D.	Mean	S.D.		
1. Explain ESPORT to clients.	6.2	1.94	4.5	2.33	5.2	2.30		
2. Show clients how to get started with ESPORT.	**6.3**	**1.97**	**5.6**	**3.99**	**5.9**	**3.12**	**3.185**	**.102**
3. Explain PLATO to clients.	6.5	2.26	5.4	3.62	5.9	3.06		
4. Show clients how to get started with PLATO.	**6.5**	**2.07**	**5.7**	**4.03**	**6.1**	**3.17**	**3.288**	**.097**
5. Explain the evaluation model (PAR) to clients.	6.8	1.94	4.6	3.11	5.6	2.82		
6. Participate in the evaluation process.	**6.7**	**2.07**	**6.1**	**4.2**	**6.4**	**3.34**	**3.038**	**.107**
7. Communicate using various technologies.	6.7	1.51	7.1	3.27	6.9	2.59		
8. Recognize outcomes or findings important to the evaluation.	8.3	1.75	8.6	1.41	8.5	1.51		
9. Contact the project administrator when necessary.	9.5	0.84	9.6	1.06	9.6	0.94		
10. Contact the PLATO trainer when necessary.	9.2	0.98	9.6	1.06	9.4	1.02		
11. Contact the project evaluators when necessary.	9.3	1.03	9.6	1.06	9.5	1.02		
12. Make time for everything the project requires me to do.	**6.0**	**1.27**	**6.8**	**2.82**	**6.4**	**2.24**	**8.528**	**.013**
13. Know where to go for assistance if needed.	9.5	0.84	9.4	0.92	9.4	0.85		
14. Have the right technology for the project.	**9.2**	**0.84**	**6.6**	**4.21**	**7.6**	**3.50**	**6.561**	**.026**
15. Be able to use the project's technologies.	7.5	1.76	8.1	1.77	7.9	1.73		

[1]*Scale: 0 = I am not at all ready; I am very uncomfortable with this; 10 = I am completely ready; I am perfectly comfortable with this*

The first training group, Cape Breton, was *more* confident about:

- Showing others how to use and get started with PLATO (items 2 and 4);
- Participating in the evaluation (item 6); and
- Having the right technology (item 14).

The Vancouver group, on the other hand, was more confident regarding only one item, making time for everything expected of them (item 12).

These results suggested that, for the most part, the training had affected the two groups about equally. Where differences were observed, they were regarded as subjects for further evaluation as the project proceeded.

Technology issues. Issues arose early over technology: almost from the beginning, facilitators experienced problems with some of the e-learning technologies used in the Cape. The project was recognized as technically innovative, for example integrating ESPORT and PLATO via a common access portal that allowed "PLATO and ESPORT [to] work together to ensure smooth transitions back and forth between the two systems" (CEP Consulting, 2004b, p. 9). While of real potential value, initially this portal was unreliable in Cape Breton, causing lost records and, consequently, learner (and facilitator) disappointment.

Another serious problem, detected first in the Cape, had to do with learner selection. Several learners directed to the program early in the project were high school graduates, and some even had post-secondary experience. ESPORT was designed for low literate, but motivated and supported, adults. Better educated learners sometimes found the limited selection of occupations demeaning: one learner commented bluntly that what he had largely been offered were "bottom-feeder jobs." While HRSDC is in the process of adding higher level occupations to the essential skills profiles, including apprenticeable trades, the present bank of Profiles (and hence, the occupations that can be pursued using ESPORT), is admittedly limited, and decidedly (and deliberately) entry-level. In recognition of this potential source of disappointment, ESPORT trainers emphasized that facilitators and program managers should screen their clients carefully on the basis of these limitations.

Community building. Communications were a central priority of the project from its start. Initially, interaction was encouraged and supported for specific reasons and groups, as follows:

- **Participants:** allowing client-learners to share experiences, ask questions, and get information or guidance on effective uses of the system.
- **Facilitators:** providing FAQs, training help, best practice tips, a means for interacting with other facilitators, a mailbox, and a communications link with the project management.
- **Evaluators:** a channel for evaluation information and feedback (questionnaires, surveys, personal communications), and for distributing reports and information.
- **HRSDC:** for monitoring the project, receiving reports, and having input.

- **Educators and the general public:** a link to information on the project.
- **For marketing in general:** providing the public with project information.

Community building continues in the form of a *community of practice* initiative, an attempt to link participants in discussions of experience and critiques of practice. The value of these interactions will be assessed in the project's final report.

Modifications to ESPORT's E-Learning Elements

Prompted by direct observation of results, the *Occasional Reports* (which attempted to highlight important outcomes in a timely manner), and by the stream of online interactions generated by the participants, various changes were made to elements of the project. The project's leaders attempted through these changes to assure that ESPORT advantages of flexibility, individualization, and responsiveness were preserved throughout the project (Kassop, 2003).

- The process for registering learners for occupation-focused PLATO courses was partially automated. The initial process required facilitator intervention, which added to workloads and could delay clients' access to PLATO elements in their learning plans (see previous). The technical solution still occasionally required some duplicate entry of information, but overall it required less time of facilitators, and gave clients more control over the learning plans.
- Evaluation results showed that HRSDC's *Online Authentic Materials* were not being used regularly with learners. These proven and familiar resources were intended to be accessed directly from the HRSDC Web site, but users found this cumbersome; as a result, links to these materials were put on the ESPORT site itself, making access easier and improving usage.
- The *Job Futures* link, permitting learners to investigate details of their occupational choices such as pay scales, employment rates, prospects for future employment, and formal qualifications, was also initially not well used. One explanation was that use of the link took clients away from the ESPORT site, making navigation too complicated for some users (who tended to become "lost in cyberspace," either confused, or distracted by the Web's many diversions). This link was also placed directly on the ESPORT site.
- Facilitator training was conducted by PLATO trainers, who were experienced with e-learning through PLATO. It was not the quality of the training but the volume of necessary information that had to be mastered that resulted in the decision to remove PLATO from initial facilitator training. ESPORT, as e-learning, and as a tool emphasizing personal exploration, presented significant new challenges for some facilitators. The training also forced all facilitators to grapple with implications for their practice

as occupational counselors. When ESPORT alone was on the training agenda, the focus on this tool was higher, and previously observed problems receded.

- Based on evaluation reports from Cape Breton and Vancouver, other significant changes were made in subsequent training: less abstract or theoretical information was provided, replaced by more actual hands-on ESPORT-related practice; facilitators were encouraged to think about application of ESPORT to authentic, familiar problems (those of their own clients); the evaluation model and immediate plans were described, but evaluation activities during training were minimized (they followed later, by e-mail and telephone).

Conclusion: ESPORT's Lessons to Date

Some major conclusions have been reached, and lessons learned, at this point in the ongoing ESPORT project, with potential value to planners of e-learning projects in Canada.

1. The importance of systematic, consultative evaluation of pilot projects has been reinforced. E-learning projects have often been accused of failing to deliver on the grandiose or extravagant promises they tend to make (Carnevale, 2004). As a result of awareness of this problem, the ESPORT project's participatory evaluation model was chosen to assure there was consensus on accomplishments claimed. While the evaluation is still ongoing, the commitment to this fundamental objective remains firm, as part of the concern of all the participants that this project contributes sound insights to the e-learning literature respecting under- and unemployed populations.
2. Some predictable (from the e-learning literature) problems were experienced in relation to the project's technologies. As noted previously, some of these issues were due to instabilities in the technologies themselves. Others, however, were related to human factors such as workload, and the complexity of the training tasks participants faced. Frankola (2001) warns that technology problems are among the most serious in any e-learning enterprise, and are among the most frequently cited reasons for participants to withdraw from technology projects. Decisions to focus and simplify training, described previously, were based on project findings, and this advice (Buckingham, 2003).
3. The adoption problems experienced by some participants were related to the impact of ESPORT as an *organizational innovation*. Welsch (2002) points out that e-learning particularly affects the financial, structural, and cultural aspects of organizations. ESPORT, as an impactful innovation, placed stresses on some aspects of organizational structures and culture, especially on staff (Molinari, 2004). Principles such as Rogers' (1983) regarding the adoption of innovations, apply in assessing the readiness for change in established institutions. Part of the evaluation included monitoring occurrences of resistance, and helping ESPORT's managers to direct project resources, including opportunities for interaction (Ferry, Hoban, & Lockyer, 1999), where they could have the most positive impact (Bates, 1995; Bates & Poole, 2003; Havelock, 1973).

4. Finally, the project, as it continues, is demonstrating the truth of Teles, Ashton, Roberts, and Tzoneva's (2001) contention that instructors/facilitators in any learning environment have four distinct roles, attention to which is especially important in "reduced-cues" e-learning environments (Walther, 1996): pedagogical, managerial, social, and technical (p. 49). In this project, the importance of facilitators adequately addressing both the *task* and the *interpersonal* aspects of their role has emerged (Keyton, 2003). Failure to address both is reflected in impaired interpersonal functioning and deterioration of the sense of community that, if present, can enrich e-learning (Rovai & Barnum 2003; Saltiel & Russo, 2001).

Although the project is still underway, it has already profited from its experiences. Important findings that have been acted upon include the observation that participants may tend to form overly optimistic impressions of a new tool; may fail to absorb the caveats and restrictions about technology's limits suggested by those with more experience; may not become sufficiently competent with the workings of the innovation during necessarily brief initial training; may underestimate, and consequently feel inadequate to, the demands on their time and energies entailed by the innovation; and may require advice, information, suggestions, encouragement, and leadership, especially in the early days of usage of an innovation such as ESPORT. These initial lessons, captured by the PAR evaluation, have helped the project evolve, and are regarded as evidence of the value of a focus on formative assessment in e-learning experiments of this nature. Future reports will describe how well these changes met the needs of the target population for finding entry-level employment.

References

Advisory Committee for Online Learning. (2001). *The e-learning e-volution in colleges and universities: A Pan-Canadian challenge.* Retrieved February 22, 2001, from http://www.cmec.ca

Aldrich, C. (2001). The state of simulations. *Online Learning, 8*(5), 52-59.

Bates, A. W. (1995). *Technology, open learning and distance education.* New York: Routledge.

Bates, A. W., & Poole, G. (2003). *Effective teaching with technology in higher education.* San Francisco: Jossey-Bass Publishers.

British Columbia, Ministry of Advanced Education. (2001). *Labour force statistics, Province of British Columbia.* Retrieved from http://www.aved.gov.bc.ca/labourmarketinfo/lf-survey/may01/may01.htm

Buckingham, S. (2003). Perspectives on the experience of the learning community through online discussions. *Journal of Distance Education, 18*(2), 74-91.

Canada. Ministry of Industry. (2002). *Achieving excellence: Investing in people, knowledge and opportunity.* Retrieved from http://innovation.gc.ca/gol/innovation/site.nsf/en/in04142.html

Canada. HRSDC. (2002). *Knowledge matters: Skills and learning for Canadians*. Retrieved from http://www11.sdc.gc.ca/sl-ca/doc/toc.shtml

Canada. HRSDC. (2004a). *Essential skills occupational profiles*. Retrieved from http://www15.hrdc-drhc.gc.ca/English/general/default.asp

Canada. HRSDC. (2004b). *National occupational classification 1992*. Retrieved from http://www23.hrdc-drhc.gc.ca/92/e/generic/welcome.shtml

Canada. HRSDC. (2005). *Essential skills*. Retrieved from http://www.hrsdc.gc.ca/en/hip/hrp/essential_skills/essential_skills_index.shtml

Carnevale, D. (2004). Report says educational technology has failed to deliver on its promises. *The Chronicle of Higher Education, 50*(43), A30.

CEP Consulting. (2004a). *Logical framework analysis*. Unpublished project document. Author.

CEP Consulting. (2004b). *Narrative*. Unpublished project document. Author.

Ferry, B., Hoban, G., & Lockyer, L. (1999). *The use of computer-mediated communication to support the formation of knowledge-building community in initial teacher education*. Retrieved March 29, 2003, from http://www.asclite.org.au/conferences/brisbane99/papers/ferryhoban.pdf

Frankola, K. (2001). Why online learners drop out. *Workforce*. Retrieved July 19, 2002, from http://www.workforce.com/archive/feature/22/26/22/index.php

Hamm, J. D. (2004). *Business breakfast in Baddeck*. Retrieved from http://www.gov.ns.ca/prem/speeches/Baddeck_Breakfast_2004JUL14.htm

Havelock, R. (1973). *The change agent's guide to innovation in education*. Englewood Cliffs, NJ: Educational Technology Pubs.

Kassop, M. (2003). Ten ways online education matches, or surpasses, face-to-face learning. *The Technology Source,* May-June. Retrieved from http://ts.mivu.org/default.asp?show=article&id=1059

Keyton, J. (2003). Observing group interaction. In R. Y. Hirokawa, R. S. Cathcart, L. A. Samovar, & L. D. Henman (Eds.), *Small group communication: Theory and practice* (8th ed.) (pp. 256-266). Los Angeles, CA: Roxbury Publishing Co.

Masters, J. (1995). *The history of action research*. Retrieved from http://www.scu.edu.au/schools/gcm/ar/arr/arow/rmasters.html

Mendelson, M. (2004). *Aboriginal people in Canada's labour market: Work and unemployment, today and tomorrow.* Caledon Institute of Social Policy. Retrieved from www.caledoninst.org/Publications/PDF/471ENG.pdf

Molinari, D. L. (2004). The role of social comments in problem-solving groups in an online class. *The American Journal of Distance Education, 18*(2), 89-101.

Moore, M. G. (2004). Constructivists: Don't blame the tools! *American Journal of Distance Education, 18*(2), 67-71.

Neal, L., & Miller, D. (2005). Distance education. In R. W. Proctor & K-P. L. Vu (Eds.), *Handbook of human factors in Web design* (pp. 454-470). Wahwah, NJ: Lawrence Erlbaum Associates.

Patton, M. Q. (1975). *Alternative evaluation research paradigm.* Grand Forks, ND: North Dakota Study Group on Evaluation.

Patton, M. Q. (1982). *Practical evaluation*. Beverly Hills, CA: Sage Publications.

Rogers, E. M. (1983). *Communication of innovations* (2nd ed.). New York: The Free Press.

Rovai, A. P. ,& Barnum, K. T. (2003). Online course effectiveness: An analysis of student interactions and perceptions of learning. *Journal of Distance Education, 18*(1), 57-73.

Saltiel, I. M., & Russo, C. S. (2001). *Cohort programming and learning*. Malabar, FL: Krieger Publishing Co.

Seymour-Rolls, K., & Hughes, I. (1998). *Participatory action research: Getting the job done.* Retrieved from http://www.scu.edu/au/schools/gcm/ar/arr/arow/rseymour.html

Sitze, A. (2001). A matter of semantics. *Online Learning, 5*(8), 6.

Statistics Canada. (2003). *Aboriginal population profile.* Retrieved from http://www12.statcan.ca/english/Profil01ab/Details/details1edu.cfm?SEARCH=BEGINS&PSGC=59&SGC=59933&A=&LANG=E&Province=All&PlaceName=Vancouver&CSDNAME=Vancouver&CMA=&SEARCH=BEGINS&DataType=1&TypeNameE=Census%20Metropolitan%20Area&ID=1251

Statistics Canada. (2005). *Latest release from the labour force survey.* Retrieved from http://www.statcan.ca/english/Subjects/Labour/LFS/lfs-en.htm

Teles, L., Ashton, S., Roberts, T., & Tzoneva, I. (2001). The role of the instructor in e-learning collaborative environments. *Technologika, 3*(3), 46-50.

Walther, J. B. (1996). Computer-mediated communication: Impersonal, interpersonal and hyperpersonal interaction. *Communication Research, 20*(1), 3-43.

Welsch, E. (2002). Cautious steps ahead. *Online Learning, 6*(1), 20-24.

Chapter XXII

EBS E-Learning and Social Integrity

Byung-Ro Lim, Kyung Hee University, South Korea

Abstract

In an effort to support public education, the Korean government utilized e-learning and established EBS e-learning system. Educational Broadcasting System (EBS) e-learning is developed especially for high school students who are preparing for the Korean college entrance examination (KSAT). This case study is to introduce EBS e-learning and analyze its merits and weaknesses in order to investigate some meaningful implications for future use of a similar learning system. First, this case study analyzes characteristics of EBS e-learning; secondly, this study identifies its outcomes and issues. Lastly, some implications are presented for further development and more effective use of e-learning system. The outcomes of the case study showed that EBS e-learning system has brought (1) cost reduction on private education on a short-term basis, (2) positive effect on social integrity, and (3) a possibility of supporting public education. Some issues identified in this case study are in the following areas: (1) contents, (2) school use, (3) learning management and op-

eration strategies, (4) faculty members, and (5) user interface. Lastly, some implications and suggestions are made to ensure the provision of quality programs in the future: (1) it is necessary to reinforce interactive ways of learning; (2) customized education and level-specific learning programs should be developed and provided; (3) it should utilize effective learning management systems; and (4) it needs to provide qualified, specialized learning contents to the learners.

Introduction

Today, we witness rapid growth of knowledge production and distribution more than any other age in human history. Also, knowledge does not belong to particular groups or dominant classes anymore, and it has become public goods to share with grassroots. In the past, social oppressions have been operated by exclusive accessibility to knowledge and information. Currently, however, the general public is able to access knowledge at their convenience and can change the quality of their lives through utilizing this accessible information and knowledge. Moreover, both accessibility and utility of knowledge and information allow even people who have limited educational opportunity to receive quality education.

However, it is obvious that there is a need to bring new communication tools in order to achieve meaningful educational experiences. People can exchange information and knowledge beyond the limit of time and space using the Internet, collaborate with other people for study at any time and any place, and take e-learning courses, which are developed in other countries for their individual achievement. E-learning, a revolutionary method of learning in this global age using the Internet, seems to have a special value in realizing meaningful learning and achieve equal educational opportunities to everyone regardless of their ethnic, local differences, and income gap. It is clear that people can be no longer competitive if they depend only upon off-line, formal education from the traditional educational institutions because of the extensive growth of information and knowledge. In order to learn newly produced knowledge along with creating new knowledge, learners need to take life-long learning and self-directed learning. E-learning can be considered as one of the best alternatives. E-learning enables people not only to get beyond the limitation of time and space, to have a good education anytime and anyplace, but also to build learning communities with other people including peers, teachers, and professionals. Building learning communities through e-learning is a realistic alternative for people to learn in authentic learning environments.

By far, e-learning has been developed in various arenas. But, the benefits of e-learning were mainly enjoyed by a few who belong to urban, middle class until now. So it is necessary to make e-learning affordable and accessible to anyone who wants to learn. In this purpose, the Korean government made a grand project in 2004 and initiated the EBS e-learning program especially for high school students who are preparing KSAT (i.e., college entrance examination in Korea). The predecessor of the Educational Broadcasting System (EBS), the Broadcasting Department of the Korean Educational Development Institute (KEDI), produced and broadcast radio programs for the Air and Correspondence High School in 1974. EBS was established as an affiliate of the KEDI with two channels (EBS TV and EBS FM) in 1990. It was separated from KEDI in 1997 and started e-learning services from the year

2004. EBS, headquartered in Seoul, Korea, is the only broadcasting corporation dedicated to public education in Korea. EBS has grown into a major broadcaster for entertaining and educational programs. Accordingly, this case study is to introduce the EBS e-learning and analyze its merits and weaknesses in order to gain some educational insights from them, especially in terms of social integrity.

EBS E-Learning Program

Background

The Korean government has energetically carried out a policy of utilizing information technology in public education since 1996, which results in connecting every school across the nation with the high-speed network, EDUNET, which provides educational portal service in national scale. Another development is EBS e-learning. From the year 2000, not only ISST (ICT Skill Standard for Teachers), and ISSS (ICT Skill Standard for Students), but also contents such as teaching guides and multimedia materials were developed and disseminated widely. In the year 2004, the EBS e-learning program and National Center for Teaching and Learning opened. Figure 1 shows e-learning history in public education from 1966 to 2004.

Traditionally, Koreans have considered the college diploma as a symbol of high status and a way of being successful in society. Therefore, high stake tests such as KSAT, which is held once a year, are highly valued and getting a good score in the test ensures a successful future to some degree. Many Korean students are willing to do their best when they come to high school.

Figure 1. History of e-learning in Korea

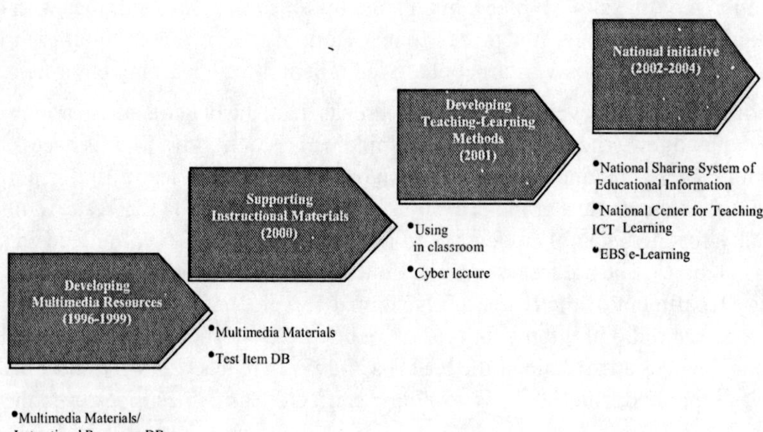

Thus, the Ministry of Education and Human Resources (MEHR) initiated EBS e-learning service to help high school students to study KSAT preparation courses in more convenient and cheaper ways. It is one of the important projects, which were planned to support public education and maintain normal schooling practices. In 2004, MEHR announced a plan to reduce cost in the private educational sector in order to normalize public education and established learner-support educational systems through e-learning. EBS was delegated to perform this plan, and it began to provide e-learning service from April 1, 2004. The purposes of EBS e-learning are as follows:

- To help students' KSAT preparation study
- To establish learner-support programs
- To support public education
- To normalize public schooling
- To reduce the cost of extra-curriculum study
- To solve the problem of social inequality

At first, EBS e-learning was considered to be a short-term measure to reduce costs in the private educational sector, which caused economic crisis and intensified social conflicts between the rich and the poor. Table 1 shows the overall cost reduction plan by MEHR.

Table 1. Plan for cost reduction in private educational sector to normalize public education

1. Short-term plan: Public education taking over private tutoring demand
    - Substituting for extracurricular studies: Establishing e-Learning systems
    - Absorbing formal, curricular studies: Level-specific supplementary learning program
    - Giving satisfaction to the gifted learning or English study programs: Using extracurricular program
    - Nursery programs: Running after-school programs to 1~3 grade students
2. Mid-term project: Substantiating public schooling
    - Rethinking reliability on public education: Hiring highly qualified faculties
    - Recovering functions of public education: Improving teaching and assessment methods
    - Supplementing educational standard for high school students: Level-specific education and expanding learner's choices
    - Normalizing public education: Improving college entrance examination and enhancing instruction for student's life goal
    - Guaranteeing the grounding knowledge of citizens: Enhancing responsibility- taking for basic knowledge-level education
3. Long-term project: Improving socio-cultural climate
    - Reforming projects for social systems and consciousness

** Source: Ministry of Education and Human Resources (2004). Plan for Cost Reduction in Private Educational Sector to Normalize Public Education.*

EBS E-Learning Menus and Programs

EBS e-learning focuses on the e-learning courses and programs for KSAT. The EBS e-learning system consists of online lectures (VOD), bulletin boards (announcement board, Q&A, FAQs, free board), diagnosis test service and personalized area ("my page"). The lectures cover almost every area of KSAT (refer to Table 2). EBS e-learning is unrivaled in the range of school courses it covers with regards to the college entrance exam. It offers a wide selection of subjects to accommodate the various needs of students, including non-regular courses for those interested in vocational colleges. In addition, EBS courses are available in three levels: beginning, intermediate, and advanced for more demanding students.

Other special lectures are also provided: Theme-based lecture, today's new lecture, this month's new lecture, special lecture, and EBSi special. In addition to the lectures, EBS e-learning provides subscribers with various menus such as news, Q&A, KSAT information, and "my page" to facilitate interaction with its users (Table 3).

EBS e-learning ensures all course materials are put together by the best, qualified writers and authors available, and takes an active part in the production process, from planning to editing. However, EBS e-learning contents are developed in VOD method, that is, the media specialist shoots the lectures and uploads them on the Internet. The instructional design is more teacher-centered and lecture-based. As shown in Figure 2, the VOD window has two parts: VOD viewer window (left half of the window) and index of the VOD (right half of the figure). It has speed control system, which enables users to control the VOD speed at their convenience, and electronic note with which users can take a note during the lecture.

Table 2. EBS e-learning lecture list

Lecture list
Korean, English, Mathematics, Social Studies, Science, Occupation education Linguistic domain, Foreign language domain, Mathematical domain Social Studies domain, Science domain, Occupation education domain, Oral interview/ Analytical writing, Entrance exam special, Listening

Table 3. Functional menus of EBS e-learning

	Content
My Page	Pre-chosen lecture, My lecture, My Q&A, My information management Personal schedule management, Personal note, My friend, My bookmark
Entrance	EBS news, Entrance examination/College-oriented info examination
Info	GPA calculation/a trial application
My teacher	EBS e-Learning teacher, Q&A teacher, Learning guide, Consulting with teacher, FAQ
EBS Empathy	New info, Thank you EBS, Excellent EBSi, Revisiting lecture, Let's get together, Let's share with, Let's recommend, Photo gallery, E-column

Figure 2. Interface of the VOD window

Characteristics of EBS E-Learning

EBS e-learning system has the following characteristics:

1. It maximizes benefits of e-learning.
    - It frees learners from constraints of time and location.
    - It utilizes a wide variety of EBS educational contents.
    - It offers two-way communication.
    - It has group discussion sessions.
2. It customizes students' learning.
    - It allows students to select video-on-demand and audio-on-demand services when they choose EBS educational contents.
    - Students can plan their own study schedule according to EBS broadcast programs.
    - Students can create their own homepage containing their history of taking EBS courses.
    - It enables learners to choose lectures suitable to their own levels.
    - It provides a caption service and Internet sites for the deaf/blind students.
3. It has other beneficial services.
    - Students can download lecture video clips around the clock, thanks to a server powerful enough to handle up to 100,000 simultaneous connections.
    - It hires cyber tutors who consult learners.
    - It provides reserved download services for online lectures.
    - It provides updated new lectures every day.

Efforts on Social Integrity

EBS provides support for students from local areas and low-income families as follows:

- Every cable TV company should provide EBS Plus.1 channel (broadcasting service of EBS e-learning).
- About 10,000 high school students from local areas were provided with a satellite broadcasting receiver, and some of them were paid for the Internet service.
- Four thousand and five hundred students who could not afford the Internet cost were provided with a satellite-broadcasting receiver and were paid for the Internet service.
- Students from low-income families (about 28,000 persons) got the textbooks for EBS e-learning for free.
- Seventy thousand students from low-income families were provided with personal computers and were paid for the Internet services.

EBS also provides support for the handicapped as follows:

- The EBS e-learning site was developed for the blind to use a screen reader so that they can read the contents.
- Textbooks for EBS e-learning were provided to the National Special Education Bureau, which in turn lets schools for the handicapped use.
- Textbooks in Braille were published for the blind.
- VOD services for about 500 lectures to the people who have hearing difficulties.

Academic and Administrative Issues

Content Related Issue

Currently, the main type of content is test-oriented VOD lectures. Just as profit-making private institutions put an emphasis on teaching for test and test-oriented learning, EBS e-learning programs focus on teaching learners how to get good test scores.

Secondly, it has a large number of faculty members from profit-making private institutions. Some instructors seem to use their popularity to advertise their own private academy. In this situation, it is hard to expect sound contents in an educational sense.

Lastly, the lecture-oriented teaching method is another issue. Since the main type of content is VOD, it is hard to use various instructional methods such as debate, small group activities, problem-based learning, and so on. The content quality is just dependent on the instructor's personal teaching ability. Relying too much on the individual competency may cause a problem in content quality, especially when the instructor is not willing to continue his/her teaching any more.

Issues Regarding School Use

The primary goal of EBS e-learning is to provide high quality of teaching and learning materials and to normalize the public education. Accordingly, it is important to effectively use these materials within the public school system. Reviews on school use of EBS e-learning programs do not guarantee that the primary goal of EBS e-learning has been achieved (KERIS, 2005). Kim (2004) worried that EBS e-learning would weaken the functions of the public education because of its extensive use in the regular class and self-study time. Current EBS e-learning experiments may have a negative effect on the public education since EBS e-learning makes teachers and students concentrate more on the EBS programs and college entrance examination instead of normal schooling.

Learning Management and Operation Strategies Issues

For the learning management strategies, there are several issues to consider:

- Lectures only depend upon teacher's individual teaching ability.
- LMS is not fully supportive, so there is insufficient learning support for the learner.
- Contents are generally unsatisfactory since they are not based on robust instructional design.
- There are insufficient learning assessment tools to evaluate learner's achievement level.

Issue on Recruiting Faculty Member

Current status of faculty members consists of middle and high school teachers (about 70%) and profit-making private institution teachers (about 30%). Moreover, the ratio of private institution teachers in faculty members is much higher than that of public school teachers in the beginner and advanced levels. From this statistics, market concerns and commercialism are likely to affect the program. This fact may cause some problems in improving the quality of EBS e-learning.

User-Interface Related Issue

User interface is not bad, but too much information on the main page can interrupt learners' choice. Also, there is a lack of clear understanding in menu structure and expression in the main page.

Program Evaluation

Statistics

The number of users and members of EBS e-learning service has rapidly increased since its providing KSAT courses on the Internet in April 2004. Access numbers tended to decrease after the KSAT in November 2004. In January 2005, an average number of signing up members per day was 3,925 and an average number of visitors per day was 1,010,168. For the membership number, total number of visitors from the beginning, average number of VOD access per day, number of download per day, and number of contents, refer to Table 4.

Figure 3 shows the changes of average number of VOD access per day during August 2004 through January 2005.

Effects of Cost Reduction on Profit-Making Private Institutions

Even though there are some differences in the amount of reduced money after taking EBS e-learning courses, researchers agreed with the cost reduction effects of EBS e-learning:

- According to the survey by "Research & Research Institute" (May 17, 2004), there happened extensive cost reduction from 237,000 won (about $230) to 194,700 won (about $190) per month after EBS e-learning programs was operated, only saved $40.
- According to the survey by "MB Zone & CNC" (November 15, 2004), research participants said that they saved 153,000 won (about $150) per month after taking EBS e-learning courses.

Table 4. Statistics of membership, access number, and number of download and contents (January 23, 2005)

N	. of membership	Total N. of visit:rs	Average N. of VOD access per day	N. of download per day	N. of contents
Number I	,433,330	127,435,643	91467 2	3,050	5,526

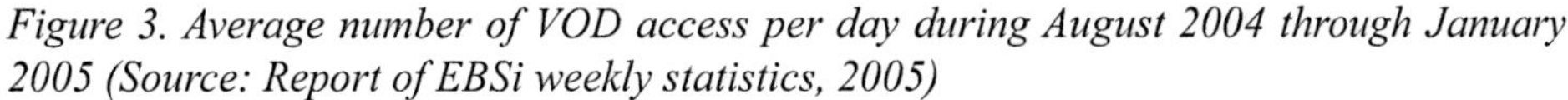

Figure 3. Average number of VOD access per day during August 2004 through January 2005 (Source: Report of EBSi weekly statistics, 2005)

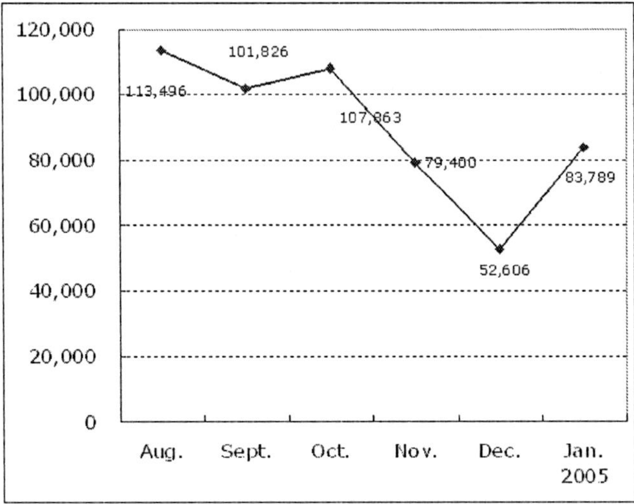

- Research by EBS (2005) show that after taking EBS e-learning programs, an average cost for private education reduced from 346,000 won ($340) to 326,000 won (about $320) per month/household, only saved 20,000 won (about $20).

Effect on the Social Integrity in Terms of Solving Inequity of Local and Class Differences

EBS e-learning seems to contribute to solving educational inequity from local and class differences. Two halves of all senior high school students used EBS e-learning or at least accessed the program. On average, students from middle class and local areas took much more EBS e-learning than others (EBS, 2005).

- Almost 80% of high school teachers and 63% of parents believed that EBS e-learning programs contributed to reduce regional differences in education.
- Seventy-seven percent of students in small and medium cities took EBS e-learning programs, while 70% of students in large cities did.
- In terms of parents' income, 32% of students who came from high-income families took private tutoring and used private institutions after school. But only 23% of students whose parents were middle class and 16% of students whose parents were low

class took private tutoring and private institutions. But, more students from the low class (24.5%) and the middle class (16.8%) than others from the upper class (11.8%) took EBS e-learning courses instead of private tutoring.

Possibility of Supporting Public Education

It seems that social and collective inquiries are not encouraged in the EBS e-learning system. The main type of learning is isolated learning, that is, listening to the lectures, memorizing, practicing, solving problems in his/her own house without any collaboration with others. When teachers introduce EBS e-learning in their classroom, students usually learn on their own, and there is little discussion, collaboration, and collective inquiry. This means that EBS e-learning is not appropriate when the learning objective is to develop higher-order thinking skills. Also, students and teachers can enjoy meaningful learning experiences when interactive methods are used appropriately. However, EBS e-learning is limited in facilitating interaction among students. It has limitation to provide students with community of learners. Currently, EBS e-learning has some limitations in realizing the ideal of public education.

Implications and Conclusion

Based on the analysis of the benefits and weaknesses of EBS e-learning systems, some implications are made to improve EBS e-learning (Lim, 2005). They include:

- It is necessary to reinforce interactive ways of learning.
- Customized education and level-specific learning should be taken place.
- It should utilize effective learning management systems.
- It needs to provide qualified, specialized learning contents to the learners.

It is necessary to reinforce interactive ways of learning.

EBS e-learning has provided one-way VOD services, which largely depend on teacher's individual teaching ability. It does not actively use interactive strategies between learners, learners and content knowledge, learners and teachers, but rather it focuses on providing learners with content knowledge in a teacher-controlled environment. Also, it does not facilitate learners to learn in interactive ways even though it tries to provide prompt feedback to the students who have questions to ask during their studies. It is necessary to develop contents in consideration of diverse interactions and to overcome teacher-directed instruction.

Customized education and level-specific learning should be taken place.

Currently, EBS e-learning provides contents on three difficulty levels: beginner, intermediate, and advanced. But it is difficult for students to perceive their learning levels in order to select appropriate contents. The reason is that EBS e-learning does not provide users with any diagnostic testing and evaluation tool. EBS e-learning needs to develop a diagnostic testing to help learners acknowledge their own level. It is also necessary to develop level-specific learning materials fitted into students' needs.

It should utilize effective learning management system (LMS).

Major e-learning institutions usually have an effective LMS so that they can provide learners with excellent services. Effective LMS should be developed so as to manage a personal learning history and help individual learners to study on their own learning patterns and learning styles, and with their own learning strategies.

It needs to provide qualified, specialized learning contents to the learners.

EBS e-learning needs to provide qualified, specialized learning contents to the learners. Specialized content, design, and method will ensure quality learning. Since the main type of content of EBS e-learning is VOD, the instructor, lecture method, and lecture organization are very important. Based on the needs analysis, it should select specialized contents, provide the best instructor, let him/her choose the appropriate method, and organize the contents in more favorable ways. Also, in order to provide quality learning, it is necessary not only to provide VOD type lectures, but also to organize lectures with various multimedia technologies.

In conclusion, EBS e-learning should go beyond simple test-oriented lectures. If it is used well enough, it has a potential to revolutionize the current educational system. In order to do that, EBS e-learning has to give up the traditional, teacher-centered paradigm of education and accept a new learner-centered paradigm. If EBS e-learning is continuously test-oriented and maintains the "teaching for test" strategy, normalization of the public education will not be realized. In order to design and develop EBS e-learning better, macro-level and long-term perspective is needed along with paradigm shifts.

Lessons Learned

1. One of the successful factors to e-learning is consistent, steady efforts by the government. Especially in the early stage, when e-learning vendors are premature and the market is not active, governmental investment can provide a momentum for e-learning development and control the direction of e-learning. Korean government initiated e-learning on a national scale already in the late 1990s. Even though the governmental efforts result in e-learning development to some degree, it does not seem to facilitate competition among vendors for the creative instructional design (remember that the content type is mainly "lecture video"). Now it is time to recognize the limitation of government's effort and to find out a way of quality assurance and creative design.

2. E-learning is not just a new type of teaching method, but also a tool for satisfying social needs. People want quality education in cheaper and more convenient way. However, in Korea too much money is wasted for extracurricular activities and private lessons, which makes Korean economy weaker and unsound. Through providing cheaper and good education programs, EBS e-learning can satisfy social needs and change the direction of money or investment to the more productive industry.
3. E-learning can contribute to social integrity. EBS e-learning experience shows that e-learning can be an effective social mechanism to lessen the differences among classes and localities. It lessens inequity between the rich and the poor and reduces the gap between the rural and the urban in terms of equal access to educational opportunities. For example, poor students who cannot afford private lessons can take KSAT courses offered by EBS e-learning instead. This is important in the Korean situation where the more educated can have a better chance to earn the money and get the power.
4. E-learning needs to be practiced with educational purposes. When we consider introducing e-learning, we need to ask what education is for. E-learning is one type of educational activity, so its purpose and methods should comply with educational purposes. Education is not simply "teaching for test," but is inspiration and should cultivate human mind. In this sense, educators criticize EBS e-learning because its main purpose is to make learners ready for the test, and its methods consist of lectures and explanation of test items. So, EBS e-learning is limited and targets only specific users who want to prepare the KSAT test. If it continues to do current practices and is not based on the sound educational principles, it can disappear after short-term, temporary glory.
5. E-learning is only a supplementary tool for normal class, and it should strengthen teachers' status in his/her classroom. In the current K-12 school system, it is difficult for teachers to get used to use technology. Many technologies have failed in the last 50 years. The main reason for the failure is mainly because of teachers' unconcern or unwillingness. If e-learning is to be used widely in schools, it should get teachers involved in the decision-making process and let them acknowledge its convenience and merits. If it is used in a way of alienating teachers, however, it will weaken public education and normal schooling in the end. Current EBS e-learning programs are good resources to teachers. The programs should not replace teachers, but supplement classroom activities.
6. E-learning can cover diverse topics and subjects beyond formal curriculum so that learners select appropriate ones and widen their knowledge. EBS e-learning has many beneficial programs that can draw students' attention. E-learning should provide students with interesting programs so that students attend (watch) the lectures when they want and where they feel comfortable.
7. E-learning can provide a different point of view or colorful explanations on a certain subject, and facilitate multiple perspectives. E-learning materials are based on multimedia, and it can represent information in many different ways. For example, historical simulation can show the dynamic situation of the historical event, which is not possible in oral or written expression. Representation of information in many different forms helps students learn the subject in a more authentic and deeper way.

8. Facilitating interactive ways of learning using Q&A, prompt feedback, and discussion ensures success of e-learning. EBS e-learning provides many ways to communicate between tutors and learners and among learners. For example, when students are puzzled, they post a question in the Q&A bulletin board. EBS tutors are supposed to answer the question within 12 hours.
9. The community of learner approach makes e-learning more dynamic and interesting. EBS e-learning uses several techniques to facilitate sense of community. For example, it provides bulletin boards such as "Buzz session', 'Postscript," "Impression after class," and "Recommending best teacher." Students use these bulletin boards to express their feelings, share stories they experienced during their study, exchange their own know-how about how to study, and express their gratitude for their tutors.
10. E-learning success depends on not only quality content, but also management for individualized learning. In the EBS e-learning system, a same content has three levels—beginning, intermediate, and advanced—and the system allows learners to choose one of them based on their competencies.

Best Practices

1. In the early stage, a consistent and comprehensive effort by the government is a very important factor to the development of e-learning.
2. E-learning is not just a method of teaching and learning, but also a way to strengthen social integrity through access to quality contents regardless of social status and regional differences.
3. Effectiveness of e-learning depends on orchestrating many factors such as level-specific contents, tutoring, community of learners, management, as well as technical infrastructure (efficient LMS, server stability, etc.).

References

EBS. (2005). *A study on strategies for activation of EBS KSAT preparation courses*. Report 2005-1.

Ministry of Education and Human Resources. (2004). *A study on mid- and long-term development strategies of EBS KSAT preparation courses project for growth of e-learning*. Report on policy study 2004 dedicated.

KERIS. (2005). *Report of Local Educational Bureau on EBS e-learning*. Unpublished report.

Kim, H. B. (2004). Educational value of EBS e-learning and analysis of its effectiveness. In *Proceedings of KAEMS Conference* (2004.12.4).

Lim, B. R. (2005). EBS e-learning: Current status, issues, and improvement strategies. In *Proceedings of KAEMS Conference* (2005.9.10)

Chapter XXIII

Case Studies on Learners and Instructors in an E-Learning Ecosystem

Vive Kumar, Simon Fraser University, Canada

Chris Groeneboer, Simon Fraser University, Canada

Stephanie Chu, Simon Fraser University, Canada

Dianne Jamieson-Noel, Simon Fraser University, Canada

Cindy Xin, Simon Fraser University, Canada

Abstract

E-learning aims to enrich learning by blending traditional and innovative learning models; conceptualizing courseware in multiple media; standardizing interoperable content representation; personalizing learning experiences to custom learning devices; integrating administrative functionalities with other academic units; and not the least, ensuring the quality of learning. Such a multifaceted ideology is construed as a learning ecosystem where knowledge is constructed, analyzed, and disseminated among members of the ecosystem. A learning ecosystem is characterized by the interactions and the flow of information across activities related to learning. Such an e-learning ecosystem would naturally include populations of learners, researchers, instructors, administrators, and technologists, among others, playing a variety of roles in an institutional setup. In this chapter, we present a number of case studies and their interrelations within an e-learning ecosystem in higher education. The case studies are presented under two subsystems: learner subsystem and instructor subsystem.

E-Learning Ecosystem

E-learning aims to enrich learning by blending traditional and innovative learning models; conceptualizing courseware in multiple media; standardizing interoperable content representation; personalizing learning experiences to custom learning devices; integrating administrative functionalities with other academic units; and not the least, ensuring the quality of learning. Such a multifaceted ideology is construed as a learning ecosystem where knowledge is constructed, analyzed, and disseminated among members of the ecosystem.

In biology, ecosystems are characterized by the interactions and the flow of matter and energy among biotic and abiotic elements. An e-learning environment can also be treated as an ecosystem characterized by the interactions and the flow of information across activities related to learning. Such an e-learning ecosystem would naturally include populations of learners, researchers, instructors, administrators, and technologists, among others, playing a variety of roles in an institutional setup. Learning resources, comparable to the abiotic elements, such as learning management system, online discussion forum, simulation software, and learner registration system play key roles in the e-learning ecosystem.

Similar to the food chains in bio-ecosystems, e-learning ecosystems enable a web of interconnecting workflow-chains. However, unlike bio-ecosystems where the flow of energy consumption is always in a single direction, the flow of information consumption in an e-learning ecosystem can potentially be multidirectional. Given the operational constraints of institutions, it is conceivable that such a multidirectional flow is necessary and advantageous. In both ecosystems, an all-encompassing reality emerges—the fittest survive. In bio-ecosystems, fitness is measured in terms of longevity and adaptability. In e-learning ecosystems, fitness is measured in terms of subject matter understanding, application of learned concepts in new situations, and ability to transfer learned knowledge, among other traits. Conceptualizing e-learning as an ecosystem enables one to explicitly identify well-defined e-learning components, to guide the flow of information across e-learning components, to measure the effectiveness of e-learning in terms of learning and teaching, and most importantly, to engage in research that assists various populations to regulate the fitness measures.

In this chapter, we present a number of case studies and their interrelations within an e-learning ecosystem in higher education. The case studies are presented under two subsystems: learner subsystem and instructor subsystem. Within each subsystem we identify topics of interest and rationalize them with cases.

Learner Subsystem

In this section we explore a key approach for supporting learners in their academic pursuits in studying.

E-Learning Support for Studying: The Learning Kit Project and gStudy

Self-regulation refers to how students are able to define tasks, set goals for learning, articulate plans to reach task goals, enact tactics and strategies to direct learning, and adapt learning approaches based on monitoring and evaluating learning processes and outcomes (Winne & Hadwin, 1998; Zimmerman, 1986). When students are given a task, information they gather while working on a task provides an opportunity for feedback both about products that are generated through studying (notes or highlights) or task products resulting from studying (i.e., an essay or response to an exam question). Feedback either internally generated by students as they study or provided externally by teachers or peers provides important information that guides students in terms of how they can direct and redirect the learning process (Butler & Winne, 1995). Although all students self-regulate, they do so to varying degrees and are not always productive or effective in how they self-regulate their learning (Jamieson-Noel, 2004). Previous research also suggests that students often have an impoverished or inaccurate knowledge base about tactics and strategies as well as entrenched beliefs about what learning is and how it occurs (Hofer, Yu, & Pintrich, 1998). Given these potential problems with students' knowledge about how to study effectively, educational researchers are interested in investigating the processes and outcomes of how students learn, with a specific emphasis on how to design instructional models or methods to help students develop more effective forms of self-regulation that may result in improved learning outcomes (Winne, 1997).

Typically research in self-regulated learning uses self-report measures where students are asked to complete a questionnaire about their methods used to study content. Current methodological chapters on self-regulation pinpoint limitations to the amount and type of information that self-report measures provide. Self-report instruments require that students reconstruct from memory how often they used various tactics and strategies for studying (Winne, Jamieson-Noel, & Muis, 2001; Winne & Perry, 1999). We know based on previous research that students' reconstructions of how often they study often lead to biased and inaccurate estimates of tactic use compared to actual studying behaviors (Winne & Jamieson-Noel, 2002). The advantage of an e-learning environment is that it can allow researchers to trace specific activities that students use to examine content. For example, we can tell how often students used various tools available within the interface. This type of data can provide additional insight into how students self-regulate their learning.

The Learning Kit project is designed to support students in their use of self-regulated learning strategies. *gStudy* (Winne, Nesbit, Kumar, Hadwin, Lajoie, Azevedo, & Perry, 2005) is a cross-platform software tool for researching learning. Researchers or instructors can assemble content (styled and hyperlinked text, graphics, and video) into kits displayed in a Web browser. Researchers can manipulate the structure and behavior of the kit's elements to operationalize experimental variables corresponding to research hypotheses. By manipulating a kit's structure we can ask specific research questions about how we can design instructional materials to determine how students examine and utilize this information to build new knowledge structures.

With *gStudy*, students can examine and annotate their individual kit's content using a number of embedded tools. These tools are designed to provide guidelines to help students determine what they can do to annotate content. For example, gStudy incorporates several different types of notes templates based on a choice of schemas (e.g., summary, question and answer, to do, debate, etc.). Each note template has different fields embedded that guide students in terms of how they can process information. For example, in a summary note the fields include providing a label for the note, filling in key ideas, and providing main ideas for the notes. A question note provides two fields: one for asking a question and one for building an answer to a question. As a final example, a debate note provides an opportunity for the students to identify the various positions presented in the text and then provide evidence to support the position. Each note template provides opportunities for the students to manipulate and transform information into their own personal understandings if they choose to use these tools to annotate the content.

Second, *gStudy* offers a highlighting tool, which allows students to select and then classify information according to various properties (e.g., important, review this, do not understand, etc.). Students highlight or underline information for any number of different purposes; for example, it could be used simply to maintain attention while reading. However, highlighting can also be used to discriminate relevant information from irrelevant information, thus reducing the overall amount of information that needs to be covered during review. This type of activity reflects a more active and generative way to examine content because it invites students to make decisions about why they need to highlight information in the text, thereby affording opportunities for students to process the content more deeply.

A third feature provides a method for students to examine the terminology embedded within the content. Students can construct new glossary entries including a variety of information within different fields similar to the note-taking template. The fields include identifying a title for the concept and providing a definition, description, and example(s). Each of these fields provides opportunities for students to elaborate on and extend their knowledge of the content.

When students examine content, there are often explicit or implicit links that can be built between conceptual ideas presented in the text. *gStudy*'s linking tool allows students to assemble information within and across elements of the content (i.e., selections in a "chapter," amongst notes, glossary items, etc.). To build connections across glossary entries, students can make links by selecting information and building connections between the two sources within the content.

The interface also offers a multi-faceted search tool, which allows students to query specific search terms to examine all of the information associated with the content. For example, to determine how often a term occurs within the body of the chapter, the student could enter the term as a search query and then set parameters on where to look within the kit. The search tool will then provide a table outlining every instance of the term within the kit, including how frequently the term occurs within the content itself, within references to notes, within glossary entries and links, and so on. The students can then select from where they would like to examine the term in relation to that content and continue to study the content.

Currently most of the tools embedded into *gStudy* focus on tactics and strategies for elaborating on content. However, we want to expand the interface by developing tools to focus on all aspects of self-regulation including defining the task, setting goals, and articulating plans. Currently we have plans to develop a task tool that will ask students to define what they think the task is about (if a task has been pre-assigned) or that will allow students to define a task for the studying episode. The task tool will provide an opportunity for students to articulate questions and outline resources required for the task. We are also considering a goal-setting tool such as a to-do list where students have an opportunity to specify what they want to achieve in learning. As well we want students to specify subtasks with a proposed due date to schedule what they want to do with the content. gStudy also includes a tool (LogReader) for analyzing gStudy log data (Hadwin, Winne, Nesbit, & Murphy, 2005).

Instructor Subsystem

Integral to the e-learning ecosystem is the instructor subsystem. Instructors or subject matter experts require a shared vision or understanding about e-learning and how it is approached within the ecosystem. To establish this and sound instructional practices, instructors benefit from professional and instructional development during initial course development and delivery and subsequent iterations. This section examines the cycle of faculty development, reflection, and refinement, and the necessary support and integration with day-to-day practices for longer-termed sustainability and evolution.

Faculty Development

Faculty development is critical for an e-learning, or any learning, ecosystem. An apparent reason for investing in faculty development is that courses are developed and taught by faculty members. Students' e-learning or learning experience in general is contingent upon the effort faculty put into developing and evolving their courses. Second, investing in faculty development establishes a basic shared understanding and foundation among faculty members. Initial faculty development can focus on the institution's overall teaching and learning goals and can help faculty acquire a shared vision and a common instructional design foundation upon which further development can be built. Providing support, resources, and instructional development up front reduces the likelihood of having to retrofit processes, procedures, and mindsets later. Moreover, faculty development provides opportunities to advance one's own understanding in teaching and learning and to refine one's teaching skills, particularly with technology in this case. Faculty development empowers faculty with knowledge and skill in course development and delivery, thereby enabling new and innovative ways of teaching; in the long run, faculty development reduces faculty members' reliance upon other resources such as support staff. Investing in faculty development results in many long-term benefits.

Universities have a diverse range of faculty members who differ in their interest and involvement in faculty development. As a result, a multi-faceted approach to instructional development may provide a means to address the varying needs of faculty. As it is, most universities have centers for university teaching, which provide workshops, seminars, guest speakers, certificate programs, and one-on-one instructional support. For the most part, these provide assistance to instructors who are already interested in and motivated to advance their instructional development. Early adopters and grassroots approaches where individual initiatives are tried and experiences shared by faculty members are also means of instructional development.

Another form is instructional development that is integrated with the development and delivery of an academic program, whereby support and services are provided in parallel with the development and delivery cycles. Furthermore, an effective faculty development program includes theory, application, and practice, such as through courses and workshops, but also incorporates the exchange of experiences and ideas among colleagues, elicits input, and provides personally relevant just-in-time knowledge and support. A posed solution to the generally available, but segmented faculty development opportunities is a multifaceted instructional development model.

The Model

In the late 1990s and early millennium, the Technical University of British Columbia (TechBC) embarked on a multi-faceted approach to faculty development (Figure 1.) In this diagram, the core focus or activity is teaching, which consists of course design and development, course delivery, and course revisions, which then feed into the next cycle of course design and delivery. To support teaching, we proposed several layers to faculty development support. These layers are interrelated, thus the boundaries between are permeable and enable influences across each layer. Though components of the model are common at various institutions, our integrated approach is unique.

The first aspect of faculty development is instructional development (professional development in teaching) through the means of a program. Faculty participated in the Mastering Educational Technology and Learning (METL) program, which consisted of face-to-face and online sessions over a semester. Topics corresponded to critical points in course design and development. For example, early in the semester when faculty members considered

Figure 1. Multifaceted approach to faculty development

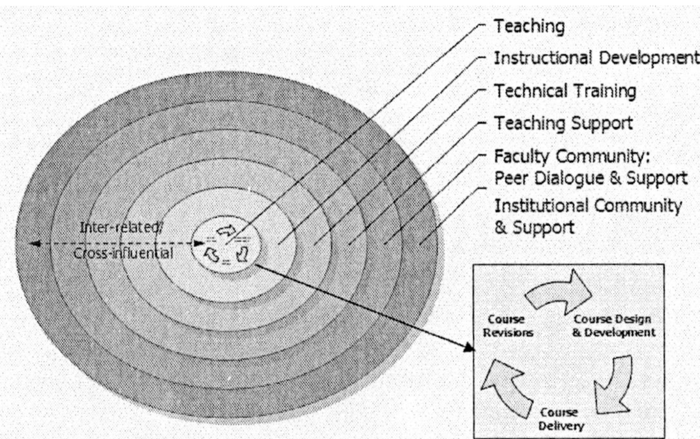

their overall goals and started high-level planning for their courses, sessions focused on institutional goals for teaching and learning (in this case e-learning) and aided faculty with their instructional objectives. The sessions aided faculty members to challenge their existing epistemological beliefs about teaching and learning, which was necessary to move toward "new" ways of teaching. As faculty members moved toward more intensive course design, sessions focused on instructional design, learning object search or development, intellectual property issues, and writing for the Web. The intent was to offer more advanced METL programs, which covered the whole teaching cycle from design to revisions and specific topics of interest for faculty members to facilitate evolution in their teaching throughout their career.

Associated with instructional development is technical training, which occurred, separate from the METL program. The rationale: It was important for faculty members to carefully consider the reasons *why* they were using certain technologies first. Training focused on authentic activities, which would help the instructors to set up or teach their course. An important note is that the institution provided and supported *select* technologies for use. This decision was geared toward providing consistency for students across their courses, enabling scalability, streamlining and to some extent, standardizing technical training and instructional support, and making the technology transparent for instructors and students over time.

Furthermore, prior to the start of a semester, workshops and open labs were available to faculty members who were unfamiliar with the technology, who desired a refresher course, or who just wanted to work on their course in the presence of support staff who could assist them. A special session demonstrated changes to existing technologies. During the semester, faculty members received teaching support from staff through e-mail, phone, or in person. Support was provided on both technical and instructional matters by staff. An instructional design drop-in clinic was also available to provide just-in-time consultation to instructors.

In addition to the instructional development and support opportunities available through staff, dialogue and collaboration among faculty colleagues was found to be just as important for successful faculty development. In the METL program and various training opportunities, faculty members were frequently paired or grouped together to discuss or work together on their course design. We found that this enabled some faculty members to speak more openly about their concerns or beliefs. The dialogue among peers appeared to enable faculty members to critique and challenge their own ideas. As well, they provided each other with useful feedback and looked at possible integration points and redundancies between their courses—all to the benefit of their students! As the faculty members faced teaching, many were seen or heard providing each other with support and advice. As the semester progressed, faculty members were asked to present their experiences to date to their colleagues and interested staff. Interestingly, the sessions were well attended. The important lesson here is that faculty members are not recipients of faculty development, but benefit greatly through participation, sharing, and leading. Faculty members bring substantial experience and input that can help their fellow faculty members, and when a sense of community has been developed, the gains are easily identifiable.

One final and critical aspect in the faculty development model is the institution. Specifically, to what extent is there a community around an e-learning direction, and what support mechanisms are in place to invest in faculty development? Bates (2000) emphasized that providing access to technology does not automatically result in innovative teaching (or instructionally sound teaching for that matter). An existing challenge is that teaching is still viewed for the most part, as secondary to a faculty member's research contributions to an institution. Teaching excellence awards are increasingly common among institutions and need to be celebrated, such as in the case of METL at TechBC where successful completion was recognized and celebrated by the institution through an awards ceremony attended by faculty colleagues, staff, the VP Academic, and President. However, the weight of teaching excellence and instructional development and change is predominantly secondary to one's research portfolio.

In order for a multifaceted faculty development model to function and be sustained, the institution, staff, and faculty members require a shared recognition of teaching and faculty growth, innovation, and experimentation. This may entail critical changes to the institution's system. Institutional motivators and realistic integration of faculty development into day-to-day work-life are needed. For example, generally faculty members are provided with sabbatical time to focus on their research, but time away from research or teaching to focus on teaching or professional development is virtually unheard of. Prospects for tenure and promotion are based less on teaching and related professional growth. These types of institutional procedures and processes require side-by-side comparison with the institution's desired direction and goals to determine necessary changes and carefully consider the actual extent to which the institution is committed to this direction.

Advantages

There are several advantages to integrating faculty development with program development and delivery.

- Instructional development opportunities can be tailored and adjusted over time to address the specific needs of a particular academic program and the instructors. Thus, instructional development can focus on specific needs at a particular time and can be adapted according to faculty needs as they develop and deliver an academic program. Integrated instructional and program development can take advantage of timelines, by providing initial scaffolding, building on previous events, and empowering faculty over time.
- Research in instructional development has indicated a relationship between changes in faculty members' teaching and changes in their epistemological beliefs and models for teaching and learning (i.e., see research by Amundsen, Saroyan, & Frankman, 1996; Saroyan & Amundsen, 2001). These foundational changes are also dependent upon time. Providing instructional development and support for the development and delivery cycles of an academic program may enable longer-term and longer-lasting effects. Without changes in personal beliefs and models, changes in teaching may be short-lived even if they are guided by a program's directives.
- As with learning in general, these changes also transpire more readily when instructors have personally meaningful experiences and opportunity for practice and reflection. Therefore, instructional development may be most effective if it is contextualized within one's work. In addition, instructional development at a program level lends

itself well to a cohort approach, whereby instructors can learn from and share ideas and experiences with their colleagues.

- Specific technologies may be implemented by academic programs to meet some program goals. Access to the technology alone may not be sufficient. Instead, faculty may benefit from opportunities for skill development in a safe, collaborative environment with their colleagues and to learn about possibilities in teaching and learning by using particular technologies. In addition, in an integrated approach to instructional development, faculty members can experience the technologies they will be using in their teaching, during their own learning.
- Staff members who support developed programs also benefit from being a part of both program development and instructional development processes. Through working with other staff that facilitates instructional development, they can gain a richer understanding of the program and its goals and provide broader support services.
- After a cycle of program development and delivery has occurred, an integrated instructional development program can be tailored further to address specific faculty or program needs and to provide advanced instructional development opportunities to faculty.

Integrating instructional development and program development and delivery is an efficient use of time and resources, although ongoing collaboration between support staff in both areas is needed. It could be argued that the line between supporting instructional and program development is artificial and that an integrated approach with the same staff provides consistent and long-term multi-faceted faculty support. An effective program includes theory, application, and practice, such as through courses and workshops, but also incorporates the exchange of experiences and ideas among colleagues, elicits input from participants, communicates opportunities, and provides personally relevant just-in-time knowledge and support.

In closing, institutional change is a long and arduous process (Bates, 2000) and may appear to be a Herculean task. One suggested first step toward building a faculty development model that supports e-learning is to start with new faculty. As an increasing number of existing faculty retire from academe, the numbers of new faculty are increasing. Given current and projected future faculty shortage (Mcleans, 1999) we cannot assume or expect faculty to have sufficient experience in instructional design or teaching proficiency. Building a multi-faceted faculty development program that works toward an institution's goal of e-learning and longer-termed institutional change may be a necessary first step to developing a faculty development program that supports the e-learning ecosystem.

Conclusion

In this chapter, we discussed examples from actual cases that were experienced by the authors. We construed the learning environment as an ecosystem of flow of information and interactions across activities related to learning. The ecosystem as a whole is oriented toward offering a personalized learning experience with the ultimate goal of sustaining and evolving knowledge. In general, sustainability can be measured in terms of the quality of the learning experience, the cost of producing the learning experience, and the infrastructure needed to offer the learning experience.

We opened our chapter with an argument that supports the notion of support e-learners in specific tasks such as studying. We advocate the need to support learners in each and every activity that they engage in as part of their learning. We have results that show the quality improvement that learners experience when a theory-oriented support tool was presented to scaffold them in their learning activities. One of the key aspects of sustainability is looking ahead and predicting the future needs. Later, we investigated how a multifaceted faculty development plays a key role in the ecosystem.

References

Amundsen, C., Saroyan, A., & Frankman, M. (1996). Changing methods and metaphors: A case study of growth in university teaching. *J. on Excellence in College Teaching, 7*(3), 3-42.

Bakardjieva, M. (1998, June 19-24). Collaborative meaning-making in computer conferences: A socio-cultural perspective. In T. Ottman & I. Tomek (Eds.), *Proceedings of Ed-Media and Ed-Telecom '98 World Conference on Educational Multimedia and Hypermedia and Educational Telecommunications*, Freiburg, Germany (pp. 93-98). Charlottesville, VA: Advancement of Computing in Education (AACE)

Bates, A. W. (2000). *Managing technological change: Strategies for college and university leaders.* San Francisco: Jossey-Bass.

Boud, D., Keogh, R., & Walker, D. (1985). Promoting reflection in learning: A model. In D. Boud, R. Keogh, & D. Walker (Eds.), *Reflection: Turning experience into learning* (pp. 18-40). New York: Nichols Publishing.

Butler, D. L., & Winne, P. H. (1995). Feedback and self-regulated learning: A theoretical synthesis. *Review of Educational Research, 65*(3), 245-281.

Carver, M., & Scheier, H. (1981). *Attention and self-regulation: A control-theory approach to human behaviour.* New York: Springer-Verlag.

Cherry, J., Fryer, B., Steckham, M., & Fischer, M. (1989). Do formats for presenting online help affect user performance and attitudes? In *Proceedings of the International Technical Communication Conference Washington, DC: Society of Technical Communication (May 10-13)*(pp. RET87- RET89). Philadelphia: Society of Technical Communications.

Coffee, P. (1997). Office Assistant is—surprise!—useful. *PC Week, 14*(3), 49.

Cole, M., & Engström, Y. (1993). A cultural-historical approach to distributed cognition. In G. Salomon (Ed.), *Distributed cognitions: Psychological and educational considerations* (pp. 1-46). New York: Cambridge University Press.

Collins, J. A., Greer, J. E., Kumar, V. S., McCalla, G. I., Meagher, P., & Tkatch, R. (1997). Inspectable user models for just-in-time workplace training. In A. Jameson, C. Paris, & C. Tasso (Eds.), *The Sixth International Conference on User Modeling (UM'97)* (pp. 327-337). Chia Laguna, Sardinia, Italy. New York: Springer Wien.

Feenberg, A. (1989). The written world. In R. Mason & A. Kaye (Eds.), *Mindweave: Communication, computers, and distance education* (pp. 22-39). Oxford: Pergamon Press.

Finnegan, D. (1997). Transforming faculty roles. In M. W. Peterson, D. D. Dill, & L. A. Mets and Associates (Eds.), *Planning and management change for a changing environment* (pp. 479-501). San Francisco: Jossey-Bass.

Greer, J. E., McCalla, G. I., Collins, J. A., Kumar, V. S., Meagher, P., & Vassileva, J. I. (1998). Supporting peer help and collaboration in distributed workplace environments. *International Journal of Artificial Intelligence in Education, 9*, 159-177.

Gwei, G. M., & Foxley, E. (1990). Towards a consultative online help system. *International Journal of Man Machine Studies, 32*(4), 363-383.

Hadwin, A. F., Winne, P. H., Nesbit, J. C., & Murphy, C. (2005). *LogReader: A toolkit for analyzing gStudy log data and computing transition metrics* (version 1.0) [computer program]. University of Victoria, Victoria, BC.

Hodgins, W. (2000). *Into the future: A vision paper* (White Paper). Technology and Adult Learning of the American Society for Training and Development.

Hofer, B., Yu, S., & Pintrich, P. (1998). Teaching college students to be self-regulated learners. In D. Schunk & B. J. Zimmerman (Eds.), *Self-regulated learning: From teaching to self-reflective practice* (pp. 57-88). New York: The Guilford Press.

Horvitz, E., Breese, J. S., Heckerman, D., Hovel, D., & Rommelse, K. (1998). The Lumiere Project: Bayesian user modeling for inferring the goals and needs of software users. In *14th Conference on Uncertainty in Artificial Intelligence* (pp. 256-265). Morgan Kaufmann Publishers. Retrieved from http://research.microsoft.com/~horvitz/lumiere.htm

Houghton, R. C., Jr. (1984). Online help systems: A conspectus. *Communications of the ACM, 27*(2), 126-133.

IMS Digital Repositories Interoperability. (2002). *Core Functions Information Model* (Version 1). Retrieved from www.imsglobal.org/digitalrepositories/index.cfm

Jambalsuren, M., & Cheng, Z. (2002). An interactive programming environment for enhancing learning performance. In *Proceedings of the Second International Workshop on Databases in Networked Information Systems. Lecture Notes in Computer Science* (Vol. 2544, pp. 201-212).

Jamieson-Noel, D. (2004). *Exploring task definition as a facet of self-regulated learning.* Unpublished doctoral dissertation, Simon Fraser University

Johnson, L. F. (2003). *Elusive vision: Challenges impeding the learning object economy.* New Media Consortium.

Kemp, J. E., Morrison, G. R., & Ross, S. M. (1998). *Designing effective instruction*. Upper Saddle River, NJ: Merrill.

Kolb, D. A., & Fry, R. (1975). Towards an applied theory of experiential learning. In C. L. Cooper (Ed.), *Theories of group processes* (pp. 33-58). London: John Wiley.

Kumar, V. (2001). *Helping the helper in peer help networks.* Unpublished doctoral theses, Department of Computer Science, University of Saskatchewan, Canada.

Kumar, V. (2004). An instrument for providing formative feedback to novice programmers. In *AERA 2004 Division I Education in the professions,* (p. 72). San Diego, CA: AERA.

Kumar, V., Groeneboer, C., & Chu, S. (2005). Sustainable learning ecosystem, tutorial. In D. Jin-Tan Yang, & Kinshuk (Eds.), *IEEE International Conference on Advanced Learning Technologies (ICALT 2005)*. Kaohsiung, Taiwan. IEEE Computer Society Press.

Kumar, V., Shakya, J., Groeneboer, C., & Chu, S. (2004). Toward an ontology of teaching strategies. In F. Akhras, & B. du Bolay (Eds.), *Workshop on modelling human teaching tactics and strategies Aug 2004*, Maceio, Alagoas, Brazil, (pp. 71-80)

Kumar, V. S., Winne, P. H., Hadwin, A. F., Nesbit, J. C., Jamieson-Noel, D., Calvert, T., & Samin, B. (2005). Effects of self-regulated learning in programming. In D. Jin-Tan Yang, & Kinshuk (Eds.), *IEEE International Conference on Advanced Learning Technologies (ICALT 2005)* (pp. 383-387). Kaohsiung, Taiwan. IEEE Computer Society Press.

Lebow, D. (1993). Constructivist values for instructional systems design: Five principles toward a new mindset. *Educational Technology Research and Development, 41*(3), 4-16.

Ledford, B. R., & Sleeman, P. J. (2000). *Instructional design: A primer.* Greenwhich, CT: Information Age Publishing.

Lee, H., Lee, C., & Yoo, C. (1998). A scenario-based object-oriented methodology for developing hypermedia information systems. *Hicss, 2*(2), 47.

Mcleans (November, 1999). Measuring excellence. In *Universities 1999*. Retrieved March 12, 2000, from http://www.macleans.ca/pub-doc/1999/11/15/Universities1999/25753.shtml

Nelson-Le Gall, S. (1981). Help-seeking: An understudied problem-solving skill in children. *Developmental Review,* 1, 224-246.

Newman, R. (1994). Adaptive help seeking: A strategy of self-regulated learning. In D. H. Schunk & B. J. Zimmerman (Eds.), *Self-regulation of learning and performance: Issues and educational applications* (pp. 283-301). Hillsdale, NJ: Lawrence Erlbaum Associates.

Newman, R. (2002). How self-regulated learners cope with academic difficulty: The role of adaptive help seeking. *Theory into Practice, 41*(2).

Rosenberg, M. J. (2001). *E-learning: Strategies for delivering knowledge in the digital age*. McGraw-Hill.

Rumelhart, V. E., & Norman, D. A. (1978). Accretion, tuning, and restructuring: Three modes of learning. In J. Cotton, & R. Klatzky (Eds.), *The collection of semantic factors in cognition*. Hillsdale, NJ: Erlbaum.

Samin, B. (2004). *Effects of self-regulated learning in programming.* Unpublished master's theses, Simon Fraser University, Burnaby, BC, Canada.

Saroyan, A., & Amundsen, C. (2001). Evaluating university teaching: Time to take stock. *Assessment and Evaluation in Higher Education, 26*(4), 341-353.

Turoff, M. (1991). Computer-mediated communication requirements for group support. *Journal of Organizational Computing, 1*(1), 85-113.

Vaid, J. M. (2005). *Cognitive psychology and computer science.* Retrieved September 20, 2005, from http://www.rtis.com/nat/user/jfullerton/school/psyc345/program.htm

Wieseler, W. (1999). *RIO: A standards-based approach for reusable information objects* (White Paper). Cisco Systems.

Winne, P. H. (1997). Experimenting to bootstrap self-regulated learning. *Journal of Educational Psychology*, *89*(3), 397-410.

Winne, P. H. (2001). Self-regulated learning viewed from models of information processing. In B. J. Zimmerman & D. H. Schunk (Eds.), *Self-regulated learning and academic achievement: Theoretical perception* (pp. 153-189). Mahwah, NJ: Lawrence Elburn Associates.

Winne, P. H., & Hadwin, A. F. (1998). Studying as self-regulated learning. In D. Hacker, J. Dunlosky, & A. Graesser (Eds.), *Metacognition in educational theory and practice* (pp. 277-304). Mahwah NJ: Lawrence Erlbaum Associates.

Winne, P. H., & Jamieson-Noel, D. L. (2002). Exploring students' calibration of self-reports about study tactics and achievement. *Contemporary Educational Psychology*, *27*(4), 551-572.

Winne, P. H., Jamieson-Noel, D., & Muis, K. (2002). Methodological issues and advances in researching tactics, strategies and self-regulated learning. In M. L. Maehr & P. R. Pintrich (Eds.), *Advances in motivation and achievement* (Vol. 12) (pp. 121-158). Greenwhich, CT: JAI.

Winne, P. H., Nesbit, J. C., Kumar, V., Hadwin, A. F., Lajoie, S. P., Azevedo, R. A., et al., N. E. (in press, 2005). Supporting self-regulated learning with gStudy software: The Learning Kit Project. *Technology, Instruction, Cognition and Learning.*

Winne, P. H., & Perry, N. E. (1999). Measuring self-regulated learning. In M. Boekaerts, P. Pintrich, & M. Zeidner (Eds.), *Handbook of self-regulation* (pp. 531-566). Orlando, FL: Academic Press.

Wise, M. (1993). Using graphics in software documentation. *Journal of the society for technical communications,* 40, 677-681.

Xin, M., & Glass, G. (2005). Enhancing online discussion through Web annotation. In G.Richards (Ed.), *Proceedings of World Conference on E-Learning in Corporate, Government, Healthcare adn Higher Education 2005.* Vancouver, BC, Canada (pp. 3212-3217.). Chesapeake, VA: AACE

Xin, M. C. (2002). *Validity-centered design for the domain of engaged collaborative discourse in computer conferencing*. Unpublished doctoral dissertation, Brigham Young University, Provo, UT.

Xin, M. C., & Feenberg, A. (2002). Designing for pedagogical effectiveness: TextWeaver. In *Proceedings of the Hawaii International Conference of System Sciences,* (Vol. 4 p. 116.2). Washington DC: IEEE Computer Society

Zimmerman, B. J. (1986). Becoming a self-regulated learner; which are the key subprocesses? *Contemporary Educational Psychology, 11*(4), 307-313.

Zimmerman, B. J., & Schunk, D. H. (2001). *Self-regulated learning and academic achievement: Theoretical perception.* Mahwah, NJ: Lawrence Elburn Associates.

Conclusion

E-Learning Best Practices and Lessons Learned: A Summary

Sanjaya Mishra, Indira Gandhi National Open University, New Delhi, India

Ramesh C. Sharma, Indira Gandhi National Open University, New Delhi, India

The 23 case studies in this volume point us to huge learning resources. But their analyses give us a set of guidelines on how planning, designing, and implementation of e-learning should be done in any organization. We group these guidelines into six groups in more generic ways so that these are applied in e-learning setting as it has been done in many of these cases.

Learner Preparation

The learner is central to any e-learning course/program, and therefore, design, development, and implementation need to be around what the requirements are of the learners. The target group should be identified through systematic market research and segmentation, and the courses and programs should be niche products. Having developed a need-based program and attracted the right learner, it is important to have the necessary "learner autonomy" built into the e-learning program and continuously support them to become better "self-directed learners." Designing flexible options to choose from a basket of content and strategies helps the learners; and it is helpful to conduct "orientation" and "de-briefing" sessions face-to-face rather than online for the first time. The success of e-learning will depend upon encouraging learners to use Web technologies and motivate them to adapt their learning styles to the new Internet pedagogy of *Experience-Reflect-Interact-Construct* (ERIC). Build the learning environment to facilitate the learner to track and monitor his or her own progress; and thus, use a learning management system (LMS) that can be a support in self-directed learning.

Teachers

The online teacher has many roles: course creators, content developers, assessors, and tutors being the prominent ones. Tutoring in an e-learning environment puts high stress on the teacher due to the ubiquity of the online systems. Messages in e-mail and discussion groups need immediate attention of the teacher; and technology use demands better time and work management strategies. It is important for the tutors to make it clear to the learners about their expected response time. This will help reduce anxiety of the learners.

The e-learning world requires continuous updating of the teachers, and hence there should be mechanisms for continuous professional development. Use online professional development models to build the capacity of e-tutors. In the *Thwarted Innovation* report, it has been pointed out that success or failure of e-learning depends much on changing the attitudes about and perceptions of e-learning by faculty and technical staff (Zemsky & Massy, 2004).

Technology

In a report on e-learning—"If We Build It, Will They Come?"—one of the recommendations was:

Ensure that frustration with e-learning technology is not a barrier to successful e-learning. (ASTD, 2001, p. 2)

Access to technology is still a problem in many developing countries. Particularly Internet bandwidth is poor in many parts of the world; and therefore the choice of platform and technology to develop and deliver e-learning should be such that it is accessible to the target group. Preparing low-bandwidth solutions and delivery of e-content through CD-ROMs are alternatives to heavy download requirements online.

Content

Content is considered to be the King in e-learning. Thus, the e-learning content should be appropriate to the needs of the target group. This demands that the curriculum design is done in a participatory mode involving various stakeholders such as the learners, subject matter experts, and industry personnel. A collaborative content design would be highly relevant. However, it is important that the content is accurate and appropriate. Thus, checking of the content before delivery is extremely essential to ensure quality. Some experts do make differentiation between content and course materials, where content being the syllabi and the latter illustrations and explanations of the content. For e-learning, we are actually concerned about both, and systematic development of multimedia course materials for online use should follow the guidelines of Clark and Mayer (2003):

- Use words and graphics rather than words alone;
- Place corresponding words and graphics near each other;
- Present words as audio narration rather than on-screen text;
- Presenting words in both text and audio narration can hurt learning;
- Adding extraneous sound/picture can hurt learning; and
- Use conversational style and virtual learning agents.

Developing scripts before implementing the course in a technology platform is a best practice.

Pedagogy

The real issue in e-learning is the pedagogy. What pedagogical strategies a course adopts decides the way it is used and looked at as a differentiating element. Pedagogy of an e-course makes it different from the static Web pages that we find through using a search engine. It is probably because of the pedagogical design; teachers are still required to teach courses. Otherwise the printing presses and textbooks would have replaced educational institutions. No matter what the technology can bring in, in terms of virtualization, it is utopian to think that teachers might get replaced. As we see in the case studies in this volume, the widely used pedagogical strategies come from the constructivist paradigm, and these are collaborative learning, case studies, problem-based learning, scenario-based learning, activity theory, and so on.

Interaction in online learning is another important issue that should be designed in such a way to facilitate both synchronous and asynchronous interaction between learner-teacher and learner-learner. Creation of learning groups is useful in management of interaction. Posting to each other's comments in asynchronous discussion is a demanding task for the learner, though it has been used successfully in some situations. The expectations of interaction should be as realistic as possible. Otherwise, the design itself may lead to student dropout. Design of authentic learning communities for interaction would be highly useful for sustainable learning. So, combine theory with practice by using a sequence of individual study/inquiry followed by large group discussion and the collaborative small group projects.

Other Issues

- It should be clear to all that e-learning is not inexpensive, though it has the potential to be cheaper than face-to-face training if we calculate the travel time, opportunity costs, and release time of the participants. Nevertheless, the right "economies of scale" of e-learning courses/programs are yet to be achieved in many institutions.
- Good e-learning programs take time to develop. No matter what rapid prototyping instructional design or rapid e-learning strategies are used, it takes enormous time and efforts to develop online courses. Most of the time for e-learning development goes in the planning phase.
- Intellectual property of the e-courses should be decided as a matter of policy up front. There are usually three options: institutional ownership of course; faculty ownership of courses; and specialized contracts (Twigg, 2000). Whatever may be the option, it is better to have clarity over the rights, usage, and revenue sharing in the beginning making clarity about what is work under hire, and how the academic freedom is applied in specific contexts.
- Share learner identities to form groups and increase collaboration. Use photos and group pages to build identity online to ensure commitments from learners. Involve the learners to share their values and expectations without masking their identities.
- Make clear agreement for technical support by assigning specific responsibilities. Involve technical staff from the beginning to avoid network and firewall related problems.
- Undertake evaluation of e-learning programs continuously at least for "reaction" and "learning" levels to gather information that is useful for improving the quality of the program.
- Promote e-learning vigorously to avoid the "B" series tag that is common to distance/correspondence courses.
- Adopt appropriate steps for adoption of innovation (e-learning in this case) in your organization.
- One of the major factors responsible for successful implementation of e-learning is consistent and steady effort of the government, policy-makers, and institutional heads. Without this, it is difficult to think about e-learning.

The analyses of the lessons learned and the guidelines just mentioned are not in order of importance. All of these are equally important. As e-learning promoters, designers, and teachers, we need to consider all these while developing programs for our clients/students to be delivered online. It is truly said in one of the chapters in this volume that, "effectiveness of e-learning depends on orchestrating many factors such as level-specific contents, tutoring, community of learners, management, as well as technical infrastructure." While this is what in essence these case studies from around the world show us, we would like to conclude with some of the advises of one of the authors in this volume:

- Do not feel disheartened (when things do not proceed in the ways you want them to be);
- Face the reality of digital divide (make provisions for those who do not have access to technology; do not avoid e-learning because of digital divide alone); and
- Learn to continue to have faith in your vision despite criticism of all kinds.

References

ASTD. (2001). *E-learning: If we build it, will they come?* (Executive Summary). Alexandria, VA: ASTD.

Clark, R. C., & Mayer, R. E. (2003). *E-learning and the science of instruction.* San Fransisco: Pfeiffer.

Twigg, C. A. (2000). *Who owns online courses and course materials?* New York: CAT, Rensselaer Polytechnic Institute.

Zemsky, R., & Massy, W. F. (2004). *Thwarted innovation: What happened to e-learning and why?* West Chester, PA: Learning Alliance for Higher Education, University of Pennsylvania.

Appendix

Framework for Writing the Case Studies

Case studies are effective instructional tools. These are useful sources of authentic learning that help to analyze situations and enable understanding of issues in context to apply the new learning in other similar situations/context. Thus, case studies present realistic situations with a balance of theory and practice. In our case, writing a case study is to faithfully record and reflect on what, when, why, and how you have planned, designed, and implemented e-learning. We expect you to follow a narrative style of story telling that gives details about actions that had influence in your e-learning practice. However, in order to have uniformity in presentation of the case studies and facilitate comparison, we suggest you to follow the format given next to present your case study in about 3,500-4,000 words.

Title of the study: This could be the name of the online program, or you can give a suitable one that reflects the central idea or focus of the case.

Introduction: Cover institutional and national context of the program; brief descriptions about the organization offering the program, its mandate, and how e-learning initiative has emerged (e.g., policy developments).

E-learning program: Give an overview of the program vis-à-vis other such program in the organization; describe objectives, entry requirements, and so forth of the program.

Academic issues: Discuss the pedagogic models (completely online/partly online (blended)/ as support to face-to-face classroom); the philosophical foundations (behaviorist/cognitivist/constructivist); approaches to program/course development; teaching-learning processes; support services to learners; use of virtual learning environment (open source/commercial) and their features; and assessment and evaluation practices.

Administrative issues: Discuss issues related to the technical infrastructure needed/used by the program, both from your end and that of the learners' end; technical, professional, and academic human resource requirements to run the program; budgetary provisions and cost-effectiveness issues (from where the money comes and where it goes?); who owns the copyright of the courses and how Intellectual Property Rights issues are resolved; quality assurance and standards (including learning objects, meta-data, learning design, etc.); accreditation of the program; staff development needs and acceptance of the program by the faculty and other colleagues.

Program evaluation: Program evaluation mechanism, opinions of stakeholders; analysis of the use of virtual learning environment, if any.

Networking and collaboration: Nature of networking and collaborative arrangements, if any to run the program.

Policy implications: Discuss policy issues that should be addressed vis-à-vis this program and your organization; influence of this program on policy development in your organization.

Sustainability and Conclusions: Sustainability of the program in terms of costs and enrollment; how to improve sustainability; future plans, if any.

Lessons learned: Based on the good and bad experiences, list at least 10 lessons *in order of priority* and explain.

Best practices: Identify *three* actions/practices (*in order of priority*) in the program that you think are best that should be emulated by others.

References: List the bibliography in APA Style, 5th edition in alphabetical order, and provide in-text references.

General Notes

1. Make the title of the Case brief; include an abstract of about 100-150 words, and give three to five keywords for the case study.
2. Preferably use headings as given previously in the framework. Only two levels of headings are allowed. Main heading should be in font size 14, subheadings in font size 12 in italics.
3. The main text should be produced in Times New Roman font size 11 and in double line spacing.
4. Tables should be included in the text at the appropriate place and centered. Caption should be between 8-10 words.
5. Give diagrams, screen shots, and illustrations wherever needed, and they should be included in the text at the appropriate place and centered. Caption below should be between 8-10 words. All figures should be presented as separate items and produced in GIF or JPEG formats.
6. Give an accurate and updated list of references. Only in-text references should be listed.
7. Please use only endnotes, if needed. They will be placed before the references at the end of each case. Footnotes at the bottom of a page will not be allowed.
8. Give one paragraph biographical sketch of about 100 words for each author at the end of the case.
9. It is the author's responsibility to obtain written permission to include any copyrighted materials in the case study. The publisher of the book requires a copy of the written permission submitted with the final version of the chapter.
10. Write the case study based on your experience and published/unpublished research/ evaluation reports of the program.
11. Use your thinking, judgment, and evaluation to critically present the case in a way that can be useful reading to students of e-learning, by the teachers, administrators, or decision-makers.
12. Make sure complete editing of the case study is conducted to ensure proper English language usage, grammatical structure, spelling, and punctuation. Attention to these details will contribute to clear, concise communication of your ideas.

About the Authors

Ramesh C. Sharma holds a PhD in education in the area of educational technology and is currently working as regional director in Indira Gandhi National Open University (IGNOU). He has been a teacher trainer also and has taught educational technology, educational research and statistics, educational measurement and evaluation, special education, and psychodynamics of mental health courses for the BEd and MEd programs. He has conducted many training programs for the in- and pre-service teachers on the use of computers, the Internet, and multimedia in teaching and instruction, and had established a Center of ICT in the college he was working. He is a member of many committees on implementation of technology in the Open University. His areas of specialization include ICT applications, computer networking, online learning, student support services in open and distance learning, and teacher education. He is the co-editor of the *Asian Journal of Distance Education* (ISSN 1347-9008, www.ASIANJDE.org). In addition to these, he is/has been on the editorial advisory board of *Distance Education*, *International Review of Research in Open and Distance Learning*, and *Turkish Online Journal of Distance Education*. He has co-authored one book on distance education research, and very recently one of his co-edited books, *Interactive Multimedia in Education and Training*, has been published by Idea Group Inc. (www.idea-group.com). He is also an advisory board member and an author for the *Encyclopedia of Distance Learning* (http://www.idea-group.com/encyclopedia/details.asp?ID=4500&v=editorialBoard).

Sanjaya Mishra holds a PhD in library and information science in the area of library networks. He has been a teacher of communication technology to distance educators. He has been involved in successful implementation of many multimedia and Internet-based courses. With professional training in distance education, television production, and multimedia, he is actively involved in collaboration at the international level. At present, he is a reader in distance education at the Staff Training and Research Institute of Distance Education, Indira Gandhi National Open University, New Delhi. He also served (2001-2003) the Commonwealth Educational Media Center for Asia at New Delhi as a program officer, where he conducted a number of workshops on multimedia and e-learning in the Asian region. He has served as consultant to UNESCO, UN-ESCAP, World Bank, and the Commonwealth of Learning. He was book review editor of *Indian Journal of Open Learning* (1997-2000) and edited a few special issues of the same journal. He is author/editor of 10 books and has contributed more than 75 research papers in reputed professional journals. He is one of the founding editors of the *Asian Journal of Distance Education*. He co-edited *Interactive Multimedia in Education and Training* (Idea Group Inc., 2005). He received the University Silver Medal for Best Research Paper for his work titled "Roles and Competencies of Academic Counsellors in Distance Education" published in *Open Learning* in 2005.

* * *

John Beaumont-Kerridge is director of online learning development at University of Luton Business School. From a background of marketing in small business management and the public sector, he teaches marketing related subjects at the University of Luton Business School. This culminated in a doctorate from The Middlesex University in 2001, focusing upon market orientation and service quality. His master's in management studies (marketing option) was gained at the University of Greenwich in 1985, and his BSc in biological chemistry was awarded in 1975 from the University of Essex. More recently, his efforts have been developing online communication and learning methods using the Internet, which have resulted in a number of successful international contracts for the Luton Business School. His main research interests include e-learning with a particular emphasis upon methods of VoiceIP integration with Internet communication tools, and aspects of marketing within the public and private sector.

Madhumita Bhattacharya teaches instructional design and learning technologies, science, and technology education at the undergraduate and postgraduate level. Madhumita supervises master's projects and doctoral thesis. Presently Dr. Bhattacharya is a senior faculty member at Massey University. She has more that 15 years of research and teaching experience in prestigious institutions in India, Japan, Singapore, Australia, Estonia, and New Zealand. Madhumita has published extensively in journals, books, monographs, and conference proceedings. Dr. Bhattacharya is a guest professor at the University of Tartu, Estonia. She is involved in a number of international projects and serves as a review board member and executive committee member of journals and academic societies.

Oliver Bohl works as a senior researcher at the Institute for Information Systems, University of Kassel/Germany (UniK). Furthermore, he works as a project manager at the Research Center for IT Design (ITeG), where he is responsible for national and international R&D projects. His research activities concentrate on business-related aspects of e-learning, economic effects of virtualization and networking, configuration of business models, and development of mobile solutions.

Bethany Bovard is an instructional designer for online learning at New Mexico State University (USA). For the past several years, she has worked on e-learning projects for RETA and the College of Extended Learning. Currently, Ms. Bovard is in a doctoral program at Capella University for instructional design of online learning. Her experience and research in the area of online professional development had a notable impact on the overall design of RETA's online instructor training program.

Dallas Brozik is a professor of finance at Marshall University. His teaching and research are within the areas of investments, derivative security pricing theory, and corporate financial management. Dr. Brozik also does extensive work in the area of simulation and game development, particularly simulations that address issues in business management.

Susan Bussmann, RETA program coordinator, was instrumental in organizing the efforts of the group and providing direction related to all aspects of the program. Bussmann is currently finishing her dissertation for a PhD in education, and her research and experience with K-12 teachers helped significantly in the selection and retention of quality teachers for the project.

K. C. Chu obtained his MPhil in electronics from the Chinese University of Hong Kong and MEd from Hong Kong Polytechnic University. He has worked in the industry for 10 years before joining the Department of Engineering, Hong Kong Institute of Vocational Education (Tsing Yi). He obtained the first Teaching Excellence Award organized by the Vocational Training Council in 2002. His current interest is focused on Web-based teaching, creative learning, and problem-based learning.

Stephanie Chu is program director of the Learning and Instructional Development Center at Simon Fraser University. Through a multitude of roles, Chu has a broad range of experience in instructional and faculty development, course and program development, and fostering innovative learning environments. Over the past decade, she has been active in the research, planning, development, design, and implementation of instructional practices using technology, at many institutional levels. This work has enabled her to recognize the value of a multifaceted approach to design that integrates professional development and support mechanisms within development processes, and includes multi-disciplinary perspectives. Currently, she is pursuing her doctorate in educational psychology with a focus on online learning and instructional design principles.

Patrick Cummins is president of CEP Consulting, Ottawa, Ontario, Canada. He is one of the developers of the ESPORT system, and is an experienced international adult educator.

Patrick J. Fahy, PhD, is a professor in the Center for Distance Education, Athabasca University, Alberta, Canada. He has worked with computer-assisted instruction systems, and in adult basic education and literacy programs, as well as in conventional K-12 education. His interests include online interaction via CMC, and the origin and support of online communities.

Carmen Gonzales is the vice provost for distance education and dean of the College of Extended Learning at New Mexico State University. In 1998, she created the RETA project from a Technology Innovation Challenge grant from the U.S. Department of Education. In her capacity as RETA program director, she designed the initial project goals and objectives. Her PhD in education is from the University of New Mexico.

Mary Griffiths has 20 years distance and flexible learning experience at Monash University, Australia, and at the University of Waikato, New Zealand. At Monash, she was a founding member, and later head, of the Faculty of Arts' international flagship program in communications. She developed courses for remote student cohorts in Australia, South Africa, Singapore, and Malaysia. At Waikato she teaches research methods, making extensive use of the university's platform for Web delivery, and a graduate course in mobile media. Her main area of research is e-democracy, and the civic effects of new mobile media uptake and uses, as well as blogging and all forms of indie publishing on the Web. Recent publications include articles on citizen literacy, New Zealand's changing identity. She co-edited a NZ issue of *Media International Australia*, and a special issue of *Southern Review: Communication, Politics, and Culture* on media and belief; and, as sole editor, a special issue of *EJEG: The Electronic Journal of E-Government* on e-citizens. In June 2006, she takes up a post at the University of Adelaide in the Department of Media.

Michael Griffiths taught for nearly 30 years as a distance and e-learning teacher, starting out as an Open University tutor in the UK in 1972, before emigrating to Australia and joining a distance delivery tertiary campus in Gippsland, Victoria. At Monash University, he was a co-founder of, first, the English program, then the communications program in 1991, and was instrumental in setting up the international writing program a few years later. He has designed over 15 full learning packages for distance students, the most recent being for the writing program: authorship and writing, writing: techniques, and writing: portfolio. Now retired, Michael's interests are in creative works, and working as a research associate on digital photo and narrative projects.

Chris Groeneboer has over 18 years experience in the post-secondary and corporate sectors. She has applied her background in computing science and psychology to learning design from several perspectives including research, teaching, project management, organizational management, and process analysis. Working with a multi-disciplinary team, she has developed models for evaluation of online learning, multi-disciplinary collaboration, and design of online learning environments. She is currently managing the Applied Research on Teaching Lab in the Learning and Instructional Development Center at Simon Fraser University. The lab supports faculty in the scholarship of teaching and learning and engages in knowledge transformation of research results in foundational areas to practice in designing, developing, delivering, and evaluating learning.

Yan Hanbing is a professor of distance education at College of East China Normal University. With a PhD in educational information technology, Dr. Yan is interested in research on distance education and IT-supported instruction. Dr. Yan has published two monographs: *IT-Supported Instructional Design*, and *IT-supported Instructional Evaluation.*

Clare Hanlon is a senior lecturer and coordinator of the postgraduate sport business course at Victoria University. Two teaching qualifications have enabled Hanlon, over the past 16 years, to implement a broad and innovative range of teaching strategies to educate primary, secondary, and tertiary students, and to train and motivate teachers to design, implement, and evaluate teaching strategies associated with sport. Hanlon's teaching practices can be placed into four categories: work-integrated learning; innovation in teaching; resources to enhance quality improvement and activate new learning experiences; and flexible teaching practices.

Alistair Inglis is a senior lecturer in flexible learning and head of the Sunbury Campus of Victoria University where he is responsible for strategic development of online learning. He has in excess of 30 years experience in instructional design and open and distance learning, has published widely in the field, and is currently deputy editor of the international journal, *Distance Education.*

Shobhita Jain studied anthropology at Oxford University and obtained a PhD at Jawaharlal Nehru University. She has done teaching and research in India, Australia, the UK, and the West Indies. During 1982-1983 she was director of the program for Women's Development at Indian Social Institute and after completing a research consultancy for FAO on farm forestry, she worked as a consultant at Multiple Action Research Group. Jain joined Indira Gandhi National Open University in 1988 and retired in 2005 as a professor of sociology, and was director of the School of Social Sciences (1998-2001). She is currently an e-learning consultant, at Jawaharlal Nehru University, New Delhi.

Dianne Jamieson-Noel is a program director in the Center for Online and Distance Education at Simon Fraser University. Currently she works with faculty members within several disciplines in the design of courses for distance delivery. Dianne's primary theoretical and research interests are in the areas of instructional design, technologies, self-regulated learning, metacognition, and assessment. Her primary interest concerns how instructors can design tasks to suit different learning purposes from those that are simple and well-defined to those that are more complex and ill-structured. She also investigates the relationship between task design and how students interpret task instructions with a specific emphasis on how task interpretation influences choices about how to self-regulate learning within the task space. This work involves investigating how technologies can be used to measure traces of task understanding and how students use tactics and strategies to self-regulate their learning.

Nancy Johnston is director of co-operative education at Simon Fraser University, Burnaby, BC, Canada. She is also founding member and current chair of the Association for Co-operative Education's Research and Initiatives Committee for BC/Yukon and a 17-year veteran co-op educator. In 2005 she was awarded the Canadian Association for Co-operative Education's Dr. Albert S. Barber Award for outstanding contributions to the philosophy and practice of co-operative education. Johnston has recently led the development of on an online co-op curriculum focusing on self-direction and skills transfer. Johnston has held many provincial and national board positions including her current positions on the Accreditation Council and Research Committee of the Canadian Association for Co-operative Education and as member of the Board of the Association for Co-operative Education of BC. Through her volunteer work and community service she has also participated in several provincial, national, and international committees, and is a frequent conference speaker and workshop presenter.

Kostas Karpouzis is with the National Technical University of Athens, Greece. His current research interests lie in the areas of human computer interaction, image and video processing, 3D computer animation, sign language synthesis, and virtual reality. He is a member of the Technical Chamber of Greece and a member of ACM SIGGRAPH and SIGCHI societies. Dr. Karpouzis has published more than 70 papers in international journals and proceedings of international conferences. He is a member of the technical committee of the International Conference on Image Processing (ICIP) and a reviewer in five international journals. Since 1995 he has participated in seven research projects at Greek and European level. Dr. Karpouzis is an associate researcher at the Institute of Communication and Computer Systems (ICCS) and holds an adjunct lecturer position at the University of Piraeus, teaching data mining and data warehousing. Dr. Karpouzis can be contacted by e-mail at kkarpou@image.ntua.gr.

Vive Kumar is a faculty member with the School of Interactive Arts and Technology, Simon Fraser University, Canada. Kumar designs mixed-initiative interfaces and ontology-oriented interactive systems that seamlessly integrate human reasoning with machine reasoning. Kumar's research is an interdisciplinary front between artificial intelligence in education and human-computer interfaces. Mixed-initiative interfaces aim to personalize user interactions in domain-specific problem-solving environments and cope with collaboration between the user and the system where the collaborative interactions are driven by the relative knowledge, preferences, and task requirements among the user and the system toward well-defined common and individualistic goals. Vive's areas of interest include mixed-initiative interfaces and interaction, human-computer interactions, artificial intelligence in education/intelligent tutoring systems, applied ontology—knowledge representation and reasoning, user modelling, applications of self-regulated and co-regulated learning, and technology-enhanced teaching, learning, and research.

Byung Ro Lim is director of the Center for Teaching and Learning in Kyung Hee University and teaches students on educational technology and e-learning. He graduated from Indiana University in Bloomington (USA) and got his PhD in the field of instructional technology. He is a consulting member of the Ministry of Education and Human Resource in South Korea and works as an editing member of several journals. His interest areas are instructional design, teacher training, e-learning, and inquiry-based learning.

Ilias Maglogiannis is a lecturer in the Department of Information and Communication Systems Engineering in University of the Aegean. His published scientific work includes five lecture notes (in Greek) on biomedical engineering, multimedia and distance learning topics, 21 journal papers and more than 40 international conference papers. He has served on program and organizing committees of national and international conferences, and he is a reviewer for several scientific journals. His scientific activities include biomedical engineering, medical informatics, image processing, multimedia, and distance learning. Dr. Maglogiannis is a member of IEEE – Societies: Engineering in Medicine and Biology, Computer, Distance Learning Task Force, and Communications, SPIE – International Society for Optical Engineering, ACM, the Technical Chamber of Greece, and the Hellenic Organization of Biomedical Engineering. Dr. Maglogiannis is also a national representative for Greece in the IFIP Working Groups 3.2 (Informatics and ICT in Higher Education) and 12.5 (Artificial Intelligence: Knowledge-Oriented Development of Applications).

Gunnar Martin is a senior consultant at the Institute for Information Systems (IWi) at the German Research Center for Artificial Intelligence (DFKI) in Saarbruecken/Germany. He is responsible for IWi's core-research field "lifelong learning" and is also co-head of the DFKI-wide "Competence Center eLearning (CCeL)." In the field of research he is co-coordinator of the "Network of Excellence for Professional Learning (PROLEARN)" of the European Union, which combines 21 core partners with more than 200 researchers and approximately 250 associated partners from industry and academia. His research activities concentrate on (process-oriented) e-learning and knowledge management as well as organizational memory (information) systems.

Elspeth McKay, PhD, is a senior lecturer with HCI Research and program coordinator, research clusters and outreach at RMIT University, Australia. McKay investigates how individuals interpret text/graphics. She earned her PhD in computer science and information systems from Deakin University, Australia. McKay identified that not all individuals cope effectively with graphical learning. Her research interests include effective human-computer interaction, specialist Web-based e-learning shells, dynamics of interactive Web-mediated knowledge sharing, ontological strategies of learning design with asynchronous Web-enabled frameworks, and development of enhanced accessibility through touch screen technologies.

Matthew Nicholson is a senior lecturer in and co-ordinator of the sport administration courses at Victoria University. In 2003 Nicholson won the Vice Chancellor's Award for Teaching Excellence and the Vice Chancellor's Award for Excellence in E-Learning at

Victoria University, in recognition of his work in establishing new and innovative online learning programs.

Julia Parra is a project co-ordinator and Web-based curriculum developer at New Mexico State University (USA). She has had the opportunity to work on a variety of projects with the NMSU's College of Extended Learning and Agricultural Communications, the Regional Educational Assistance Program (RETA), and STAR-Online. Her research and experience with K-12 educators, Web-based curriculum development, and project management was instrumental during the co-design and implementation of the RETA Online Training program. Currently, Ms. Parra is a doctoral student in the Educational Technologies Program at Pepperdine University.

Donna L. Russell has a BA in elementary education, a master's degree in curriculum and instruction, and a doctoral degree in educational psychology with an emphasis on cognition and technology. She has 14 years experience in classroom teaching and has implemented research in varied K-12 educational settings. Dr. Russell is an assistant professor in the Curriculum and Instructional Leadership Department at the School of Education at the University of Missouri - Kansas City where she has designed a new master's degree in curriculum and instruction with an emphasis on learning technologies. Her research areas and interests include the systemic qualitative analysis of technology integration and innovation in diverse educational settings using cultural historical activity theory, designing research and the evaluation of advanced learning processes in technology-based educational settings, and the design and evaluation of online learning environments.

August-Wilhelm Scheer is a professor and the director and founder of IWi, and also holds the chair for business administration and business information systems at the Saarland University. Professor Scheer is the founder and the chairman of the supervisory board of IDS Scheer AG and chairman of imc information multimedia communication AG, both sited in Saarbruecken. Since 1999, Scheer is a member of the foundation council of the Hasso-Plattner-Foundation for software system technology (HPI) of the University in Potsdam. From 1988-1998 he was, and since 2002 is again, a member of the supervisory board of SAP AG, Walldorf. Prof. Scheer was awarded the "Medal of National Education" in Warsaw (1996), the "TMBE'96 Award for Achievement and Contribution to the Industry" in Washington (1996), "IT-Precursor Award" by the magazine "IT.Services" in Cologne (1999), and received the Research Award of the Phillip Morris Foundation (2003). In 1997, he received the honorary doctor by the University of Pilsen (Czech Republic) and in 2001 by the University of Hohenheim (Germany Republic) for his scientific achievements in the development of methods for the configuration of information systems and for the analysis of business processes. Since 1999, he has been the representative for innovation, technology, and research of the Prime Minister of the Saarland. He has written more than 300 essays and more than 10 books, among them standard works like "Architecture for Integrated Information Systems (ARIS)," "ARIS: Business Process Frameworks," and "ARIS: Business Process Modeling." These books are best-sellers in research, education, and practice, and have already been translated into English, Japanese, Chinese, Russian, Czech, and Polish.

Raffaella Sette (PhD, criminology specialized in online education) is a researcher at the Faculty of Political Science of the University of Bologna (Italy) and a teacher of "criminal sociology" in the degree course in "social service" of the same faculty. She is the author of various essays and articles on the sociology of deviant behavior, victimology, and the teaching of applied criminology.

Jarkko Suhonen is an acting professor with the Department of Computer Science, University of Joensuu. He has been involved in creating, managing, and evaluating the ViSCoS (virtual studies of computer science; http://cs.joensuu.fi/viscos/?lang=eng) online study program at the University of Joensuu. He is currently the leader of ViSCoS. In his PhD thesis, Suhonen constructed and evaluated the FODEM method, which was used to develop ViSCoS. He has co-authored and published about 30 scientific papers.

Erkki Sutinen is a professor and the leader of the Educational Technology Research Group at the University of Joensuu (http://cs.joensuu.fi/edtech). His research interests include the use of technologies for clearly defined needs such as for complex subject domains such as programming in developing countries and within special education. Such applied techniques cover visualization, information retrieval, data mining, robotics, and design models. He has co-authored and published about 100 academic papers. In 2005 alone, annual external funding for his research team amounted to about 800,000 EUR.

Katia Tannous obtained her Bachelor of Chemical Engineering degree from Caxias do Sul University, Master of Science in Process Engineering from State University of Campinas, and her PhD in the same field from the École Nationale Polytechnique de Toulouse - INP, France. She realized also a post-doctorate at the University of Waterloo in Canada. She is accredited as a specialist in education and human resource from PUC-Campinas. Since 1994, she has been teaching extensively in different subjects in undergraduate and graduate courses (transport phenomena and particulate systems) in the School of Chemical Engineering, using distance education software. She is responsible for a research group involving fluidization and particles technologies and simulator software with integration to specific Web sites.

Lucio Teles holds a PhD in computer applications in education, University of Toronto. His master's degree is from the University of Geneva, and he completed his undergraduate degree at the Johan Wolfgang University, Frankfurt, Germany. He conducted research on the use of online classrooms learning and the role of the instructor in online collaborative environments as principal investigator for TeleLearningNetworks of National Centers of Excellence, Canada. He has been a professor in the Faculty of Education and director of the LohnLab for Online Teaching at the Center for Distance Education, Simon Fraser University, in British Columbia, Canada. He is a co-author of *Learning Networks: A Guide for Teaching and Learning Online*, MIT Press, 1995. Currently he is a professor, Faculty of Education, University of Brasilia (www.unb.br) and adjunct professor at the Faculty of Education, Simon Fraser University. He is interested in how cyber culture, virtual art, and online games can impact and facilitate the process of learning.

Colette Wanless-Sobel has a PhD in American studies from the University of Minnesota and currently teaches in independent and distance learning at the University of Minnesota and at Inver Hills Community College, Inver Grove Heights, MN. Her research interests are in intellectual history, specifically gender and sexuality, and online education.

Mitchell Weisburgh was founding president and CEO of Personal Computer Learning Centers of America, Inc. (1981-1999); CTO (2000 to 2004), CollegePilot.com; and designer of the PILOT online learning system and the CollegePilot online SAT Prep Course. He is founder of PILOT Online Learning online curriculum design and management. Weisburgh has developed and taught over 100 courses on the use of PCs in business, including spreadsheets, word processors, databases, presentation software, project management, decision making, and course development. He has led discussions for the International Forum of Educational Technology & Society of the IEEE Learning Technology Task Force, and a Board member of mid-Hudson ASTD chapter.

Hilary Wilder teaches educational technology courses in the Department of Elementary and Early Childhood Education in the College of Education, William Paterson University, New Jersey (USA). She has also worked for many years as an instructional technologist and designed and developed multimedia and Web-based corporation. In 2001, she volunteered in schools in Namibia and worked with students and teachers using computers in K-12 schools. She returned to Namibia in 2003 to give workshops for the students and professors in the Faculty of Education at the University of Namibia. It was through these trips that she made contact with others involved in this case study.

Udo Winand has been a professor and head of the chair for information systems of Kassel University (Germany) since 1993. The research activities of Professor Winand are concentrated on business networks and partnerships, virtual organizations, eB2C-business, trust in information systems, knowledge management and e-learning. Professor Winand is the manager-in-chief of the Working Group Managerial Partnership of Schmalenbach Society, German Society for Management. He is co-editor of several journals and series of books.

Cindy Xin is a program director at the Learning and Instructional Development Center, Simon Fraser University. Dr. Xin has been conducting research and development in e-learning for higher education since 1996. Her previous work includes researching on new models of e-learning and communication, developing evaluation and assessment tools and instruments, and conducting quantitative and qualitative analysis on large field site data. She led the development of a number of open source e-learning applications. These include CourseReader, an online discussion tool for International Labor Organization of the United Nations; TextWeaver, an enhanced discussion forum under a fund from the U.S. Education Department; and Marginalia, a Web annotation tool under a fund from BC Campus, a British Colombia learning organization in Canada. She has fruitfully collaborated with researchers from Canada, the U.S., Europe, and China. Her current research focuses on new models and theories of online collaborative discourse and inquiry. She holds a PhD in instructional psychology and technology, an MS in computer science, and a BS in mathematics.

Alina M. Zapalska is a professor of economics at the U.S. Coast Guard Academy. She has published numerous academic papers in professional refereed journals and book chapters. Her primary interests of teaching and research are in the areas of macroeconomics, entrepreneurship, international business, international trade and finance, transitional economies, experimental economics, and pedagogy. Her international work and study experience have enabled her research to be focused on analyzing economies of Poland, Hungary, Czech Republic, Sweden, Thailand, China, New Zealand, Australia, Bangladesh, and South Korea.

Zhu Zhiting worked with the University of Twente, The Netherlands with a research focus on cross-cultural influences of networked learning and received his PhD. He is now a professor of educational technology in the School of Educational Sciences and director of the Educational Information Center and vice dean of Cyber-Education College, East China Normal University. He also owns professorships awarded by Beijing Normal University and Nanjing Normal University. He is the director of the China E-Learning Technology Standardization Committee, vice chairman of the Instructional Steering Committee of Educational Technology Higher Education, and member of National Steering Committee for Teachers' E-Education. He also worked with UNESCO-APEID for three years as an expert in teacher training on the Technology-Pedagogy Integration Project. His research interests involve e-education theories and models, system architectures and standardization of e-learning technology, knowledge management technology in education, and technology philosophy.

Index

D

E

F

G